BENCH BOSSES

MATTHEW DIBIASE

BENCH BOSSES

THE NHL'S COACHING ELITE

With a Foreword by Scotty Bowman

FENN
M&S

Library and Archives Canada Cataloguing in Publication

DiBiase, Matthew, author
Bench bosses : the NHL's coaching elite / Matthew DiBiase.

Issued in print and electronic formats.
ISBN 978-0-7710-2508-2 (bound).--ISBN 978-0-7710-2509-9 (html)

1. Hockey coaches--Biography. 2. Hockey--Coaching.
3. National Hockey League. I. Title.

GV848.5.A1D523 2014 796.962092'2 C2014-904600-6
C2014-904601-4

Published simultaneously in the United States of America by FENN,
a division of Random House LLC, a Penguin Random House Company, New York

Library of Congress Control Number is available upon request

ISBN: 978-0-7710-2508-2
ebook ISBN: 978-0-7710-2509-9

Typeset in Fournier by M&S, Toronto
Printed and bound in the USA

FENN/McClelland & Stewart,
a division of Random House of Canada Limited,
a Penguin Random House Company
www.penguinrandomhouse.ca

1 2 3 4 5 19 18 17 16 15

FENN
M&S
Penguin Random House

This book is dedicated to the late Rudy DiMemmo (1930–2012): born American, first son, grandson, brother, cousin, husband, father, grandfather, great-grandfather, uncle, and best friend to those who loved him and love him still.

IN MEMORIAM

Maryann Barbara Heavener DiBiase

Frank Fortunato DiBiase Sr.

They both died too soon to see this book in print.

Rest in Peace.

"Excellence is an art won by training and habituation. We do not act rightly because we have virtue or excellence, but we rather have those because we have acted rightly. We are what we repeatedly do. Excellence, then, is not an act but a habit."

Aristotle

"Perfection is not attainable, but if we chase perfection we can catch excellence."

Vince Lombardi

"The will to win, the desire to succeed, the urge to reach your full potential . . . these are the keys that will unlock the door to personal excellence."

Confucius

CONTENTS

PART THREE: HONOURABLE MENTION

PART FOUR: THE BEST OF THEIR TIMES

PART FIVE: FACTS AND FIGURES

PART SIX: THE WORST OF THEIR TIMES

FOREWORD

After having coached in the National Hockey League (NHL) for nearly 30 years, it is a privilege and an honour to write this foreword for a fascinating book on coaching personalities and their careers.

At the beginning of my coaching career, to stand behind the bench and try to match wits with the legendary Punch Imlach of the Toronto Maple Leafs and Toe Blake of the Montreal Canadiens was a dream job.

The tactics of Roger Neilson, with his innovative style applied to so many different teams; to the successes of Glen Sather, with the four-time Stanley Cup champion Edmonton Oilers in the mid- to late 1980s; preceded by the victories of Al Arbour, with his four-time Stanley Cup champion New York Islanders in the early 1980s, are stories all by themselves.

Moving on to coaches such as Jacques Lemaire, winning with the New Jersey Devils and then enjoying expansion success with the Minnesota Wild, and Joel Quenneville, coaching the St. Louis Blues, the Colorado Avalanche, and winning Stanley Cups with the Chicago Blackhawks; to Ken Hitchcock of the Stanley Cup champion Dallas Stars (who now is with the St. Louis Blues) provides great insights into what methods and styles are successful in hockey these days.

The book also delves into two of my former players: Dave Tippett of the Arizona Coyotes and Lindy Ruff of the Dallas Stars, who are lifers in the art of longevity because of their coaching philosophies and abilities.

Readers will be able to realize the successes of Mike Babcock of the Toronto Maple Leafs, the only coach in the Triple Gold Club: winning the World Junior, the Stanley Cup, and Olympic gold in his illustrious coaching career.

I am sure all of these coaches will have the same feelings I have always had when leading a team: having skillful players with a work ethic makes coaching such a rewarding profession.

We have all had the same ingredients to allow us the careers we have.

Scotty Bowman

INTRODUCTION

Sports debates usually focus on the best players at any given position in any particular sport; seldom do the debates extend to head coaches or managers. Though there are books that have examined the great head coaches or managers in the four major North American sports (baseball, football, basketball, and hockey), the majority of them consist of biographical, anecdotal, and occasionally humorous portrayals without any systemic analysis based on the coach's actual performance.

In the past 16 years, only two published books have undertaken such analyses: one for baseball managers and the other for pro football head coaches (more on both shortly). The book you are about to read marks the first attempt at rating the most successful head coaches in the history of professional hockey by using a disciplined, systemic approach to evaluating coaching excellence.

Bench Bosses lists the 50 most successful hockey coaches of all time and examines former coaches who once ranked among the top 50 but have been displaced in recent years. The book both ranks the coach in question and reveals his stats in the regular season and the playoffs. It also includes the coach's awards, the names of his players who received notable individual awards and All-Star honours by their respective leagues, how many playoff appearances he made, and whether he competed for and won the Stanley Cup or the Avco Cup.

Bench Bosses also contains personal profiles of the coaches featured, each with biographical information drawn from a variety of sources that shed light on the coach's background, character, personality, and leadership style. It provides readers with insights into the strengths and weaknesses of the coaches profiled: which coaches led teams that were strong offensively or defensively, or were well balanced; which coaches were good at power-play offence or the penalty-kill; which coaches were good at emphasizing on-ice discipline or had the nastiest squads on the ice.

After you read this book, you will know the highest-ranked coach who never won a Stanley Cup, the most successful coach of the 1990s, the most successful coach during the Original Six era, and much more.

Will *Bench Bosses* end all debate on who were the greatest hockey coaches of all time? Of course not; hockey coach ratings, like the stock market, are constantly fluctuating, and certain coaches will rise in greatness while others fall into obscurity. If I were to revisit my ratings five or ten years down the road, there is no doubt that they would look different than they do now. However, *Bench Bosses* provides a rational starting point for future discussion on the topic and allows hockey fans and historians of today and tomorrow a solid, proven basis for further analysis of hockey coaching greatness.

I hope you enjoy reading this as much as I have enjoyed writing it.

Matthew DiBiase
2009–2015

AUTHOR'S NOTE

This book's information is current up to June 30, 2015. The author is solely responsible for all its content. Any errors (unless otherwise noted) are also the sole responsibility of the author.

PART ONE

BACKGROUND

METHODOLOGY

Bench Bosses follows in the wake of previous sports research that ranked head coaches or managers using proven methodological approaches to managerial success. Two of the most noteworthy sports historians who have attempted this are Bill James, who published in 1997 *The Bill James Guide to Baseball Managers: From 1870 to Today*, and Sean Lahman, who published in 2008 *The Pro Football Historical Abstract: A Hardcore Fan's Guide to All-Time Player Rankings*.

Bench Bosses is a continuation of this process and broadens its scope into the realm of major league hockey by synthesizing and modifying the methods and criteria used by James and Lahman. The end result builds upon their work and expands the envelope of sports analysis to create a new field of sports research: the evaluation and ranking of head coaches.

James was the first to establish a basic rating system for evaluating baseball managerial success using the following six standards of coaching excellence:

1. Coached a winning season
2. Finished 20 games above .500%
3. Won 100 or more games in a season
4. Won the division
5. Won the league
6. Won the World Series

Managers were rated using the criteria and awarded a point each time they met any or all of the standards. The points were totalled and the managers ranked. Although James did not claim that his system was foolproof, he felt that it at least provided a solid starting point for the future research and evaluation of managers – and as of 2015 no other sports historian I know of has refuted his methodology.

In 2008 football historian Sean Lahman endorsed James's system and modified it toward rating the most successful pro football coaches of all time. His system awarded points based on the following:

1. Coached a winning season
2. Had a winning percentage of .650 or higher in the regular season
3. Earned a playoff berth
4. Earned a league championship game or Super Bowl berth
5. Won the league championship or Super Bowl
6. Historical factor

The "historical factor" was Lahman's personal contribution to the rating process, about which he writes, "I did a pretty rigorous review of what was written about each coach by his contemporaries, looking for specific citations of his innovations or contributions that had a significant impact on the way the game was played.

"Points were awarded based on some specific criteria I came up with and a scale for measuring their ultimate impact. It's subjective, but based on a defined methodology."[1]

MY SYSTEM

The system I created to rate hockey coaches evolved slowly through trial and error over the course of the six years it took to research and write this book. In the beginning, I resorted more to Bill James's system than Sean Lahman's: my method eschewed Lahman's historical factor because I felt that the coaches featured in this book all had significant historicity in their backgrounds and that the historical factor was too subjective – too vulnerable to external debate and potential personal bias to serve as an effective rating standard.

---

1 *The Pro Football Historical Abstract*, Sean Lahman, pp. 255–256.

The standards I used, meanwhile, were based on hard numbers that could be verified by any interested hockey researcher. During my research, I determined six standards of success, with a point awarded every time a hockey coach achieved the following:

1. Coached a winning season
2. Had a winning percentage of .600 or better in a season
3. Finished first in the division or league
4. Earned a Stanley Cup playoff spot
5. Reached the Stanley Cup finals
6. Won the Stanley Cup

I wanted to create a system that would be fair to hockey coaches from *all* eras. The one major complaint I had about James's system was that it was biased more to 20th- and 21st-century managers than 19th-century managers. His standard of awarding a point every time a manager won 100 games is a prime example of this: only one baseball manager in the 19th century had a 100-win season because baseball seasons were seldom lengthy enough for a team to be able to win 100 games until very late in the century. If James had substituted winning percentage in lieu of winning 100 games, the system would have afforded greater balance for managers for all eras.

This is why my first rating method did not rely on standards like awarding a success point if a team earned 100 team points in a season, as such a standard would have been biased against NHL coaches who coached in the early days when NHL seasons were only 24, 36, or 48 games in length.

Nonetheless, after I rated all the hockey coaches in the NHL, PCHA, WCHL/WHL, and WHA – coming up with a top 50 list and considering my work complete – I ran into some interesting problems.

THE PROBLEMS

For a rating method to succeed, it must withstand critical analysis – even one's own. After I had completed my first run at the hockey coaches, I began to uncover certain flaws on relying solely on success points (as James and Lahman did in their books). One hockey coach above all exposed those flaws in stark relief: the late Clarence Henry "Hap" Day (head coach of the Toronto Maple Leafs from 1940 to 1950). Using my first rating method, I was able to award Day only 30 success points even though he had coached *five* Stanley Cup winners. In my first top 50 list, Day rated only #23.

How could this be?

Furthermore, when first ranking the best hockey coaches of the 1940s, Day wasn't even the top-ranked head coach of the decade. His 28 points finished second to Dick Irvin's 30 points.

Again, how could this be? The calculations according to my standards were correct.

After a while I tabled my concerns and proceeded on – only to find new problems in the 1917–1926 period.

When the National Hockey League (NHL) began operations in 1917, it coexisted with the Pacific Coast Hockey Association (PCHA), which had been operating since 1911. The two leagues vied with each other for the Stanley Cup from 1917/18 to 1923/24. Later, in 1921, the Western Canada Hockey League/Western Hockey League (WCHL/WHL) joined the fray and from 1921/22 to 1923/24 made the Stanley Cup playoffs a three-way dance. Even after the PCHA folded in 1924, the WCHL/WHL continued to vie with the NHL for the Stanley Cup until 1926.

This interleague competition posed potential problems, as the coaches who led teams in the PCHA and WCHL/WHL had to win their respective league championships in order to compete for the Stanley Cup.

Shouldn't extra points be awarded to those coaches who won league championships in the PCHA and WCHL/WHL?

Also, from 1921/22 to 1923/24, the PCHA and WCHL/WHL engaged in an interleague playoff to determine which *league* would compete against the NHL for the Cup.

Shouldn't extra points be awarded to those coaches in the PCHA and WCHL/WHL who competed in that interleague playoff?

Finally, what about the NHL?

During the 1922/23 and 1923/24 Stanley Cup playoffs, the NHL champion had to engage in a round-robin playoff tournament with *both* the PCHA and WCHL champions to determine which two teams would compete in the Stanley Cup finals.

Shouldn't extra points be awarded to those NHL coaches who competed in those two interleague playoffs?

It was back to the drawing board for me. I updated my coaches ratings accordingly, but the end still wasn't in sight.

FAILURE POINTS

Both James and Lahman chose to award zero points in their respective methods whenever a manager had a losing season. During my first attempt at rating hockey coaches, I did the same – but was that really the right way to do it?

If there can be gradations of success, shouldn't there also be gradations of failure? Can failure even be quantified, delineated, and evaluated? While I was focusing on determining the greatest hockey coaches of all time, I was also wondering who were the worst. I pondered the problem and developed four standards for determining coaching failure. A failure point was awarded every time a hockey coach did the following:

1. Coached a losing season
2. Had a winning percentage of less than .400 in a season
3. Finished in last place in the division or league
4. Failed to reach the playoffs

Again, I ranked and rated every hockey coach using this method, totalling their failure points. The first results were fascinating, and as I was reviewing these results a new idea caused me to re-evaluate (again) my entire rating method.

The NHL uses the plus–minus system for rating a player's two-way skills, wherein a player is awarded a point if his team scores during an even-strength or short-handed situation while he's on the ice, and a minus point is counted against him if the opposition scores against his team during an even-strength or short-handed situation. If you can use a method like that to evaluate players, why not use a plus–minus system for evaluating hockey coaches?

I decided to combine the success and failure points into a combined score to determine the 50 greatest hockey coaches of all time.

I recalculated the rankings using this plus–minus system, and the results astonished me even more. Certain coaches I had rated highly on my original top 50 list were now reduced in rank; other coaches were eliminated altogether – and some of the ones who took their places surprised me.

And there was still one nagging problem: Hap Day.

Even a plus–minus system for evaluating hockey coaches still didn't solve the dilemma of why Day rated so poorly despite winning five Stanley Cups. The way I saw it, this questioned the legitimacy of my project.

I nonetheless carried on until one evening in the winter of 2012 when I caught the luckiest break of all my research that resolved the Hap Day problem once and for all.

It happened on a Saturday night at a bar and grill in Deptford, New Jersey. I was having a drink while sitting next to a couple at the bar. The guy (whose name escapes me) was a former college football player from Rider University who had unsuccessfully tried out for the New York Jets in the early 1980s and was now working as an accountant. We got to talking about sports in general, and while telling him about my book project, I found myself lamenting my Hap Day problem.

It was then that the accountant provided me with a key clue, opining that my present system of awarding a single success or failure point every time a coach achieved a certain result was fundamentally sound – but the basic flaw was that each act of success or failure was *equal in value*. He posed some rhetorical questions to me: Is having a winning season truly equal to winning the Stanley Cup? Is making the playoffs truly equal to winning your division or league? And on the debit side, should having a losing season be as equally bad as finishing in last place?

He made a wonderful suggestion: Why not use *weighted* values for each of the categories and award success and failure points using a sliding scale?

The mental gears in my head began formulating the system, and when he finished talking I knew right then and there that I had found my breakthrough. After thanking him profusely, I made my way home at breakneck speed, fired up my computer, and began formulating the weights and measures I wanted to use when ranking hockey coaches.

WEIGHTS AND MEASURES

Since I had six standards of success, I decided that the scale would also be from 1 to 6. The problem was in fixing the value of each standard of success. I reviewed the raw data from my rating forms and made the following determinations:

1. Reached the playoffs: *1 point*
2. Coached a winning season: *2 points*
3. Had a winning percentage of .600 or better in a season: *3 points*
4. Finished first in the division or league: *4 points*
5. Reached the Stanley Cup finals: *5 points*
6. Won the Stanley Cup: *6 points*

And for my four standards of failure, I allotted the following:

1. Coached a losing season: *1 point*
2. Failed to reach the playoffs: *2 points*
3. Had a winning percentage of less than .400 in a season: *3 points*
4. Finished in last place in the division or league: *4 points*

My premise was this: The more common an act of success or failure was, the lower its point value should be.

My research showed that hockey coaches were likely to have more playoff appearances than winning seasons (especially given the high percentage of NHL teams that advance to the post-season); hence, playoff appearances would rank lower than winning seasons. I also found that hockey coaches were more likely to coach a season where the team's winning percentage was .600 or better than they were to finish in first place; hence, the reason why first-place finishes would outrank having a winning percentage of .600 or better in a season.

The same went for failure points, where, for example, a hockey coach was far more likely to have a losing season than to fail to make the playoffs.

Armed with this new insight, I began re-ranking all of the hockey coaches. The results (again) astonished but also gratified me. In the weighted plus–minus system, Hap Day finally achieved the rank befitting his great accomplishments.

The only remaining issue was how to rate the head coaches in the PCHA and the WCHL/WHL.

After some experimentation, I decided upon the following:

1. Competing in the PCHA and WCHL/WHL league playoffs: *1 point*
2. Winning the PCHA and WCHL/WHL league championship: *5 points*
3. Competing in the interleague playoffs from 1921/22 to 1923/24: *1 point*

I applied the same standard to the two NHL head coaches (Pete Green and Leo Dandurand) who competed in the 1922/23 and 1923/24 interleague playoff tournaments.

Both men were awarded 1 point for competing in the interleague playoff tournament and 5 points for winning the NHL league championship.

Why did I do this for Green and Dandurand and not for the other NHL coaches who competed against the PCHA and the WCHL/WHL during the 1917–1926 era?

The reason is this: From 1917/18 to 1921/22, the NHL champion was *guaranteed* a slot in the Stanley Cup finals; the same goes for the 1924/25 and 1925/26 playoffs. But since in the 1922/23 and 1923/24 seasons the NHL had to compete in a round-robin tournament with both the PCHA and WCHL champions in order to earn a slot in the Stanley Cup finals, the NHL coach faced a risk (albeit a small one) of being eliminated from Stanley Cup finals competition altogether.

In view of this, I felt it was only fair that Pete Green and Leo Dandurand should be awarded 5 success points for winning the NHL championship because they were facing a risk the other NHL coaches weren't facing from 1917/18 to 1921/22 and from 1924/25 to 1925/26.

THE WORLD HOCKEY ASSOCIATION

There were no problems in rating and ranking those head coaches who led teams in the World Hockey Association from 1972/73 to 1978/79. Since the WHA never competed with the NHL for the Stanley Cup, I adopted the following system for rating and ranking its head coaches:

1. Made a playoff appearance: *1 point*
2. Coached a winning season: *2 points*
3. Had a winning percentage of .600 or better in a season: *3 points*
4. Finished first in the division or league: *4 points*
5. Reached the Avco Cup finals: *5 points*
6. Won the Avco Cup: *6 points*

The failure point standards are the same four standards for NHL coaches, with the same values.

PARTIAL SEASONS

A note should be made about how hockey coaches who coached partial seasons were rated. I chose to err on the side of conservatism.

If a hockey coach had a partial season where *he* had a winning record but his team finished with a losing season, he would not be awarded 2 points; if the team finished with a winning season, 2 points would be awarded.

The same rule applies for winning percentage. If a coach's winning percentage was .600 or better in a partial season but the team's final winning percentage was below .600, 3 points would not be awarded. If the team did finish with a final winning percentage of .600 or better, 3 points would be awarded.

With regards to finishing first, earning a playoff spot, reaching the Stanley Cup finals, or winning the Stanley Cup in a partial season, the following rules apply: Only the coach who was in place when the regular season ended with the team in first place gets the credit. The same goes for the playoff spot, Stanley Cup or Avco Cup finals appearance, and Stanley Cup or Avco Cup victory. Only the coach who was there at the time gets the plus points awarded for those standards.

The rules for assessing minus points during a partial season are as follows: If a coach had a losing record and the team finished with a losing record, a minus point would be assessed – but if the team in question didn't finish with a losing record, a minus point would not be assessed. Additionally, if a coach coached a partial season for a team and had a winning record even though the team finished with a losing record, a minus point would not be assessed.

If the coach of a partial season's winning percentage was below .400 and the team's final winning percentage was also below .400, 3 minus points would be assessed – but if the team finished above .400, 0 minus points would be assessed.

If a coach was fired before the regular season ended, his team was in last place when the firing took place, *and* the team finished in last place when the regular season ended, 4 minus points would be assessed to the coach in question.

If the team was not in last place when the coach was fired but the team eventually finished last, the 4 minus points would not be assessed to that particular coach.

When assessing 2 minus points for failing to reach the playoffs, only the coach who was in place when the regular season ended would be penalized.

TIE-BREAKERS

Invariably while rating and ranking the coaches, I encountered situations in which coaches were tied in terms of their coaching value. My solution for resolving ties was as follows: The coach with the higher average season rating got the nod. If there was also a tie in average season ratings, the coach with the higher winning percentage in the regular season would get the higher rating.

THE PROCESS IN ACTION

Now that I've articulated my rating system, I would like to give two examples of how the system works.

Former Toronto Maple Leafs head coach Ron Wilson coached 18 seasons in the NHL. During those years, Wilson did the following:

1. His teams made eight playoff appearances: *8 points*
2. His teams had 11 winning seasons: *22 points*
3. His teams finished at .600 or better five times: *15 points*
4. His teams finished first four times: *16 points*
5. His teams made one Stanley Cup finals appearance: *5 points*

His overall plus points total is 66.

On the debit side, Wilson's teams did the following:

1. Had losing seasons seven times: *7 points*
2. Failed to make the playoffs nine times: *18 points*
3. Finished below .400 only once: *3 points*
4. Finished last four times: *16 points*

Wilson's overall minus points total is 44; when you deduct his 44 minus points from his 66 plus points, Wilson's overall value as a coach is +22.

The second example is former Edmonton Oilers head coach Tom Renney. Renney coached nine seasons in the NHL, and his teams did the following:

1. Made three playoff appearances: *3 points*
2. Had four winning seasons: *8 points*
3. Finished at .600 only one time: *3 points*

Renney's overall plus points total is 14.

On the debit side, Renney's teams did the following:

1. Had five losing seasons: *5 points*
2. Failed to make the playoffs four times: *8 points*
3. Finished below .400 twice: *6 points*
4. Finished in last place three times: *12 points*

Renney's minus points total is 31. When you deduct his 31 minus points from his 14 plus points, Renney's overall coaching value is -17.

TROPHY TERMS

NHL hockey is unique among the four major North American sports in that its major trophies are named after famous players, owners, or executives. Throughout this book you see trophy names being invoked many times: die-hard hockey fans will understand the meaning of a trophy term, but what about those readers who cannot tell the difference between a Norris Trophy winner and a Conn Smythe Trophy winner?

The following lists the names of the trophies mentioned in this book.

THE JACK ADAMS AWARD: awarded annually to the NHL coach "adjudged to have contributed the most to his team's success"; first awarded in 1973/74.

THE LADY BYNG MEMORIAL TROPHY: awarded annually to the NHL player "adjudged to have exhibited the best type of sportsmanship and gentlemanly conduct combined with a high standard of playing ability"; first awarded in 1924/25.

THE CALDER MEMORIAL TROPHY: awarded annually to the NHL Rookie of the Year; first awarded in 1932/33.

THE HART MEMORIAL TROPHY: awarded annually to the NHL's Most Valuable Player; first awarded in 1923/24.

THE WILLIAM M. JENNINGS TROPHY: awarded annually to the NHL goalkeeper(s) having played a minimum of 25 games for the team with the lowest goals scored against it during the regular season; first awarded in 1981/82.

THE JAMES NORRIS TROPHY: awarded annually to the NHL's best defenceman; first awarded in 1953/54.

THE PRINCE OF WALES TROPHY: awarded for a variety of purposes, but for this book I have focused on the period when it was awarded to the NHL League Champion during the 1925/26 Stanley Cup playoffs and when it was awarded annually from 1938/39 to 1966/67 to the NHL team that had the best regular season record. Today, the Prince of Wales trophy is awarded to the winner of the Eastern Conference title in the Stanley Cup playoffs.

THE PRESIDENT'S TROPHY: awarded annually to the NHL team that has the best regular season record; first awarded in 1985/86.

THE MAURICE "ROCKET" RICHARD TROPHY: awarded annually to the leading goal-scorer in the NHL; first awarded in 1998/99.

THE ART ROSS TROPHY: awarded annually to the NHL's leader in scoring points at the end of the regular season; first awarded in 1947/48.

THE FRANK SELKE TROPHY: awarded annually to the NHL's best defensive forward; first awarded in 1977/78.

THE CONN SMYTHE TROPHY: awarded annually to the most valuable player during the Stanley Cup playoffs; first awarded in 1964/65.

THE VEZINA TROPHY: awarded annually to the NHL goaltender "adjudged to be the best at this position"; first awarded in 1926/27.

PART TWO

THE TOP 50

THE TOP 50

Here it is. This part profiles the 50 most successful professional hockey coaches from the 1917/18 season to the 2014/15 season. Each entry lists the following information:

1. The coach's name and rank on the top 50 list
2. Total number of plus points
3. Total number of minus points
4. The coach's value
5. The coach's peak rank on the top 50 list and the season when he reached it
6. The highest peak value the coach ever reached and the season he reached it
7. Coaching experience in the NHL, WHA, PCHA, or WCHL/WHL
8. Career regular season record in wins, losses, ties, and overtime losses. If the coach in question coached in the WHA, PCHA, or WCHL/WHL, then their coaching record in that particular league is listed separately.
9. Career playoff record in wins, losses, and ties. Again, if the coach in question coached in the WHA, PCHA, or WCHL/WHL, then their playoff coaching record in that particular league is listed separately.
10. Jack Adams Awards won (if applicable) and their respective seasons
11. Prince of Wales trophies (for the 1925/26 NHL season and/or the time period of 1938/39 to 1966/67) or President's trophies won (if applicable) and their respective seasons. If a coach won the league championship in

the PCHA, WCHL/WHL, or the WHA, the season they won the league championship is listed.

12. Divisional titles won
13. PCHA, WCHL/WHL, WHA, and Stanley Cup playoff appearances.
14. Stanley Cup and/or Avco Cup finals appearances
15. Stanley Cup and/or Avco Cup victories

Each entry also includes a biographical sketch providing insights on the coach's accomplishments, innovations, tactics, and styles and characteristics of the teams they coached – not to mention their foibles, weaknesses, and personalities.

These insights are drawn from published sources and interviews conducted by me or others, which are listed in the Bibliography.

SCOTTY BOWMAN RANK #1

PLUS: 316
MINUS: 7
VALUE: +309
PEAK RANK: #1 in 1992/93
PEAK VALUE: +309 in 2001/02

COACHING EXPERIENCE: St. Louis Blues, 1967–1970, 1971[2]; Montreal Canadiens, 1971–1979; Buffalo Sabres, 1979/80, 1982[3]–1985, 1986[4]; Pittsburgh Penguins, 1991–1993; Detroit Red Wings, 1993–2002

REGULAR SEASON W–L–T–OL: 1,244–573–314–10
PLAYOFF W–L: 223–130

JACK ADAMS AWARDS: 1976/77, 1995/96

PRESIDENT'S TROPHIES: 1992/93, 1994/95–1995/96, 2001/02

WESTERN DIVISION TITLES: 1967/68–1969/70
EASTERN DIVISION TITLE: 1972/73
NORRIS DIVISION TITLES: 1974/75–1978/79
ADAMS DIVISION TITLE: 1979/80
PATRICK DIVISION TITLE: 1992/93
CENTRAL DIVISION TITLES: 1993–1996, 1998/99, 2000/01–2001/02

PLAYOFF APPEARANCES: 1967/68–1979/80, 1981/82–1984/85, 1991/92–2001/02

---

2 Bowman coached the last 28 games of the 1970/71 season.

3 Bowman coached the last 35 games of the 1981/82 season.

4 Bowman coached the last 37 games of the 1985/86 season and the first 12 games of the 1986/87 season.

STANLEY CUP FINALS: 1967/68–1969/70, 1972/73, 1975/76–1978/79, 1991/92, 1994/95, 1996/97–1997/98, 2001/02
STANLEY CUP VICTORIES: 1972/73, 1975/76–1979, 1991/92, 1996/97–1997/98, 2001/02

When I was tabulating the ratings to determine which coach was number one, I first sorted alphabetically. It didn't take long to get to Scotty Bowman and, as I continued, to realize that Bowman was not only the most successful hockey coach of all time, but he also totally annihilated the competition – just as he did when he was coaching in the NHL. The complexity of my research was basically devoted to which coaches would occupy slots 2 to 50.

Bowman ranked among the top three coaches in the 1970s and the 1990s (to know where he ranked, see "Decades" in Part Four) and remains (as of 2015) the greatest head coach of the NHL's second half-century, which began in 1967.

No other NHL coach has won more divisional titles (16) than Bowman.

Since the President's Trophy was first awarded in 1986, no other NHL coach has equalled Bowman's four trophy wins. (Conversely, Scotty Bowman is one of only two NHL coaches who have defeated three President's Trophy-winning teams in Stanley Cup playoff competition.)

Bowman reached the Stanley Cup finals 13 times, winning a record nine Cups, and is the only NHL coach to win Stanley Cups for three different teams: Montreal, Pittsburgh, and Detroit.

He (along with Lester Patrick) remains one of the most influential coaching legends in the game, inspiring others to become great coaches in their own right: Jacques Lemaire, Lindy Ruff, Roger Neilson, Al Arbour, and Mike Keenan, to name a few.

How did he succeed?

Ken Dryden, in his masterpiece *The Game*, quotes Bowman as saying that his secret was "to get the right players on the ice." A rather simplistic explanation, but when you look deeper, a picture emerges of how Bowman triumphed where others failed.[5]

Bowman rang the line changes with abandon, tenacity, and infinite patience. The late Roger Neilson once said that Bowman was willing to wait 59 minutes to

---

5 *The Game*, Ken Dryden, p. 45.

make the right line change that would score the goal that won the game – and history bears this out. Other times Bowman would keep certain lines out for extra-long shifts, testing the limits of his opponent's physical and spiritual endurance (along with his own team's).

A prime example of this is the legendary Game 7 of the 1978/79 semifinals, when Don Cherry's Bruins committed a bench penalty by having too many players on the ice. It was Bowman's insistence that his top line do a double shift that caused the Bruins to bollix up their own line rotations, drawing the penalty that led to their eventual defeat.

Bowman's Cup-winning teams always possessed depth, strength, speed, and variety. While Bowman's St. Louis and Buffalo teams had the talent to reach for the Cup, neither had the necessary depth to *win* the Cup (only St. Louis made the finals).

Unlike Pat Burns or Roger Neilson (who were defensive coaching geniuses); or Marc Crawford (who lived and died with his offence), Bowman demanded (and usually got) tactical balance from his teams. Not just in even-strength situations but also from his special teams. Bowman always believed that if a team had well-balanced and strong special teams, then it could win the Stanley Cup. His early St. Louis Blues teams were weak on the power play while strong on the penalty kill; it was the same with his Buffalo Sabres teams in the 1980s. That's why they failed to win the Stanley Cup for Bowman.

His Cup-winning teams, however, did *everything* superbly.

Bowman (like Lester Patrick before him) was the epitome of tactical fluidity, constantly adjusting his line assignments on a game-by-game basis. Ken Dryden writes, "He believes a championship team needs all kinds of players, and that too many players of the same type . . . make a team vulnerable."[6]

Bowman was particularly ahead of the curve with his conversion to emphasizing on-ice discipline during the early 1970s. In his early years with the St. Louis Blues, his teams were very physical and could rack up the penalty minutes, but by 1970 Bowman did a complete turnaround. While the majority of NHL teams were increasing their on-ice brutality (most exemplified by the Philadelphia Flyers), Bowman's teams went out of their way to reduce their penalty minutes.

---

6 *The Game*, Ken Dryden, p. 46

This was especially true with Bowman's Montreal Canadiens, who were always at the bottom when it came to team penalty minutes. Only once (in 1974/75) were the Canadiens in the top five in team penalty minutes. When Bowman left Montreal, he took his on-ice discipline with him: his Sabres, Penguins, and Red Wings teams all exhibited superb on-ice discipline, avoiding the penalty box.

Bowman swam against the tide and was rewarded richly for it. He did not invent on-ice discipline, nor was he the only NHL coach to practise it (Emile Francis, Billy Reay, and Al Arbour also followed his lead). But it was Bowman who put it on page one in his playbook and made it an essential staple in his team's makeup.

Another key aspect of Bowman's teams was their ability to *control the game*. A prime example is, again, the Montreal Canadiens' Game 7 victory in the 1979 semifinals against Boston. In the footage of the closing minutes of the game, what's most striking is that although the Habs were losing 4–3 with two minutes to go, they had total control of the flow of the game. They maintained possession of the puck and never allowed Boston to get any significant scoring opportunities against Ken Dryden. And after a bench penalty gave the Canadiens a power-play opportunity, they converted effortlessly, thus forcing the game into overtime.

Even in the overtime period, Montreal never lost control. Again, Boston never got a decisive shot on goal, while Montreal relentlessly worked the puck until scoring the inevitable game-winner.

The game remains one of the purest displays of professional hockey in the history of the sport.

But it wasn't just tactics that made Bowman the greatest. He also used psychological alchemy to work his magic. Steve Shutt states that "the key guy on the team was Scotty. He realized that the only team that could beat our team was ourselves. We had such a good team that petty grievances could develop that might bring the team down. So what Scotty did, he made himself the focal point. The one thing we had in common was that everybody hated Scotty."[7]

That was Bowman during the 1970s, but by the 1990s his style had evolved. Chris Chelios writes, "Bowman had clearly softened by the time he landed in Detroit. . . . I found Scotty quite entertaining, and he was awesome at handling our

---

7 *The Habs*, Dick Irvin, pp. 281–282.

very talented team. It wasn't Bowman's style to confront players individually. He made his points by the way he played guys or what he said to the entire group."[8]

Though Jack Adams and Punch Imlach had done the same thing earlier, Bowman was the antithesis of the volcanic duo they were. Bowman, by nature, was (and is) a shy, enigmatic figure: more intellectual and subtle than Adams or Imlach ever were – but still he had a steely edge. Bowman would not tolerate any player failing to play up to his potential.

In the book *Simply the Best*, Bowman told the authors Mike Johnston and Ryan Walter a story about coaching Jacques Lemaire in the minors.

Lemaire back then was a solid scorer with indifferent two-way skills. Bowman brought Lemaire into his office and bluntly told him that if he had hopes of making it to the NHL, he had better improve his defensive skills.

Lemaire was shocked at Bowman's lecture but did improve his defensive game – and later became not only a stalwart presence with the Canadiens but also ultimately one of the finest coaches of defensive hockey in NHL history. Lemaire's teammate Guy Lafleur was another challenge: a late bloomer whom Bowman considered trading but instead managed to unlock Lafleur's box of skills in the nick of time. In return, Lafleur provided the offensive spark for the Canadiens.

Bowman went against the grain yet again by not showing any prejudice against European players (unlike many of his peers, such as Chicago's Bob Pulford). When he coached the Red Wings especially, his European contingent was sizable and highly talented: players such as Sergei Fedorov, Nicklas Lidstrom, and, later, Dominik Hasek all played key roles in his three Cup wins for Detroit.

When Bowman took over as head coach at Detroit, he inherited a team riven with cliques. He broke the cliques through subtle genius. He began by secretly changing all the locker assignments. Most of the players accepted the new locker assignments without complaint, but those who did complain were later quietly traded away from Detroit, thus solving a long-term problem with the team.[9]

In addition to tactics and psychology, there was also Bowman's fanatical attention to seemingly insignificant details that had the potential of winning or losing games for his teams. When Bowman was coaching the Red Wings, he once urged

---

8 *Made in America*, Chris Chelios with Kevin Allen, p. 163.

9 *Gordie Howe's Son*, Mark Howe with Jay Greenberg, p. 233.

Detroit general manager Ken Holland to petition ESPN to reduce the size of its cutouts (where the TV cameras were set up) along the boards to prevent the puck from hitting them or going through them – which might result in a faceoff in the Detroit zone. Holland, bemused by Bowman's request, did so.

Bowman later told Mike Johnston and Ryan Walter, "I want the edge; I don't want the other guy to have the edge." [10] Very rarely did that happen.

Scotty Bowman began coaching at a young age. Legend has it that Bowman's playing career in the Montreal Canadiens farm system ended because of a severe head injury, but biographer Douglas Hunter maintains that – although Bowman did suffer a scalp injury inflicted by future Habs player Jean-Guy Talbot – it wasn't serious enough to end his playing career: Bowman missed only one game with the injury and instead quit the game when he realized he would never make it to the NHL.

Hunter adds that Bowman worked for a brief time as a salesman for Sherwin-Williams before Canadiens director of player personnel Sam Pollock, sensing Bowman's potential, encouraged him to take up coaching. Bowman coached at all levels and excelled from 1956 to 1967.

When the NHL expanded in 1967, the fledgling St. Louis Blues hired Bowman as an assistant coach to Lynn Patrick (the son of Lester Patrick). Eighteen games into their inaugural season, Patrick made the most brilliant decision of his hockey career when he resigned as head coach to work in the front office while asking Bowman to take his place.

The Blues had been moribund and punchless under Patrick; Bowman changed all that. Shaking off the cobwebs, Bowman energized the team by hiring retired Habs legend Dickie Moore to ignite the offence and scored another coup by stealing Red Berenson from the Rangers. Berenson had been used for defensive purposes in Montreal and New York, but under Bowman he became the big gun the Blues badly needed.

The Blues were a rarity among the six expansion teams: a team that won with its defence. Hockey legend Glenn Hall was also lured out of retirement and repaid

10 *Simply The Best*, Mike Johnston and Ryan Walter, p. 266.

the Blues with some of the most inspired goaltending of his career – winning the 1968 Conn Smythe Trophy in the process. The next year Bowman added Jacques Plante to the goalie rotation, whereupon Plante and Hall shared the 1969 Vezina Trophy. In front of them was a superb blue-line corps of Al Arbour, former Habs legend Doug Harvey, and Barclay Plager.

Bowman led the Blues to three consecutive Stanley Cup finals appearances from 1968 to 1970 (the only ones in their franchise history). However, after 1970 the honeymoon ended. Bowman wanted to become general manager and turn over the coaching reins to Al Arbour but encountered resistance from the Blues front office. Bowman, seeing the writing on the wall, found the ultimate golden parachute: he accepted Sam Pollock's offer to coach the Montreal Canadiens.

From 1971 to 1979, Bowman moulded, developed, manipulated, and cajoled his players into becoming one of the most dominant dynasties in NHL history. Still, it was slow going in the beginning – relatively speaking. From 1971/72 to 1974/75, Bowman got only one Stanley Cup win (in 1972/73).

During that time he integrated future Habs greats Larry Robinson, Steve Shutt, and Bob Gainey into the lineup; coped with Ken Dryden's holdout in 1973/74 (and slow comeback in 1974/75); endured the defections of J. C. Tremblay, Marc Tardif, and Réjean Houle to the WHA; and weathered the retirement of Habs legend Henri Richard. The team played great hockey, but it took time for all the right pieces to fall into place.

In 1975/76 it finally clicked, and for the remainder of the decade the Canadiens were in a league of their own – playing at a heightened pitch of omnipotence that not even the Habs dynasty of 1955/56 to 1959/60 had matched. (Dick Irvin Jr., in his book *The Habs*, considered the Bowman dynasty the greatest of all time.)

(It was also during those four years with the Canadiens and his first season with the Sabres that Bowman broke Toe Blake's record of ten straight playoff series wins when he led the Habs and the Sabres to 14 consecutive playoff series wins as a coach.)

However, when Sam Pollock retired in 1978 and Bowman was denied the Habs general manager position, he again saw the writing on the wall and, seeking a new challenge, became the head coach and general manager of the Buffalo Sabres. It was the sole challenge Bowman wouldn't meet.

The 1980s were the only dead zone in Bowman's career. Although he became the winningest coach in Sabres history until Lindy Ruff passed him, Bowman never got the Sabres to the Stanley Cup finals (although he did reach the conference finals in 1979/80). Bowman himself was tiring of coaching, but while wanting to seek a permanent career in the front office, Bowman was cursed by his own greatness: he was unable to find a coach who could match his magnificent skills in leading a team.

By 1986 Bowman left the Sabres for good and was in limbo doing broadcasting work before finding a position in the front office of the Pittsburgh Penguins. By 1991 his coaching career was a distant memory. According to my rating system, he wasn't even the most successful coach in hockey history at this point (for more, see "The Progressive Chart" in Part Four).

The Penguins had won the 1990/91 Stanley Cup under Bob Johnson and were primed to defend it when Johnson learned he had cancer (to which he would eventually succumb). Entering the breach once again was Scotty Bowman. Harnessing the skills of Mario Lemieux and Jaromir Jagr, the Penguins repeated as Stanley Cup champions, with Bowman winning his sixth Stanley Cup as a coach. However, the Penguins failed to accomplish a three-peat in 1992/93 after a stunning upset loss to Al Arbour's New York Islanders.

Bowman had regained his love for coaching. He reaffirmed his genius to the hockey world (he truly was now the greatest head coach in hockey history), but it was time once again to move on. Coaching genius demands stern challenges, and in 1993 the Detroit Red Wings (through the good offices of Bowman's close friend and former St. Louis Blues colleague Jim Devellano) presented Bowman with a challenge (and coaching offer) no hockey coach could possibly refuse: end the Red Wings' Stanley Cup drought.

Though the Wings under Jacques Demers and Bryan Murray had made the playoffs six out of seven years (and made the conference finals twice), they could never reach the Cup finals. Bowman took on the task, was given the power and responsibilities to meet it, and by 1994/95 had led the Red Wings to their first Stanley Cup final since 1965/66. Though they lost to New Jersey (Bowman's fourth – and last – Cup loss, and first since 1969/70), in the years that followed, Bowman made the Red Wings the best team in the NHL, earning more Cup finals appearances than any other franchise.

In 1996/97 Bowman's Wings finally ended Detroit's 42-year Stanley Cup drought. They repeated in 1997/98 (the last NHL team to do so), which tied Bowman and Toe Blake for the most Cup wins (eight).

Bowman struggled with minor health problems during the next four years but kept going, and in 2001/02 he won his ninth and final Stanley Cup. At 68 years old, it was time to leave the bench.

As of 2015, Bowman lives in semi-retirement, dividing his time between upstate New York and Florida, doing consulting work: first for the Red Wings and now for the Chicago Blackhawks (where his son Stan is now general manager – and a very good one too).

HECTOR "TOE" BLAKE RANK #2

PLUS: 195
MINUS: 0
VALUE: +195
PEAK RANK: #1 in 1967/68
PEAK VALUE: +195 in 1967/68

COACHING EXPERIENCE: Montreal Canadiens, 1955–1968

REGULAR SEASON W–L–T: 500–255–159
PLAYOFF W–L: 82–37

PRINCE OF WALES TROPHIES: 1955/56, 1957/58–1961/62, 1963/64, 1965/66, 1967/68

PLAYOFF APPEARANCES: 1955/56–1967/68
STANLEY CUP FINALS: 1955/56–1959/60, 1964/65–1967/68
STANLEY CUP VICTORIES: 1955/56–1959/60, 1964/65–1965/66, 1967/68

For a quarter-century, Hector "Toe" Blake was the greatest hockey coach ever (see "The Progressive Chart" in Part Four).

Although Scotty Bowman eventually surpassed Blake by a wide margin, Blake still holds an edge over Bowman in terms of maintaining consistent optimum performance with his teams (see "Average Season Rating" in Part Four).

Let's examine these numbers. Blake's five greatest consecutive seasons were from 1955/56 to 1959/60, where he scored +98 out of a possible +105, for an average season rating of +19.60.

Meanwhile, Bowman's greatest five-year stretch was from 1974/75 to 1978/79, where he scored +94 out of a possible +105, for an average season rating of +18.80.

Now let's examine Blake's *worst* five-year stretch. His leanest period was from 1960/61 to 1964/65, where he scored +47 out of a possible +105, for an average season rating of +9.400.

Compare that with Bowman's worst five-year stretch from 1982/83 to 1986/87, where he scored +5 out of a possible +105, for an average season rating of +1.000.

Now let's look at it all another way. It took Blake 13 seasons to accumulate his +195 value, while Bowman's coaching value after 13 seasons was +170 (in 1979/80). Bowman's lean period during the 1980s slowed down his progress in terms of coaching value, and it took Bowman 21 seasons to do what Blake was able to do in 13. Bowman suffered the peaks and valleys that almost all NHL coaches must suffer from time to time, but amazingly Blake never did. Even during his worst period, Blake's ability to get optimum performance from his players was astounding (see "Average Season Rating" in Part Four).

Blake's record is stunning: he had a winning season and made the playoffs every year he coached. Nine times in 13 seasons his Canadiens had the best regular-season record in the NHL. He won eight Stanley Cups (an NHL record until Scotty Bowman won his ninth in 2001/02). In Blake's first five seasons of NHL coaching, he won five consecutive Stanley Cups – the greatest coaching debut and the greatest dynastic run in hockey history; a record never to be matched, let alone broken. (Also during that epic quinquennium Blake broke the NHL record of six playoff series wins held by Tommy Gorman and Hap Day when he led the Habs to ten straight playoff series wins.)

How did he do it?

When I interviewed many former Habs who played for Blake, they all recited the same sentence when asked what Blake's offensive tactics were: *advance the puck, hit the open man, and converge on the net.* It was a continuation of the tactics honed by Blake's predecessor, Dick Irvin, but with a significant change. Hockey writer Todd Denault notes: "Blake also subtly changed the way the Canadiens attacked the opposition by stressing constant motion. By going on the attack, Blake made the most of his offensive strength up front. Under Irvin, the Canadiens defence was instructed to circle around the red line, while the forwards were in the opponent's end of the rink. Now, Blake wanted his defence-men to move up towards the blue line."[11]

Or as former Habs defenceman Terry Harper tells Stephen Cole, "Our game was built around our centres. . . . He knew with our centres, we'd score, but if we

---

11 *Jacques Plante*, Todd Denault, pp. 80-81.

managed to allow fewer than anyone else, everything else would fall into place. On defense, one man stayed in front, the other went into the corner. Simple, but if you screwed up, you didn't play. . . . We kept a defenceman in front. What we did was bring the centre back in the corner. And he'd bring the puck up. Or he and the defenceman would bring it out. The other defenceman stayed back. We made our centres work the entire rink, all game. No floating the blueline. Our centres started and finished everything. And we only used three."[12]

(When your team has three centres like Jean Beliveau, Henri Richard, and Ralph Backstrom, three is all you really need.)

The end result was a cannonade that left the NHL shell-shocked. From 1955/56 to 1962/63, the Canadiens had the best offence in the NHL as Habs legends Maurice "Rocket" Richard, Jean Beliveau, Henri Richard, Bernie Geoffrion, and Dickie Moore generated points with ruthless abandon.

Blackhawks legend Bobby Hull later told hockey historian D'Arcy Jenish, "They were an awesome group. They just kept coming at you. Five after five, right down to their so-called third and fourth lines. They'd come back in their own end and they wouldn't stop. . . . Going into Montreal, if we could keep the score under double figures we considered ourselves lucky."[13]

Blake's tactical disposition did not compromise his defence, however; it enhanced it. From 1955/56 to 1959/60, the Habs also had the best *defence* in the NHL. Jacques Plante rewrote the book on NHL goaltending with his innovative style. Blue-liners Doug Harvey, Tom Johnson, and Jean-Guy Talbot were the best in the game.

Blake's magic came from his leadership style, which over the course of time took on a mystical patina that earned him a prominent place in the pantheon of Montreal sports heroes. Blake led his players with an intricately balanced mixture of sternness, strength, subtlety, intensity, silence, anger, passion, and occasional humour. In return, his players gave him their hearts, minds, souls, and bodies – along with their collective blood, toil, tears, and sweat.

Blake forged those primal ingredients into the greatest assemblage of hockey talent in NHL history.

---

12 *The Last Hurrah*, Stephen Cole, p. 215.

13 *The Montreal Canadiens*, D'Arcy Jenish, p. 155.

No other hockey coach during the Original Six era was as *beloved* by his players as Toe Blake was. That is not hyperbole. When interviewing his former players, I was struck by the reverence they still accorded him. Never did I hear a complaint or a harsh word about him. Other coaches were spoken about in terms of fear and respect – and Blake could inspire both in the right moments – but he was largely spoken of in the same way a loving son describes his father.

A 2007 interview with former Montreal Canadien Bobby Rousseau bears this out. Blake had a rule that if a player had personal troubles outside the rink, they *stayed* outside the rink. Rousseau had two young sons who developed stomach ailments that required hospitalization. Needless to say, Rousseau was anguished, but mindful of Blakes's edict he kept his troubles to himself. Still, his hockey play suffered.

After a sub-par game, Rousseau was summoned to Blake's office and asked what was wrong. Rousseau, apologetically, told Blake about his boys being in the hospital, whereupon Blake asked if the boys were still there. When Rousseau said yes, Blake held up a hand and told him: "Go to your sons and don't come back until they're out of the hospital." Rousseau went to his sons, who pulled through okay, and the day after the meeting a team representative came to the hospital with two boxes of Montreal Canadiens hockey equipment: uniforms, gloves, sticks, and pads autographed by all the members of the Canadiens team. (Can you imagine what that equipment would be worth in today's sports memorabilia market?)

That was Toe Blake, the father figure.

When the Habs' Henri Richard was asked in a 2007 interview who was the unsung hero of the Montreal Canadiens dynasty from 1955/56 to 1959/60, he said laconically that it was Toe Blake – and gave the interviewer a stern look to let him know that he wasn't kidding.

When the late Tom Johnson was asked in 2006 how Blake kept his players hungry during their dynastic run, he said that Blake would pose a simple question to his players in training camp: *Is this the year you're going to let them take it away from you?* No fire-and-brimstone speeches. No threats or ultimatums, just a simple question.

No player ever put Toe Blake to the test when it came to discipline, but the closest was probably the late Jacques Plante – whose eccentricities exasperated coaches and teammates alike during his illustrious goaltending career. Still, Blake kept him for seven seasons, until Plante was traded to the Rangers in 1963.

Even a roguish imp like Bryan "Bugsy" Watson toed the line while playing for Blake. Watson said in a 2006 interview that Blake influenced his own managerial style when it comes to running his businesses (Watson is a successful restaurateur in Alexandria, Virginia).

Toe Blake's entire hockey life was dedicated to the Montreal Canadiens. He began his playing career for the Habs in 1937 – the late Cecil Hart's last great gift to hockey.

He endured the bad years of the late 1930s and the early 1940s, when the Canadiens were the doormats of the NHL.

Blake won the Hart Trophy in 1938/39 and the Lady Byng Trophy in 1945/46 (the only NHL player to win both trophies and later coach a Stanley Cup winner). He was also a five-time NHL All-Star.

As a player, Blake is best remembered for his legendary scoring line. When Dick Irvin took over as the Canadiens coach in 1940, he kept Blake and eventually paired him with two future Habs icons: Elmer Lach and Maurice "Rocket" Richard.

The Punch Line was born.

Blake played the same role in the Punch Line as Sid Abel did in the Production Line in Detroit: his experience and intelligence complementing the superb playmaking skills of Lach and the ballistic scoring talent of Richard. Montreal soon won the Stanley Cup in 1943/44 (with Blake scoring the Cup-winning goal) and again in 1945/46.

When Blake's NHL playing career ended in 1948, he took up coaching in the Canadiens farm system. His big break came in 1955 when the Habs were at a crossroads and Blake was asked to succeed Dick Irvin as head coach. Irvin had led the team to nine Stanley Cup finals appearances in 15 seasons, with three Cup wins and six defeats. The talent was definitely still there, and there was no questioning Irvin's coaching genius. The problem was the passion of Maurice "Rocket" Richard.

The Rocket had been sailing on winds of fire for 13 glorious seasons, but now the flames were threatening to consume his career and his team's chances for victory. The Richard–Hal Laycoe stick-fight and the ensuing suspension of Richard for the remainder of the season and the playoffs (not to mention the Richard Riot that followed) cost the Canadiens the 1954/55 Stanley Cup.

Dick Irvin had spent 13 years fuelling the Rocket's flames. Now the Habs needed someone to key the Rocket down.

Enter Toe Blake.

Blake relieved Richard from the burden of carrying the entire team while nonetheless making the Rocket the team captain and pairing him with his younger brother, Henri. In 1960 the Rocket finally retired with five more Cup wins; his place in the Hockey Hall of Fame guaranteed; his apotheosis complete as a player.

The early 1960s, however, were lean years for Blake. The Habs still won, but always failed to reach the Cup finals, as the stalwarts from the dynasty years had either retired or were traded away. The team was in transition as veterans such as Bernie Geoffrion, Doug Harvey, Tom Johnson, and Jacques Plante were weeded out while youngsters such as Jacques Laperrière, Gilles Tremblay, Yvan Cournoyer, Bryan "Bugsy" Watson, Bobby Rousseau, and the late John Ferguson were integrated into the team.

Blake believed in bringing rookie players up slowly, using them as role players until they gained maturity and confidence. Bryan Watson states that he and Red Berenson were used exclusively in penalty-killing situations during his rookie season. Even the future Hall of Famer Cournoyer was used on the power play before becoming an offensive mainstay.

Still, when emergency situations arose, Blake would not hesitate to start a rookie. His use of goalie Rogie Vachon during the 1966/67 season is a case in point.

The 1964/65 season had marked the beginning of four straight Cup finals appearances (and three Cup wins) for Toe Blake and the Canadiens, and the 1964/65 Cup win was a record-setter for Blake – his sixth victory, surpassing Hap Day's mark of five.

The only blot was the loss to Toronto in 1966/67. By that time, Blake had become drained by the emotional burdens of maintaining Montreal's dynastic reign: even victory can become as burdensome and destructive as defeat.

If the Habs had won the 1966/67 Stanley Cup, Blake would have retired – but the loss to Toronto stung Blake and his players.

The greatest coach of them all could not bear to end his career in defeat.

Blake steeled himself for one more campaign and led the Canadiens to a final glorious season in 1967/68. They were the best team in the NHL that year and were 12–1 in the playoffs, sweeping the upstart St. Louis Blues in four games.

Blake then went into a furtive retirement, and in his final years he was plagued with Alzheimer's disease. Yet before he died, he was given one final gift by the Montreal fans.

In 1989 Montreal fans selected the all-time Montreal Canadiens dream team, and the man they chose to lead that team was not Scotty Bowman – as one might expect, considering it was only ten years after his dynastic run.

It was Toe Blake.

DICK IRVIN RANK #3

PLUS: 219
MINUS: 30
VALUE: +189
PEAK RANK: #1 in 1943/44
PEAK VALUE: +199 in 1954/55

COACHING EXPERIENCE: Chicago Blackhawks, 1929[14], 1930/31, 1955/56; Toronto Maple Leafs, 1931–1940; Montreal Canadiens, 1940–1955

REGULAR SEASON W–L–T: 692–527–230
PLAYOFF W–L–T: 100–88–2

PRINCE OF WALES TROPHIES: 1943/44–1946/47

CANADIAN DIVISION TITLES: 1932/33–1934/35, 1937/38

PLAYOFF APPEARANCES: 1930/31–1946/47, 1948/49–1954/55
STANLEY CUP FINALS: 1930/31–1932/33, 1935/36, 1937/38–1939/40, 1943/44, 1945/46–1946/47, 1950/51–1954/55
STANLEY CUP VICTORIES: 1931/32, 1943/44, 1945/46, 1952/53

Dick Irvin is curiously an obscure figure in Montreal Canadiens history: a hockey coach overshadowed by more luminous personalities such as Scotty Bowman and Toe Blake – a rather unfair view when you consider his record. He ranked among the top three NHL coaches in the 1930s, 1940s, and 1950s (to know where he ranked, see "Decades" in Part Four). When his coaching career ended in 1956, he stood at the summit while everyone else tried to catch up with him (for more, see "The Progressive Chart" in Part Four).

Irvin took two struggling franchises and made them not only contenders and

14 Irvin coached the last 12 games of the 1928/29 season.

Stanley Cup champions but also flagship franchises. He was even starting to rebuild a third struggling franchise when his career and life were suddenly cut short by bone cancer. He was the most innovative hockey coach of his time – indeed, a coach way *ahead* of his time.

It was Irvin who made hockey coaching a true profession, not solely as an enforcer of discipline and making sure the players made the train on time but also as a teacher and inculcator of the proper fundamental skills.

No detail escaped Irvin's eye. He would always quiz his players about the rules of hockey and how a player should play his position. When a player wasn't eating right and was gaining unnecessary weight, he would speak to him about it.

Hal Laycoe told Dick Irvin Jr.: "Dick was always after you about your weight. . . . He told me I had played well the year before but that I wasn't playing as well then because I was three to four pounds heavier. . . . Dick was always thinking up ways to keep us on our toes. . . . He used to test us on the rules.

"One time he had the defencemen write down six things that made a good defenceman. It was interesting because usually players don't think that way."[15]

Irvin was reaffirming personal and tactical discipline. Excess weight on a player reduced speed and quickness, thus the need to diet properly. Testing his players on their hockey IQ was a subtle way of reinforcing the fundamentals he demanded.

Like baseball's John McGraw, Irvin loved to take raw, hungry hockey talent and teach them how to play the game the way he wanted it to be played. He was the doyen of offensive hockey of his era, introducing hockey fans to some of the most legendary players that ever stepped on the ice.

It was Irvin who established the traits that defined the Habs for decades to come: speed, depth, superb two-way skills from forwards, aggressive checking from defencemen, and superior goaltending.

Irvin led his teams to 17 consecutive playoff appearances (an NHL record) and 24 playoff appearances overall in 27 seasons of coaching.

His teams reached the Stanley Cup finals 16 times – which is not only an NHL record (which will never be broken) but also a record in all four major North American sports (Phil Jackson made 12 NBA finals appearances, Casey Stengel appeared in 10 World Series, and Steve Owen appeared in eight NFL championship games).

---

15 *The Habs*, Dick Irvin, pp. 60–61.

But even more fascinating is that in those 16 Stanley Cup finals appearances, Irvin won the Cup only *four* times, enduring 12 losses. Again, a record not only in NHL hockey but also in all four major North American sports (if you're wondering who is second with the most Stanley Cup finals losses, it's a three-way tie at four between Scotty Bowman, Sid Abel, and Lester Patrick).

And not only that: Irvin (along with Bowman) is the only NHL coach to lose three consecutive Stanley Cup finals (1937/38–1939/40). Furthermore, he is also the only NHL coach to lose Stanley Cup finals coaching three different teams.

Three of his Cup defeats were decided in the final game of the series (1930/31, 1953/54, and 1954/55). Another defeat came at the hands of the legendary Bill Barilko goal in 1950/51. Finally, his loss in 1953/54 was decided by a fluke shot by Tony Leswick, which bounced off the glove of Doug Harvey into the Montreal net.

When looking at Irvin's Cup losses, I am reminded of something former NBA player Tom Meschery told author Terry Pluto (in the book *Tall Tales*) about the late Wilt Chamberlain losing so many times in the playoffs to Bill Russell's Boston Celtics. Meschery said, "But Wilt really finished second all the time. Does that make him a loser? That makes him second best – at the worst."[16]

The same is true for Dick Irvin.

During the 1910s and 1920s, Irvin had been one of the finest hockey players in the game. He was a scoring wizard who played for the Portland Rosebuds in the PCHA and earned All-Star honours in 1916/17. Later he played for the Regina Capitals in the WCHL/WHL, earning All-Star honours in both 1921/22 and 1923/24. Irvin joined the Chicago Blackhawks in 1926, serving as the Hawks' first team captain before a skull fracture ended his playing career in 1929.

Irvin took up coaching, leading the Blackhawks to their first Stanley Cup finals appearance ever in 1930/31 (losing to Cecil Hart's Canadiens). The following season, he took over the reins of the Toronto Maple Leafs, who had not won the Stanley Cup since 1921/22. Owner Conn Smythe was determined to shake up the team, and Irvin did not disappoint. He teamed youngsters Busher Jackson, Joe Primeau, and Charlie Conacher into the legendary Kid Line and got solid defensive work from King Clancy, Hap Day, and Red Horner. Playing in the newly

---

16 *Tall Tales*, Terry Pluto, p. 344.

opened Maple Leaf Gardens, the Leafs won the 1931/32 Stanley Cup against Lester Patrick's New York Rangers.

But it would be 12 years before Irvin coached another Cup winner. Irvin suffered Cup losses in 1932/33, 1935/36, 1937/38, 1938/39, and 1939/40 – even while the Leafs frequently dominated the Canadian division standings (and the offensive stats) during the regular season. Still, Irvin augmented his team with more bright rookies such as Syl Apps, Gord Drillon, and legendary goalie Turk Broda. Nonetheless, by 1940 Leafs owner Conn Smythe, tired of being second best, decided to make a coaching change. Rather than humiliate Irvin by summarily firing him, Smythe eased Irvin out by encouraging him to coach the Montreal Canadiens, who were suffering through the worst period of their illustrious history.

It's hard to contemplate the Habs historically being in desperate straits – but that's where they were at. The team was in danger of folding and badly needed a change of fortune.

They got it in Dick Irvin. Like he did in Toronto, Irvin combed the minors for young talent. Forwards Elmer Lach, Toe Blake, and Ray Getliffe supplied the offence while Butch Bouchard, a crushing checker, anchored the blue-liners. In 1943 Irvin discovered Bill Durnan, the greatest goaltender of the 1940s, who won six Vezina trophies in seven seasons for Irvin in Montreal.

Irvin took advantage of the rules changes in 1943, which introduced the red line and the two-line offside to hockey – thus speeding up the game and opening up the dikes offensively. Still, he needed a catalyst to make his brand of fire-wagon hockey work.

In 1942, he found him in a French-Canadian son of Montreal named Maurice "Rocket" Richard.

Richard struggled through injuries during his rookie season, but as a sophomore he suddenly launched himself and his team to the greatest performance in Habs franchise history. Montreal's winning percentage of .830 in 1943/44 is still a team record. The Rocket became the first NHL player to score 50 goals in a season. And the Habs won their first Stanley Cup since 1930/31. They added another in 1945/46.

Irvin hit a rough patch in 1947/48 but kept rebuilding thanks to the flood of talent being signed into the Montreal farm system by Habs general manager Frank Selke. More immortals arrived: Doug Harvey, Tom Johnson, Jean Beliveau,

Jacques Plante, and Dickie Moore. But Irvin didn't rely solely on talented rookies, seasoning his team with key acquisitions from other teams. Players such as Ray Getliffe, Ken Mosdell, and Bert Olmstead were acquired in trades, working wonders for the Habs during Irvin's reign as coach. Irvin won his fourth and final Stanley Cup in 1952/53 over the Boston Bruins.

The Canadiens that subsequently won five straight Cup wins from 1955/56 to 1959/60 were coached by Toe Blake – but it was Dick Irvin who built that team. It was Irvin who put the pieces together, honed his young talents into hardened, determined hockey players, and gave them the experience needed to become future champions. Dick Irvin was the Frank Lloyd Wright of the NHL: an architect of winning teams.

He was also the Glen Sather of his own era: he lived and died with his offence. Irvin's Toronto teams, despite possessing talented blue-liners and decent goaltending, never dominated defensively. It was only when Irvin coached Montreal that his teams became more balanced. Even so, they lost twice to the Leafs dynasty teams that were defensive wizards in 1946/47 and 1950/51 and fell three times in 1951/52, 1953/54, and 1954/55 to the well-balanced Detroit Red Wings dynasty.

Meanwhile, Irvin got his players to excel by constantly stirring the pot. Irvin could be barbed, sarcastic, caustic, and, on occasion, tactless in leading his players.

When interviewing hockey legend Jean Beliveau, I asked him what the differences in coaching styles were between Irvin and Toe Blake. Beliveau answered obliquely, "One [Blake] was more tactful in criticizing his players than the other one was [Irvin]."

Irvin was the first coach to use stats as a tool to evaluate his players and his opponents, and if he were coaching today he would be ecstatic at the revolution and proliferation of hockey statistics. His training camps and team practices were crisp and efficient, devoted to inculcating the players with Irvin's tactics and methods (whereas most other NHL coaches' training camps and practice methods were still crude and informal) and more focused on getting the players into physical shape.

Another interesting aspect of Irvin's teams is the fact that they were among the *nastiest* in the NHL: finishing either first or second in team penalty minutes 20 times in 27 seasons of coaching. Is it any coincidence that two of the greatest stick-fighting incidents in NHL history – the Eddie Shore–Ace Bailey fight of

1933 and the Maurice Richard–Hal Laycoe imbroglio of 1955 – both involved teams led by Dick Irvin?

(What's interesting about the Richard–Laycoe stick-fight is that Irvin showed no displeasure to Richard over the incident and instead excoriated Richard's teammates for not coming to Richard's aid during the fight.)

When the Habs failed to win the 1954/55 Stanley Cup, general manager Frank Selke decided to make a change.

Like Conn Smythe before him, Selke could not bear to humiliate the coach who had made his team a contender – and again Irvin got a golden parachute. This time it was the head coaching job of the Chicago Blackhawks: the Siberia of the NHL during the 1950s.

Irvin, seeing the writing on the wall, accepted the offer and began the task of rebuilding the Hawks, just as he'd done twice before. He lasted one season before learning of the bone cancer that would eventually kill him in 1957.

His parting from the Hawks was a poignant one.

Hawks player Forbes Kennedy later told Irvin's son, Dick Jr.: "You could see he was getting sick. . . . We were getting ready for a morning practice when Dick came into the room. 'Fellows,' he said, 'you know I've always told you if you didn't give me 100 per cent you couldn't play on this team. Well, now I can't give you 100 per cent so I'm leaving. I can't coach any more. I have to go home. Good luck.' There were a few guys in the room, including Dick, with some tears in their eyes. What with the record he had I figured I was in on some hockey history, sad as it was. I'll never forget it."[17]

---

17 *Behind the Bench*, Dick Irvin, pp. 46-47.

GLEN "SLATS" SATHER RANK #4

PLUS: 137
MINUS: 13
VALUE: +124
PEAK RANK: #4 in 1987/88
PEAK VALUE: +131 in 1988/89

WHA COACHING EXPERIENCE: Edmonton Oilers, 1977[18]–1978/79

WHA REGULAR SEASON W–L–T: 95–76–7
WHA PLAYOFF W–L: 8–15

WHA LEAGUE CHAMPIONSHIP: 1978/79

WHA PLAYOFF APPEARANCES: 1976/77–1978/79
AVCO CUP FINALS: 1978/79

NHL COACHING EXPERIENCE: Edmonton Oilers, 1979–1989, 1993–1994; New York Rangers, 2003[19]–2004[20]

NHL REGULAR SEASON W–L–T–OL: 497–307–121–7
NHL PLAYOFF W–L–T: 89–37–1

JACK ADAMS AWARD: 1985/86

PRESIDENT'S TROPHIES: 1985/86–1986/87

SMYTHE DIVISION TITLES: 1981/82–1986/87

NHL PLAYOFF APPEARANCES: 1979/80–1988/89

---

18 Sather coached the last 18 games of the 1976/77 WHA season.

19 Sather coached the last 28 games of the 2002/03 NHL season.

20 Sather coached the first 62 games of the 2003/04 NHL season.

STANLEY CUP FINALS: **1982/83–1984/85, 1986/87–1987/88**
STANLEY CUP VICTORIES: **1983/84–1984/85, 1986/87–1987/88**

"You can tell it's getting close to the playoffs – Glen Sather is getting bitchy and yelling at everybody."[21]

Vic Hadfield

"Is there another coach who would've gotten as much out of me?"[22]

Wayne Gretzky

The last true dynasty in NHL history was the Edmonton Oilers, who won five Stanley Cups in seven seasons from 1983/84 to 1989/90. The man who built that dynasty and coached four of those Stanley Cup wins (while serving as general manager for the fifth in 1989/90) is Glen Sather.

Sather orchestrated a revolution in offensive tactics, assembling the most awesome array of scoring talent since the NHL expanded in 1967. His teams set scoring records that endure today – and will likely never be broken. But his most enduring legacy to hockey was the way he harnessed, focused, and unleashed the on-ice genius of Wayne Gretzky.

Glen Sather had been a journeyman defensive forward who played for seven hockey teams in the NHL and WHA and was called "Slats" because of his gritty, intense play.

He began his NHL career with the Boston Bruins as one of the many bright young players who flourished under Harry Sinden's tutelage.

Sinden's style of physical, aggressive offensive-oriented hockey with an emphasis on the transition game heavily influenced Sather's own playing style in the decade to come. His longest stay as a player was with the Rangers during their heyday under Emile Francis. Sather was a solid reserve player who made his teams better: what he lacked in talent he made up for with intelligence, hard work, and an inquisitive mind for learning how to make a team win in all facets of hockey management.

---

21 *Vic Hadfield's Diary*, Vic Hadfield with Tim Moriarty, p. 109.

22 *Gretzky: An Autobiography*, Wayne Gretzky with Rick Reilly, p. 187.

Sather ended his playing career with the Edmonton Oilers in 1977 when they were still in the WHA, serving as a player-coach for the team during the 1976/77 season. In the WHA, he saw first-hand the offensive wizardry of Bobby Hull, Anders Hedberg, and Ulf Nilsson of the Winnipeg Jets. The trio (using their synthesis of North American and European offensive tactics) set the WHA ablaze with their transition game, and Sather saw the future of hockey. He immediately adopted the Jets tactics, but to make it work he needed the talent – which he didn't have . . . yet.

The transition game eliminated the old rules demanding that forwards stay within their lanes while playing. Instead, the whole ice became a canvas upon which a team could create new ways of advancing, passing, and shooting the puck. The boundaries of the transition game existed solely in the limits of the imagination of the puck-carrier: the more creative a player was, the more opportunities there were to score.

Wayne Gretzky writes, "Our game was speed and skating and finesse. Our game was using all five people in the play. We knew the more we had the puck on offense, the better off we'd be. So we decided we'd go all out on the forecheck, cut the rink in half, and not give them center ice. We also picked up the centreman early and left the wingers to the defensemen."[23]

Sather ultimately merged the North American tactics he learned at the knee of Harry Sinden with the European tactics used by Hedberg and Nilsson, and from 1979/80 to 1993/94 hockey fans were treated to new heights of scoring prowess – not only from the Edmonton Oilers but also from legends Mario Lemieux and Brett Hull.

Sather's first full season as a coach was a losing one, but very early in the 1978/79 season he found the catalyst to start the offensive engines of the Oilers: a blond-haired, slight-looking teenaged centre from Brantford, Ontario, named Wayne Gretzky, whose personal services contract had just been purchased from the doomed Indianapolis Racers franchise. During the next two decades, Gretzky didn't rewrite the hockey record book – he *became* the hockey record book.

Glen Sather's task in coaching and developing the Great One focused more on the mental and emotional aspects of the game rather than the tactical. Gretzky's

---

23 *Gretzky: An Autobiography*, Wayne Gretzky with Rick Reilly, p. 76.

physical talents and hockey IQ were self-evident and inter-stellar. What Gretzky needed was the maturity to become THE MAN he was meant to be. He was only 17 years old and he had a lot to learn.

Sather began by having Gretzky living in his home during the first few weeks after he arrived in Edmonton. Every day Wayne was inculcated with the responsibilities and expectations he would have to bear every game for the rest of his career.

Slats augmented Gretzky's education by having veteran players like the late Garnet "Ace" Bailey provide peer group instruction and correction whenever the Great One lost focus. In return Gretzky learned what it meant to be a teammate and a leader on and off the ice.

Sather gave Gretzky ample playing time but was not afraid to bench Gretzky if he felt that his mind was not on his work.

There is an oft-told story that in Gretzky's rookie year in the WHA, he failed to pick up an opponent on defence and allowed the man to score. Sather benched him for an entire period before allowing Gretzky to play in the third – whereupon the Great One responded with a hat trick that won the game. It was the last time Gretzky was ever benched.

Sather was a study in contrasts. He could play the cool self-made millionaire sophisticate (who never had a hair out of place) and the sophomoric prankster with equal passion.

But make no mistake, behind the sartorial splendour was a ruthless, cunning, driving competitor who did not tolerate losing. Sather had a cruel, cutting tongue that spared no one: his players, opponents, referees, and any fan or sports writer who crossed him were all cut to the quick. Slats never stopped demanding more from his players. In the beginning, it helped make the Edmonton Oilers Stanley Cup champions. In the end, it broke the team apart.

The Oilers finished first in the final season of the WHA but still lost the 1978/79 Avco Cup finals to the Jets. Along with Winnipeg, Edmonton merged with the NHL in 1979, but it cost Sather nearly his entire team (save for Gretzky) to the expansion draft. Starting from scratch, he added Mark Messier, Paul Coffey, Jari Kurri, Kevin Lowe, Andy Moog, and Grant Fuhr to the team.

All of these men were artists on the ice, and every night during the 1980s they would create a body of work that endures in the hockey record books and is etched forever on the Stanley Cups they would win together.

By 1981/82 the Oilers were winning again and began a streak of six straight Smythe Division titles. By 1982/83 they had reached the Stanley Cup finals for the first time – only to be swept by the Islanders at the tail end of New York's dynasty.

Then the Oilers began their own dynastic run: they avenged their loss to the Islanders by beating them for the Cup in 1983/84, and they beat Mike Keenan's Flyers in 1984/85. After a fluke second-round loss to Bob Johnson's Calgary Flames in 1985/86, they bounced back with a tough win over the Flyers again in 1986/87, followed by a crushing sweep of the Boston Bruins a season later. Throughout that period the Oilers dominated the standings: from 1982/83 to 1986/87, they were the best regular-season team in the NHL three times and were the recipients of the first two President's trophies in NHL history.

Glen Sather's Oilers were a rarity: a hockey dynasty that won solely with its offence. From 1982 to 1987, they led the NHL in that category, and their best defensive showing was in 1984/85, when they finished seventh. A major reason for their loss in the 1982/83 finals was that the Islanders were a well-balanced team with the defence and goaltending to shut down Gretzky and company.

Interestingly enough, Sather's Oilers never led the NHL in power-play offence – but they were one of the best teams in converting power-play opportunities. They weren't prolific, but they were certainly accurate.

Edmonton's *real* secret weapon, however, was their short-handed offence. This was one of Sather's greatest innovations: in a penalty-killing situation, he would put his top guns (Gretzky and Jari Kurri) on the ice. Both men were able to capitalize on turnover opportunities, get the odd-man rush, and make the quick score. Talk about a morale killer for your opponents. From 1981/82 to 1989/90, the Oilers led the NHL in short-handed offence seven times in eight seasons.

What's surprising, though, is the fact that Sather's Oilers still lacked the invincibility that other great hockey dynasties had possessed. Their second-round loss to the Flames in 1985/86 came about because an Oiler blue-liner accidentally banked the puck off goalie Grant Fuhr's skate into his own net. There was a lack of cohesion in the team's chemistry. Doug Hunter in his book *Champions* writes that "Paul Coffey was fed up with Glen Sather. . . . Coffey alleged that the team observed a double standard in its treatment of players – some were coddled while others were dumped on."[24]

Wayne Gretzky writes, "Slats loved trying to get the upper hand so much that he went over the line. He'd do sleazy things, like trying to get a player to come in and do a contract one-on-one, rather than with his agent. . . . They'd come out of his office a lot poorer."[25]

Coffey was traded to Pittsburgh in 1987. The Oilers then failed to win the Cup in 1988/89 when they lost in the first round to Robbie Ftorek's Los Angeles Kings – led by none other than Wayne Gretzky (who had been sent there in 1988 in the most famous trade in NHL history). There were also off-ice problems, exemplified by Grant Fuhr's suspension for substance abuse.

Also, Sather's pressure-cooker nature was wearing thin with the Oilers veterans, who resented his tirades against them both in the locker room and in the press.

And then there was Sather's desire to leave coaching and focus on the front office. During the 1980/81 season, he had briefly yielded the bench to Bryan "Bugsy" Watson but returned to coaching when the Oilers started out poorly. Sather later used high-powered coaches such as John Muckler, Roger Neilson, and Ted Green to help him during the glory years.

After 1989, Sather gave up the head coaching job while remaining as general manager. The Oilers still regained the Cup in 1989/90, but afterwards the rot set in. Many of the Oilers stars were traded away, and by 1993/94 Edmonton was in the basement (while several of the team's former stars were en route to winning the Cup with the Rangers). Sather returned to coach the Oilers in 1993/94 but couldn't salvage the team. He stayed as Oilers general manager, however, until 2000, when he also returned to New York to become the Rangers general manager (until he resigned after the 2014/15 season).

Sather's true legacy to hockey is that he was the greatest coach of the 1980s. He was the greatest offensive coach of his time and earned the admiration of his peers.

Years later Jacques Demers would state, "I liked Glen Sather's ability to coach a bunch of superstars and make them perform at a high level every single night. I liked Glen Sather's approach to the game and the creativity he allowed for all those

---

24 *Champions*, Douglas Hunter, p. 203.

25 *Gretzky: An Autobiography*, Wayne Gretzky with Rick Reilly, p. 122.

players. . . . I thought that Glen Sather changed our game in a positive way in the '80s. He made our game more interesting, and he gave every one of those players the opportunity to express themselves every night, no matter where the game was played. I liked his cockiness behind the bench. That little smirk that he knew he was going to beat you. I hated it, but I liked that."[26]

---

26 *Simply The Best*, Mike Johnston and Ryan Walter, pp. 147–148.

JOEL QUENNEVILLE RANK #5

PLUS: 124
MINUS: 2
VALUE: +122
PEAK RANK: #5 in 2013/14
PEAK VALUE: +122 in 2014/15

COACHING EXPERIENCE: St. Louis Blues, 1997[27]–2004; Colorado Avalanche, 2005–2008; Chicago Blackhawks, 2008–present

REGULAR SEASON W–L–T–OL: 754–438–77–106
PLAYOFF W–L: 115–89

JACK ADAMS AWARD: 1999/00

PRESIDENT'S TROPHIES: 1999/00, 2012/13

CENTRAL DIVISION TITLES: 1999/00, 2009/10, 2012/13

PLAYOFF APPEARANCES: 1996/97–2002/03, 2005/06, 2007/08–2014/15
STANLEY CUP FINALS: 2009/10, 2012/13, 2014/15
STANLEY CUP VICTORIES: 2009/10, 2012/13, 2014/15

When Joel Quenneville (pronounced *kwen-ville*) was hired by the Chicago Blackhawks four games into the 2008/09 season, his coaching value was +42 and he ranked #31 on my coaches list. Quenneville had had a decent, respectable coaching career up to that point: a Jack Adams Award here, a President's Trophy there, a bunch of playoff appearances, but no Cup win or even a Cup final for that matter. There was nothing really to suggest that seven years after his

27 Quenneville coached the last 40 games of the 1996/97 season.

hiring by Chicago, Quenneville would end the Blackhawks 49-year Stanley Cup drought, win two additional Stanley Cup titles and become the best active coach in the NHL in terms of career value.

Oddly enough, though Quenneville's greatest success has been in Chicago, he also remains the winningest coach in St. Louis Blues franchise history. (Not bad when you consider that Scotty Bowman, Al Arbour, and Mike Keenan, to name a few, all tried their hands in coaching the Blues one time or another in their illustrious careers.)

His coaching career has been one of consistent excellence. Quenneville has never had a losing season in his 18 seasons of NHL coaching.

Despite Quenneville's reputation for being a strong defensive coach, his teams have been much stronger offensively than they are defensively. In 18 seasons, they have finished in the top ten for offence thirteen times but for defence only seven times. Meanwhile, Quenneville's teams never have great strength in their special teams. He got decent power-play and penalty-kill quality from his Blues teams, but his years with Chicago have seen considerable inconsistency in special teams. The 2009/10 and 2012/13 Cup-winning Blackhawks teams were only 19th and 20th in power-play production respectively, whereas they finished fourth and third in penalty-killing during those same two years. Nonetheless, the Blackhawks exhibit enormous offensive strength in even-ice situations and have great on-ice discipline (nearly always finishing in the bottom five in the NHL in team penalty minutes).

Joel Quenneville had been a journeyman defenceman: drafted by the Maple Leafs in 1978, he bounced around with Toronto (led by Roger Neilson) and the Colorado Rockies (where he played under Don Cherry) before finding a home with the Hartford Whalers. Quenneville's playing career was similar to Lindy Ruff's in that it was solid and steady but never spectacular. He stopped playing in 1992 and immediately took up coaching, working in the Leafs organization before establishing ties with rising coaching prospect Marc Crawford.

In 1994 Quenneville linked up with Crawford and spent the next three years working as an assistant coach for him. Just as Darryl Sutter developed his coaching identity serving under Mike Keenan, Quenneville sharpened his coaching skills under Crawford, playing a supporting role in the Colorado Avalanche's 1995/96 Stanley Cup triumph.

That Cup victory gave Quenneville his first big break: in January 1997 the St. Louis Blues hired him to replace the fired Mike Keenan. Quenneville inherited a team that had seen fan favourites Curtis Joseph and Brendan Shanahan traded to other teams and superstar Brett Hull at loggerheads with their volatile ex-coach. Quenneville had his work cut out for him.

He faced the challenge superbly, and in an excellent display of coaching he got the Blues playing at a higher pitch, with a solid two-way effort from Brett Hull (whose defensive skills were at best indifferent prior to his new coach's arrival).

Quenneville's best season in St. Louis was in 1999/00, when the Blues set franchise records in both wins and team points and won the President's Trophy. They also had the best defence in the NHL, with Chris Pronger having a career year, winning the Norris and Hart trophies. Forward Pavel Demitra and goalie Roman Turek excelled, and Quenneville himself won the Jack Adams Award as the NHL's coach of the year.

On paper the Blues were a shoe-in to reach their first Stanley Cup final since 1969/70. But it wasn't to be, as the first-seed Blues were upset in the first round of the playoffs by Darryl Sutter's eighth-seeded San Jose Sharks. The Blues would do better the following season, making it to the conference finals for the first time since 1985/86, only to be swept aside by Bob Hartley's Colorado Avalanche, who later won the Stanley Cup.

Quenneville never reached those levels again in St. Louis. He was fired in 2004 by the Blues, but in 2005 he took over as head coach for the very same Colorado Avalanche. Although he had winning seasons with the Avalanche, Quenneville's playoff performances were mediocre. As the 2000s continued, Quenneville was acquiring a reputation for not being able to lead his teams to the big one – let alone *win* the big one (see "Heartbreak Coaches" in Part Four).

In 2008 the Avalanche fired Quenneville, and he then replaced Denis Savard behind the bench in Chicago. He was joining a Hawks franchise that was determined to end the dry rot of the Bob Pulford years, and the accession of Hawks owner Rocky Wirtz to power in 2007 resulted in a tsunami of change for Chicago. Gone were the decades of penury and icing squads that were always one player shy of winning the Stanley Cup. Gone was the xenophobia that kept talented European players from playing in Chicago and the restrictive TV packages that kept local Chicagoans from watching their Hawks in the comfort of their own homes. Attendance subsequently soared, and Chicagoans redoubled their love for their beloved Hawks.

Wirtz had talented managers in Dale Tallon and, later, Stan Bowman, who brought in bright, young players.

What he needed was the right coach to lead this team into the 2010s . . . and victory.

Surprising many, Joel Quenneville became the icing on the cake.

In 2008/09 the Blackhawks made their first conference final appearance since 1994/95. The following year they put it all together: Chicago was the third-best team in the NHL and ranked in the top five in offence, defence, penalty-killing, and short-handed offence.

The Hawks had All-Star talent in forward Patrick Kane and Norris Trophy winner Duncan Keith. In the playoffs, Jonathan Toews led the Hawks offensively while goalie Antti Niemi stifled the opposition with key saves. In the end, the Blackhawks simply possessed too much firepower for their opponents to contain, and Quenneville did what Billy Reay, Bob Pulford, Mike Keenan, and Darryl Sutter could not do: win the Stanley Cup when Patrick Kane scored in overtime of Game 6.

Still, Quenneville and the Hawks stumbled a bit after that. The Hawks lost key talent to free agency immediately after winning the championship, which compromised their goaltending and defence significantly. Chicago remained competitive and playoff-bound, but they were forced to rebuild, thus preventing Chicago from repeating as Stanley Cup champions.

More than anything in the next couple of years, Quenneville was waiting for goalie Corey Crawford to grow into his goalie pads. It took time, but by 2012/13 Chicago roared out of the gate by going undefeated in its first 24 games. The team's winning percentage of .802 was the greatest in Hawks franchise history, and in a lockout-shortened season Chicago had the President's Trophy all sewn up. (Quenneville's second President's Trophy makes it only the third time in NHL history that a coach has won two President's trophies for two different teams. Scotty Bowman and Mike Keenan are the others.)

But the question remained: How would they fare in the playoffs?

The Hawks breezed by Minnesota handily in the first round, but then it started getting ugly.

Chicago allowed seventh-seeded Detroit to outgrind and outdefend them in the first four games of the second round. The Red Wings had a 3–1 series lead, but the Blackhawks determinedly came back. Still, in Game 6 in Detroit, they found themselves in a 2–1 deficit going into the third period.

It was there that Chicago showed their real secret weapon: an unquenchable, doggedly absolute, indefatigable desire and will to win.

It wasn't talent alone that helped Chicago win Games 6 and 7 against Detroit. It was a triumph of the will.

One could see it in Chicago's fanatical willingness to go any distance in order to win, to pay the brutal price that must be paid by all teams who strive for and seek the Stanley Cup. Though only eight players on that Hawks team were present in 2009/10, the newcomers shouldered their collective responsibility and rose to the challenge.

The conference finals against the defending champion Los Angeles Kings would go only five games, but each win was the nearest run for the Blackhawks – especially the final game, when Chicago finally solved the style of stellar Kings goalie Jonathan Quick in double overtime.

The Stanley Cup finals between Chicago and Boston was not only the first Original Six matchup in Cup finals since 1978/79 but also the ultimate showdown between the two best franchises in the young 2010s for primacy in the NHL.

Again, Chicago was tested. The Blackhawks topped their double-overtime defeat of Los Angeles with a triple-overtime series-opening victory over Boston. But the Bruins then beat Chicago in the Windy City to steal home-ice advantage, and after Boston stoned Chicago in Game 3 and appeared to be in control in Game 4 after the first period, one could sense the postmortems being written up for the Blackhawks.

Up to that moment Boston was controlling the pace of the game (and the series) by forcing Chicago to engage in a defensive battle. Although Chicago had the best defence in the NHL in 2012/13, they were unable to generate any points against the Bruins impenetrable blue line and goaltending. Boston was out-hitting them.

Quenneville had started the series by splitting Patrick Kane and Jonathan Toews into separate lines, but in Game 4 he put them back together. He ordered the rest of the team to flood the Boston zone in the hopes of getting more scoring chances, more rebounds, and placing greater pressure on Bruins goalie Tuukka Rask.

In the second and third periods, it worked. Chicago finally turned the tide against Boston and scored five goals. Although Boston came back with four goals of their own, they fell into Chicago's trap perfectly. Now Boston was engaged in a battle of the *offences*: Chicago's strength.

It took overtime yet again for Chicago to win the game, but they regained home-ice advantage – and their confidence.

They needed it: Boston would have them down 2–1 with 1:16 left in Game 6.

Then Chicago scored two goals in 17 seconds to win their second Stanley Cup.

Though Patrick Kane was awarded the 2013 Conn Smythe Trophy it should have been awarded to the entire Blackhawks team. Forwards Bryan Bickell, Patrick Sharp, Marian Hossa, and Jonathan Toews supplied the firepower. Blueliners Duncan Keith, Johnny Oduya, and Niklas Hjalmarsson were rock solid on defence, and goalie Corey Crawford had the best goals against average (GAA) of the playoffs.

The 2013/14 season was not as kind to Quenneville and the Hawks. Chicago struggled in a more dense Central Division, vying for the division lead with the St. Louis Blues and a newly resuscitated Colorado Avalanche team. Quenneville led Chicago to his sixth triple-digit team point season as a coach, but the Hawks could only finish third in the Central division stakes.

The playoffs saw Chicago beat the Blues and the Minnesota Wild in six games in rounds one and two, but when they faced their new decade rivals – the Los Angeles Kings, whom they beat the season before in the Western Conference finals – the team saw itself extended way beyond their own fevered imaginings. After winning Game 1 at home, Chicago saw Los Angeles win the next three games to put them in a 3–1 series hole. Their offence was stymied by the Kings' smothering defence.

Once again Chicago showed character by winning Games 5 and 6, forcing Game 7 at sweet home Chicago. The Hawks controlled the first period with a 3–2 lead, forcing the Kings to wage a battle of the offences (much to the Hawks' liking), but the Kings turned the tables on the Hawks – outhitting and outfighting Chicago – tying the game in the third period to force an overtime.

When the Kings won the overtime period and the series (and eventually the Stanley Cup), it showed that Chicago's supremacy as the greatest team of the 2010s is not without challengers; that sustaining that championship spirit is the toughest test in hockey at this present time. A test that Joel Quenneville and the Chicago Blackhawks still needed to learn.

In 2014/15 Chicago finished third again in the Central Division and faced Nashville in the first round. Although the Blackhawks won in six it was tough going; then the Hawks swept the Minnesota Wild in the second round. The Western Conference finals against Anaheim was another struggle. Chicago was down 3–2 in the series but regained their offensive firepower in Games 6 and 7 to win the series.

The Stanley Cup finals against the upstart Tampa Bay Lightning was another surprise. The Lightning took a 2–1 series lead; playing with the same insouciance a young Blackhawks Cup winning team possessed in 2009/10. But Chicago rebounded strongly to win the series.

Throughout the playoffs Joel Quenneville urged his players to be patient on the ice and they were. Chicago's second and third liners scored game-winning goals and controlled the boards while Duncan Keith won the Conn Smythe trophy by playing marathon minutes, leading his team in assists and was a +16 on the ice throughout the playoffs.

Quenneville's third Cup win elevated him in ways unimaginable. He became the 11th head coach to coach three Stanley Cup winners and, most significant of all, he surpassed Mike Babcock as the greatest NHL coach of the 21st century. Since 2007/08 Babcock had always stood atop all coaches according to my calculations but throughout the 2010s Quenneville advanced by leaps and bounds until he passed Babcock in terms of coaching value during this century.

Joel Quenneville has reached that place where every game he coaches (and wins) he makes history by surpassing some august hockey figure. Quenneville himself is now part of the ranks of the august and the exalted and the view from the summit of Mount Olympus is limitless and wonderful to behold.

AL ARBOUR RANK #6

PLUS: 137
MINUS: 32
VALUE: +105
PEAK RANK: #4 in 1982/83
PEAK VALUE: +121 in 1985/86

COACHING EXPERIENCE: St. Louis Blues, 1970[28]–1972[29]; New York Islanders, 1973–1986, 1988–1994, 2007[30]

REGULAR SEASON W–L–T: 782–577–248
PLAYOFF W–L: 123–86

JACK ADAMS AWARD: 1978/79

PATRICK DIVISION TITLES: 1977/78–1978/79, 1980/81–1981/82, 1983/84

PLAYOFF APPEARANCES: 1971/72, 1974/75–1985/86, 1989/90, 1992/93–1993/94

STANLEY CUP FINALS: 1979/80–1983/84
STANLEY CUP VICTORIES: 1979/80–1982/83

"He was as sensitive and considerate as a coach can be. I always thought Al really hated it when people were mad at him. He was always in control of every area of coaching and he never seemed to seek the gratification of external praise. His real strength, though, was that he didn't burn his teams out. You did feel a kind of pressure from him, sure, and sure, I saw

---

28 Arbour coached the first 50 games of the 1970/71 season.

29 Arbour coached the last 44 games of the 1971/72 season and the first 13 games of the 1972/73 season.

30 Arbour coached one game of the 2007/08 season.

him discipline people. But he did it in a way, usually, that let the player keep his dignity.

"He's the best coach of our time. He made you play your best, but he wasn't mean. He didn't have to harass or ridicule you to make you play better. He simply made you a better person and a better player."[31]

Glenn "Chico" Resch

Al Arbour is the greatest coach in the history of the New York Islanders franchise – and of any New York area franchise. In one of the most remarkable franchise-building efforts in NHL history, he (along with his players and general manager Bill Torrey) made the Islanders into a powerhouse.

Arbour had been a defenceman and one of the first NHL players to wear eyeglasses. In a 2008 interview, Arbour describes himself as "a fifth defenceman (when NHL teams usually carried four) who filled in when someone got hurt."

In truth, he is being unduly modest. Arbour in his playing days was much like Glen Sather and Emile Francis: a useful reserve player who always made his team better. It wasn't a fluke that he played for the Detroit Red Wings during their glory years in the 1950s.

He also played for the Chicago Blackhawks team that won the 1960/61 Stanley Cup; he played for Punch Imlach's Maple Leafs when they won the 1961/62 and 1962/63 Stanley Cups; and he ended his career playing for Scotty Bowman's St. Louis Blues teams that made three consecutive Stanley Cup finals appearances from 1967/68 to 1969/70.

It was only near the end of his career, though, that he got the idea of becoming a coach.

Arbour later told Dick Irvin Jr. that "Scotty Bowman was the one who got me interested in coaching. I was playing for him in St. Louis at the end of my career, and he wanted to step aside and become the general manager. He wanted me to take over."[32]

Arbour certainly had the right role models to become a coaching legend, learning from Tommy Ivan and Scotty Bowman the value of having a well-balanced team offensively and defensively.

---

31 *Coaches*, Stan Fischler, p. 170.

32 *Behind the Bench*, Dick Irvin, p. 183.

He learned from Bowman the secret that strong special teams can make teams champions. The Islanders finished in the top ten in power-play offence eight times and in penalty-killing 11 times. (In penalty-killing situations, the Islanders' transition game was astounding: they led the NHL in short-handed offence three times and finished in the top ten 14 times.) He also learned from Scotty Bowman the value of on-ice discipline. Like Bowman's Canadiens, Arbour's Islanders swam against the thuggish tide in the NHL during the 1970s and 1980s by reducing his team's penalty minutes (with the two clubs taking the lion's share of the Cups). Arbour's teams were second only to Scotty Bowman's Buffalo Sabres in having the fewest penalty minutes during the 1980s.

Tommy Ivan taught Arbour how to be a father figure to his players. Duane Sutter later told Greg Prato: "Al would take you in on one-on-one situations in his office and talk to you about your game and your life, and life in general."[33]

Arbour learned from Rudy Pilous (his coach in Chicago) the necessity of leavening his intensity with humour: he became a congenial and engaging raconteur with a potent and sometimes earthy sense of humour.

And he learned from Bowman and Punch Imlach the necessity of maintaining intensity and discipline when it came to leadership – and how to keep his players focused and hungry. In his first NHL coaching gig, Arbour didn't do too badly with the St. Louis Blues. In 1971/72 he led them to their fourth Stanley Cup semifinal appearance in five seasons, only to be swept by the eventual champion Boston Bruins team. But the Blues wouldn't come that close to the Stanley Cup again until 1985/86, and Arbour's stay in St. Louis was undermined by front office interference that led to the departures of both Scotty Bowman and Arbour himself.

St. Louis's loss was the fledgling New York Islanders' gain. After an awful start in their inaugural season in 1972/73, Islanders general manager Bill Torrey offered Arbour the head coaching job. Arbour, despite some personal misgivings, agreed to take it.

It was the start of a beautiful professional friendship, and together Arbour and Torrey would assemble one of the greatest teams in NHL history. Winger Bob Nystrom and goalies Billy Smith and Glenn "Chico" Resch were already in the organization, but the Islanders used the draft with great skill to add Denis Potvin

33 *Dynasty*, Greg Prato, p. 275.

in 1973, Clark Gillies and Bryan Trottier in 1974, Ken Morrow in 1976, and Mike Bossy in 1977.

These players formed the heart and soul of the Islanders dynasty from 1980 to 1983.

By 1974/75 the Islanders had their first winning season, the first of what proved to be 12 consecutive playoff appearances, and the first of nine Stanley Cup semi-final appearances in the next ten years (they were denied only in 1977/78). Moreover, they ended the Montreal Canadiens domination of the regular-season standings when they finished the 1978/79 season as the best team in the NHL (a feat they would repeat again in 1980/81 and 1981/82). By 1979/80 they finally reached the Stanley Cup finals and won their first championship over Pat Quinn's Philadelphia Flyers.

What can be said about their dynastic run? They were 16–3 in the finals during those four years: losing two games to the Flyers, one game to the Minnesota North Stars in 1980/81, and sweeping both Roger Neilson's Vancouver Canucks in 1981/82 and Glen Sather's Edmonton Oilers in 1982/83.

But the most amazing aspect of the Islanders' dynasty was that they won 19 consecutive playoff series, breaking Scotty Bowman's record of 14 set in 1979/80. Since then – up to 2015 – no NHL coach has remotely come close to that astronomical figure. Glen Sather won nine straight from 1984 to 1986 and Bowman won nine straight from 1996/97 to 1998/99. One can safely conclude that this is an NHL coaching record that will never be broken.

Arbour's Islanders were the only NHL team to come close to matching Toe Blake's NHL record of five consecutive Stanley Cup wins. While the 1979/80 Canadiens lost in the quarterfinals, in 1983/84 the Islanders again reached the finals for a fifth straight time, facing the Edmonton Oilers. Slowed down by age and injuries, the Islanders fell in five games. Earl Ingarfield Sr. (who worked in the Islanders front office during those years) speculated in a 2009 interview that one reason why they lost in 1983/84 was the 2–3–2 playoff format instead of the 2–2–1–1–1 format of the past. Ingarfield said that if the Islanders had been able to play Game 5 at home, they might have won and turned the series around.

Even so, the fact that they were in a position to equal Toe Blake's Stanley Cup quintet has to be seen as one of the supreme coaching accomplishments since 1967. Today, with a 30-team league and free agency, there is no way for a team to equal what Al Arbour tried to do in 1983/84. Indeed, since 1983/84 no NHL team has even made *three* consecutive Stanley Cup finals appearances.

However, after 1984, the Islanders' fortunes declined. By 1986 Al Arbour retired from coaching, but in the years that followed the team began to flounder.

Arbour returned to coach the Islanders in 1988/89 but couldn't stop the slide. The only bright spot in Arbour's second term as head coach came in 1992/93 – and never was Arbour's intensity more evident than in the 1992/93 Stanley Cup playoffs. The Islanders had just had their first winning season since 1987/88 and were making their first playoff appearance since 1989/90. The team was filled with mostly raw youngsters sprinkled with a few veterans. Only one player, Pat Flatley, had played in their last Cup final squad in 1983/84.

In Game 1 of the first round against Terry Murray's Washington Capitals, the Islanders lost 3–1 in a listless effort.

What followed is best chronicled by Stan Fischler: "On the day off before Game 2, Arbour had his players get on the bus. . . . Arbour asked the driver to get off the bus, then closed the doors. For the next 10 minutes, it was a miracle the windows didn't crack. Arbour gave it to his team, and gave it to them good."[34]

"'I think Al wanted to drill home the message that we shouldn't just be happy to be in the playoffs,' recalled Pat Flatley. 'He knew we could win the series, but he was questioning if we knew that. It was quite a lecture.'"[35]

Arbour supplemented his tongue-lashing, however, by calling out Islanders top gun Pierre Turgeon and injured forward Ray Ferraro to stand up and make a difference. They did, promptly pulling off the last great playoff run in Islanders franchise history. New York beat the Caps in six and faced the defending champion Pittsburgh Penguins in the second round, defying all odds and coming back from a 3–2 series deficit to win Games 6 and 7 (the last game was won in Pittsburgh in overtime) in one of the most stunning upsets in Stanley Cup playoff history.

Although the Islanders ultimately lost the conference finals to eventual champion Montreal in five games, honour was served. The 1992/93 Islanders proved themselves worthy of their glorious forebears. Arbour got his team to give everything they could possibly give.

---

34 *Pride and Passion*, Stan Fischler and Chris Botta, p. 212

35 *Ibid.*

He left coaching for good in 1994, although he made a fleeting one-game appearance in 2007, and today he lives in quiet retirement in Florida (although it was reported in August 2014 that Arbour is suffering from dementia).

As of 2015, Arbour's final post-season remains the last time the Islanders reached the conference finals in the Stanley Cup playoffs. It also represents a summary lesson about how coaching genius can inspire a team to excel in the face of long odds.

KEN HITCHCOCK RANK #7

PLUS: 125
MINUS: 23
VALUE: +102
PEAK RANK: #7 in 2014/15
PEAK VALUE: +102 in 2014/15

COACHING EXPERIENCE: Dallas Stars, 1996[36]–2002[37]; Philadelphia Flyers, 2002–2006[38]; Columbus Blue Jackets, 2006[39]–2010[40]; St. Louis Blues, 2011[41]–present

REGULAR SEASON W–L–T–OL: 708–429–88–97
PLAYOFF W–L: 76–72

JACK ADAMS AWARD: 2011/12

PRESIDENT'S TROPHIES: 1997/98–1998/99

CENTRAL DIVISION TITLES: 1996/97–2000/01, 2011/12, 2014/15

ATLANTIC DIVISION TITLE: 2003/04

PLAYOFF APPEARANCES: 1996/97–2000/01, 2002/03–2003/04, 2005/06, 2008/09, 2011/12–2014/15
STANLEY CUP FINALS: 1998/99–1999/00
STANLEY CUP VICTORY: 1998/99

---

36 Hitchcock coached the last 43 games of the 1995/96 season.

37 Hitchcock coached the first 50 games of the 2001/02 season.

38 Hitchcock coached the first 8 games of the 2006/07 season.

39 Hitchcock coached the last 62 games of the 2006/07 season.

40 Hitchcock coached the first 58 games of the 2009/10 season.

41 Hitchcock coached the last 69 games of the 2011/12 season.

When Ken Hitchcock became head coach of the St. Louis Blues early in the 2011/12 season, he was ranked 19th on my top 50 list. Four solid seasons later he has vaulted twelve steps in rank despite failing to win the Stanley Cup, with an even greater chance to crack the top five coaching ranks if he can continue his winning ways.

Hitchcock never played in the NHL but established his reputation as a coaching wizard in the minor leagues. From 1991 to 1993, he served as an assistant coach to Philadelphia Flyers head coach Bill Dineen. In 1995/96 he got his first NHL head coaching gig when he was chosen to take over the Dallas Stars, a team in transition under general manager Bob Gainey. The Stars hadn't been to the Stanley Cup finals since 1990/91 (when they were still the Minnesota North Stars) and had never won a Cup.

Hitchcock engineered one of the most remarkable turnarounds in NHL franchise history. The Dallas Stars had finished last in the Central Division in 1995/96. But during the next five seasons they would win five consecutive divisional titles, two consecutive President's trophies in 1997/98 and 1998/99, three straight Stanley Cup conference final appearances from 1997/98 to 1999/00, two trips to the Stanley Cup finals in 1998/99 and 1999/00, and the 1998/99 Stanley Cup – the only Stanley Cup win in their history (as of 2015).

During those glory years, Hitchcock's Stars won with defence and penalty-killing – but not by using a trapping defence like Jacques Lemaire did. Hitchcock described his system in the 1990s as "a counter-attack game."

Today, Hitchcock's defensive strategy has evolved from a counter-attack to a speedier, more aggressive game.

In a 2013 interview with this writer, Hitchcock explained, "It's how fast you can play and it's based on numbers. You try to outnumber the opposition in and around the puck. If they've got two players near the puck, we have three. If they have three, then we have four. It's more in your face. Today's game is more about forechecking. How hard we can forecheck. We want greater physicality on the forecheck."

Offensively, Hitchcock stressed, "We emphasize that there is more to hockey than puck possession. We try to shoot it as much as possible. My philosophy is the more you shoot it, the more you get it back." (It's ironic that Hitchcock is a defensive maven. During his minor league coaching years, Hitchcock's teams won with a run-and-gun offence. He tried to use the same system during his rookie season with the Stars but got badly burned by the opposition – a key reason why the Stars finished last that season – and Hitchcock was forced to readjust his tactics.)

The mainstays to Hitchcock's success in Dallas were goalie Ed Belfour, defensive forward Jere Lehtinen, and centres Joe Nieuwendyk (who won the Conn Smythe Trophy during the 1998/99 Stanley Cup playoffs) and Mike Modano (who earned NHL All-Star honours in 1999/00). Of the four, Belfour and Nieuwendyk eventually attained Hall of Fame status. Still, with the exception of Brett Hull, there were no superstars on Hitchcock's teams.

Hitchcock's motivational style when interacting with his players draws heavily from his old mentor, Bill Dineen. He states, "I worked through the team leaders and used a gradual approach whereby I would guide the players to turn to the team leaders for guidance. I would let the veteran players teach. I'm not in the locker room that much, but I try to develop a bond and trust with the players through the veterans.

"In Dallas, the team was really committed to winning, both offensively and defensively. They really bought into it. They were really hungry and eager to learn what it takes to win."

Interestingly, Hitchcock adds, "I learned a lot about how to motivate my players through my veteran players and my assistant coaches. In Dallas, I had Rick Wilson and Doug Jarvis. In Philadelphia, I had Craig Hartsburg and Terry Murray. Today [in St. Louis] I have Brad Shaw and they really gave me an understanding about the players' mindset."

Terry Murray states, "Ken is a great person to work for. He's a great delegator who's great at communicating with the players and coaches while always looking for a better way to handle situations."

The Stars failed to defend the Stanley Cup in 1999/00 – losing to the New Jersey Devils in six games.

The 21st century was rough on Hitchcock. In 2000/01 the Stars were swept in the second round by Joel Quenneville's St. Louis Blues, and by 2001/02 Hitchcock was fired halfway through the season.

He returned to Philadelphia to become the head coach of the Flyers, who had been underachieving in the playoffs since 1999/00. He got great results.

Using the same methods he used in Dallas, Hitchcock relied heavily on Keith Primeau to stand up and be a team leader. Hitchcock says, "When Keith Primeau came it became so easy to lead the team. Primeau found a new calling as a leader and he made the team so much better through his example."

Jeremy Roenick wrote in his memoir, *J.R.*: "Although Hitchcock and I would battle over issues, I always felt like there was mutual respect between us. Hitchcock primarily liked the way I played, although he was always trying to convince me that I needed to be more defensive-minded. Probably he was right. I've always said that Hitchcock was the smartest coach I ever had."[42] (Considering that Roenick played for Mike Keenan, Darryl Sutter, Ron Wilson, and Todd McLellan, that is high praise indeed.)

The Flyers responded with three straight seasons of earning 100 or more team points, a divisional title, and a conference final appearance in 2003/04 – losing to John Tortorella's Tampa Bay Lightning, who won the Cup that year in seven games. Hitchcock maintains it was injuries to five key players that killed the Flyers' chances of beating Tampa in the playoffs.

Unfortunately, Hitchcock could not sustain his success. A first-round playoff elimination in 2005/06 and then a horrendous start to the 2006/07 season cost him his job in the wake of a Flyers blood purge.

Three weeks after his firing, Hitchcock was hired by the Columbus Blue Jackets, who had yet to have a winning season since their NHL debut in 2000/01. In only four years he became their best coach ever, and thanks to the goaltending efforts of NHL All-Star and Calder Memorial Trophy winner Steve Mason, Hitchcock led the Blue Jackets to their first winning season and first playoff appearance in 2008/09.

In 2009/10 the Blue Jackets could not get untracked, but on February 4, 2010, in a shocking move, Hitchcock was fired.

He did not return to NHL coaching until 2011/12 when the St. Louis Blues fired head coach Davis Payne and reached out to Hitchcock to restore discipline and focus to the underachieving Blues. It was a challenge worthy of his talents.

Despite the team's losing record, they possessed superb goaltending, a solid

---

42 *J.R.*, Jeremy Roenick with Kevin Allen, p. 148.

defence, and plenty of young talent. Just like he did with Dallas, Hitchcock engineered a turnaround that resulted in the Blues winning their first division title since the 1999/00 season while leading the NHL in overall defence, thus earning Hitchcock his first Jack Adams Award.

The resuscitated Blues featured bright players such as forward Alex Steen and Ryan Reaves. Steen displayed excellent two-way skills while Reaves was a crushing, punishing power forward.

The Blues also had a solid blue-line corps with Alex Pietrangelo, Kevin Shattenkirk, and veteran Barret Jackman. Pietrangelo was especially sterling, earning All-Star honours for his efforts.

But the real jewels in the Blues roster were goalies Brian Elliott and Jaroslav Halak. Hitchcock rotated the two brilliantly; achieving stunning performances from both resulted in the goalies being awarded the Jennings Trophy in 2011/12. Of the two, Elliott was the most spectacular, leading the NHL with a 1.56 goals against average (GAA) and a save percentage of .940 (and second only to Jonathan Quick of the Los Angeles Kings in shutouts, with nine).

The Blues were only two points behind the President's Trophy–winning Vancouver Canucks and appeared poised to go far in the playoffs.

Sadly for Hitchcock and the Blues, they were humiliated in the second round by the eighth-seeded Los Angeles Kings – who swept them in four games, outdefending the best defence in the NHL.

Still, Hitchcock's return to the NHL was a solid comeback and a glorious reaffirmation of his coaching genius.

The following season the Blues failed to repeat as Central Division champions but continued to play strong until beaten again by the Kings. There were disturbing signs during their first-round loss to the defending Stanley Cup champions. The Blues gave up a 2–0 series lead and were leading 3–2 after two periods in Game 3 before giving up two goals in 76 seconds to lose the game and eventually the series as the Kings swept Games 4 through 6, outhitting and outworking the Blues in key situations.

In 2014/15 the Blues showed great strength throughout the season and surged at the end to win the Central Division title but once again faltered in the first round of the playoffs, falling to the Minnesota Wild in six, their offence only scoring two goals in the last two games.

The question remains whether St. Louis can bear down and develop greater strength in the face of adversity. As Hitchcock puts it, "The essential element in being a great coach is being able to build a team before it can begin to win games. Being able to win and control the hearts and minds of your players while building a bond and trust that helps you win championships."

Ken Hitchcock is building that team right now in St. Louis; the emotional bonds and the trust are there. What is required now is the will to win.

TOMMY IVAN RANK #8

PLUS: **109**
MINUS: **14**
VALUE: **+95**
PEAK RANK: **#3 in 1953/54**
PEAK VALUE: **+109 in 1953/54**

COACHING EXPERIENCE: **Detroit Red Wings, 1947–1954; Chicago Blackhawks, 1956–1958**[43]

REGULAR SEASON W–L–T: **288–174–111**
PLAYOFF W–L: **36–31**

PRINCE OF WALES TROPHIES: **1948/49–1953/54**

PLAYOFF APPEARANCES: **1947/48–1953/54**
STANLEY CUP FINALS: **1947/48–1949/50, 1951/52, 1953/54**
STANLEY CUP VICTORIES: **1949/50, 1951/52, 1953/54**

The late Jack Adams devoted 20 years to coaching and running the Detroit Red Wings: building them up from an expansion team to an established NHL franchise, developing an organization to recruit and sign available hockey talent, and establishing a viable farm system to nurture and harness that talent. By 1947 it was time for the Red Wings to take the next step and become a flagship franchise on par with the Montreal Canadiens and the Toronto Maple Leafs, and Adams decided to give up coaching and devote himself fully to the front office. The man Adams selected to lead the Red Wings during the most glorious chapter in their franchise history was the late Tommy Ivan.

Ivan is unfortunately remembered today for making one of the dumbest trades in NHL history when (as Chicago Blackhawks general manager) he sent Phil

43 Ivan coached the first 33 games of the 1957/58 season.

Esposito and three other players to the Boston Bruins for four players who did nothing to improve the Blackhawks fortunes: while Esposito would lead the Bruins to two Stanley Cup victories, the Blackhawks endured a Stanley Cup drought that lasted 49 years.

But before Ivan made that clunker of a trade in 1967, he was one of the greatest coaches in NHL history. He ranked among the top three coaches during the 1950s (to know where he ranked, see "Decades" in Part Four), and he ranked third in the Original Six era (1942–1967) behind Blake and Dick Irvin. Ivan's ability to get maximum effort from his players was exceeded only by Blake and Pete Green (see "Average Season Rating" in Part Four).

From 1948/49 to 1953/54, Ivan's Detroit Red Wings won a record six consecutive league championships (today's equivalent would be six consecutive President's trophies – an impossible task in this day and age). They made seven playoff appearances and five Stanley Cup finals appearances and won three championships.

Ivan was a coaching rarity for his time in that he had never played a minute in the NHL. His minor league playing career was ended by a severe injury, and taking up coaching instead, Ivan developed his reputation during the Second World War coaching hockey teams at the Canadian Army training base in Cornwall, Ontario (the late Punch Imlach worked alongside him). Many Canadian Army base teams included NHL players or players who would eventually make it to the NHL.

After the war, Jack Adams hired Ivan to coach the Wings farm team in Omaha, Nebraska, where a young Gordie Howe was on the roster. After one season in Omaha, Ivan moved up the ladder to the Wings farm team in Indianapolis, and by 1947 (at the age of 36) he was tapped to coach the Red Wings themselves.

Tommy Ivan was beloved in the eyes of his players (only Blake exceeded him in that regard). His truest strength as a coach was his positivism: his willingness to allow his players to be creative on the ice without hamstringing their talents. Red Wings icon Ted Lindsay said in a 2006 interview that Ivan allowed him, Howe, and Abel to design their own line rushes and work out new tricks and combinations on the ice. Their teammates were allowed the same leeway, and in return his players gave Ivan and the Detroit fans some of the greatest on-ice artistry in the sport.

What's amazing about Ivan's Red Wings was how well balanced they were tactically – and the exceptional depth of talent they possessed. During the glory years, the Wings were always in the top two for offence and defence (leading the

NHL in offence from 1948/49 to 1952/53 and defence from 1951/52 to 1952/53). Ivan was actually the best defensive coach of the Original Six era – but his genius was not based on tactical or strategic wizardry. Ivan himself summed up his defensive philosophy thusly: "Fundamentally there are only two basic manouevres in hockey. Either you knock the puck away from the man, or you knock the man away from the puck."[44]

Wings defencemen Red Kelly and Marcel Pronovost embodied both approaches.

Red Kelly was hardly a tough checker (he was a three-time Lady Byng Trophy winner), but his ability to force turnovers, gain possession of the puck, play the points, and set up his forwards was legendary. Kelly was the finest scoring blueliner of his era and the first recipient of the Norris Trophy.

His defensive linemate Marcel Pronovost, meanwhile, was the opposite. He was a ferocious, durable, hardy checker and a great shot-blocker – quite capable of knocking opponents away from the puck.

Together they made one of the greatest blue-line tandems in NHL history.

Forwards Gordie Howe, Sid Abel, Ted Lindsay, and Alex Delvecchio were the vanguard of the Red Wings offence. Lindsay led the NHL in goals scored in 1947/48 and in assists in 1949/50 (while winning the Ross Trophy as well that same season). Sid Abel won the Hart Trophy in 1948/49 after leading the NHL in goals scored.

And then there was Gordie Howe. "Mr. Hockey" dominated the NHL during Ivan's reign as Wings head coach, generating points with ruthless skill and effortless ease. He led the NHL in goals scored from 1950/51 to 1952/53, led the NHL in assists three out of four years from 1950/51 to 1953/54, and won the Ross Trophy four years in a row from 1950/51 to 1953/54.

Behind them all, the late Terry Sawchuk was the greatest goaltender of the Original Six era: twice winning the Vezina Trophy while playing for Tommy Ivan.

All of these men entered the Hockey Hall of Fame – a veritable wing in its own right.

And yet the Red Wings were more than their Hall of Fame cast. Defencemen Jack Stewart, Bill Quackenbush, and Leo Reise Jr. earned All-Star honours as well.

Forward Dutch Reibel was a Calder Trophy runner-up (Ted Lindsay would later state that Reibel was an unsung hero of the Red Wings).

---

44 *Gordie: A Hockey Legend*, Roy MacSkimming, p. 69

Even more significant is that Tommy Ivan got clutch performances from the players who never made the headlines. It was Pete Babando, for instance, who scored the Cup-winning goal in the 1949/50 Stanley Cup finals. Then when Red Kelly was knocked out of the 1951/52 playoffs with injuries, blue-liner Benny Woit took his place and performed brilliantly in Games 2 through 4 of the finals, checking his opponents with abandon and blocking shots.

(The Red Wings' 1951/52 Stanley Cup win must be considered one of the supreme defensive performances in Stanley Cup playoff history – holding their opponents to only five goals scored in eight games.)

And then there is what happened in the overtime period of Game 7 of the 1953/54 Stanley Cup finals against Montreal . . .

In interviews with former members of the Red Wings dynasty teams of 1949/50–1954/55, several players pointedly discussed the key role played by the Red Wings checking line of Marty Pavelich, Glen Skov, and Tony Leswick.

Vic Stasiuk stated that the checking line (along with the Production Line of Howe, Lindsay, and Abel) was never changed throughout the entire dynastic period and was a secret weapon of the Wings dynasty.

Bill Dineen said that when the Wings played Montreal and Rocket Richard took the ice, Pavelich, Skov, and Leswick took the ice too.

And so when it came time to score the Cup-winning goal for Detroit in the 1953/54 Stanley Cup finals, it was Tony Leswick (with Glen Skov getting the assist) who came through in the clutch.

Tommy Ivan may have been the head coach of the Detroit Red Wings, but it was still Jack Adams's team – and Adams never let Ivan forget it. Ivan never had to chew out his team when they slumped: Adams was always there to crack the whip for him. Ivan was the first of a trio of Wings coaches who had to play the role of good cop to Adams's bad cop (the others were Jimmy Skinner and Sid Abel), and it was Ivan who salved the wounds caused by Adams's tirades. By 1954 Ivan had had enough, and when the Chicago Blackhawks needed someone to run their club and help rebuild the team, he accepted their offer.

Ivan took over as Hawks general manager in 1954 and spent the next 23 years of his life serving in that capacity. He took over a team that hadn't won the Stanley Cup since 1937/38 and built up the organization. He established a farm system that developed the new talent signed by the Hawks scouts, and

– until 1967 – made shrewd trades with other NHL teams for hidden gems on their rosters.

Ivan returned to coaching for a brief time in the wake of Dick Irvin's death, but midway through the 1957/58 season Ivan handed over the reins to Rudy Pilous and never returned to coaching. By 1958/59 the Hawks were playoff contenders; by 1960/61 they won the Stanley Cup, and in the 12 years that followed made four more Stanley Cup finals appearances – all the while providing Chicago with some of the most entertaining hockey ever played during their franchise history.

Tommy Ivan was inducted into the Hockey Hall of Fame as a builder in 1974, and when he stepped down as Hawks general manager in 1977 (handing the job over to Bob Pulford), he devoted himself to developing the U.S. Olympic hockey team – the same U.S. Olympic hockey team that would win the gold medal in the 1980 Winter Games at Lake Placid – the Miracle on Ice.

Ivan died in 1999.

MIKE BABCOCK RANK #9

PLUS: 98
MINUS: 3
VALUE: +95
PEAK RANK: #9 in 2013/14
PEAK VALUE: +95 in 2014/15

COACHING EXPERIENCE: Anaheim Ducks, 2002–2004; Detroit Red Wings, 2005–2015; Toronto Maple Leafs, 2015–present

REGULAR SEASON W–L–T–OL: 527–285–19–119
PLAYOFF W–L: 82–62

PRESIDENT'S TROPHIES: 2005/06, 2007/08

CENTRAL DIVISION TITLES: 2005/06–2008/09, 2010/11

PLAYOFF APPEARANCES: 2002/03, 2005/06–2014/15
STANLEY CUP FINALS: 2002/03, 2007/08–2008/09
STANLEY CUP VICTORY: 2007/08

Until now, Mike Babcock was the greatest NHL coach of the 21st century, occupying the top slot from 2007/08 until he was surpassed by Joel Quenneville in 2014/15. He was the greatest coach of the 2000s; and, as of 2015, sits as the eighth-best coach of the 2010s. During the 2013/14 season Babcock surpassed the late Jack Adams to become the greatest head coach in the history of the Detroit Red Wings.

Since his NHL coaching debut in 2002/03, Babcock has won five divisional titles, made nine playoff appearances, and as of 2015 is the only active NHL coach with three Stanley Cup finals appearances to his credit. He coached the 2007/08 Stanley Cup champions (and was two goals shy of winning his second Stanley Cup in 2008/09), and in 2010 he led the Canadian Olympic hockey team to the gold medal at the Winter Olympics in Vancouver (becoming only the second man ever to coach a Stanley Cup winner and an Olympic gold-medal-winning team).

Mike Babcock is a coaching *wunderkind*. In 2011/12 he became the third-fastest NHL coach to win 400 games (following Scotty Bowman and Glen Sather, respectively).

Babcock never played a minute in the NHL. He played collegiate hockey at McGill University (like fellow McGill alumnus Lester Patrick) as a defenceman, twice earning All-Star honours.

He began his coaching career in 1991 in the WHL (with a brief one-season flirtation with the Canadian college ranks) and spent eight seasons in the league, twice leading his teams to the WHL finals.

In 1997 he was named head coach of Team Canada and led them to the gold medal at the World Junior Championships. (As Scotty Bowman noted earlier, Babcock is the only coach in hockey history to be a Triple Gold Club member: winning the World Junior, the Stanley Cup, and Olympic gold.)

In 2000 Babcock turned to professional coaching, leading the Anaheim Ducks' minor league affiliate in Cincinnati.

Throughout his apprenticeship in junior, college, and the minors, Babcock demonstrated the drive and excellence that distinguishes him today. Significantly, whenever Babcock faced a rare losing season, his teams always rebounded strongly.

In 2002, when Ducks general manager Bryan Murray needed a new coach to invigorate the team, he picked Babcock, later saying, "He just came across as a very strong, confident type of guy. I knew he had great ambition. He's a driven guy."[45]

In a 2013 interview, Murray adds, "I chose Mike because I had a feel for his talent. He was confident, knowledgeable. He was great at talking to his players, earning their respect, and listening to them."

When Babcock took over the Ducks, the team was in the doldrums, finishing last in the Pacific Division three years in a row.

Babcock wasted no time making his presence and authority felt.

When Ducks defenceman Mike Commodore showed up at training camp in less than tip-top shape, Babcock sent him to the minors and later traded Commodore

---

45 http://sports.espn.go.com/nhl/columns/story?columnist=burnside_scott&id=3387051

to Calgary for Rob Niedermayer, who helped the Ducks during their 2002/03 playoff run.

In his rookie season, Babcock led the Ducks to franchise records in wins and team points, getting splendid performances from Paul Kariya and Petr Sykora and a career year from goalie Jean-Sébastien Giguére, who won the 2002/03 Conn Smythe Trophy.

The Ducks swept through the first three rounds with a 12–2 record before succumbing to the veteran New Jersey Devils in a hard-fought seven-game series.

The following season was rough. The Ducks had a losing season and failed to make the playoffs (the only time in Babcock's NHL coaching career this has happened). Despite this setback, Babcock wanted a long-term contract from the team. Instead, the Ducks' new general manager Brian Burke wanted his own man at the helm.

When Burke lowballed Babcock with a one-year contract offer, Babcock resigned as Ducks coach and was immediately hired by the Detroit Red Wings, who had been underachieving since Scotty Bowman's retirement as coach in 2002.

Babcock, as a young coach coming off a losing season, was entering a pressure-cooker situation, trying to lead a veteran team with a rich tradition. A lesser coach might have faltered, but Babcock led the Wings to a President's Trophy season only to be upset by the Edmonton Oilers in the first round of the 2005/06 playoffs.

Again, a lesser coach may have cleaned house, making wholesale trades to shake up the team. Instead, Babcock readjusted the coaching reins, allowing his veterans more input in the team's leadership. The Red Wings responded with three more Central Division titles, a second President's Trophy, and the 2007/08 Stanley Cup.

In 2013 NHL.com managing editor Shawn Roarke told *Bleacher Report*'s Steve Silverman that Babcock is the best coach in the NHL, explaining, "The reason is because he relates to all kinds of players and gets the most out of them by finding a role for them in the team that best suits their skill set. Plus, as he proved at the [2010] Olympics, he has the requisite ego and the cult of personality to deal with superstar players and bend them to the good of the club."[46]

---

46 http://bleacherreport.com/articles/1621175-why-detroit-red-wings-playoff-berth-proves-mike-babcock-is-best-coach-in-nhl

Wings forward Dan Cleary says, "What you see is what you get and he's got a great pulse for the locker room. He knows when to push and when not to push. I think he's the best coach in the league. It's his work ethic. His staff cares about the little things that go unnoticed and win games."[47]

Even those players who saw their roles reduced by Babcock gave him his due. Chris Chelios in his memoirs notes the differences he had with Babcock about his playing time being reduced by Babcock but adds thoughtfully, "How can I argue that Babcock doesn't properly use his personnel? Look at his record. The NHL is a bottom-line business. It's about winning, and Babcock has gotten results."[48]

Another aspect of Babcock's greatness is his ability to foster and develop substantial coaching talent.

San Jose Sharks head coach Todd McLellan is one of the first fruits of the Mike Babcock coaching tree. Pittsburgh's Dan Bylsma (who finished his NHL playing career under Mike Babcock) is another.

Babcock's Red Wings teams have been well balanced in terms of offence and defence. His most significant strength has been on power-play offence. His biggest weakness has been in short-handed offence.

Babcock emphasizes puck possession, defence, and on-ice discipline. Defensive stalwarts such as former blue-liner Nicklas Lidstrom, forward Pavel Datsyuk, and goalies Dominik Hasek, Chris Osgood, and Jimmy Howard all flourished and excelled under Babcock's systems.

The 2010s, however, have proven to be a stern test for Babcock and the Wings.

The team has been forced to cope with aging players, the retirement of Nicklas Lidstrom, and injuries to key personnel. In short, the team is slowly rebuilding and yet Babcock has kept the team competitive: still capable of blinding flashes of brilliance, still adept at stealing victories over more vaunted opponents.

The 2012/13 NHL season is a brilliant case in point. Before the season began, there were doubts expressed (to me personally) by an insider in the Wings organization whether the team could make the playoffs. Indeed, when the lockout ended and play began, the Wings looked clipped and caged: hovering slightly above .500 and out of playoff contention. By the Ides of March, the team came to life, going

---

47 http://espn.go.com/espn/conversations/_/id/4189181

48 *Made in America*, Chris Chelios with Kevin Allen, p. 191.

12–6–3 in the final stretch (winning the last four games of the regular season) to gain the seventh seed in the Western Conference.

More amazingly, Babcock took on the Anaheim Ducks, who had had a dazzling season under Bruce Boudreau (and were highly favoured to win), and slowly ground the Ducks into the ice, winning the series in seven games, with three of their four wins coming in overtime.

Babcock refused to be swayed by the Ducks' firepower. He rotated his players with abandon and bagged the Ducks with raw fundamentals. There was nothing pretty in Detroit's approach. It was proletarian, hard-hat hockey at its best. Greybeards (like Pavel Datsyuk and Johan Franzen) and fuzzy-cheeked youngsters (like goalie Jimmy Howard and centre Damien Brunner) alike displayed Babcock's indomitable work ethic to pull off *the* greatest upset of the 2012/13 playoffs.

Then even more amazingly the Red Wings almost knocked off the Chicago Blackhawks in the second round. After suffering a Game 1 defeat, they won the next three games and were leading 2–1 going into the third period of Game 6 in Detroit. Had Detroit hung on to win, it would have been an upset of even greater proportions. Sadly, it wasn't to be. Chicago erupted with three goals to start the third period and won Games 6 and 7 and, eventually, the Stanley Cup.

And yet the fact that Babcock and Detroit gave the Blackhawks their hardest test during the 2012/13 playoffs represents another piece of evidence of Babcock's coaching genius. The following season saw Babcock be named (once more) as head of Team Canada Men's Hockey team in the 2014 Winter Olympics in Sochi, Russia. Blessed with a sterling assistant coaching staff of Claude Julien, Lindy Ruff, and Ken Hitchcock (a veritable coaching dream staff); NHL superstars Sidney Crosby, Jonathan Toews, Shea Weber, Corey Perry; and a goal-tending troika of Carey Price, Roberto Luongo, and Mike Smith; Mike Babcock guided Team Canada handily through the Men's Tournament with only Team Finland extending Team Canada to overtime. In classic Babcock fashion, Team Canada had the best defence of all the Men's Olympic hockey teams.

In their final three games against Latvia, the United States, and Sweden, Team Canada only allowed one goal (scored by Latvia). Babcock's gold medal victory was a first in the history of Canadian Men's Olympic hockey. No other coach of Team Canada had coached two gold medal victories in Men's Olympic competition.

Babcock wasn't finished yet. During the 2013/14 NHL season the Detroit Red Wings were again battling age and trying to rebuild with youngsters. The Wings were further tested by being transferred to the Eastern Conference (along with Columbus) as part of the realignment of the NHL that season. Competing in the crowded Atlantic Division, Detroit hung tough and became the eighth seed in the Eastern Conference during the 2013/14 Stanley Cup playoffs. Although Detroit suffered a first-round defeat at the hands of Claude Julien's Boston Bruins, Babcock's refusal to allow Detroit to fall short of reaching the playoffs earned the respect and admiration of the hockey press that season. Babcock was named one of three candidates eligible for the 2013/14 Jack Adams Award but finished second to winner Patrick Roy in the voting.

Mike Babcock has the right to call himself a coaching genius, and that coaching genius will one day lead him to be inducted into the Hockey Hall of Fame as a builder.

In 2014/15 Babcock led the Wings to their strongest performance in three years. For a time they vied for the President's Trophy but after the All-Star break the Wings began to fade, eventually finishing third in the Atlantic Division. In the first round of the playoffs the Wings were clipped by the youthful and insurgent Tampa Bay Lightning. Detroit had a 3–2 lead but failed to close the deal, losing games 6 and 7 and the series.

Not only did the Wings first-round defeat mark the end of the season it also marked the end of Mike Babcock's stay as head coach of the Detroit Red Wings. One of the great mysteries of the 2014/15 season was whether the Wings would offer a contract extension to Babcock and (if the Wings did make an offer) would Babcock accept it. Speculation was rife all season long about where Babcock might go (with Toronto always taking precedence in the rumors). Babcock, himself, remained mum all season long.

After the Red Wings' season ended, Babcock rested for a time. Meanwhile Detroit Red Wings general manager Dave Holland did the proper and respectful thing by making a lucrative contract extension offer to Babcock. But after nine days of rest and consulting with his family, Mike Babcock asked permission from the Red Wings to seek other offers from NHL teams – which was granted.

Now the speculation grew to a fever pitch. For a time it looked like the Buffalo Sabres were the frontrunners for his services but on May 20, 2015, the Toronto

Maple Leafs announced that Mike Babcock would become their new head coach with an eight year contract worth $50 million – the greatest coaching contract in NHL history.

The challenge of ending the Leafs' 48-year Stanley Cup drought has long been the Eve of NHL coaches – alluring, tantalizing, enticing, seductive but fraught with enormous risks. Many a great coach made the attempt. Men like Roger Neilson, Floyd Smith, Pat Burns, Pat Quinn, Ron Wilson, and Randy Carlyle all tried their hands at restoring Toronto back to Stanley Cup greatness and they all failed. In the case of Wilson and Carlyle their coaching records suffered greatly because they coached the Maple Leafs.

And now Mike Babcock has left one of the most efficiently run teams in the NHL in order to become the head coach of a team that has seethed with locker-room tension and front office intrigue for decades. He is accepting the ultimate coaching challenge in the NHL today – a challenge that will either elevate his already lofty coaching reputation to even greater levels or else cast him from the plinth he has occupied with dignity and greatness throughout the 21st century.

In Act V, Scene I of Shakespeare's *Othello* the character Iago speaks, "This is the night that either makes me or fordoes me quite."

The same can be said for Mike Babcock.

LESTER "THE SILVER FOX" PATRICK RANK #10

PLUS: 133
MINUS: 44
VALUE: +89
PEAK RANK: #1 in 1937/38
PEAK VALUE: +89 in 1938/39

PCHA COACHING EXPERIENCE: Victoria Senators, 1911–1913; Victoria Aristocrats, 1913–1916, 1918–1922; Spokane Canaries, 1916/17; Seattle Metropolitans, 1917/18; Victoria Cougars, 1922–1924

PCHA REGULAR SEASON W–L–T: 120–149–3
PCHA PLAYOFF W–L–T: 1–5–1

PCHA LEAGUE CHAMPIONSHIPS: 1912/13–1913/14

PCHA PLAYOFF APPEARANCES: 1917/18, 1922/23

WCHL/WHL COACHING EXPERIENCE: Victoria Cougars, 1924–1926

WCHL/WHL REGULAR SEASON W–L–T: 31–23–4
WCHL/WHL PLAYOFF W–L–T: 8–4–4

WCHL/WHL LEAGUE CHAMPIONSHIPS: 1924/25–1925/26

WCHL/WHL PLAYOFF APPEARANCES: 1924/25–1925/26

NHL COACHING EXPERIENCE: New York Rangers, 1926–1939

NHL REGULAR SEASON W–L–T: 281–216–107
NHL PLAYOFF W–L–T: 32–26–7

AMERICAN DIVISION TITLES: 1926/27, 1931/32

NHL PLAYOFF APPEARANCES: **1926/27–1934/35, 1936/37–1938/39**

STANLEY CUP FINALS: **1913/14, 1924/25–1925/26, 1927/28–1928/29, 1931/32–1932/33, 1936/37**

STANLEY CUP VICTORIES: **1924/25, 1927/28, 1932/33**

The annual Lester Patrick Trophy acknowledges the recipient's contribution to ice hockey in the United States – aptly named after Lester Patrick because Patrick (along with his brother, Frank) did more to bring hockey to the United States while making the game more exciting and entertaining than any other person in the history of the sport.

One could write an entire book listing the innovations Lester and Frank contributed to hockey. They did not invent the game, but their improvements certainly made it more enjoyable to watch.

Some of their ideas were subtle but had greater long-term significance: the penalty shot; the awarding of a point for assisting a goal; the creation of a playoff system; allowing goalies to fall to the ice to make saves. Imagine hockey today without these innovations.

The Patrick brothers also brought hockey to the west coast of Canada and the United States, developing the Pacific Coast Hockey Association (PCHA), which went toe-to-toe with the National Hockey Association and later the National Hockey League for 13 seasons. Such was the quality of its play that they were able to compel the NHA and NHL to allow the PCHA – and later the Western Canada Hockey League/Western Hockey League (WCHL/WHL) – to vie for the Stanley Cup until 1926.

When the WHL folded, many of its best players went east to join the burgeoning NHL, which now had sole control over the Stanley Cup. The Americanization of the game was by then in full swing, and Lester Patrick's big break came in 1926 when the fledgling New York Rangers, skeptical about the personnel signed to the team by Conn Smythe, fired Smythe and hired Patrick to take his place as coach and general manager (thus affecting the destinies of the Rangers and Toronto Maple Leafs in unfathomable ways).

Patrick initially confounded Rangers ownership by retaining the players Smythe had signed, but for the next 13 seasons he led the Rangers through the most successful and glorious period of their existence. The Rangers were a team to be reckoned with in the NHL: making 12 playoff appearances in 13 seasons, earning five Stanley Cup finals appearances, and winning two championships in 1927/28 and 1932/33.

Patrick never owned the Rangers, but he (like Art Ross in Boston and Jack Adams in Detroit) made the team in his own image. The Rangers were *his team*, and he would serve in any capacity to help his team win. The story of Patrick removing his street clothes, donning a uniform and goalie pads, and replacing his injured goalie in the 1927/28 Stanley Cup playoffs (while performing well) is part of NHL folklore.

One element of Patrick's greatness as a coach was his tactical fluidity in finding ways to win games and championships. Though he would later be known for offence, when he coached in the PCHA and the WHL he relied mostly on goaltending and defence. Patrick helped make Harry Holmes of the Victoria Aristocrats (later Cougars) a Hall of Fame goalie, and in 1924/25 and 1925/26 when Patrick led Victoria to the Stanley Cup finals, both times he had the best defence in the WCHL/WHL. In fact, Patrick was the best defensive coach in the five-year history of the league.

Another interesting note is that during that same time period Patrick became the first hockey coach to win five consecutive Stanley Cup playoff series – the previous record had been three set twice by Pete Green from 1919/20 to 1920/21 and during the 1922/23 season.

When the Victoria Cougars became the only non-NHL team to win the Stanley Cup by defeating the Montreal Canadiens in 1924/25, they used another Patrick family innovation: line changes. Before line changes, teams put their best six men on the ice and let them play the full 60 minutes with extremely limited substitution, or without substitution at all.

Patrick's rotation of his players kept the Cougars fresh while the Canadiens faltered with fatigue. Along with their stellar goaltending and a crushing defence, the Cougars won the best-of-five series in four games.

When Patrick coached the Rangers, however, he won predominately with offence. His Rangers finished in the top three in offence in the NHL eight times. Bill Cook led the NHL in scoring twice. The "A" or "Bread" Line of brother wingers Bill and Bun Cook, combined with the immortal Frank Boucher, was one of the deadliest scoring lines of the NHL's first quarter-century (1917–1942).

Boucher was a legendary centre. A superb playmaker, he led the NHL in assists three times in his career and was a four-time NHL All-Star.

(When you adjust Boucher's scoring totals to today's 82-game schedule, he ranks among the all-time greats.)

Boucher was a widely respected player, winning the Lady Byng Trophy seven times for gentlemanly play. He was also one of the most intelligent players in the game, and when Patrick stepped down as head coach, he chose Boucher to succeed him. Boucher became one of the most innovative coaches in NHL history himself.

Patrick's Rangers also had a respectable blue-line corps led by All-Stars Ching Johnson and Earl Siebert; another All-Star was Davey Kerr, who was a solid goalie during the final years of Patrick's coaching career.

Lester Patrick was to hockey what Connie Mack was to baseball: a courtly, wily, educated, gentlemanly coach. Boucher wrote in his memoir *When the Rangers Were Young*, "He struck dramatic poses and was in turn kind, sarcastic, pompous, vain, callous, and contrite, depending on the circumstances. He had both a compelling arrogance and a winning humility. By all odds, he was the most knowledgeable hockey man I have ever met."[49]

Patrick family biographer Eric Whitehead quotes Patrick himself on his coaching philosophy: "I look for the leaders. Then I let them lead. I give my last instructions in the dressing room just before the game, then I sit and let them think whatever they like . . . then I just tag along and enjoy it."[50]

Patrick was skilled not only in leading his players but also in handling the New York press.

The Rangers decision to replace Conn Smythe with Lester Patrick was an inspired one because Patrick (unlike the acerbic Smythe) was the perfect man to sell a Canadian sport to the media hub of the United States. Patrick made good copy, and the fact that the Rangers were contenders during his reign helped solidify his relations with the New York press. Getting positive feedback in New York influenced press coverage in many other American NHL franchise cities. The best evidence of Patrick's superb relations with the media can be found in his first team All-Star coaching honours seven times in eight seasons, from 1930/31 to

---

49 *When The Rangers Were Young*, Frank Boucher with Trent Frayne, p. 101

50 *The Patricks*, Eric Whitehead, p. 180

1937/38 (from 1930/31 to 1945/46, coaches as well as players were awarded All-Star honours).

Simply put, Lester Patrick became the best PR man for the NHL during its salad days. The NHL is playing today in cities Patrick never dreamt to be possible because of his groundwork as a coach.

When Patrick retired from coaching in 1939 (remaining as Rangers general manager until 1946), he was the best coach in hockey history (see "The Progressive Chart" in Part Four). Though seven other hockey coaches would surpass him in the 73 years that followed, that shouldn't dim the lustre Patrick brought to all aspects of hockey. When he died in 1960, all of hockey mourned.

Patrick saw his sons Lynn and Muzz establish solid careers in the NHL, and his grandsons Craig and Dick continue to maintain the Patrick family connection with the league. Craig served as general manager of the Pittsburgh Penguins from 1989 to 2006, and Dick has served as president of the Washington Capitals since 1982.

But Lester Patrick's legacy rests not only with his descendants. He (along with Scotty Bowman) inspired many of his players to become coaches and executives in the NHL and the minors.

The Lester Patrick coaching tree is one of the most influential and enduring ones in the NHL today. Future coaches like Frank Boucher, Alf Pike, and Phil Watson (as well as Patrick's sons Lynn and Muzz) all played for Patrick. They, in turn, would inspire many of their own players to become coaches and executives. Coaches Emile Francis, Harry Sinden, Glen Sather, and the late Fred Shero are all descendants of Patrick's coaching wisdom.

Wherever hockey is played, you are seeing the enormous gifts Lester Patrick gave to the sport and to hockey fans around the world.

CLARENCE HENRY "HAP" DAY RANK #11

PLUS: 91
MINUS: 4
VALUE: +87
PEAK RANK: #3 in 1949/50
PEAK VALUE: +87 in 1949/50

COACHING EXPERIENCE: Toronto Maple Leafs, 1940–1950

REGULAR SEASON W–L–T: 259–206–81
PLAYOFF W–L: 49–31

PRINCE OF WALES TROPHY: 1947/48

PLAYOFF APPEARANCES: 1940/41–1944/45, 1946/47–1949/50
STANLEY CUP FINALS: 1941/42, 194/45, 1946/47–1948/49
STANLEY CUP VICTORIES: 1941/42, 1944/45, 1946/47–1948/49

Clarence Henry "Hap" Day was the first NHL coach to win five Stanley Cups (a record later broken by Toe Blake in 1964/65) and the first to three-peat his team as Stanley Cup champions. From 1946/47 to 1948/49, Day's Toronto Maple Leafs were the NHL's first dynasty since the original Ottawa Senators in the early 1920s.

When he quit coaching, Day was the greatest coach in Maple Leafs history (today he ranks third) and was the third greatest hockey coach of all time, according to my rating system. Many of the players he coached became immortals in the pantheon of hockey.

Day did what his coaching predecessors in Toronto had failed to do: make the Leafs an NHL dynasty while giving the team a rich tradition that the Leafs today still strive (and fail) to live up to.

He was a company man. Day spent almost his entire playing career with Toronto, starting in 1924 when the team was still called the Arenas (later to be renamed the St. Patricks) and Maple Leaf Gardens did not exist. In 1926 he became captain and remained so until 1937, when he was traded away to the New York Americans – only George Armstrong served longer as captain. In 1927 Day struck up a fortuitous friendship with Conn Smythe, who had bought the Toronto St. Patricks that same year and renamed them the Maple Leafs. Day was retained by Smythe, who began to rebuild the entire team around Day and Ace Bailey. When Day wasn't playing for Smythe on the ice, he was working at Smythe's sand and gravel business (in time Day became a limited partner in the company).

Hap was a defenceman on Dick Irvin's Leafs teams during the 1930s and was a member of their 1931/32 Stanley Cup champion team.

In 1940 Smythe – dissatisfied with the Leafs' six Stanley Cup losses in eight seasons – allowed Irvin to leave to become head coach of the Montreal Canadiens and replaced him with Hap Day.

Later, Smythe wrote in his memoir *Conn Smythe: If You Can't Beat 'Em in the Alley*, "Hap was everything I wanted. He could do things I couldn't: fire people; bench them; live always on what a man could do today, not on what he had done a few years ago."[51]

Day and Smythe were opposites in personality. Smythe was combative and intense. Day was quiet in tone and, as former Leaf Gaye Stewart said in a 2008 interview, "not into fire and brimstone." Yet both Stewart and Fleming Mackell state that Day was a disciplinarian who played no favourites.

Although Day coached the Leafs, it was always Conn Smythe's team.

Mackell said in a 2007 interview that Smythe used injured players as messengers, relaying instructions to Day during a game. Later Smythe installed a special phone line to the Leafs bench. When Smythe picked up the phone, a light on Day's end came on, informing him that Smythe wanted to talk to him.

Under Dick Irvin, the Leafs never finished higher than third in defence. In Hap Day's first season, they had the best defence in the NHL (in seven of Day's ten seasons, the Leafs finished either first or second in the NHL in defence). But it wasn't solely defence that helped the Leafs win. Day also got decent offensive efforts from his teams. That comes as a surprise (considering Toronto's long tradition of not

51 *Conn Smythe: If You Can't Beat 'Em In The Alley*, Conn Smythe with Scott Young, p. 143.

being an offensive powerhouse), but during the 1940s – with the exception of the 1948/49 season when they finished fifth in offence – Day's Leafs were always among the top three teams in offence (finishing either first or second in the NHL four times). Indeed, Day's Leafs were second only to Art Ross's Boston Bruins in offence. Ross led the decade with 3.82 goals scored per game, with Day in second with a 3.38 average.

Howie Meeker told Dick Irvin Jr. in his book *Behind the Bench* that "his [Hap Day's] main area of discipline, though, was on the ice, especially behind our blue line. He was in total control of the team, when we didn't have the puck. Once we got over the blue line he was no longer in control. You were. If you did what he wanted, knew what to do behind your own blue line, then you were always in the hockey game. I just think it was the greatest system to play under because he didn't put any pressure on you to score goals. He put pressure on you to keep the puck out of your net."[52]

In the book *Total Hockey,* Roger Neilson says, "Hap Day . . . was a conditioning maniac, and he would drive those guys until they were sick at practice. You had to be tough, but it really helped the Leafs win Cups."[53]

During the 1940s, the Leafs were two teams playing on the same ice: the regular-season Leafs, with a modest .549 winning percentage; and the playoff Leafs, with a powerful .613 winning percentage. Metaphorically speaking, the team took after its goalie, the legendary Turk Broda, who yielded 2.53 goals per game during the regular season but only 1.98 goals per game during the playoffs. It seems that the Leafs only displayed the full panoply of their hockey talents during playoffs.

In a sense, the regular season didn't provide enough stimuli for the Leafs to dominate. It took the pressure-cooker atmosphere of the playoffs to bring out the untapped reserves of on-ice energy and innate brilliance the Leafs possessed.

The four times that Day's Leafs lost in the playoffs, they did so in the semifinal round. When the Leafs reached the Stanley Cup finals, the Cup was theirs – though they had to fight, scratch, gouge, kick, and beat their opponents in the alley to get it.

During the dynasty years of 1946/47 to 1948/49, the Leafs won 24 of 29 playoff games and Hap Day was a perfect 5–0 in Stanley Cup finals competition. No other

---

52 *Behind the Bench*, Dick Irvin, pp. 36–37.

53 *Total Hockey*, Dan Diamond and Associates, p. 379.

NHL coach (except Joel Quenneville) with three or more Stanley Cup wins can make such a claim. (During that same period, Day also equalled Tommy Gorman's NHL record of winning six consecutive playoff series.)

Still, his sternest test as a coach came in the 1941/42 finals against the Detroit Red Wings. It was the closest Day ever came to suffering defeat in the finals. The Red Wings, taking advantage of Toronto's total lack of offence from forwards Gord Drillon, Syl Apps, and Bob Davidson, roared out to win the first three games.

His back to the wall, Day resorted to the unorthodox: replacing Gord Drillon and Bucko McDonald with two young sophomores, Don Metz and Hank Goldup, in Game 4.

Despite the fact that Game 4 was a seesaw battle (with Detroit taking a 2–0 and, later, a 3–2 lead), Toronto rallied to tie the game before Metz scored the game-winning goal to keep the Leafs alive. (It was after this game that Detroit head coach Jack Adams slugged a referee and was suspended by NHL president Frank Calder for the duration of the series.)

Day's line-tinkering paid off handsomely for the Leafs. Metz was the offensive sparkplug, scoring goals and setting up scoring chances for his teammates. Toronto won Games 5, 6, and 7, becoming the first team to successfully rally from a 3–0 series deficit to win a playoff series – a feat repeated three times since in NHL history. Day, after winning the Cup, told the press: "We won it the hard way." Indeed, they did.

Like all sports dynasties, Day's Leafs were an amalgam of solid veterans, rookies, and key acquisitions from other teams. Forwards Syl Apps and Ted "Teeder" Kennedy supplied the offence and leadership. Apps was a dignified leader who brought maturity and gravitas to the team.

Kennedy was the hardest-working player on the Leafs, a catalytic presence both on and off the ice. He succeeded Apps as team captain.

Bill Ezinicki was one of the toughest defensive forwards in the NHL, while shooters Harry Watson and Max Bentley were key acquisitions from other teams to help augment the offence.

The Leafs blue-line corps was incredibly rich and talented. Gus Mortson, Jimmy Thomson, and the ill-fated Bill Barilko were punishing hitters. From 1946/47 to 1950/51, a Maple Leaf always led the league in penalty minutes.

Hap Day was superb in developing rookie players, coaching four Calder Memorial Trophy winners, an NHL record he shares with Frank Boucher and Punch Imlach. He was a great teacher of hockey fundamentals. Fleming Mackell says that when he joined the Leafs, he didn't know how to play defence, so Hap Day worked with him on his two-way skills.

After 1950, Day yielded the coaching reins and moved to the front office, where he worked as assistant general manager under Conn Smythe. He briefly became the Leafs general manager but was coldly removed by Smythe in favour of Smythe's son, Stafford.

Day left the Leafs for good and spent the rest of his life as a private businessman – forever embittered by the Smythe family he had once loyally served and by the team he had helped make champions.

GEORGE "PUNCH" IMLACH RANK #12

PLUS: 95
MINUS: 9
VALUE: +86
PEAK RANK: #4 in 1968/69
PEAK VALUE: +92 in 1968/69

COACHING EXPERIENCE: Toronto Maple Leafs, 1958[54]–1969, 1980[55]; Buffalo Sabres, 1970–1972[56]

REGULAR SEASON W–L–T: 402–337–150
PLAYOFF W–L: 44–48

PRINCE OF WALES TROPHY: 1962/63

PLAYOFF APPEARANCES: 1958/59–1966/67, 1968/69, 1979/80

STANLEY CUP FINALS: 1958/59–1959/60, 1961/62–1963/64, 1966/67
STANLEY CUP VICTORIES: 1961/62–1963/64, 1966/67

His nickname said it all.

He was as subtle and graceful as a punch in the mouth. The title of his memoirs, *Hockey Is a Battle,* defined his personality. One line in particular from his book – "When I was winning Stanley Cups" – speaks volumes about his ego.

And yet he became (and still remains) the greatest coach in Toronto Maple Leafs franchise history and as of 2015 was the last man to lead the Leafs to a Stanley Cup victory.

Decades later, George "Punch" Imlach still inspires debate and controversy.

---

54 Imlach coached the last 50 games of the 1958/59 season.

55 Imlach coached the last 10 games of the 1979/80 season.

56 Imlach coached the first 41 games of the 1971/72 season.

Name another NHL coach who deliberately drove his best scorer to nervous collapse and yet resurrected the careers of many other players who were denied a chance to become champions for other teams.

Name another NHL coach who engineered one of the great franchise turnarounds in hockey history and yet was responsible for its decline and fall, which endures today.

Name another NHL coach and general manager who could take an expansion franchise and make them Stanley Cup contenders in only five years.

Imlach remains a disturbing figure. His behaviour bordered on the pathological. A clinical psychiatrist would have a field day diagnosing Imlach's personality traits.

Punch Imlach was not a lovable figure. He was crude, obscene, boorish, tactless, deliberately hostile, and almost desperate in his need to engage in combat. To paraphrase the late U.S. general George Patton, the off-season must have been hell on Imlach. I suspect he would have been happier if hockey seasons were endless.

Even when his teams won the Stanley Cup, there was no joy, no exultation, and no release from the relentless urge to scrape, kick, bite, and gouge the opposition. One sensed in Imlach an emptiness; a psychic void that no victory or dynastic run could ever fill.

To say that Imlach was intense is a gross understatement. It wasn't just bile he vented: it was also viscera, gall, entrails, and excrement. Although Imlach's memoirs fail to capture his hardcore personality, Stephen Cole's book *The Last Hurrah* does a better job at portraying Imlach in his roiling, sulfuric magma state.

It has been said before, and it bears repeating, that Imlach coached the Leafs at the wrong time in their history. If he had led the team in the 1930s, 1940s, or 1950s, then his reputation would have shone even brighter because his brass-knuckle style was the norm for that era.

His older players never chafed as much from his abrasiveness as did his younger players, who had joined the Leafs during the 1960s in what became hockey's generation gap.

Like all enigmas, Imlach was a man of contradictions.

His reputation for penuriousness is legendary, and yet it was a selective penury. (One of the reasons why Imlach drove Frank Mahovlich to a nervous breakdown was because Mahovlich demanded a sizable raise after scoring 48 goals during the

1961/62 season. Mahovlich was one of many who felt the lash from Imlach because he wanted to earn a championship wage for his labours.)

Imlach was not afraid to open up his pocketbook when necessary. Hockey legend Red Kelly said in a 2008 interview that he never signed a written contract with Imlach; that he played for Toronto on a handshake deal. Marcel Pronovost stated in his memoirs that he made the best money of his career under Imlach. Punch lured Dickie Moore out of retirement by offering him a blank contract. Al Arbour, in another interview, said that, yes, negotiating a contract with Imlach was tough, but if he gave you his word when it came to money, you could take it to the bank – his word was his bond.

Punch was famed for his preference for veteran players. Emile Francis once said laughingly in a 2009 interview that Imlach reminded him of the late NFL coach George Allen (who coached the Over the Hill Gang in Washington). Yes, Imlach liked veterans and sought them out to man his teams, but he was not averse to playing a rookie if the player in question had the requisite skills and mental toughness.

Imlach coached eight Calder Memorial Trophy candidates (four winners and four runners-up) during his career (only Dick Irvin coached more). Rookies Carl Brewer, Bob Nevin, Dave Keon, Ron Ellis, and Gilbert Perreault all achieved stardom under Imlach's stern tutelage.

Punch was famous for his rigorous training camps and the high number of exhibition games his Leafs played before the regular season, which is why the number of pre-season exhibition games all NHL teams play is now limited.

Imlach wrote in his memoirs: "I figured the same as those track coaches who say that, if you're going to run a mile, you practice for it not by running one mile, but by running ten miles. If you're going to play a hockey game in an hour, you should be able to practice two hours. That's the way you build endurance. You can't build it in half-hour practices."[57]

What Imlach did was hardly unique in the sports world during the 1960s. Rigorous training camps were an intrinsic part of Vince Lombardi's legend when he coached the NFL's Green Bay Packers. And the late Red Auerbach of the Boston Celtics in the NBA not only ran his players hard in camp but also had them

57 *Hockey Is A Battle*, Punch Imlach with Scott Young, p. 115

play a lot of exhibition games to get them into shape quicker and help them roar out of the blocks when the regular season began.

Punch's training method may have worn his players down physically, but it fortified their souls psychologically.

During the glory years of 1958/59 to 1966/67, the Toronto Maple Leafs went 9–3 in overtime games in the Stanley Cup playoffs. Two of those wins are part of Leafs folklore: the Game 6 win against Detroit during the 1963/64 Stanley Cup finals and the Game 3 win against Montreal in the 1966/67 Stanley Cup finals.

The former saved the Leafs from losing the Cup against the Wings and led to a Game 7 victory. The latter stands even brighter in the Leafs legend. In 1966/67 the Leafs and Canadiens were tied at one game apiece going into Game 3. The Leafs (worn by age, injuries, and psychic exhaustion from Imlach's tyranny) battled the Habs to a standstill. For 88 minutes they withstood the younger Canadiens: refusing to tire, refusing to wilt; refusing to be outworked, before scoring the winning goal.

That Game 3 triumph was the turning point of the entire series. Had they lost then, they would have been thrown into an inescapable hole. The Game 3 win captures forever the mental toughness and physical endurance of the Leafs dynasty teams. The workouts and the poundings Imlach put them through in training camp and practice made the pressures of playing the game itself seem like child's play.

Imlach's Maple Leafs dynasty teams should be viewed as a layer cake. The first layer consisted of veteran holdovers from previous Leafs regimes such as George Armstrong, the late Tim Horton, and Ron Stewart.

The second layer was made up of the relative newcomers: young, home-grown Toronto prospects in their sophomore or junior years such as Bob Baun, Dick Duff, Bob Pulford, and Frank Mahovlich. In time, they became part of the team's veteran layer.

The third layer included the first cadre of veteran player acquisitions who formed a vital part of Imlach's team nucleus: Allan Stanley, Johnny Bower, Bert Olmstead, and Red Kelly.

The fourth layer was composed of the rookie stars: Carl Brewer, Bob Nevin, Dave Keon, and Ron Ellis.

The icing on the cake came from veteran castoffs acquired from other teams. These were players who fixed holes in the team's roster during the regular season and playoff time, such as Terry Sawchuk, Marcel Pronovost, Andy Bathgate, and Don McKenney – the latter two acquired in the infamous trade that sent future stars Duff and Nevin to New York (a trade seen as the beginning of the decline and fall of the Leafs dynasty).

Put together, these layers formed a recipe for greatness.

Imlach's formula for success was based on defence and penalty-killing. Former Montreal Canadien Gilles Tremblay said in a 2007 interview that Imlach's system was "hooking and trapping and cycling the bloody puck!"

This system also allowed for Leafs goalie Johnny Bower to achieve the NHL stardom and recognition he so richly deserved. The acquisition of goalie Terry Sawchuk from Detroit in 1964 brilliantly augmented the goaltending position.

Toronto finished either first or second in the NHL in defence from 1960/61 to 1962/63 and from 1964/65 to 1965/66.

Between 1962/63 and 1967/68, the Leafs led the NHL in penalty-killing three times, although there was a weak period from 1964/65 to 1966/67 when the Leafs penalty-killing effectiveness declined. Ironically, the Leafs finished last in the NHL in penalty-killing during the 1966/67 season, which is amazing considering how well they played defensively during the playoffs.

Toronto had one of the greatest blue-line corps in NHL history. From 1959/60 to 1968/69, a Leafs defenceman always received NHL All-Star honours, with Allan Stanley, Carl Brewer, and Tim Horton sharing the glory. Those three, along with Bob Baun, Marcel Pronovost, and Larry Hillman, were integral to the Leafs' dynastic glory.

Complementing the blue-liners was the solid two-way play of forwards Keon, Pulford, Kelly, and Pete Stemkowski. Bryan "Bugsy" Watson said in a 2006 interview that Dave Keon was the secret weapon of the Maple Leafs dynasty from 1961/62 to 1966/67.

Hockey legend suggests that Toronto was always weak offensively. In truth, the Leafs had an average offence, usually finishing behind Chicago and Montreal. But the Leafs power-play offence was the weakest in the NHL during the 1960s. Ron Ellis would later tell Kevin Shea that "we very seldom practiced the power play. We never had a set power play unit during the '60s. Punch's approach was to send out whichever line was next up when a penalty was called. That's why the Leafs never had a scoring leader; Punch wanted to have balanced scoring from all three lines. And it paid off. But if you put Frank Mahovlich or Davey Keon on the point during a power play, they would have quickly moved into the top ten scoring leaders."[58]

When it came to his forwards, Imlach always sought depth at the centre position. Johnny Bower wrote in his memoirs, *The China Wall*: "Punch always said, 'If I can get three strong centremen down the middle, I can win the Stanley Cup.' And he did."[59]

Actually, Imlach usually had more than three strong centremen on his teams. He had George Armstrong, Red Kelly, Bob Pulford, and Dave Keon at centre. Later he shifted Armstrong to left wing, but during the early years of his coaching reign, Armstrong was a centre. In later years he added Pete Stemkowski, Mike Walton, and Norm Ullman to the mix. Still, Imlach's desire for depth down the middle was not unique. His nemesis, Toe Blake, also insisted on (and got) great depth at the centre position.

If there was one factor that helped Toronto win four Stanley Cups in six years, it was their collective hockey IQ. When it came to hockey intelligence, the Leafs dynasty was one of the greatest in hockey history. Several of Imlach's players would go on to become coaches themselves, such as Red Kelly and Bob Pulford. When researching Imlach's Leafs, one is amazed at how well his players could analyze their opponents, sniff out their weaknesses, and devise tactics to overcome them.

The 1966/67 Cup win is a prime example. The Leafs, using their collective intelligence and summoning up their remaining physical and emotional reserves of strength, overcame the fearsome cannonading of the Chicago Blackhawks and the great speed and intimidating winning tradition of the Montreal Canadiens to win. It remains one of hockey's most epic legends.

After the Stanley Cup victory in 1966/67, Imlach's world slowly fell apart. The Leafs were gutted badly by the 1967 expansion draft, then came the drying up of

58 *Over the Boards: The Ron Ellis Story*, Ron Ellis and Kevin Shea, p. 84.

59 *The China Wall*, Johnny Bower with Bob Duff, p. 68.

the Leafs farm system coupled with the mismanagement of the team's finances by the front office. Imlach compounded the disaster by fighting the emergence of the present-day players' association and then denuding the team of its stars through a series of massive and unwise trades.

Imlach was fired in 1969 and remained unemployed until 1970 when the expansion Buffalo Sabres hired him to be their first coach and general manager. He did a great job in building the Sabres from the ice up: drafting youngsters Gilbert Perreault and Rick Martin and combining them with veteran expansion draftees. Imlach stepped down as coach in 1972 but remained as general manager.

In 1974/75 the Sabres reached the Stanley Cup finals in only their fifth season of existence – an NHL record that lasted until 1995/96 when the Florida Panthers reached the Cup finals in only their third year.

Imlach did not go gentle into that good night. Battling ill health since the 1960s, he was fired from Buffalo in 1978 and returned to Toronto, trying to recapture lost glory; all to no avail. He was fired for good in 1981 and spent the last six years of his life in unhappy retirement before dying in 1987.

Punch Imlach remains controversial to this very day.

He wouldn't have had it any other way.

"IRON" MIKE KEENAN RANK #13

PLUS: 105
MINUS: 20
VALUE: +85
PEAK RANK: #7 in 1994/95
PEAK VALUE: +95 in 1994/95

COACHING EXPERIENCE: Philadelphia Flyers, 1984–1988; Chicago Blackhawks, 1988–1992; New York Rangers, 1993/94; St. Louis Blues, 1994–1997[60]; Vancouver Canucks, 1997[61]–1999[62]; Boston Bruins, 2000/01[63]; Florida Panthers, 2001[64]–2003[65]; Calgary Flames, 2007–2009
REGULAR SEASON W–L–T–OL: 672–531–147–36
PLAYOFF W–L: 96–77

JACK ADAMS AWARD: 1984/85

PRESIDENT'S TROPHIES: 1990/91, 1993/94

PATRICK DIVISION TITLES: 1984/85–1986/87
NORRIS DIVISION TITLES: 1989/90–1990/91
ATLANTIC DIVISION TITLE: 1993/94

PLAYOFF APPEARANCES: 1984/85–1995/96, 2007/08–2008/09
STANLEY CUP FINALS: 1984/85, 1986/87, 1991/92, 1993/94
STANLEY CUP VICTORY: 1993/94

---

60 Keenan coached the first 33 games of the 1996/97 season.

61 Keenan coached the last 63 games of the 1997/98 season.

62 Keenan coached the first 45 games of the 1998/99 season.

63 Keenan coached the last 74 games of the 2000/01 season.

64 Keenan coached the last 56 games of the 2001/02 season.

65 Keenan coached the first 15 games of the 2003/04 season.

"Playing for Mike Keenan in Chicago was like camping on the side of an active volcano."[66]

Jeremy Roenick

"Negative energy is better than no energy at all."[67]

Mike Keenan

Hypothetical question: What would Scotty Bowman's coaching career have looked like if he hadn't coached nine Stanley Cup winners?

What if Bowman had coached only one Stanley Cup winner and had either gone down in defeat in all his other Cup finals or else failed to reach the finals at all? What would his coaching career have looked like then?

Answer: Like "Iron" Mike Keenan's coaching career.

I pose this hypothetical question because Mike Keenan has always patterned himself after Scotty Bowman, repeatedly expressing his admiration for the legendary nine-time Stanley Cup winner's coaching style.

The tragedy of Mike Keenan's coaching career is that he aspired to match Bowman's greatness but fell short – done in mostly by himself.

His coaching career can be split into two parts.

In part one, from 1984 to 1994, Keenan was the most successful coach in the NHL: he developed many young stars and helped three different teams reach the Stanley Cup finals four times in nine seasons. Three times during this glory period, Keenan's teams had the best regular-season record in the NHL.

His teams were exceptionally well balanced, but his real strength lay in his ability to get great goaltending and defensive work from his players. For these ten seasons, Keenan got All-Star work from goalies Pelle Lindbergh, Bob Froese, Ron Hextall, and Ed Belfour. Both Froese and Belfour won the Jennings Trophy in 1985/86 and 1990/91, respectively. Lindbergh, Hextall, and Belfour each won the Vezina Trophy in 1984/85, 1986/87 and 1990/91, respectively. Hextall also won the 1986/87 Conn Smythe Trophy while Belfour collected the 1990/91 Calder Memorial Trophy. (Ironically, Keenan became infamous for

66 *J. R.*, Jeremy Roenick with Kevin Allen, p. 51.

67 Ibid, p. 60.

his penchant for pulling and benching his goalies during the course of a season.)

Defencemen Mark Howe, Doug Wilson, and Chris Chelios all earned All-Star honours (with Howe a three-time Norris Trophy runner-up and a 2011 Hockey Hall of Fame inductee) for Keenan.

Keenan was a throwback from another era. While other coaches during the past 30 years were reducing their teams' penalty minutes, Keenan's teams were always the bad boys of the NHL. In fact, Keenan's squads exceeded all others in team penalty minutes during the 1980s, 1990s, and 2000s and, according to my ratings, earned more penalty minutes per game (23.14) than any other.

Like Glen Sather's squads, Mike Keenan's teams were dangerous in penalty-killing situations. He was second only to Sather in short-handed offence during the 1980s and to Bryan Murray during the 1990s.

When it came to leadership, "Iron" Mike was tension and release.

He could be the cool, detached, professorial type (he was a school teacher before he became a hockey coach) while showing an unrelenting eagerness to mix it up with his players, the press, and management.

Jeremy Roenick writes:

> He was always hard on his players, like a drill sergeant trying to ready recruits for the dangers ahead. . . . Keenan was a screamer who thought nothing of singling out one of his players for a personal attack, just to let the team know how upset he was with how the team was performing. . . . Mercy was not on the table when Keenan had a lock on a player . . . Keenan seemed to like to have his dressing room filled with tension.
>
> He believed his team performed at a higher level if they were on edge. He liked to push his players to that edge any way he could. He clearly seemed to believe that keeping his players shoulder-deep in adversity at all times kept them sharp. . . . Most coaches coach from behind the bench, but Keenan wanted to coach from inside your head.[68]

Keenan wanted his teams to intimidate the opposition as much as he intimidated his players.

---

68 *J. R.*, Jeremy Roenick with Kevin Allen, pp. 51–58.

Mark Howe writes, "Every day – and I mean every day – Keenan was with the Flyers, I drove to work wondering what shit was going to hit the fan. Anybody who says he wasn't intimidated the first year would be lying."[69]

Keenan craved size and strength in a player. If a player didn't have the requisite size, then he would make the player wear larger pads to create the impression of bulk and might.

Most of all, he loved players who had moxie and were chippy on the ice. One of the reasons why Keenan supplanted Flyers goalie Bob Froese with Ron Hextall was because Hextall was one of the scrappiest goaltenders who ever manned the pipes.

Hextall was a perfect fit for the Broad Street Bully atmosphere in Philadelphia, and Keenan recognized and savoured the catalytic qualities that Hextall brought to the team on and off the ice.

But Keenan wanted more than willingness to fight the opposition; he wanted players *who were also unafraid to fight him.*

Keenan would excuse defiance and insubordination as long as the player in question was not undermining his control of the team. Conversely, Keenan would eagerly unload any player who stood in his way of having complete control of the team or else lacked the martial ardour he demanded. Chris Chelios notes, "Keenan wasn't interested in guys who were magicians with the puck or had eyes in the backs of their heads. He wanted warriors. He wanted to run opponents into the boards and then right out of the building."[70] (His trade of Denis Savard to Montreal for Chris Chelios is a case in point.)

Still, Keenan's assets could easily turn into liabilities.

Keenan's consistent willingness to shake things up to get results was his best and his worst quality. When he was right (which he often was up to 1994), the results were astounding. When he was wrong (which he often was after 1994), the results were disheartening.

If there was one quality that he deserves high marks for (and the quality I most admired about him when he was coaching the Flyers), it was his courage in developing rookie players. If you were a talented prospect, Keenan would give you the time you needed as long as you gave him the effort and results he wanted. Goalies

---

69 *Gordie Howe's Son*, Mark Howe and Jay Greenberg, p. 165.

70 *Made in America*, Chris Chelios with Kevin Allen, p. 123.

Ron Hextall and Ed Belfour and centre Jeremy Roenick were prime examples. All three men owe a lot to Mike Keenan, especially Belfour, who was inducted into the Hockey Hall of Fame in 2011.

Jeremy Roenick summed up his feelings toward Keenan this way: "I love the man for moulding me into the player I became. . . . He was a father figure for me, and he nurtured my game through a tough-love approach."[71]

Mike Keenan played collegiate and, later, senior hockey in Canada but never played in the NHL. He began coaching in 1979 in the minors, and during the 1980s he coached the Buffalo Sabres' minor league team in Rochester (when Scotty Bowman was Sabres head coach and general manager), leading them to a Calder Cup win in 1982/83. (Keenan is one of six hockey coaches who led teams to both a Calder Cup and Stanley Cup win during their careers. If you want to know who the other five are, please keep reading.)

He was coaching Canadian collegiate hockey when he applied for the vacant head coaching position with the Philadelphia Flyers in 1984. The Flyers had been underachieving since 1979/80, experiencing three consecutive first-round playoff eliminations.

The talent was there, but the leadership wasn't. Flyers legend Bobby Clarke had just retired as a player and was now the Flyers' new general manager. He wanted to make his first head coaching selection a special one.

After weighing a number of candidates, Clarke narrowed his choices to two men: Ted Sator and Mike Keenan. Sator had served as an assistant to the departed Bob McCammon and had had coaching experience in Europe. Flyers management had prepared for Sator and Keenan written philosophical questionnaires that both men were asked to fill out. Keenan, knowing the enormity of this last test, responded with a 19-page essay that must rank as the hockey equivalent of Oscar Wilde's *De Profundis*. (Bobby Clarke would later quip, "He wrote a book.")

Keenan wrote, "Personally, I have experienced a contagious phenomenon whereby the more I win, the more I want to win. Nothing short of this objective is

---

71 *J.R.*, Jeremy Roenick with Kevin Allen, p. 68.

acceptable. . . . My approach to motivating the athlete is to maintain an imbalance of predictability by incorporating incentive, fear, and attitudinal methods employed in a very dynamic environment."[72]

Keenan's confessional, along with his more extensive North American coaching experience (as opposed to Sator's European coaching experience), sealed the deal.

Bobby Clarke had found his man.

Iron Mike's first training camp was a model of modernity. Every detail bore Keenan's personal stamp. While he was busy developing his team's mental synergy, he personally made sure that each player had their own personal water bottle.

(It was Keenan who placed water bottles atop the nets for his goaltenders to use during stoppages in games – a feature used by all hockey teams today.)

Keenan saw everything and missed nothing. Every practice was up-tempo, intense, with no wasted motion. The players young and old bought into his passion. Mike Keenan was a master mechanic fine-tuning a Lamborghini sports car.

With Keenan displaying a crisp, decisive, bold, edgy style of leadership and a keen eye for talent, the Flyers roared out of the blocks, playing fantastic hockey. Sadly though (like Don Cherry in the late 1970s), it was Keenan's misfortune to begin his coaching career during the Edmonton Oilers dynasty era. Keenan's Flyers were the second-best team in the NHL from 1984/85 to 1986/87.

His two Stanley Cup defeats at the hands of Edmonton proved fateful in many ways. He was the only opposing coach to extend the Oilers to a full seven games in the finals during their dynastic run. Had the Flyers been able to win either in 1984/85 or 1986/87, or both, then Keenan might have been able to attain the Scotty Bowman–like status he aspired to.

But the fact was he didn't, and as a result the Flyers ended up bridling against the psychological gamesmanship that was Keenan's métier.

Sports psychology is a high-wire act without a net; a thin membrane stands between glory and disaster when leading, manipulating, and controlling an athletic team. As the old French proverb goes, "Success can hide many errors."

Players will forgive a multitude of "sins" as long it results in championship glory. Punch Imlach lasted as long as he did in Toronto because he led the Leafs to

---

72 *Full Spectrum*, Jay Greenberg, p. 182.

four Cups in six seasons. Once the Cups stopped coming, he was gone two years after his last Cup victory.

Scotty Bowman was never beloved by his Montreal players like Toe Blake was, but he was always respected because he won five Cups in seven seasons. If Bowman had not been able to lead the Habs to victory, would his players have been so patient and forbearing with his leadership style?

Would they?

Suffering from psychic exhaustion, the Flyers lost in the first round of the 1987/88 playoffs and Mike Keenan was fired. The Chicago Blackhawks immediately hired him.

Keenan did what no other Blackhawks coach had done since 1972/73: led the team to the Stanley Cup finals.

Again, it was Iron Mike's misfortune to play against the Pittsburgh Penguins mini-dynasty team – losing four straight to his idol, Scotty Bowman, in 1991/92. Keenan (feuding with Bob Pulford) was forced to yield the coaching reins to his protegé, Darryl Sutter, while serving as Hawks general manager. By 1993 Keenan was gone, on his way to New York.

Having failed to end the Blackhawks' 31-year Stanley Cup drought, he now sought to end the longest Stanley Cup drought in NHL history. The Rangers hadn't won since 1939/40. In 1993/94 Keenan finally got it right, leading the Rangers to the President's Trophy and the Stanley Cup. It was his greatest moment, and if he had chosen to retire from coaching at that moment, then his place in the NHL coaching pantheon would have been far loftier than it is now.

He didn't, however.

After 1994, part two of his coaching career began.

Keenan became an accursed vagabond coach and/or general manager: coaching five different teams, shaking them up either by trading away fan favourites such as Brendan Shanahan from St. Louis to Detroit (where Shanahan played for three Stanley Cup winners) or else getting into petty, unnecessary feuds with team stars such as Brett Hull in St. Louis and Trevor Linden in Vancouver. Keenan experienced a 12-year gap between playoff appearances.

The sad truth was that many good coaches, such as Joel Quenneville, Marc Crawford, Jacques Martin, and Darryl Sutter, were called upon at one time in their careers to put back together what Mike Keenan had torn asunder.

His last post was with the Calgary Flames, managed by his former pupil, Darryl Sutter. Despite two winning seasons, the Flames underachieved in the playoffs and the pupil had to fire the master.

Keenan reluctantly took up broadcasting work with the MSG Network in New York and, later, with NBC Sports Network. Watching him on camera, you could sense the unease, the unhappiness. You got the feeling that if some NHL team would only offer him a coaching or managing position, he would have taken it in a New York minute, but no offers were forthcoming. Given his peregrinations throughout the league (and the ensuing debris left in his wake), Keenan had pretty much exhausted his possibilities.

On May 13, 2013, he signed a contract to become the head coach of Metallurg Magnitogorsk (located in the Southern Ural Mountains of Russia) in the Kontinental Hockey League (KHL).

It's a long way from coaching in the NHL, but in the heart and soul of every person who has ever coached in hockey, the ultimate place (correction, the *only* place) to be is standing behind the bench, leading and teaching young people how to play hockey – and how to play like champions.

Mike Keenan once more demonstrated his coaching genius, leading his team to a 15-point improvement in team points, leading the Eastern Conference overall in team points (while possessing the best defence in the Eastern Conference). Metallurg Magnitogorsk steamrolled through the playoffs: going 12–2 to reach the Gagarin Cup finals. In a tense seven-game series, Keenan guided his Foxes to the 2013/14 Gagarin Cup title.

Even in exile in the frozen Russian wastes, Mike Keenan still knows how to make his teams champions.

FRED "FOG" SHERO RANK #14

PLUS: 87
MINUS: 4
VALUE: +83
PEAK RANK: #8 in 1979/80
PEAK VALUE: +84 in 1979/80

COACHING EXPERIENCE: Philadelphia Flyers, 1971–1978; New York Rangers, 1978–1980[73]

REGULAR SEASON W–L–T: 390–225–119
PLAYOFF W–L: 63–47

JACK ADAMS AWARD: 1973/74

WEST DIVISION TITLE: 1973/74
PATRICK DIVISION TITLES: 1974/75–1976/77

PLAYOFF APPEARANCES: 1972/73–1979/80
STANLEY CUP FINALS: 1973/74–1975/76, 1978/79
STANLEY CUP VICTORIES: 1973/74–1974/75

"Win together today and we walk together forever."

What Fred Shero wrote on the blackboard before Game 6 of the 1974 Stanley Cup finals

On May 19, 1974, the Philadelphia Flyers were playing the Boston Bruins in Game 6 of the Stanley Cup finals at home in Philadelphia. I watched the game on TV, thrilled at the prospect that for the first time in my conscious memory a Philly sports team had a shot at being a world champion.

When Rick Macleish scored in the first period, my heart jumped even further

---

73 Shero coached the first 20 games of the 1980/81 season.

for joy. For the remaining 45 minutes and 12 seconds of the game, I held my breath, hoping the Flyers could win but not really believing it because for years (like so many other Philly sports fans) I had been inculcated with the sad reality that Philadelphia sports teams always failed to win the big ones. And after all, the Flyers were playing the Boston Bruins: two-time Stanley Cup champions who had Bobby Orr and Phil Esposito on their roster.

On paper the Flyers didn't stand a chance. But when the final buzzer sounded and the Flyers had won, 1–0, I was now a devoted fan of a world championship team – a rare moment of happiness in an otherwise unhappy childhood.

And then the Flyers did something even more extraordinary – they repeated as Stanley Cup champions again! (They were the last Philadelphia sports team to do so as of 2015.)

During the championship years of 1973/74 to 1974/75, the Flyers were not so much a team as they were a menagerie littered with an oddball assortment of characters named Moose, Rosco, Big Bird, Little O, Cowboy, Hound, and the Hammer – and the man who rode herd on that menagerie and led them to the only Stanley Cup victories in Flyers franchise history was Fred "Fog" Shero – their greatest head coach.

Shero was a product of the New York Rangers organization. He was a defenceman who played briefly with the Rangers, including when they lost the 1949/50 Stanley Cup finals to Detroit in a hard-fought series.

After 1950, Shero was sent back to the minors and ended his playing career in 1958, whereupon he immediately took up coaching, serving a very long (in his eyes) apprenticeship in the Rangers farm system. Shero excelled in the minors, winning two championships in the International Hockey League (IHL) and one in the Central Hockey League (CHL). In 1969/70 Shero coached the Buffalo Bisons in the American Hockey League (AHL) to a Calder Cup win (Shero is another one of the six coaches who have coached a Calder Cup and a Stanley Cup winner).

The Flyers hired Shero to be their head coach in 1971. Since their inception in 1967, the Flyers had not had a winning season. Shero got off to a slow start with another losing season – but the elements for future greatness were already there. The Flyers had a wealth of young hockey talent. Most of the members of the 1973/74 Cup champions were already on the roster – what they needed was leadership and seasoning. Shero was the perfect man to give it to them.

The following season Shero led the Flyers to the first of six consecutive Stanley Cup semifinal appearances. By 1974/75 they had won two Stanley Cups. By 1975/76 they were poised to win a third but were beaten by Scotty Bowman's Montreal Canadiens. In 1976/77 and 1977/78 the Flyers failed to reach the finals, and Shero left the Flyers to become the New York Rangers head coach and general manager.

In 1978/79 Shero led the Rangers to their first Stanley Cup final since 1971/72, only to fall to the Habs in five games. Shero is the only NHL coach since 1967 to make seven consecutive Stanley Cup semifinal or conference final appearances – six with the Flyers and one with the Rangers.

Despite all the maledicta heaped against the Flyers for their *Fight Club* style of hockey, the Flyers were a well-balanced team. From 1973/74 to 1977/78, the Flyers were always among the top six in offence and defence (from 1973/74 to 1974/75, they had the best defence in the NHL). The Flyers also showed high marks in power-play offence and penalty-killing. But Shero's teams' greatest strength was in short-handed offence. When it came to short-handed goal production, Shero's teams were the finest of the 1970s.

Under Shero, Flyers centre Bobby Clarke won three Hart trophies; goalie Bernie Parent (my favourite Flyer) won two Vezina and two Conn Smythe trophies during the Flyers Cup years. Winger Bill Barber was an NHL All-Star, as were Clarke and Parent. All three players became Hockey Hall of Fame inductees.

When the Montreal Canadiens swept the Flyers in four games in 1975/76, hockey purists to this day celebrate it as the hockey equivalent of Luke Skywalker vanquishing Darth Vader.

But what about the time when the Soviet Red Army hockey team toured the NHL during the 1975/76 season? The Habs blew a 3–1 lead against the Red Army team and salvaged a tie, whereas the Flyers beat the same Red Army team handily, 4–1 (in fact, the Flyers victory forced the Russian teams to alter and improve their tactics in future confrontations with North American hockey teams).

Flyers critics base their objections on hockey aesthetics, but one wonders if the real source of their hate is based more on the fact that the Flyers won two Stanley Cups with their brawling style. One also wonders if the criticism of the Flyers would be as vehement if the Flyers had never won the Stanley Cup.

Nothing is more galling than when a team succeeds using a system that other teams deem anathema. From 1994/95 to 2002/03, the New Jersey Devils won three

Stanley Cups with their neutral-zone trap. Critics claimed it made for boring and stultifying hockey – which it did – but without it New Jersey would never have won.

Douglas Hunter, in his book *Champions,* writes, "It was no-nonsense lunch-bucket hockey, molded to the skills of tier-two players who needed to follow a disciplined game plan. Don't think, just do, was the method behind his strategies. . . . And though he [Shero] had nothing good to say about dump-and-chase hockey . . . it remained a cornerstone of the Flyers' game. . . . No stylish retreating and regrouping was allowed in the Shero playbook. If people wanted to see fancy skating, he once said, they should go to the Ice Capades."[74]

Shero himself was more succinct in his approach. He told his players, "Take the shortest route to the puck carrier and arrive in ill humor."

Physicality is vital to championship hockey. What the Flyers did was take physicality, kick it up several notches, and make it page one in their playbook. The Flyers were not the only NHL team to play a rough brand of hockey, but they played the roughest brand of hockey of their time – that is why they won two Stanley Cups and that is why their opponents cried foul.

It was brutal, savage, ugly . . . but it worked.

In terms of coaching style, Fred Shero was the ultimate player's coach. He never embarrassed his players and defended them to the nth degree before the press and the public.

When Shero noticed a player having trouble executing assignments, he would use team captain Bobby Clarke and other veteran players to convey the message and help the player in question improve his game. Shero felt peer pressure worked better than cracking the whip, and given the Flyers' unique chemistry, his methods worked beautifully.

He was notorious for his Delphic utterances, but his oracular manner was a shrewd tool to defuse and release tension. He was a psychological alchemist who used verbal distraction to counter the external emotional distractions and pressures that could undermine the team's focus.

He was not afraid to drink with his team (which in itself was a clever ploy: he could bond with his team while at the same time keeping his players in line because no player wants to get uncontrollably drunk in front of his coach).

---

74 *Champions*, Douglas Hunter, p. 171.

Shero, like Emile Francis and Roger Neilson, was a wizard at analyzing film to deduce an opponent's weaknesses. His decision to force Boston's Bobby Orr to carry the puck at all times was vital in the Flyers' 1973/74 Cup win.

He studied Russian hockey tactics for years and was an avowed admirer of their systems. (In fact, immediately after the Flyers won their first Stanley Cup, Shero took a three-week trip to the Soviet Union to observe the Russian team practice and to attend seminars given by Russian coaching legend Anatoli Tarasov.)

That study helped the Flyers beat the Red Army team in 1975/76.

Author and Flyers historian Jay Greenberg writes, "Shero assured his players that their system was tailor-made to counter the Soviets. The key was for the third Flyer forward to stay at the attacking blue line, cutting off the Army's long passes up-the-middle. When the Soviets would weave to regroup around center ice, Philadelphia wingers and defensemen were told to drop back and wait at the blue line. Shero was certain the opposition would become disoriented if unable to pass or skate the puck into the offensive zone. Since the Soviet idea of defense was a poke check and a trapping pass to a cherry-picking forward, the Flyers figured gaining possession would not be a problem and keeping the puck would be the key. The Red Army was not expected to challenge much along the boards, leaving Philadelphia plenty of time to make good, safe plays. Shero believed his team could negate the Soviets' speed advantage by shooting judiciously and avoiding errant, diagonal passes."[75]

The game turned out exactly as Shero predicted, and the Flyers defended the NHL's and North America's honour with a decisive win. In retrospect, Fred Shero's game plan was a wicked foreshadowing of the neutral-zone trapping, clutch-and-grab defensive style used from 1994/95 to 2003/04.

He was the first NHL coach to use an assistant coach [Mike Nykoluk] to help run the team, thus allowing him to have greater one-on-one contact with his players. (Today, NHL teams have at least three to four assistant coaches on staff.)

Shero left the Flyers because he craved an opportunity to coach and be general manager at the same time for the Rangers, but by fall 1980 he was gone.

At his retirement, Shero was among the top ten greatest coaches in hockey history.

---

75 *Full Spectrum*, Jay Greenberg, p. 100.

Shero took up broadcasting and never returned to NHL coaching. His son Ray Shero grew up to become one of the finest team executives in the NHL. (He was general manager of the Pittsburgh Penguins until he was fired in 2014. Today he is the general manager of the New Jersey Devils.)

In the 1980s Fred Shero battled a closet drinking problem and in 1990 succumbed to stomach cancer. When he died, Flyers fans mourned his death – this writer included.

It took the hockey world a long time to give Fred Shero his just due, but on July 9, 2013, he finally earned his well-deserved reward when he was inducted into the Hockey Hall of Fame.

Rest in peace, Freddie.

PETER "PETE" GREEN RANK #15

PLUS: 84
MINUS: 2
VALUE: +82
PEAK RANK: #1 in 1922/23
PEAK VALUE: +82 in 1923/24

NHL COACHING EXPERIENCE: Ottawa Senators, 1919–1925

NHL REGULAR SEASON W–L–T: 94–52–4
NHL PLAYOFF W–L–T: 14–9–1

LEAGUE CHAMPIONSHIPS: 1919/20, 1921/22–1923/24

PLAYOFF APPEARANCES: 1919/20–1923/24
STANLEY CUP FINALS: 1919/20–1920/21, 1922/23
STANLEY CUP VICTORIES: 1919/20–1920/21, 1922/23

We live in an age where with a few clicks of a computer mouse we can obtain the most detailed, intimate, and sometimes embarrassing facts about a person's life (whether they are famous or obscure).

Peter "Pete" Green, the first NHL coach ever to win three Stanley Cups, is neither famous nor obscure. He is a near-mystery.

Hockey writer Paul Kitchen, who wrote *Win, Tie, or Wrangle*, the definitive history of the original Ottawa Senators (and who graciously lent me his notes on Pete Green), found precious little in the way of background information.

Green was born in Quebec either in 1863 or 1868 (sources differ). Even the spelling of his last name inspires debate. Kitchen found some sources that spelled his name as "Greene." In his notes, Kitchen quotes an Ottawa newspaper stating that Green was "one of the most astute lacrosse players of his day and had considerable success coaching the Capitals in lacrosse, the Ottawas in hockey, and the Ottawa football club."

Green's whole life did not revolve solely around hockey. Green worked roughly forty years in the Post Office Department in Ottawa, from 1895 to the mid-1930s. (This was not an uncommon thing for hockey players and team personnel during that era. Eddie Gerard also worked as a civil servant for the Canadian government when he wasn't playing hockey.)

Green's involvement with Ottawa hockey began in 1903, serving as a trainer for the Ottawa HC's Stanley Cup wins in 1903 to 1906 and later as the coach for the Ottawa Senators during their Stanley Cup wins in 1909, 1910, and 1911. Green stopped coaching in 1913. (The Ottawa Senators of that era are not related to the present-day Ottawa Senators franchise. Today's Senators are an expansion team that has operated since 1992 while resurrecting the original team's name in the process.)

The original Ottawa Senators dominated Canadian hockey during the early 20th century and became the NHL's first dynasty team when the fledgling league began in 1917 (winning Stanley Cups in 1919/20, 1920/21, 1922/23, and 1926/27).

Pete Green was at the helm for the first three Cup titles.

When he returned in 1919 to take over the team once more, the Senators were stocked with veteran holdovers from the National Hockey Association era such as Clint Benedict, Eddie Gerard, Cy Denneny, and Frank Nighbor (all future Hall of Famers and the best players in the league at that time).

Still, Green was not afraid to start a rookie if the player showed promise. King Clancy biographer Brian McFarlane quotes a story from the late hockey journalist Basil O'Meara about how Green saw Clancy do well in amateur hockey and asked Clancy to play for the Senators. O'Meara wrote that Green was a "keen judge of hockey talent."

Another example is when goalie Clint Benedict left Ottawa for the Montreal Maroons in 1924. Green replaced Benedict with rookie (and future Hall of Famer) Alec Connell.

Hall of Fame centre Frank Boucher also started his professional hockey career playing for Green.

Indeed, Paul Kitchen states in his book that Green, before and after his coaching stints with the Senators, kept close ties with the team, recommending promising hockey prospects from time to time.

Green's Senators were not just physically talented but also hockey smart. Gerard, Boucher, and Denneny would later coach Stanley Cup winners in their own right. King Clancy worked in the NHL his entire life as a player, referee, coach, and team executive.

The Senators of that era (like all great hockey dynasties) were a total package. Forwards Frank Nighbor (recipient of the first Lady Byng and Hart trophies) and Cy Denneny supplied the scoring punch. Due to their efforts, Green was the best offensive coach of the 1920s and of the NHL's first quarter-century. Eddie Gerard played defence with great physical skill and intelligence. King Clancy and Georges Boucher were splendid blue-liners themselves, with Clancy supplying the bench strength. Clint Benedict was the finest goalie in the NHL's first decade of existence. Even the Senators front office was excellent. Ottawa manager Tommy Gorman was one of the best general managers during the league's first quarter-century, a hands-on executive who worked closely with Green to run the team (and who would later coach two Stanley Cup winners in the 1930s).

Green's Senators won games with superb goaltending and defence. The late hockey historian Stanley Coleman wrote in his trilogy *The Trail of the Stanley Cup* that the 1920/21 Senators used a "Kitty bar the door technique which their opponents found very frustrating."

In *Win, Tie, or Wrangle*, Paul Kitchen writes that the Senators always strove to get an early lead on their opponents. Once they did so, they would then go into their Kitty-bar-the-door defence, which consisted of the forwards and blue-liners literally forming a wall in front of the goaltender to prevent their opponents from getting any significant shots on goal.[76]

This led to the NHL passing new rules that limited the number of defenders a team could keep in its own zone.

Indeed, the Senators led the NHL in defence from 1919/20 to 1922/23, which begs the question: Was this a reflection of Green's hockey philosophy or did he simply lead with his strength and push the right buttons?

And what was Green's coaching personality like?

Was he intense like Punch Imlach? Or beloved like Toe Blake?

Green was certainly not a tactician like NHL coaches are today – not in that era of hockey, when rosters were small and substitutions minimal. Still, Green did have a system for substitutions. King Clancy told Brian MacFarlane that when the

---

76 *Win, Tie, Or Wrangle*, Paul Kitchen, p. 270.

Senators played at home, the three substitute players (Frank Boucher, Clancy, and Morley Bruce) would sit in the dressing room, waiting to be summoned. A buzzer system installed by Green for that very purpose would signal which player was needed. One buzz meant that Boucher would go in. Two buzzes meant Clancy himself had to go in, and three buzzes meant that Bruce went in.[77]

And yet he was a disciplinarian. In his notes on Green, Kitchen quotes a 1919 *Ottawa Journal* article: "The return of Green to the game means that the men who were inclined to hoist the odd noggin betimes will be given scant encouragement. Green doesn't believe in alcohol as an athletic aid and in the old days when it was more common than at the present had many a hard encounter with recalcitrant players."

The Senators won the Stanley Cup in 1919/20 and 1920/21 (the first NHL team ever to repeat as Stanley Cup champions) but lost the NHL finals to Toronto in 1921/22, even though they had won the league championship. The Senators rebounded powerfully the following year, winning the 1922/23 Stanley Cup while earning high praise from Frank Patrick, who thought the Senators were "the greatest hockey team he had ever seen."

Things began to slip for Pete Green. The Senators lost the NHL finals to the Canadiens in 1923/24 and in 1924/25 fell to fourth place, not making the playoffs.

Green stopped coaching in 1925. Kitchen writes that Green was in his sixties and may have been battling ill health. We have no idea when he passed away.

When Green resigned in 1925, he was the best hockey coach of all time (according to my rating system) and remained so until the 1930s. He was among the top five greatest coaches of all time until 1959/60 and among the top ten until 1985/86 (see "The Progressive Chart" in Part Four).

It's sad that we don't know more about Pete Green. Considering the fact that in this day and age we know the most lurid and insipid details about the most trivial things and arcane individuals, it's regrettable that we cannot have a complete portrait of the NHL's first truly great coach; it prevents us from paying homage to him and according Pete Green the respect and admiration he so richly deserves.

---

77 *Clancy: The King's Story*, Brian McFarlane, p. 48.

"TRADER" JACK ADAMS RANK #16

PLUS: 117
MINUS: 36
VALUE: +81
PEAK RANK: #4 in 1944/45
PEAK VALUE: +81 in 1945/46

COACHING EXPERIENCE: Detroit Cougars, 1927–1930; Detroit Falcons, 1930–1932; Detroit Red Wings, 1932–1947

REGULAR SEASON W–L–T: 413–390–161
PLAYOFF W–L–T: 52–52–1

PRINCE OF WALES TROPHY: 1942/43

AMERICAN DIVISION TITLES: 1933/34, 1935/36–1936/37

PLAYOFF APPEARANCES: 1928/29, 1931/32–1933/34, 1935/36–1936/37, 1938/39–1946/47
STANLEY CUP FINALS: 1933/34, 1935/36–1936/37, 1940/41–1942/43, 1944/45
STANLEY CUP VICTORIES: 1935/36–1936/37, 1942/43

In his book *The Reckoning*, the late Dave Halberstam titled his first two chapters on the Ford Motor Company "Henry Ford: The Builder" and "Henry Ford: The Destroyer." If one were writing a history of the Detroit Red Wings, the same chapter titles could aptly apply to the late "Trader" Jack Adams because Adams made the Detroit Red Wings into an NHL dynasty and then dismantled that dynasty and condemned the Wings to a 42-year Stanley Cup drought.

The man responsible for the Red Wings becoming the greatest American franchise in the NHL was a feisty centre who played for the 1917/18 Stanley Cup–winning Toronto Arenas, then for Frank Patrick's Vancouver Millionaires in the

Pacific Coast Hockey Association (PCHA), where he led the league in scoring once while helping the Millionaires reach the Stanley Cup finals both times.

Adams returned to the NHL in 1922 to play again for Toronto and, later, the original Ottawa Senators team that won the 1926/27 Stanley Cup.

Retiring a champion, Adams (showing the savvy and self-confidence that defined his hockey career) went to the fledgling Detroit Cougars franchise, offering his services as coach and general manager. The struggling team gratefully accepted.

For the next 35 years, Adams ceaselessly made, remade, and re-remade the team into his own image.

It was rough going. His first winning season and playoffs appearance came in 1928/29, but the following two seasons saw him finishing last. The Cougars changed their name to the Falcons, and in 1932 James E. Norris bought the Falcons and renamed them the Red Wings.

Norris did two important things:

1. He had the financial resources to build a winning team as well as a burgeoning hockey farm system where future stars could be bred.
2. He was trustful enough (within certain limits) to give Jack Adams carte blanche to run the Red Wings as he saw fit.

Adams now had the same total control that Art Ross in Boston and Lester Patrick in New York enjoyed – and he exercised it ruthlessly until 1962.

The Red Wings slowly took flight, making their first Stanley Cup finals appearance in 1933/34 (losing to the Chicago Blackhawks); then came the motherlode.

Detroit and Montreal were the only NHL teams to win consecutive Stanley Cups from 1927 to 1942. Detroit dominated the regular-season standings from 1934/35 to 1936/37 while winning the Stanley Cup in 1935/36 and 1936/37.

When it came to leadership, Jack Adams was a bull who brought his own china shop. He led with the same feistiness and volcanic temperament that defined his playing style. (He cost his team the 1941/42 Stanley Cup when he slugged a referee during Game 4 of the finals. The NHL suspended him for the duration of the series, and the Toronto Maple Leafs – down 3–1 in the series – won the next three games in one of the greatest comebacks in Stanley Cup playoff history.)

The stories of his verbal, emotional, and psychological excesses are part of NHL folklore. Adams seldom ruled by fear when he could rule by terror because terror was a much better motivator. Coaching in an era where there were no agents, no NHL Players' Association, fewer teams (and roster slots), and very low wages, Adams had many ways to push his players hard.

Adams's winning formula was unlike what his dynasty teams of 1949/50 to 1954/55 possessed: great balance on offence and defence. During his coaching reign, the Wings had only an average offence but superb defence and great goaltending.

Adams's genius was in finding and developing superior goaltending talent. Long before Terry Sawchuk came along, Jack got All-Star performances from goalies John Roach, Norm Smith, and Johnny Mowers. And long before defenceman Red Kelly joined the Wings, blue-liner Ebbie Goodfellow became a three-time NHL All-Star for Adams.

Another key ingredient was on-ice discipline. Considering Adams's volcanic, bellicose personality, you would expect his teams to have racked up a lot of penalty minutes. Not so. Adams was superb at instilling on-ice discipline and was among the pioneers who made it an essential part of a team's tactical makeup. Adams's system did not die with him. His coaching successors Tommy Ivan, Jimmy Skinner, and Sid Abel continued the trend. Today, on-ice discipline and reducing penalty minutes are now essential NHL strategy.

Another Adams's innovation was fire-wagon hockey. During the Second World War, Adams took advantage of his team's superb forechecking ability.

Hockey historian Brian McFarlane writes, "Every time the Red Wings whipped the puck into the opposing team's zone all five skaters would pour into the attacking zone.

"Other teams had used this 'every man up' strategy on the power play, but the Wings began to do it all the time."[78]

Fire-wagon hockey nipped the opponent's line rushes even before they began, helping the Red Wings win the 1942/43 Stanley Cup.

Former Montreal Canadien Ray Getliffe would state in a 2006 interview that whole games would be played in one team's zone. This tactic resulted in the creation of the red line, which reduced offside calls and opened up the game offensively.

---

78 *Best of the Original Six*, Brian McFarlane, p. 137.

The war years were a boon for the Red Wings, who made the Stanley Cup finals four times from 1940/41 to 1944/45 while Adams sowed the seeds for future Red Wings greatness. Centre Sid Abel joined the team, followed in 1944 by a brash, determined left winger named Ted Lindsay.

Then, in 1946, came Adams's magnum opus: a shy eighteen-year-old right winger from Floral, Saskatchewan, who asked for a Red Wings jacket as part of his signing bonus.

The player's name was Gordie Howe, and he got the jacket . . . and the uniform . . . and a spot on the roster . . . and the NHL was changed forever.

Adams stayed as head coach to shepherd Howe through his rookie season, but in 1947 he yielded the coaching reins to Tommy Ivan while remaining as Wings general manager.

In the 1950s the Red Wings became the dynasty they were destined to be, and through it all Adams traded and shifted players with reckless abandon (he wasn't called "Trader" Jack for nothing).

After 1955, Adams's trades weren't working, and the Red Wings, no longer a dynasty, moved forward solely on inertia.

After 1955, they stopped winning Stanley Cups.

After 1966, they stopped winning altogether.

Jack Adams was fired as general manager in 1962, and he died in 1968.

Until Mike Babcock surpassed him in 2013/14, Adams had been the greatest coach in the Detroit Red Wings franchise history. His team win totals exceeded those of other Red Wing coaching luminaries such as Scotty Bowman, Sid Abel, Tommy Ivan, Jacques Demers, and Bryan Murray to name a few.

Today, Jack Adams's name lives on in the form of the trophy named after him that was first introduced by the NHL in 1973/74 and is awarded every season to the NHL coach "adjudged to have contributed the most to his team's success."

DARRYL SUTTER RANK #17

PLUS: 91
MINUS: 11
VALUE: +80
PEAK RANK: #17 in 2013/14
PEAK VALUE: +80 in 2013/14

COACHING EXPERIENCE: Chicago Blackhawks, 1992–1995; San Jose Sharks, 1997–2002[79]; Calgary Flames, 2002[80]–2006; Los Angeles Kings, 2011[81]–present

REGULAR SEASON W–L–T–OL: 547–404–101–69
PLAYOFF W–L: 88–77

NORRIS DIVISION TITLE: 1992/93
PACIFIC DIVISION TITLE: 2001/02
NORTHWEST DIVISION TITLE: 2005/06

PLAYOFF APPEARANCES: 1992/93–1994/95, 1997/98–2001/02, 2003/04, 2005/06, 2011/12–2013/14
STANLEY CUP FINALS: 2003/04, 2011/12, 2013/14
STANLEY CUP VICTORIES: 2011/12, 2013/14

The Sutter family of Alberta is one of the great families in NHL hockey. Louis and Grace Sutter raised six sons to be NHL players: Brian, Darryl, Duane, Brent, Rich, and Ron. Of the six, four Sutter boys (Brian, Darryl, Duane, and Brent) eventually became NHL coaches.

Darryl Sutter was the second of the Sutter boys to play in the NHL. He had the shortest playing career and the lowest stats of all his brothers. And yet Darryl

---

79 Sutter coached the first 24 games of the 2002/03 season for San Jose.

80 Sutter coached the last 46 games of the 2002/03 season for Calgary.

81 Sutter coached the last 49 games of the 2011/12 season for Los Angeles.

remains (as of 2015) the best coach of all the Sutter boys, with a coaching value of +80 (Brent is second, with a coaching value of +16; Brian is third, with +9; and Duane is last, with -7).

As a coach, Darryl is an inspirational figure who has repeatedly motivated his teams to overcome more talented opponents. He is a Giant Killer *par excellence*. Since 1985/86 (when the President's Trophy was first awarded), only two NHL coaches have beaten three President's Trophy winners in Stanley Cup playoff competition. One is Scotty Bowman and the other is Darryl Sutter.

A prime example of this was during the 2011/12 playoffs when Sutter took the eighth-seeded Los Angeles Kings to their first Stanley Cup win, defeating the top three seeds in the Western Conference in the process to reach the finals.

Hockey historian Stan Fischler quotes Sutter (on his coaching philosophy) in his book *Coaches*: "If you look at teams who win the Stanley Cup, you see it starts with the goaltender and a hell of a team defence."[82]

Indeed, goalie Ed Belfour won a Vezina and two Jennings trophies for Sutter in Chicago, while the Blackhawks had the best defence in the NHL two of the three years he coached there.

In San Jose, Sutter got solid goaltending from Mike Vernon and later Evgeni Nabokov (winner of the 2000/01 Calder Memorial Trophy). Calgary's Miikka Kiprusoff won the 2005/06 Vezina and Jennings trophies under Sutter.

When Sutter returned to coaching in Los Angeles in 2011, it was the stellar goaltending work of young Jonathan Quick that propelled the Kings to their Stanley Cup victories in 2011/12 and 2013/14.

In addition to superb goaltending, Sutter's teams were usually among the best in penalty-killing. But it wasn't solely defence and penalty-killing that distinguished his teams. Sutter's squads were always physical, aggressive, and unafraid to duke it out to win.

Darryl played eight seasons in the NHL, solely with the Chicago Blackhawks. He was an injury-prone left winger who (when healthy) was a dependable goal-scorer. Sutter was the Blackhawks team captain from 1982 to 1987. When his playing career ended, Sutter became an assistant coach for the Hawks and later coached in the minors before becoming an associate coach under Mike Keenan (who took

82 *Coaches*, Stan Fischler, p. 123.

over the coaching reins of the Blackhawks in 1988). When Keenan became the Hawks general manager in 1992, Sutter became head coach.

The relationship between Keenan and Sutter is significant.

Again, Stan Fischler quotes Sutter, who said that "being Keenan's assistant was not hard for me and no adjustment was necessary since Mike and I are a lot alike in terms of our expectations of players and our expectations of ourselves. . . . When Mike and I discussed a game, I knew exactly what he was going to say. If we have a difference it's in the way we're demonstrative."[83]

The Hawks won the Norris Division title in Sutter's rookie season as a coach, only to suffer first-round elimination in the playoffs. His idyll ended when Keenan left Chicago after a bitter power struggle with Bob Pulford. Like so many coaches before and after him, Sutter had to make do with the players Pulford dealt him. In his last season in Chicago, he made it as far as the conference finals of the 1994/95 Stanley Cup playoffs before succumbing to the Detroit Red Wings in five games. (It would be another 14 years before the Blackhawks made another third-round appearance.) Sutter resigned as head coach but remained in the Hawks' front office before moving on to San Jose in 1997.

The San Jose Sharks hadn't made a playoff appearance since 1994/95. In his first five seasons with them, Sutter got the Sharks into the post-season five times, but it was tough going. Sutter didn't have his first winning season until 1999/00. Still, the Sharks showed their grit that year when they upset the President's Trophy recipient St. Louis Blues with a first-round playoff victory. Two years later Sutter coached the Sharks to their first Pacific Division title. By 2002 Sutter became only the second coach in NHL history to increase his team's season points total five straight years (the other was Al Arbour of the New York Islanders).

The 2002/03 season started poorly for Sutter. In nature, sharks must move constantly in order to survive. When they stop moving, they die. By December 2002, the San Jose Sharks had stopped moving, and Darryl Sutter was fired. Four weeks later Sutter was hired by the Calgary Flames to be their head coach (and later their general manager).

The man from Viking, Alberta, had finally come home.

---

83 Ibid.

By 2003 the Flames had been doused. They hadn't made the playoffs since 1995/96 and hadn't had a winning season since 1994/95. The team needed re-igniting. Led by sharpshooter Jarome Iginla and goaltender Miikka Kiprusoff, the Flames did a slow burn, with a 19-point upsurge and a playoff appearance in 2003/04.

It was here that Sutter's Flames started to burn brighter. They advanced all the way to the Stanley Cup finals, beating Vancouver, Detroit, and (what must have been sweet revenge for Sutter) the San Jose Sharks through three bitterly fought rounds. It was Sutter's first Stanley Cup finals appearance as a head coach.

The Flames took on the Tampa Bay Lightning and had a 3–2 series lead going into Game 6, which was played in Calgary. At the end of regulation time, the score was tied 2–2 and the Flames needed only one goal to win their first Stanley Cup since 1988/89. It never came.

Thirty-three seconds into the second overtime period, Tampa's Martin St. Louis scored to win Game 6, thus forcing a Game 7 at Tampa (which the Lightning won 2–1).

The Flames continued to win, but Sutter stopped coaching after 2006 to focus solely on his general manager duties. His coaching successors, however, failed to duplicate his magical touch.

Interestingly, Sutter hired his old mentor, Mike Keenan, as head coach but fired him after two seasons, replacing him with his younger brother Brent (who failed to match what Darryl had done as a coach himself).

In December 2010, Sutter stepped down as the Flames general manager, but in the fall of 2011, it was déjà vu all over again when he got a call from Dean Lombardi (who had hired him to coach in San Jose and was now the general manager of the Los Angeles Kings), asking him to resume his coaching career and take over the helm of the stagnant Kings.

The Kings, despite having several young, talented players, were in a state of abdication; their offence was non-existent, and their players utterly lacked a sense of identity and focus. The fan base and press were disillusioned and demanding a tactical makeover. When the hiring of Darryl Sutter was announced, it was greeted with considerable skepticism.

Amazingly, Sutter peeled off six years of rust and turned the Kings into hard-hitting, tight-fisted, well-motivated contenders for the Pacific Division title.

Although they finished second, the Kings showed toughness, courage, and determination along the way.

The changes Sutter made were not tactical. The Kings' offence remained peashooter weak. At no time did they dominate the division. What Sutter did was to get the Kings to look at themselves and make up their minds about what sort of team they were going to be.

Gone was the lotusland atmosphere. Sutter demanded (and got) the Kings to commit to his work ethic. The Kings had shown defensive prowess under Terry Murray. Sutter now demanded (and got) an even greater defensive effort from everyone.

Although the Kings failed to win the divisional title and only drew the eighth seed in the Western Conference, what followed was one of the greatest playoff runs since the NHL went to four rounds of playoffs in 1975. In only 20 games, the Kings humiliated the Vancouver Canucks (who had won their second consecutive President's Trophy), swept the St. Louis Blues (who had the best defence in the NHL), skinned the Phoenix Coyotes (who had edged out the Kings for the Pacific Division title), and overcame a late, desperate surge by the New Jersey Devils to win the 2011/12 Stanley Cup.

What was amazing about the Kings' domination of their opponents was that Sutter showed nothing new in his tactical bag of tricks during the playoffs. What fans saw was the classic Darryl Sutter oeuvre of superb goaltending coupled with a crushing defence supplemented by aggressive, relentless two-way play by his forwards.

Sutter's tactics were predictable; what was fascinating was how his opponents utterly failed to respond and motivate their teams to overcome them.

Ken Hitchcock, who coached the Blues in their loss to Los Angeles, states perceptively: "Darryl Sutter's team played with a sense of desperation and a real edge of commitment. They played hard, consistent hockey. It's really revealing to see his teams play because the way they play exposes the flaws and weaknesses and the strengths of their opponents."

The Kings won through execution. It was beautiful to see how the Kings played their game, using a five "P" system: pressure, possession, passing, penalty-killing, and power play, all executed with a crisp coolness that froze their opponents. The only time the Kings lost their cool was during Games 4 and 5 of the Stanley Cup finals when they suffered two consecutive defeats to the New Jersey Devils. Kings captain Dustin Brown later told the press that Sutter had told the team to cool down and regain their composure, which they did wonderfully in the deciding Game 6.

Jonathan Quick earned his Conn Smythe Trophy with a 1.41 playoff GAA. Dazzling, acrobatic, and youthfully exuberant, Quick earned All-Star honours while carrying the team on his padded shoulders and showing that he truly represents the future of NHL goaltending.

Dustin Brown, Anze Kopitar, and late-season acquisition Jeff Carter supplied the goalscoring. Drew Doughty, Justin Williams, and Mike Richards (along with Brown and Kopitar) set up many a Kings goal. The two Dustins, Brown and Penner, supplied the muscle when muscle was needed (but surprisingly the Kings seldom committed stupid penalties throughout their playoff run).

The Kings penalty-killing unit was sensational, allowing only five power-play goals in 20 games while scoring five short-handed goals in the process.

By leading the Los Angeles Kings to the Stanley Cup title, Darryl Sutter had done what Bob Pulford, Pat Quinn, Marc Crawford, and Terry Murray could not do: win it all.

Sutter had finally elevated his players and himself to a place from which they had long been denied: the summit of NHL hockey, with the Stanley Cup beside them, their names etched forever in the annals of hockey history – the ultimate award for a great hockey team and a great hockey coach.

The Kings failed to repeat during the strike-shortened 2012/13 season but managed to reach the Western Conference finals where they fell in five to the Chicago Blackhawks (with three of their four losses decided by one point).

If winning the 2011/12 Stanley Cup was the good and failing to retain the Cup in 2012/13 was the bad, then the Kings' 2013/14 season was the ugly. Even though the team finished in the triple digits in team points, they still finished third in the Pacific Division. What followed during the playoffs was one of the most brutal grinds in Stanley Cup playoff history.

The Kings were forced to play 26 out of a possible 28 games. Seven times they faced elimination at the hands of their opponents during the first three rounds of the playoffs. Seven of their 26 games went into overtime (three of those games going into double overtime), with the Kings winning five of the seven of the matchups. The Kings won three Game 7s on the road just to reach the Stanley Cup finals.

In the first round against Todd McLellan's San Jose Sharks, they fell into a 3–0 series deficit before doing what had only been done three times before in NHL history: winning the next four games to win the series – an honour Darryl Sutter shares with Hap Day, Al Arbour, and Peter Laviolette. During the four-game comeback, the Kings held the Sharks to two goals in three games.

During the second round, the Kings allowed Bruce Boudreau's Anaheim Ducks to rally from a 2–0 deficit to gain a 3–2 series lead, but again the Kings rallied to win Games 6 and 7 by a combined 8–3 margin in goals in both games.

Then came the Western Conference finals where the Kings faced the defending champion Chicago Blackhawks. The Kings had a 3–1 series lead before allowing Chicago to rally back to force a Game 7 in Chicago. In a violent struggle, the Kings rallied to force an overtime, which they won.

In a historic matchup with Alain Vigneault's New York Rangers (the first time these two teams had ever faced each other in the Stanley Cup finals), the Kings beat the Rangers to win their second Stanley Cup in three seasons.

Unlike the 2011/12 Cup win that featured a dazzling, beautiful display of defensive hockey by the Kings, the 2013/14 Cup win was anything but beautiful. The Kings won it ugly. It was brutal, savage trench warfare that saw the Kings draw upon their reserves of mental toughness and dish out violence and punishment against their foes.

Their first-round comeback against San Jose was triggered by vicious brawls against the Sharks in Game 4 of the series. The Kings pummelled the Sharks into submission. In Game 7 of the Western Conference finals, the Kings got extremely physical with the Blackhawks and won.

It was not pretty to watch by any means. It was an ordeal, a trial by fire, but it also showed the Darryl Sutter touch. Only Darryl Sutter could take a team that had enjoyed the California lifestyle for so long and teach them how to win a war of attrition on the ice.

Only Darryl Sutter could take a team of raw youngsters and make them two-time Stanley Cup champions – defeating teams that had outperformed them during the regular season.

Only Darryl Sutter could instill the requisite rage and white-hot anger in his players that could inspire them to overcome crisis situation after crisis situation.

With Darryl Sutter, the man and the team and the moment have met.

(In 2014/15, the Kings became the tenth team in NHL history to fail to reach the playoffs after winning the Stanley Cup the season before. Injuries and internal disarray – two of its players suffered brushes with the law off the ice – cost the team dearly. Even victors can be undone by victory itself.)

BILLY REAY RANK #18

PLUS: 95
MINUS: 17
VALUE: +78
PEAK RANK: #9 in 1975/76
PEAK VALUE: +82 in 1975/76

COACHING EXPERIENCE: Toronto Maple Leafs, 1957–1958[84]; Chicago Blackhawks, 1963–1976[85]

REGULAR SEASON W–L–T: 542–385–175
PLAYOFF W–L: 57–60

PRINCE OF WALES TROPHY: 1966/67

EAST DIVISION TITLE: 1969/70
WEST DIVISION TITLES: 1970/71–1972/73
SMYTHE DIVISION TITLE: 1975/76

PLAYOFF APPEARANCES: 1963/64–1967/68, 1969/70–1975/76
STANLEY CUP FINALS: 1964/65, 1970/71, 1972/73

From 1961/62 to 1972/73, the Chicago Blackhawks were a dynasty that never was. The man leading the team during that era was the late Billy Reay, who was (and remains) the winningest coach in Blackhawks history. No other Hawks coach won more games, served as long, achieved such sustained excellence, and was loved more by his players than Reay was.

But he never won the Stanley Cup. The Blackhawks made the Stanley Cup finals three times – in 1964/65, 1970/71, and 1972/73 – and all three times

84 Reay coached the first 20 games of the 1958/59 season.

85 Reay coached the first 34 games of the 1976/77 season.

they fell to the Montreal Canadiens in hard-fought series with epic displays of hockey therein.

According to my rating system, Billy Reay is the greatest hockey coach never to have won the Stanley Cup.

Reay was not only a first-rate hockey coach but also a solid hockey player. He came out of the Red Wings farm system but found his niche after the Second World War with the Montreal Canadiens. He played centre for the Habs from 1945 to 1953, helping them win the 1945/46 and 1952/53 Stanley Cups. During those years he was exposed to the offensive style of Dick Irvin, who emphasized speed, power, and a relentless assault on the opponent's net.

When his playing career ended, Reay coached in the minors and by 1957 became the head coach of the Toronto Maple Leafs. He was caught in the doldrums that dogged the Leafs during the 1950s; his days were numbered when Punch Imlach became general manager in 1958. Twenty games into the 1958/59 season (with the Leafs in last place), Reay was fired. He returned to the minors, coaching in the Chicago Blackhawks farm system – where he excelled.

Reay returned to the NHL in 1963 when the Blackhawks hired him to replace the fired Rudy Pilous.

For the next 13 seasons, Reay led the Hawks through the most illustrious period in their franchise history, in the process getting the Hawks to produce some of the finest all-around hockey in NHL history.

These were the glory years for Hawks icons such as Bobby Hull, who led the NHL in goals scored five times, winning one scoring title while twice being named NHL MVP. Stan Mikita won four scoring titles and was twice named NHL MVP as well. In 1966/67 Mikita pulled a rare trophy-winning triple crown: collecting the Ross, Hart, and Lady Byng. Before the arrival of Bobby Orr, Pierre Pilote was one of the finest shooting defencemen in the NHL and a two-time Norris Trophy winner.

And then there was "Mr. Goalie," Glenn Hall, who revolutionized NHL goaltending with his butterfly style and who set an NHL endurance record at goalie that will likely never be broken. Hall was succeeded in net by Tony Esposito, who won three Vezinas for Billy Reay and was a mainstay of the 1970/71 and 1972/73 Stanley Cup teams.

All of these men were NHL All-Stars and were elected to the Hockey Hall of Fame. But they were not the only quality players Reay coached. Players such as

Kenny Wharram, Moose Vasko, Pat Stapleton, Bill White, and Dennis Hull (Bobby's brother) earned All-Star honours too; and let's not forget that the young Phil Esposito got his start in the NHL playing for Reay as well. Although Espo never won All-Star honours for Reay, he was a vital part of the team's offensive punch until he was traded in 1967.

Reay as a coach was a study in coolness. He was not volcanic like Punch Imlach or feisty like Emile Francis. He did not lead with the controlled tension-and-release emotionalism of Toe Blake.

Former Hawk Doug Mohns says, "I thought Billy Reay was a rather stoic person until I got to know him on practice days and behind the bench. . . . He arranged his lines so that each line had a certain amount of chemistry and could complement one another. The defensive pairs were established in the same manner. . . . Billy's emphasis was on maintaining possession of the puck. He wanted the opposition to chase us and NOT us to chase them. He also wanted us to play a physical game to slow the opposition down where they couldn't freewheel without any concern of getting hit."

Mohns's statement is borne out by the composition of Reay's first two lines: the Hem Line of Bobby Hull, Phil Esposito, and Chico Maki; and the Scooter Line of Doug Mohns, Stan Mikita, and Kenny Wharram. Reay balanced the playmaking skills of Esposito and Maki with Hull's incredible shooting ability and killer instinct for the net. Hull became the first NHL player to score 50 goals in two consecutive seasons.

The Scooter Line was just as devastating. Reay balanced Stan Mikita's indefatigable playmaking talent with Kenny Wharram's speed and shooting ability and Doug Mohns's superb two-way skills, hypersonic speed, and knack for scoring in the clutch. During the 1966/67 season, the Blackhawks occupied three of the top five spots in goals scored and points.

As a team, Reay's Blackhawks dominated the NHL in offence, power-play offence, and short-handed offence from 1963/64 to 1966/67. Even after the 1967 NHL expansion, the Hawks were usually near the top in all the major offensive and defensive categories.

With regards to on-ice discipline, Reay's Hawks during the final years of the Original Six era were average in team penalty minute totals, but what is fascinating is that post-expansion, their on-ice discipline improved steadily.

By 1976 Reay's Hawks were near the bottom of the NHL in team penalty minutes. Only Emile Francis and Scotty Bowman exceeded Reay in on-ice discipline at that point.

And yet they still couldn't win the Stanley Cup.

The question is why?

When former Blackhawks who played for Reay were asked in interviews for their opinion on why they didn't win more Stanley Cups after 1961, their responses varied, with some intriguing insights.

Players such as Eric Nesterenko and Doug Jarrett expressed confusion and bewilderment about the team's failure. Nesterenko said, "We should have won more Cups." When asked why it didn't happen, he expressed mystification, shrugged his shoulders, and replied, "I don't know, but we should have won more Cups." Jarrett was more histrionic. He looked to the heavens and cried out, "The fates were against us!"

Lou Angotti felt that bad luck and poor officiating played a role in the Hawks' upset loss at the hands of Detroit in the 1965/66 Stanley Cup semifinals when Bryan "Bugsy" Watson drove Bobby Hull to total distraction with his sneaky tactics.

Hawks legend Glenn Hall was more trenchant on the poor officiating issue. He said in 2008 that "horseshit officiating" cost the Hawks the 1965/66 series: "You can't win with horseshit officiating!"

But bad luck and poor officiating were only half of the problem. Many former Hawks spoke volumes about how nice and personable Billy Reay was, but it was Glenn Hall who made a telling point about Reay's coaching personality: "Reay was nice, very nice. He never embarrassed you in front of the team, but he never kicked ass."

Which leads to another point: Reay's inability to crack the whip allowed certain players to play selfish hockey to the detriment of the team. Both Eric Nesterenko and Lou Angotti alluded to this. Glenn Hall biographer Chico Adrahtas said in a 2009 interview that Hall lost out on winning two more Vezina trophies because he never got the same defensive zone support that Johnny Bower, Terry Sawchuk, or Gump Worsely received.

Former Maple Leaf Ron Ellis offered another insight into the mystery in a 2008 interview: The Hawks "were not set up for the playoffs. They were set up for regular season hockey when you're entertaining the crowds but they were not set up for the playoffs. . . . They had to change their game and that's what screwed them up."

Doug Mohns stated earlier that Reay wanted the Hawks to play physical hockey, but in 1964/65, 1965/66, and 1966/67 the Hawks suffered playoff defeat because they allowed their opponents to out-hit them in key situations.

In Game 7 of the 1964/65 Stanley Cup finals, Canadiens forward Claude Provost blunted the Hawks offensively because he was able to shadow Bobby Hull's every move.

In 1965/66 Detroit's blue-line tandem of Bryan "Bugsy" Watson and Bill Gadsby played the series of their lives, and Wings goalie Roger Crozier won the Conn Smythe Trophy that year while beating the Hawks.

And then there was the playoff loss to Toronto in 1966/67.

By all rights Toronto was the weaker team, yet the Leafs used a vigorous checking game, superb defensive work from their forwards, yeoman efforts from their blue-liners, and some of the greatest goaltending in Stanley Cup playoff history to beat the Hawks.

The Hawks may have played physical hockey, but when it came to be playoff time, it wasn't physical enough.

After 1974, the Hawks declined into mediocrity. The team, the coach, and the general manager were all getting old.

Billy Reay was the first to go: summarily fired a few days before Christmas 1976 with a terse note slipped underneath his hotel room door. Hawks general manager Tommy Ivan followed him in 1977 – though at least Ivan was allowed to resign gracefully.

The man who succeeded both men would inaugurate a lesser, sterner, more heartbreaking era for Blackhawks fans: Bob Pulford (see #53).

CECIL "CECE" HART RANK #19

PLUS: 78
MINUS: 1
VALUE: +77
PEAK RANK: #2 in 1930/31
PEAK VALUE: +78 in 1937/38

COACHING EXPERIENCE: Montreal Canadiens, 1926–1932, 1936–1939

REGULAR SEASON W–L–T: 196–125–73
PLAYOFF W–L–T: 16–17–4

CANADIAN DIVISION TITLES: 1927/28–1928/29, 1930/31–1931/32, 1936/37

PLAYOFF APPEARANCES: 1926/27–1931/32, 1936/37–1937/38
STANLEY CUP FINALS: 1929/30–1930/31
STANLEY CUP VICTORIES: 1929/30–1930/31

The Hart Memorial Trophy is awarded each year to the NHL's Most Valuable Player. Named after Dr. David A. Hart, who first presented it to the NHL in 1923 as the Hart Trophy, it was retired to the Hockey Hall of Fame in 1960 and then renamed as the Hart Memorial Trophy. Dr. Hart was the father of Cecil "Cece" Hart, who was head coach of the Montreal Canadiens in the 1920s and 1930s.

When Hart's coaching career ended in 1939, he was the most successful head coach in Canadiens history and the third-greatest head coach in hockey history (according to my rating system).

Hart is one of four NHL coaches (along with Pete Green, Tommy Gorman, and Hap Day) with two or more Stanley Cup wins to go undefeated in Stanley Cup finals competition – which begs the question: why isn't he in the Hockey Hall of Fame?

Montreal Canadiens historian D'Arcy Jenish writes that Hart was an insurance broker who helped develop amateur hockey and baseball leagues in Montreal, ultimately becoming a close friend of Montreal Canadiens co-owner Leo Dandurand. When Dandurand purchased the Canadiens from the estate of the late George Kennedy in 1921, it was Hart who represented Dandurand's interests and handled the negotiations.[86]

Hart served as the team's director, getting his name etched onto the 1923/24 Stanley Cup in that capacity. He also helped recruit potential talent and was responsible for the signing of future NHL legend Howie Morenz to the Montreal Canadiens. In short, he was the team's troubleshooter.

By 1926 the Habs were in the doldrums and in need of reviving. So Hart manned the bench and for the next six seasons led the Canadiens through their finest run in Habs franchise history up to that point. His teams earned six playoff appearances, five division titles, and two consecutive Stanley Cups in 1929/30 and 1930/31 (the first NHL coach to do so since Pete Green's success with the original Ottawa Senators in 1919/20 and 1920/21).

It was also during that same time period that Cecil Hart tied Lester Patrick's record of winning five consecutive playoff series. (Patrick's and Hart's record would be broken in 1934/35 by Tommy Gorman, who became the first NHL coach to win six consecutive playoff series.)

Had it not been for the absurd playoff structure that existed in the NHL from 1928/29 to 1937/38, Hart might have been able to win more Stanley Cups. Like Art Ross, Hart was undermined by the fact that the divisional title winners had to face each other in the opening round of the Stanley Cup playoffs. Like Ross, Hart lost the opening round three times: in 1928/29, 1931/32, and 1936/37.

More significantly, from 1926 to 1932, Hart's Canadiens had the best regular-season record in the NHL three times (Ross was the only NHL coach who exceeded that total when he did it five times during the Expansion and Contraction Era from 1926 to 1942). And Hart, Jack Adams, and Tommy Gorman were the only NHL coaches to win back-to-back Cups from 1926 to 1942 – which again begs the question: Why isn't he in the Hockey Hall of Fame?

Hart's Habs teams combined superb speed and offensive punch with a tight defence complemented by magnificent goaltending. Winger Aurel Joliat was a

86 *The Montreal Canadiens*, D'Arcy Jenish, p. 54.

four-time NHL All-Star and future Hall of Famer. Defenceman and team captain Sylvio Mantha anchored the blue-line corps and was also an NHL All-Star and future Hockey Hall of Famer.

But the twin pillars of Hart's Montreal Canadiens were centre Howie Morenz and goalie George Hainsworth. Morenz had already played three seasons with the Habs when Hart became head coach, but it was under Hart that he reached his peak as the NHL's top gun and its most popular player, winning three Hart trophies and two NHL scoring titles. Morenz was the Bobby Hull of his era, combining great speed and physical strength with excellent shooting skills. His basic stats pale in comparison with today's stars, but when you adjust them toward an 82-game season, they become astounding.

In the 1927/28 season, playing in 43 games, Morenz scored 33 goals and 18 assists for 51 points. When you adjust his stats to today's game, he ends up with 67 goals and 123 assists, for an astonishing 190 points. On the all-time list of most adjusted points scored in a single season, Morenz's offensive performance is the greatest of all time, which is why he was called the "Babe Ruth of Hockey" and was the first link in a chain of Montreal hockey icons such as Rocket Richard, Jean Beliveau, and Guy Lafleur.

When Habs legend Georges Vezina died in 1926, George Hainsworth filled the void between the pipes, winning three consecutive Vezina trophies from 1926/27 to 1928/29 while playing under Hart. Playing in an era with major restrictions on forward passing in the zones, Hainsworth set NHL goaltending records that will likely remain unbroken.

During the 1928/29 season, Hainsworth (in a 44-game season) won 22 games – all by shutout – and had a goals-allowed average of 0.92. Even when you adjust Hainsworth's average to today's era, it's still a sizzling 1.91. His season record of 22 shutouts will also likely never be broken.

Until the arrival of Martin Brodeur and Terry Sawchuk, Hainsworth had more career shutouts (94) than any other NHL goalie. He remains third on the all-time list of career shutouts today. Hainsworth was a major reason why Hart was the best defensive coach of the 1920s and of the NHL's first quarter-century (1917–1942).

When you consider the great hockey talent that flourished during Hart's coaching reign, it once more begs the question: Why isn't he in the Hockey Hall of Fame?

Jenish writes that Hart resigned as head coach in 1932 for two reasons:

1. Hart had never stopped working as an insurance broker, so the NHL expansion and the lengthening of the regular season and playoffs were undermining his business interests.
2. His friendship with Leo Dandurand had cooled significantly, and by 1932 the two men were no longer on speaking terms.[87]

Hart returned to the Canadiens in 1936 when the new Habs owners begged him to revive the franchise. Serving as head coach and general manager, Hart did his best, leading the Canadiens to another Canadian division title in 1936/37, but the magic of the earlier years was gone. The team had grown old. George Hainsworth was gone, and the death of Howie Morenz in 1937 robbed the Habs of their big-gun star attraction. The team sank in the standings and lost fan support. Hart was fired in 1939 and died in the summer of 1940.

Considering all that he achieved as a coach, that one nagging question still begs to be answered: Why isn't Cecil Hart in the Hockey Hall of Fame?

---

87 *The Montreal Canadiens*, D'Arcy Jenish, pp. 80-81.

CLAUDE JULIEN RANK #20

PLUS: 80
MINUS: 5
VALUE: +75
PEAK RANK: #20 in 2013/14
PEAK VALUE: +75 in 2013/14

COACHING EXPERIENCE: Montreal Canadiens, 2002[88]–2006[89]; New Jersey Devils, 2006/07[90]; Boston Bruins, 2007–present

REGULAR SEASON W–L–T–OL: 470–278–10–102
PLAYOFF W–L: 61–47

JACK ADAMS AWARD: 2008/09

PRESIDENT'S TROPHY: 2013/14

NORTHEAST DIVISION TITLES: 2008/09, 2010/11–2011/12
ATLANTIC DIVISION TITLE: 2013/14

PLAYOFF APPEARANCES: 2003/04, 2007/08–2013/14
STANLEY CUP FINALS: 2010/11, 2012/13
STANLEY CUP VICTORY: 2010/11

During the past eight years, Claude Julien has risen up the ranks of the NHL coaching fraternity with a dazzling swiftness, vying with Chicago's Joel Quenneville for primacy in the 2010s and for NHL coaching supremacy for the 21st century.

---

88 Julien coached the last 36 games of the 2002/03 season.

89 Julien coached the first 41 games of the 2005/06 season.

90 Julien coached the first 79 games of the 2005/06 season.

When Julien took over as Bruins head coach in 2007, his coaching value was only +7 and he wasn't even on the charts in terms of coaching greatness. By 2009 his value was at +20 and he was ranked #57, according to my rating system. Five years later he vaulted up to #20 on the charts. At the end of the 2014/15 season, he was the fifth-best active NHL coach in terms of career value and average season rating. His stock has soared in the 2010s, and he continues to lead a team that possesses youth, potential, and a limitless upside for future growth.

Still, to get to where he is today, Julien was forced to endure a long apprenticeship and some very nasty hits and crosschecks along the way.

Julien was a career minor league defenceman who had two brief cups of coffee with the Quebec Nordiques in the 1980s. When his playing career ended in the 1990s, Julien took up coaching in junior hockey before working his way up to the minors, coaching the Hamilton Bulldogs in the AHL from 2000 until January 2003 when the Montreal Canadiens hired him to replace Michel Therrien as head coach. Julien had mixed results. He failed to reach the playoffs in 2002/03, took the Habs to a second-round loss in 2003/04, and was fired as head coach midway through the 2005/06 season.

In 2006/07 Julien went to New Jersey, where he seemed to do well. The Devils won the Atlantic Division title that season and were the second seed in the Eastern Conference. Martin Brodeur thrived on Julien's defensive systems, winning his third Vezina Trophy. All this was achieved despite the fact that the Devils had a sub-par offence and struggled with injuries suffered by Patrik Elias, John Madden, Scott Gomez, and Brian Gionta.

Then, suddenly, with three games remaining in the regular season, Julien was fired as head coach.

Devils general manager Lou Lamoriello was cryptic in his explanation, stating, "I don't think we're at a point of being ready both mentally and [physically] to play the way that is necessary going into the playoffs." (As of 2015, Lamoriello has yet to provide a detailed explanation as to why he canned Julien, remaining unrepentant about making the move in the first place. His motive remains a great mystery.)

Lamoriello had done this before when he replaced Robbie Ftorek with Larry Robinson mere days before the 1999/00 playoffs (Robinson led the Devils to the Stanley Cup), but one cannot ascribe the reasons for firing Ftorek to Claude Julien. Ftorek and Julien are polar opposites in terms of tactics and personality. Also, the motives for firing Ftorek were well known and played out before the hockey world. The ambiguous nature of Julien's dismissal remains vexing.

There are unconfirmed rumours that Julien failed to properly discipline a Devils player who had deliberately shot a puck at him during a practice session (which might have resulted in a collective loss of respect for Julien by the players). What is more likely is the possibility that Lou Lamoriello hired Julien but immediately repented his decision because the Devils management later admitted that they had been talking to Julien's eventual successor, Brent Sutter, *18 months before he was officially hired by the team in July 2007.* If this is true, then it means that Julien never had a chance in New Jersey to begin with, and Lou Lamoriello needed to pull the trigger before Julien could possibly upset the apple cart by succeeding in the playoffs (the Devils lost in the second round in 2007).

Also, the Devils were playing inconsistently, at 7–6–2, when Julien was let go.

Whatever the reason for his firing, Julien was on a precipice, his NHL coaching future in doubt. If he failed once more, it's likely he would never coach in the NHL again.

Julien was not unemployed for long. Two months after the Devils had fired him, the Boston Bruins hired him.

Working hand in glove with Pete Chiarelli, one of the finest general managers in the game, Julien led the team to four division titles, seven playoff appearances, two Eastern Conference titles, the 2013/14 President's Trophy, and the Bruins' first Stanley Cup win since 1971/72.

His greatest regular-season performances as a coach came in 2008/09 and 2013/14. In 2008/09 the Bruins were the second-best team and had the best defence in the NHL. Julien won the Jack Adams Award for his sterling efforts. In 2013/14 Boston won the President's Trophy and displayed amazing tactical balance in all the key offensive and defensive categories.

Most importantly, Julien got the Bruins players to believe in his systems and to believe in themselves. Joe McDonald from ESPNBoston.com writes pertinently, "Julien is an honest coach. He doesn't play mind games with his players and he doesn't have that old-school mentality of 'it's the coach's way or no way.' Time and again, Julien will talk to his players and get their take on certain things, an exercise that always ends with a collaborative effort. Julien never leaves his players wondering where they stand."[91]

Bruins mainstay Brad Marchand tells McDonald, "He wants me to be able to play my game, and he gives me the rope and leniency to play that way. He knows when to reel me back in and when to calm me down."[92]

During his early years in Boston, Julien's teams won games with pure defence and great goaltending. Tim Thomas won the Vezina Trophy in 2008/09 and 2010/11, and Thomas and fellow net-minder Manny Fernandez combined to win the Jennings Trophy in 2008/09; and the following season Thomas and Tuukka Rask combined to win the Jennings again in 2009/10. (Tuukka Rask won the Vezina in 2013/14.)

Julien demanded (and got) solid two-way work from the entire team. Defenceman Zdeno Chara won the Norris Trophy in 2008/09 and earned All-Star honours in 2010/11, 2011/12, and 2013/14 while forward Patrice Bergeron won the Selke Trophy in 2011/12, 2013/14, and 2014/15.

But it's Julien's work with Tim Thomas that deserves notice. Whereas Julien inherited goaltending legend Martin Brodeur when he coached the New Jersey Devils, Tim Thomas made his name under Julien's tutelage.

Thomas was drafted by the Quebec Nordiques in 1994, yet he spent nearly a decade playing in the minors and in Europe before being signed as a 31-year-old free agent by the Bruins in 2005. He was already the starting goalie for the Bruins when Julien arrived, but it took Julien's defensive systems and the acquisition of veteran blue-liners Zdeno Chara, Tomas Kaberle, Andrew Ference, and the young Adam

---

91 http://espn.go.com/boston/nhl/story/_/id/7292119/claude-julien-boston-bruins-mutual-respect-breeds-success

92 Ibid.

McQuaid to give Thomas the defensive support he needed to excel between the pipes.

Under Julien, Thomas had career years and gained recognition with his stalwart presence in the net. When Thomas was awarded the Conn Smythe Trophy as MVP of the 2010/11 Stanley Cup playoffs, it was the culmination of the long years of hard effort in the minors and in Europe and the patience and dedication to make the most of his opportunities.

Before the 2010/11 season, Julien's major weaknesses were in power-play offence and, to a lesser extent, penalty-killing and overall offence.

With the exception of the 2008/09 season, his teams always finished near the bottom of the NHL in power-play offence and in the top ten in penalty-killing only four times in 12 seasons.

It's ironic that the Bruins finished third during the 2009/10 season in penalty-killing, yet one of the main reasons they lost four straight games to the Flyers in the second round of the 2009/10 Stanley Cup playoffs was their inability to contain the Flyers' power-play offence. Time and again the Bruins – renowned for their on-ice discipline – committed penalties and failed to stop the Flyers.

Another Achilles heel of Julien's teams during the early years was their weak offence. In 2009/10 they had finally cracked the top ten in offence only once. Indeed, the Bruins finished next-to-last in offence during the 2009/10 season.

Until 2010/11, Julien was snake-bit in playoff competition, never going beyond the second round of the Stanley Cup playoffs. In 2003/04, he was beaten by the Tampa Bay Lightning. In 2008/09, he lost to the Carolina Hurricanes, and in 2009/10, he fell to Peter Laviolette's Flyers.

The summer of 2010 was a long one for Julien and the Bruins. There was much to think about, much to ponder and brood upon, but when autumn came and the 2010/11 season began, Julien and the Bruins had retooled themselves dramatically.

In 2009/10, the Bruins finished 29th in offence. In 2010/11, they were eighth in the NHL in offence due to the solid work from Milan Lucic, Patrice Bergeron, Nathan Horton, and Brad Marchand. Their efforts were complemented by David Krejci's superb playmaking skills.

Gargantuan defenceman Zdeno Chara led the NHL in the plus–minus factor (and teammates Adam McQuaid, Horton, Lucic, and Marchand also finished in the top 20 in that category).

The Bruins also improved their transition game, finishing fourth in the NHL in short-handed offence thanks to Marchand and Bergeron. (When Bergeron scored the third goal in Game 7 of the Stanley Cup finals against Vancouver while the Bruins were short-handed, it was not a fluke occurrence. The Bruins scored three short-handed goals during the finals.)

But the biggest surprise came when Boston (noted for its on-ice discipline) did a 180-degree turnaround of their on-ice demeanour.

Whereas the season before they had finished 20th in team penalty minutes, now they became nastier, finishing eighth in the NHL in penalty minutes. Julien got the Bruins to play with greater emotional and physical ferocity.

Never was this more evident than in their four regular-season meetings with the Philadelphia Flyers. The Bruins went 3–1 in their matchups, shutting down the Flyers' offence and out-hitting the Broad Street Bullies.

Never was revenge more sweet than in the second round of the 2010/11 playoffs when they swept the Flyers in four games, chewing them up and spitting them out, outscoring the Flyers 20–7 in four games.

It was the conference finals that gave Boston its biggest scare. They faced a young and raw Tampa Bay Lightning, led by its equally young and raw head coach, Guy Boucher. The Bruins were taken to the very limit and had to win Game 7 by a 1–0 margin, with the winning goal coming in the third period.

And yet their Game 7 win should be seen as a triumph for the Boston Bruins. They were able to assert their defensive skills and force the Lightning (who won games with a high-octane offence) to engage in a battle of defence – which played directly to the Bruins' collective strength. In such a contest, the Lightning could not win. And so Claude Julien earned his first appearance in the Stanley Cup finals as a head coach.

The Bruins lost the first two games against Vancouver, even though they allowed only four goals in two games. They were playing tentatively, allowing Vancouver to press the action in their zone. Even worse, the Canucks seemed to be winning psychologically as well: Alexandre Burrows bit Patrice Bergeron in Game 1 and was not disciplined by the league, and Canucks goalie Roberto Luongo dissed Tim Thomas (the future Vezina Trophy winner) in the press.

The tinderbox was full; all it needed was a spark to ignite it.

It came in the form of Game 3, when Canucks defenceman Aaron Rome flattened Nathan Horton with a late hit early in the match in Boston. The sight of Horton being taken away on a stretcher in restraints and knocked permanently out of the series galvanized the Bruins, made them look deep into themselves, and re-elicited their inner hockey talents, which had been lying dormant in Games 1 and 2. Their backs to the wall, the Bruins returned to the controlled rage and physical play that got them to the Stanley Cup finals in the first place.

The Bruins won four of the remaining five games (their sole loss was a 1–0 thriller in Game 5), outscoring the Canucks 21–4 in the process. Tim Thomas stoned the Canucks in Games 4 and 7 (Thomas had four shutouts and the lowest GAA during the 2010/11 playoffs). Shorn of Nathan Horton's scoring talents, the Bruins rallied with a brilliant collective offensive effort.

Thomas wasn't the only defensive star. Zdeno Chara led all players, with a +16 rating in the playoffs. Boston held the Canucks (who had the best power-play offence in the NHL) to only two power-play goals throughout the series while the Bruins (who had one of the weakest power-play units during the regular season) scored six power-play goals themselves.

When the final buzzer sounded in Game 7 with the Bruins earning a convincing 4–0 win, it exorcised the demons of their 2009/10 playoff loss forever; the Bruins were shriven by their fans and justified by their collective faith in themselves.

By leading the Bruins to the 2010/11 Stanley Cup title, Claude Julien did what Bep Guidolin, Don Cherry, Terry O'Reilly, and Mike Milbury could not do (they had led the Bruins to the Stanley Cup finals in 1973/74, 1976/77–1977/78, 1987/88, and 1989/90, respectively, only to lose in the process): he ended the Bruins' Stanley Cup drought and vaulted the team to greatness, elevating himself to greatness in the process.

(In 2014/15, the Bruins failed to reach the playoffs. It was the third time in NHL history that a President's Trophy winner failed to reach the playoffs the following season.)

FRANK PATRICK RANK #21

PLUS: 84
MINUS: 14
VALUE: +70
PEAK RANK: #1 in 1918/19
PEAK VALUE: +70 in 1923/24, 1935/36

PCHA COACHING EXPERIENCE: Vancouver Millionaires, 1912–1922; Vancouver Maroons, 1922–1924

PCHA REGULAR SEASON W–L–T: 143–127–2
PCHA PLAYOFF W–L–T: 18–20–2

PCHA LEAGUE CHAMPIONSHIPS: 1914/15, 1917/18, 1920–1924

PCHA PLAYOFF APPEARANCES: 1917/18–1923/24

WCHL/WHL COACHING EXPERIENCE: Vancouver Maroons, 1924–1926

WCHL/WHL REGULAR SEASON W–L–T: 22–34–2

NHL COACHING EXPERIENCE: Boston Bruins, 1934–1936

NHL REGULAR SEASON W–L–T: 48–36–12
NHL PLAYOFF W–L: 2–4

AMERICAN DIVISION TITLE: 1934/35

NHL PLAYOFF APPEARANCES: 1934/35–1935/36

STANLEY CUP FINALS: 1914/15, 1917/18, 1920/21–1921/22
STANLEY CUP VICTORY: 1914/15

Frank Patrick was the younger brother of Lester Patrick, but he differed from his more illustrious sibling in subtle ways. While Lester was charming and convivial, Frank was sombre and introspective. However, both brothers did share the same intellectual, cultural, and athletic versatility and the same genius, passion, and inventiveness for the playing, promoting, coaching, and administration of professional hockey.

Frank Patrick ranked among the top three hockey coaches during the early years of professional hockey (1917–1926) – and for a brief, shining time during that era, Patrick was the greatest coach in all of hockey, according to my rating system (see "Decades" and "The Progressive Chart" in Part Four).

Patrick's coaching value is figured from 1917 to 1936. If you count his Pacific Coast Hockey Association (PCHA) record before 1917, his coaching value would be +90. He remained in the top five until 1945 and was among the top ten until 1974, also according to my rating system.

Frank and Lester brought Canadian hockey to the Pacific Northwest, expanded the wage potential for hockey's best players at that time, and rewrote the hockey rulebook. In the process, they developed a style of hockey that competed and eventually won over the more conservative Eastern style of Canadian hockey, all the while becoming two of the finest coaches of offensive hockey of their era.

Frank Patrick is credited with 22 rule changes that are still in effect. He invented the blue line, the penalty shot, forward passing, the playoff system, the boarding penalty, and even the gesture of raising one's stick after scoring a goal. He was not only innovative but also prescient. He predicted that teams would dress two goalies for games and even proposed the formation of women's hockey leagues.

Frank (like his brother) was a defenceman during his playing days and (also like his brother) revolutionized the position, making bold rushes with the puck and expanding the envelope of what a defenceman could do on the ice.

When the PCHA began operation in 1912, Patrick's Vancouver Millionaires franchise swiftly became a powerhouse in the fledgling league, winning the league title six times in 13 seasons. In 1913 Patrick also became the president of the PCHA, a post he held until 1924, representing and defending the league's interests while negotiating with the NHA and later the NHL.

His greatest moment came in 1914/15 when the Millionaires took on the original Ottawa Senators for the Stanley Cup. In an awesome display of offensive hockey, Patrick's Millionaires beat the Senators in three games, outscoring them 26 goals to 8.

Ottawa had some of the greatest defensive players in the game in Clint Benedict, Art Ross, and Eddie Gerard, and yet the Vancouver Millionaires got a composite offensive team effort from their forwards: Cyclone Taylor (who scored six goals in the series), Mickey Mackay, Frank Nighbor, and Barney Stanley together accounted for 21 of Vancouver's 26 goals in the series.

It was a landmark moment in hockey history: it was the first time that the upstart PCHA had won the Stanley Cup – and they had beaten one of the most powerful franchises at that time to do so. And they did it with one of the mightiest displays of offensive hockey of the 1910s. (As of 2015, it remains the only time a Vancouver hockey franchise has ever won the Stanley Cup.)

For the remainder of his coaching career, Patrick always tried but failed to repeat that magical moment. He had three more chances to win the Cup, in 1917/18, 1920/21, and 1921/22, but fell short each time. He won the PCHA playoffs in 1922/23 and 1923/24 but lost in the interleague playoff rounds to the Western Canada Hockey League (WCHL) winner both times.

Frank Patrick was the Glen Sather of his era. His teams always led the PCHA in offence. Patrick got high-octane output from the best scorers of his time. Players such as Newsy Lalonde, Gordon Roberts, Cyclone Taylor, Jack Adams, and Art Duncan flourished under his tutelage. All of these men enjoyed Hall of Fame careers, as did goalie Hugh Lehman.

Conversely, Patrick's teams only led the league in defence four times and finished last five times. This imbalance is one reason why Patrick failed to win the Stanley Cup when competing against the NHL from 1917 to 1926.

Was Patrick the greatest offensive coach of his time?

The answer is no. Examining the average goals per game of Patrick's teams versus the league leaders of the NHL and the WCHL/WHL from 1917 to 1926, his teams failed to surpass those in the other two leagues.

But Patrick did dominate (and quite possibly innovated) in one area: demanding on-ice discipline from his players. His Vancouver teams were notable in that they didn't accumulate a lot of penalty minutes. In fact, no other coach was as good at getting his players to avoid the penalty box as Frank Patrick was.

It's also interesting to note that other coaches who practised on-ice discipline, such as Newsy Lalonde, Jack Adams, and Frank Boucher, all played for Patrick during their careers.

Is it possible that these men may have derived their ideas of on-ice discipline from him?

For 13 seasons the Patrick brothers shared in the glories and tribulations of running the PCHA together, but after 1924 an imperceptible parting of the ways began: Frank's star began to dim while Lester's gained in radiance.

The collapse of the PCHA and the merger with the WCHL/WHL went badly for Frank. His teams finished poorly in 1924/25 and 1925/26. When the WHL collapsed, Frank did not join Lester in establishing himself in the NHL, even though there were standing offers from the Chicago Blackhawks and the Detroit Red Wings for Frank to coach and/or manage their teams.

He ignored the offers and remained in the Pacific Northwest to run and maintain the Patrick family's arena in Vancouver along with various mining and business interests – with precious little success.

Patrick agreed to work in the NHL in 1933 when he was named managing director of the league during the 1933/34 season. His job was to hire, supervise, or discipline referees and handle other tasks assigned to him by the league governors. (Patrick, along with NHL president Frank Calder, personally investigated the Ace Bailey–Eddie Shore stick-fight to see whether Shore merited further punishment in addition to the 16-game suspension he received. In the end, Frank exonerated Shore of the charge that he deliberately tried to hurt Bailey during the fight.)

After one season of league office work, Patrick returned to coaching: this time it was for the Boston Bruins. Long-time Bruins coach Art Ross left the bench to work solely as general manager – yielding the position to Patrick.

Eight years away from coaching hockey had not diminished his genius. He led the Bruins to two winning seasons, one divisional title, and two playoff appearances but failed to reach the Stanley Cup finals both times. (In 1934/35 Frank Patrick, like Cecil Hart and Art Ross, was another victim of the absurd NHL playoff system that was in effect from 1928/29 to 1937/38, which required the two division title winners to play each other in the opening round of the playoffs. Patrick's Bruins lost the opening round to Dick Irvin's Toronto Maple Leafs.)

Patrick was popular with his players, achieving MVP work from the legendary Eddie Shore twice. His Bruins had the best defence in the NHL in the 1935/36 season. He was still innovative in manipulating his player talent.

Patrick's conversion of Earl Siebert from forward to defenceman was a stroke of genius. Siebert (an NHL All-Star at forward) earned All-Star honours as a blue-liner.

Patrick only coached two years in Boston. The reasons why he left are varied.

Art Ross (who made the Boston Bruins in his own image) could not remain in the shadows quietly and was a formidable figure in his own right. Patrick family chronicler Eric Whitehead recorded this tense exchange between Art Ross and Lester Patrick about Frank:

> "Do you let him do the job, Art?"
>
> "You're talking like a coach, Lester. *I'm the boss and this is my hockey club* [emphasis mine]. I like to keep close to things. That's my job. It's my obligation to Mr. [Weston] Adams."
>
> "What about your obligation to your coach?"
>
> "For chrissake, Lester, there you go again. Thinking like a goddamn coach. I'm looking at it like a general manager, and I think Frank is too goddamn soft. He's too chummy with the players, and he thinks every referee is his best friend. He protects everybody. He's too goddamn nice . . . and he's drinking."[93]

Whitehead wrote that Frank began to drink in his 40s, although not constantly or excessively. Still, as time passed, it became a growing, lurking problem within and without the family, a problem that he couldn't handle, a weakness that diminished him.

Whitehead quoted Frank Patrick's son, Joseph Patrick Jr.: "It is true that my father did have a drinking problem in his later years, but he never drank what is normally considered to be excessively. He simply couldn't hold the stuff. What would be a relatively harmless amount to the average social drinker was damaging to him. In his declining years when things were going badly for him, he could and

93 *The Patricks*, Eric Whitehead, pp. 210-211.

did stay completely away from liquor for months at a time. But when he brooded and slipped back just a little, it hurt him."[94]

Henry David Thoreau once wrote, "Public opinion is a weak tyrant compared with our private opinion. What a man thinks of himself, that is what determines . . . his fate."

Let us theorize that sometime between 1924 (when the PCHA folded) and 1933, Frank Patrick – as noted before, always sombre and introspective – examined himself thoroughly, ruthlessly, unsparingly; weighing his inner self on scales – as did the ancient gods of Greece.

On the one hand, there were decades of personal and professional triumphs as a hockey player, coach, manager, and businessman; a lifetime in which he enjoyed the love, loyalty, and affection of his parents, siblings (especially his brother, Lester), his wife and children, and those of his players and peers in the world of hockey.

On the other hand, there were the negative counterweights that existed solely in his mind, unseen and unrecognized by those who knew and loved him.

Is it possible that Frank Patrick compared himself unfavorably with his brother, Lester?

Or perhaps he compared himself unfavorably with other illustrious hockey figures such as Art Ross (a dear friend of the Patrick family)?

Or maybe it was the shocking premature death of his former PCHA compatriot Pete Muldoon in 1929 that might have had a shattering effect on him. (Authors Morey Holzman and Joseph Nieforth wrote that "Frank Patrick was crushed" by Muldoon's death.)[95]

We will never know, but one can postulate that Frank Patrick, for unfathomable and inconceivable reasons, may have dismissed his magnificent attainments. He deemed himself a failure and, repulsed by his own self-indictment, occasionally sought refuge in alcohol – which merely compounded his personal damnation.

Is it possible that Patrick spent the rest of his life as a man at war with himself? (With people with low self-esteem, no amount of outside love or praise can ever mitigate the finality of one's own internal judgment.)

---

94 Ibid. p. 211.

95 *Deceptions and Doublecross*, Morey Holzman and Joseph Nieforth, p. 294.

The greatest loss to society is when a talented person (such as Patrick) cannot find peace and contentment with their own accomplishments but instead become their own worst enemy, thus destroying themselves and denying the world the benefits of their talents.

If Patrick were alive today, he could have gone to a rehabilitation centre to conquer his inner demons. He would have had his choice of psychiatric counselling options and therapeutic drugs to help him resolve the conflicts in his heart and soul. Patrick could have been cured and a great hockey mind rescued to bring even greater glory to the game.

Sadly, these options were non-existent during the final 24 years of Patrick's life.

After 1936 Patrick drifted into obscurity as his business interests failed and his personal problems undermined his standing within his family and the hockey world in general.

Eric Whitehead writes that Lester had to step into the breach to help Frank's family move forward with their lives. All of this was done quietly and discreetly.[96]

The only bright spot in Frank's latter years came in 1958 when he was elected to the Hockey Hall of Fame.

When Lester Patrick died on June 1, 1960, his death was mourned widely.

When Frank Patrick died on June 29, 1960, his death was little noted.

Rest in peace.

---

96 *The Patricks*, Eric Whitehead, p. 250.

ALAIN "A. V." VIGNEAULT RANK #22

PLUS: **90**
MINUS: **20**
RATING: **+70**
PEAK RANK: **#22 in 2014/15**
PEAK RATING: **+70 in 2014/15**

COACHING EXPERIENCE: **Montreal Canadiens, 1997–2000[97]; Vancouver Canucks, 2006–2013; New York Rangers, 2013–present**

REGULAR SEASON W–L–T–OL: **520–341–35–74**
PLAYOFF W–L: **61–61**

JACK ADAMS AWARD: **2006/07**

PRESIDENT'S TROPHIES: **2010/11, 2011/12, 2014/15**

NORTHWEST DIVISION TITLES: **2006/07, 2008/09–2012/13**
METROPOLITAN DIVISION TITLE: **2014/15**

PLAYOFF APPEARANCES: **1997/98, 2006/07, 2008/09–2014/15**
STANLEY CUP FINALS: **2010/11, 2013/14**

Before he was fired in 2013, Alain Vigneault was the greatest coach in Vancouver Canucks history: twice setting team records in wins and team points, dominating the Northwest division, winning the President's Trophy two consecutive seasons (the seventh NHL coach to do so), and leading the Canucks to their third Stanley Cup finals appearance in 2010/11.

How did he do it?

Although the Canucks were strong offensively from 2009/10 to 2011/12, Vancouver's real strength was their defence and their physicality (from 2006/07 to

97 Vigneault coached the first 20 games of the 2000/01 season.

2012/13, Vigneault's Canucks finished in the top ten in defence four times – leading the NHL in 2010/11 – and in team penalty minutes four times as well. Goalie Roberto Luongo had the best seasons of his career under Vigneault (and Cory Schneider emerged as a top goaltending prospect).

Still, the Canucks had a flaw in their defensive makeup: penalty-killing.

With the exception of 2006/07 (where they led the NHL), their penalty-killing ability was average at best. It explains why Vigneault and the Canucks, in the 2006/07, 2008/09, and 2009/10 playoffs, never went beyond the second round: in power-play situations, they were burned repeatedly by their opponents.

But in 2010/11, Vigneault corrected the team's penalty-killing deficiency when Canucks general manager Mike Gillis acquired defenceman Dan Hamhuis from the Nashville Predators. Hamhuis, working with Kevin Bieksa, Christian Ehrhoff, and Alexander Edler, gave Vancouver a shot in the arm in defence and helped the Canucks become the third-best penalty-killing team in the NHL.

When Vigneault took over in 2006, the Canucks' offence was weak, near the bottom of the NHL. It took A. V. three seasons to build up his team's offensive capability, and the 2010/11 season was proof that genuine progress was made. The Canucks led the NHL in offence and power-play offence. Vigneault gained a solid offensive effort from Ryan Kesler and the Sedin twins: Henrik and Daniel.

And yet the end result of this patient rebuilding was that Vigneault earned the dubious distinction of being the only NHL head coach to win two President's trophies without also winning the Stanley Cup – a distinction that cost him his job with Vancouver.

Alain Vigneault was a defenceman who played in the Quebec Major Junior Hockey League before being drafted in the eighth round by the St. Louis Blues in 1981. Vigneault only had two brief playing stints with the Blues, spending most of his time in the minors. By 1984 his playing career was over, and in 1986 he took up coaching in junior hockey. In 1992 he became an assistant coach with the expansion Ottawa Senators, remaining there for four seasons before returning to coach junior hockey once more.

His first big break came in 1997 when the Montreal Canadiens hired him to become their head coach. Vigneault spent three whole seasons and part of a fourth with the Habs. His performance was uneven. He led the Canadiens to a playoff spot in his rookie season but failed to reach the playoffs for the remainder of his stay. Still, A. V. was runner-up to Joel Quenneville in the voting for the 1999/00 Jack Adams Award because he had managed the Canadiens to a winning season and barely missed out on the playoffs despite coping with serious injuries to his players.

This didn't save Vigneault, however. He was fired after a poor 20-game start to the 2000/01 season.

A. V. briefly scouted for the St. Louis Blues before returning to junior and minor league coaching until he was tabbed to replace Marc Crawford as head coach of the Vancouver Canucks in 2006.

The 2010/11 season was meant to be the culmination of both Alain Vigneault and the Canucks. This was the greatest Canucks team ever created.

There were individual honours aplenty for the organization. Daniel Sedin won the Ross Trophy, Ryan Kesler won the Selke Trophy, and Roberto Luongo and Cory Schneider combined to win the Jennings Trophy. Even Canucks general manager Mike Gillis won GM of the year honours. This was the franchise's 40th season of competition, and what would be a better way to celebrate than to win the Stanley Cup?

The talent was there, and the Canucks were never seriously challenged during the regular season, but when the playoffs began, there were signs that in retrospect heralded a less than august finish to what had been a glorious season.

In the first round against the defending Stanley Cup champion Chicago Blackhawks, the Canucks roared out to a 3–0 series lead. The Hawks looked like easy pickings. But, strangely and disturbingly, the Canucks allowed the Blackhawks to win the next three games, giving them a chance to do what the 1941/42 Toronto Maple Leafs, the 1974/75 New York Islanders, and the 2009/10 Philadelphia Flyers had done before: come back from a 3–0 series deficit and win the series.

Even more significantly, the Canucks allowed the Blackhawks not only to win but also to drive the Canucks to the point of collapse. The Canucks lost Games 4 and 5 by 7–2 and 5–0, respectively. The only squeaker was in Game 6, which they lost 4–3 in overtime.

What augured poorly for the Canucks was the fact that the Hawks were able to shake, rattle, and roll goalie Roberto Luongo from the nets in Game 4, forcing Alain Vigneault to play musical goaltenders in Games 5 and 6. In addition, the Canucks were playing undisciplined hockey during the two blowout losses, allowing the Hawks to score four power-play goals during those two games. Chicago's rally proved that the Canucks could be knocked off their game when the opposition was able to apply great pressure on offence and defence. In retrospect, one suspects that the Boston Bruins (and their coach, Claude Julien) derived insight and inspiration on how to play the Canucks based on what had happened in this series.

The Canucks rallied at home to beat the Blackhawks 2–1 in Game 7, and Canucks fans collectively wiped their brows in relief. Vigneault marshalled his team through the next two rounds: beating the Nashville Predators in six games and the San Jose Sharks in five. But, again, there were still disturbing portends along the way. The Predators were making their first second-round playoff appearance in their franchise history and really didn't stand a chance against the Canucks, and yet they played gutsy hockey and made the Canucks earn every single one of their four victories in the six-game series. The Canucks had the best offence in the NHL, but they couldn't dominate the defensive-oriented, well-disciplined Predators. In six games they outscored the Predators by only 14–11. Again, one suspects that the Boston Bruins (and Claude Julien) derived insight and inspiration about how to play the Canucks based on the Predators series.

By the third round, the Canucks seemed to have settled down defensively. Goalie Roberto Luongo had shaken off the blows from the first round and played every minute of every game in rounds two and three. Offensively, the Canucks appeared to have woken up as well, scoring 20 goals in five games during the conference finals against the Sharks.

When it came time to play the Boston Bruins for the Stanley Cup, the Canucks on paper seemed to hold all the aces. Most experts predicted a Canucks victory and the end to the Curse of Marty McSorley.

(During Game 2 of the 1992/93 Stanley Cup finals between the Los Angeles Kings and the Montreal Canadiens, Kings player Marty McSorley was penalized in the closing minutes of the game for having an illegal stick. The Habs promptly scored on the ensuing power-play, thus tying the game and eventually winning Game 3 in overtime. This sparked a Canadiens comeback in the series because Montreal had been down 1–0 in the series before winning Game 2. They would take Games 3 through 5 to win the Stanley Cup – the last time a Canadian team has ever won the Stanley Cup, hence the Curse of Marty McSorley, which is now a part of NHL folklore.)

The Canucks won the first two games and were seemingly in control, stoning the Bruins in Game 1 and winning Game 2 in overtime; it seemed that nothing could stop the Canucks' tidal wave.

But what followed had all the aspects of a nightmare for Alain Vigneault, the Canucks players . . . and their fans. In Game 3, the Vancouver tidal wave crested; dashed itself against the immovable object; collapsed, receded, and dissolved into nothingness.

The Bruins had given way in the first two games, but when Canucks blue-liner Aaron Rome knocked Boston's Nathan Horton into the hospital with a late hit early in the match, and thus earning a suspension for the remainder of the series, it hardened the Bruins, made them dig and grasp deeper into themselves . . . and emerge stronger.

Just like the Blackhawks did in the first round, the Bruins got their offence going and chased Luongo from the net in Games 4 and 6, significantly outscoring the Canucks in the remaining five games. The Bruins (like the Predators) played well-disciplined, superb defensive hockey. Putting it all together, the Bruins denied the Canucks the Stanley Cup, their loss rendering meaningless all the previous success the Canucks had gained during the 2010/11 season.

The following season, Vancouver repeated as President's Trophy winners in a brilliant stealth campaign in which they won the trophy by a two-point margin. The Canucks had not lost any strength tactically; their offence and defence were still strongly balanced, as were their special teams.

And yet the Canucks were humiliated in the first round by the Los Angeles Kings, who won the Cup that year. The Canucks were held to only eight goals in five games. They allowed the Kings' pop-gun offence to beat them on the power play and score two short-handed goals against them in Game 2. They were shut out in Game 3 by Jonathan Quick. The Canucks' Game 4 victory merely prolonged the agony, ensuring they would lose the series on their own home ice.

Things began to slip for Vancouver and Alain Vigneault. The lockout-shortened 2012/13 season saw the Canucks face powerful competition from the resurgent Minnesota Wild. For the first time in years, the Canucks had to fight for the Northwest Divisional title. They won, but it was tough going.

In truth, Vancouver had lost its strength. The team's productivity in offence, defence, and power-play offence declined significantly. They struggled with injuries and the controversy over what to do with goalie Roberto Luongo's oversized contract. In the end, the Canucks suffered another first-round playoff defeat – a pathetic four-game sweep by the San Jose Sharks.

Canucks general manager Mike Gillis swung the axe on Vigneault on May 22, 2013. One month later, in a game of musical coaches, the New York Rangers hired Vigneault to replace John Tortorella, who became Vigneault's replacement in Vancouver!

A. V. had a rough time of it in the Big Apple. The Rangers started off poorly and were below .500 in the early weeks of the season. By New Year's Eve 2013, the Rangers were 20–19–2, but during the months of January and February, New York went on a 13–5–1 tear, which got them out of the doldrums.

The Rangers won with defence and penalty-killing. Goalie Henrik Lundqvist was stalwart in the nets. Winger Rick Nash personally won nine games with his shooting, and blue-liner Ryan McDonagh was wicked in scoring in penalty-killing situations.

The Rangers were lucky in that the Metropolitan division was very weak in 2013/14. Even though the Rangers were playing barely above .500 during the stretch run of the regular season, they still managed to finish in second place.

The Rangers astounded the hockey world by reaching the Stanley Cup finals. Like their opponents – Darryl Sutter's Los Angeles Kings – the path was not easy. Their first- and second-round triumphs went the full seven games. The second-round victory was particularly hot. The Rangers were facing the Pittsburgh Penguins – a team everyone thought was going to win the Stanley Cup. The Penguins certainly thought so themselves, taking a 3–1 series lead.

It was then that the Rangers begged to differ. In between Games 4 and 5, the venerable Martin St. Louis (who had been a late-season acquisition from Tampa) was rocked by the death of his mother. The entire team went to the funeral in a show of solidarity to St. Louis. There was doubt that St. Louis would play, but after consulting with his father, he decided to do so. In that moment of grief and loss there came a quiet collective team resolution and determination that could not and would not be quenched.

The Rangers won the next three games to take the series, outscoring Pittsburgh 10–3 in the process. Games 5 and 6 were Pier-Six brawls, with the Rangers showing no mercy to the Penguins. Centre Derrick Brassard stepped up to score three goals in Games 5 and 6. Martin St. Louis did his part when he scored the opening goal in Game 6.

But it was Henrik Lundqvist who dazzled the hockey world by holding the Penguins to three goals in three games.

The Rangers were again underdogs in the Eastern Conference finals – facing a resurgent Montreal Canadiens who had just beaten the President's Trophy – winning Boston Bruins in the second round. The series went six games and, again, Lundqvist shut the door on the Habs, holding them to 2.50 goals per game in the series, shutting them out in Game 6 to clinch the Eastern Conference finals.

The 2013/14 Stanley Cup final was a battle of the defences. The Rangers fell in five, but it was so close. If the Rangers had won, then goalie Henrik Lundqvist would have won the Conn Smythe Trophy (he would have deserved no less).

It was Alain Vigneault's second Stanley Cup finals defeat, but the fact that he got the Rangers there was a personal triumph and a brilliant reaffirmation of his coaching genius.

The Rangers did even better in 2014/15, winning their first President's Trophy since 1993/94. For Alain Vigneault it was his third President's Trophy win in five seasons – a feat exceeded only by Scotty Bowman who did it three times in four seasons from 1992/93 to 1995/96. Vigneault also become the third NHL coach (the others were Mike Keenan and Joel Quenneville) to coach President's Trophy winners for two different teams.

New York were well balanced tactically and were highly favored going into the playoffs. They won handily in the first round but were given a bad scare by the Washington Capitals who had the Rangers down 3–1 in the second round. It was déjà vu all over again for the Rangers and, amazingly, they rallied to win the next three games – holding the Caps to 5 goals in 3 games – and the series.

In the conference finals the Rangers were facing an upstart Tampa Bay Lightning team that had beaten Detroit and Montreal in the first two rounds. In a see-saw series, New York allowed the Lightning to steal their thunder and even humiliate the stalwart Hendrik Lundqvist in the process. The Rangers rallied to force a game seven at home in New York but the strain of trying to perform two great series rallies was too much for the Rangers and they ended their season with a flaccid, inert, and sloppy performance, allowing the Lightning (an offensive-minded team) to win a battle of the defences against the Rangers.

PAT QUINN RANK #23

PLUS: 92
MINUS: 24
VALUE: +68
PEAK RANK: #14 in 2005/06
PEAK VALUE: +78 in 2005/06

COACHING EXPERIENCE: Philadelphia Flyers, 1979[98]–1982[99]; Los Angeles Kings, 1984–1987[100]; Vancouver Canucks, 1991[101]–1994, 1996[102]; Toronto Maple Leafs, 1998–2006; Edmonton Oilers, 2009–2010

REGULAR SEASON W–L–T–OL: 684–528–154–34
PLAYOFF W–L: 94–89

JACK ADAMS AWARD: 1979/80, 1991/92

PATRICK DIVISION TITLE: 1979/80
SMYTHE DIVISION TITLES: 1991/92–1992/93
NORTHEAST DIVISION TITLE: 1999/00

PLAYOFF APPEARANCES: 1978/79–1980/81, 1984/85, 1990/91–1993/94, 1995/96, 1998/99–2003/04
STANLEY CUP FINALS: 1979/80, 1993/94

---

98 Quinn coached the last 30 games of the 1978/79 season.
99 Quinn coached the first 72 games of the 1981/82 season.
100 Quinn coached the first 42 games of the 1986/87 season.
101 Quinn coached the last 26 games of the 1990/91 season.
102 Quinn coached the last 6 games of the 1995/96 season.

Pat Quinn has the most wins of all NHL coaches who never coached a Stanley Cup winner. He is presently fifth on the all-time list in regular-season wins, sixth in playoff-game wins, and still holds the record for coaching the longest unbeaten streak in NHL history when the 1979/80 Flyers went undefeated in 35 consecutive games.

How did his teams win?

They won with offence and the power play: his teams' short-handed offence was above average but not on the same scale as his power-play offence.

When it came to on-ice nastiness, Pat Quinn, like Mike Keenan, was a throwback to the old NHL. His teams were always near the top for visits to the penalty box, finishing among the top five in penalty minutes ten times during his coaching career.

Quinn was a journeyman defenceman in the NHL. He played two seasons with the Leafs (where he is best remembered for a vicious bodycheck of Bobby Orr during the 1968/69 playoffs that knocked Orr out and provoked a bench-clearing brawl) before being drafted by the expansion Vancouver Canucks in 1970.

After two seasons with Vancouver, he was drafted by the expansion Atlanta Flames in 1972, where he spent five seasons until injuries forced him to retire in 1977. When his playing career ended, he took up assistant coaching with the Flyers under Fred Shero while attending law school.

When Shero left the Flyers in 1978, Quinn stayed on as an assistant under Bob McCammon. When the Flyers got off to a slow start, McCammon was fired and Quinn took over as head coach.

The following season was Quinn's greatest moment as a coach. Not only did the Flyers finish with the best record in the NHL, but they did so as a result of a 35-game unbeaten streak.

Phil Myre (who played and coached with Pat Quinn) states, "Pat Quinn was a player's coach. If you couldn't play for Pat Quinn, then you couldn't play for anyone. Pat brought great structure to the team and he let the players be creative, to be themselves. He allowed them to express themselves on the ice. Pat always emphasized puck possession. He loved offence and he worked hard on breakouts and entries."

Goalie Bernie Parent had retired, so Quinn brilliantly rotated net-minders Pete Peeters (a bright, promising rookie) and Phil Myre (a solid veteran and former

Atlanta Flames teammate of Quinn). Quinn was judicious and brilliant in integrating Peeters into the goaltending mix. Myre says, "During the early part of the streak, Pat handpicked the opponents for Peeters, but when Pete got more confident, then Pat choose who was in goal based on how well they played against the team in question."

Peeters responded brilliantly. He had the best GAA of all Flyers goalies during the regular season and manned the nets in two-thirds of the games during the 1979/80 playoffs.

What's amazing about the streak was that the Flyers were a team in transition. Quinn balanced the old-guard holdovers Bobby Clarke, Bill Barber, and Rick Macleish from the Cup years of 1973/74 and 1974/75 with the talented youngsters Brian Propp, Ken Linseman, and Paul Holmgren. Every game a different player would step up and make the key goal, pass, hit, block, or save that kept the streak alive.

In the 1979/80 playoffs, the Flyers rolled into the Stanley Cup finals with an 11–2 record to face the New York Islanders – and trouble. It was Quinn's misfortune that he was facing the Islanders team that would win four straight Stanley Cups. Two of the Flyers' losses against the Islanders came in overtime. The Game 6 loss was particularly galling when the non-call of a blatantly offside Islander resulted in their second goal. (To this day, Flyers fans boil in anger about that play – this writer included.)

That was the high point of Quinn's stay in Philadelphia. By 1982 he was gone and stayed out of hockey for two years while completing his law studies.

In 1984 he became head coach of the Los Angeles Kings but failed to equal his success with the Flyers. In 1986 he ran afoul of the Kings' front office and the NHL when he admitted that he had signed a contract with the Vancouver Canucks to be their coach and general manager. Quinn was suspended for the remainder of the 1986/87 season and was banned from coaching the Canucks until 1990.

In 1987 Quinn joined the Canucks front office and began rebuilding the team. During his stint as general manager, Quinn drafted Canucks stars Pavel Bure and Trevor Linden. In 1991 Quinn took over as head coach (ironically replacing Bob McCammon), leading the Canucks to two consecutive divisional titles and in 1993/94 the second Stanley Cup finals appearance in Canucks franchise history.

Again, Quinn was unlucky in having to face Mike Keenan's New York Rangers, who had won the President's Trophy that same season. The Canucks were down 3–1 in the series but rallied to force a Game 7, only to lose 3–2 in the final game.

By 1997 he was gone from Vancouver, and in 1998 he became head coach of the Toronto Maple Leafs, where he stayed for seven years. During the 1999/00 season, he led the Leafs to their first division title win. The last time the Leafs had finished in first place was in 1962/63 when they won the Prince of Wales Trophy.

In 2001/02 he became the last Leafs coach to lead the team to the conference finals – where they lost to the Carolina Hurricanes. (Quinn had better luck in the 2002 Winter Olympics, coaching Team Canada to the Olympic gold medal in Salt Lake City.)

Quinn's stock began to fall during the 2005/06 season. The Leafs failed to reach the playoffs and he was let go.

He then worked for Team Canada, reaching the 2006 Spengler Cup finals and then leading Team Canada to International Ice Hockey Federation (IIHF) gold medal wins for the U18 and U20 teams in 2008 and 2009, respectively. Quinn made an abortive comeback with the Edmonton Oilers in 2009/10, only to see his lustre dull even further. He never coached in the NHL again.

In April 2013, Quinn was named chairman of the board of the Hockey Hall of Fame by the NHL and officially took over the post in August 2013. But in the months that followed, his health began to fail, and on November 23, 2014, Pat Quinn passed away. His death was mourned by the entire hockey world.

BILL "FOXY" DINEEN RANK #24

PLUS: 75
MINUS: 9
VALUE: +66
PEAK RANK: #13 in 1978/79
PEAK RATING: +75 in 1978/79

WHA COACHING EXPERIENCE: Houston Aeros, 1972–1978; New England Whalers, 1978/79

WHA REGULAR SEASON W–L–T: 318–199–28
WHA PLAYOFF W–L: 44–27

WHA COACH OF THE YEAR: 1976/77–1977/78

WHA WEST DIVISION TITLES: 1973/74–1976/77

WHA PLAYOFF APPEARANCES: 1972/73–1977/78
AVCO CUP FINALS: 1973/74–1975/76
AVCO CUP VICTORIES: 1973/74–1974/75

NHL COACHING EXPERIENCE: Philadelphia Flyers, 1991–1993
NHL REGULAR SEASON W–L–T: 60–60–20

Bill Dineen is the greatest coach in the seven-year history of the World Hockey Association (WHA). He was there when the first puck dropped in 1972, and he was still working in the WHA when the final buzzer sounded for the league in 1979. As coach and general manager of the Houston Aeros, he helped bring major league professional hockey to Texas 21 years before the Minnesota North Stars moved to Dallas.

Dineen won two Avco Cups for the Houston Aeros; no other WHA coach won as many. Twice he was named WHA coach of the year; again, no other WHA coach achieved this. And that's not all: he also played a vital role in altering the face of hockey with regards to drafting young amateur hockey talent, as well as giving a retired hockey immortal another chance to bring joy to hockey fans.

Dineen played forward for the Detroit Red Wings from 1953 to 1957, backing up Gordie Howe, Ted Lindsay, and company while getting his name etched twice onto the Stanley Cup in 1953/54 and 1954/55. During those years he struck up a fortuitous and lasting friendship with Howe.

Dineen, like many other Red Wings, was victimized by the fallout of Lindsay's doomed attempt at forming the first NHL Players' Association. He was exiled to the Chicago Blackhawks in one of Jack Adams's massive house-cleaning trades. After 1958, Dineen was sent back to the minors, never to return to the NHL as a player. Dineen never contemplated a coaching career until 1971 when the head coach of the Denver Spurs (in the Western Hockey League, or WHL) was fired and Spurs management prevailed upon Dineen to take over. Dineen served as a player-coach, and as he later put it, "I enjoyed it and learned I had a feel for coaching." The Spurs made the playoffs under Dineen's tutelage. The following season, with Dineen coaching full-time, the Spurs won the 1971/72 WHL title.

When the WHA was formed in 1972 as a rival professional major league, Dineen was hired by the Houston Aeros to be their head coach and general manager. Unlike what most of the other WHA teams did to find players – sign one superstar and surround him with 22 low-cost nobodies – Dineen put his minor league coaching experience to good advantage. He knew where to find players who had major league potential (but were overlooked by the NHL) and would be hungry and grateful for the opportunity. As a result, Dineen was able to field a successful squad without exhausting the limited financial resources of the Aeros franchise. As Dineen put it succinctly, "I built the team from scratch."

When it was time for Dineen to splurge, however, he made hockey history.

Dineen's friendship with Gordie Howe and his family had endured. By 1973 Howe's sons Marty and Mark were top prospects in Canadian junior hockey, but NHL rules at the time mandated that a player had to be 20 years old to be eligible for the NHL draft. (Today, the minimum draft age is 18.) In 1973 Marty was 19 and Mark was 18.

The WHA, desperate to trump the NHL in its quest for talent, allowed its teams to draft players under the age of 20. So Dineen drafted Marty and Mark

Howe – which gave the father of the Howe boys the greatest excuse to end an unhappy two-year retirement as a player.

Gordie Howe's return to hockey is part of hockey legend and remains one of the greatest comebacks in sports history. His arrival in the WHA (along with the signing of Bobby Hull) gave the new league desperately needed legitimacy. Other NHL stars followed suit. Howe played six happy years in the WHA, receiving the mega-star wages he never got in the NHL.

Dineen's investment had paid off handsomely. Gordie was named the league MVP and Mark Howe was named the WHA's rookie of the year during the 1973/74 season. (Mark would eventually become a three-time WHA All-Star.) From 1973/74 to 1976/77, the Aeros dominated the WHA, making three straight Avco Cup finals appearances from 1973/74 to 1975/76 and winning the title twice, in 1973/74 and 1974/75.

But the Aeros were more than the Howes: in the 1972/73 season (before the Howes' arrival) and the 1977/78 season (after their departure), Dineen got quality play from his personnel, leading the Aeros to winning seasons and playoff appearances both times.

Wingers Frank Hughes and John Tonelli were superb shooters alongside Gordie and Mark Howe. (Tonelli later became an integral member of the New York Islanders dynasty teams of the 1980s.)

Centres Larry Lund and Terry Ruskowski were first-rate playmakers who created innumerable scoring chances for the Aeros offence (Ruskowski, like Tonelli, excelled in the NHL in the 1980s).

In a league that stressed high-octane offence, the Aeros led the WHA in defence three times. Defenceman Poul Popiel was a two-time WHA All-Star and another solid playmaker while his linemate John Schella was a crushing hitter.

Houston goalies Don McLeod and Ron Grahame earned league honours as the best goaltenders in the WHA: McLeod, once; Grahame, twice. Indeed, Grahame would also be named MVP of the 1974/75 WHA playoffs. Ernie Wakely earned WHA All-Star honours in 1977/78 while playing goalie for Dineen in Houston.

Significantly, the Aeros during their glory years had solid special teams, finishing in the top five in the WHA in both power-play offence and penalty-killing from 1973/74 to 1976/77.

Dineen was not a tactician like Emile Francis or Roger Neilson. Instead, he was more of a motivator. Dineen stated in a 2013 interview that "my job was to keep the players happy and in top condition. I modeled myself after Tommy Ivan because that's what he did when he coached in Detroit. The main element to my coaching was in keeping my players motivated to win at all times."

What ruined the Aeros was a lack of money. Despite Dineen's best efforts, the Aeros folded in 1978.

Dineen became head coach of the New England Whalers (and reunited with the Howes). The Whalers had a winning season, but Dineen suffered problems he did not encounter in Houston.

Mark Howe writes, "Unlike in Houston, where Bill could bring in guys he wanted and who wanted to play for him, many Whalers thought he was a bad coach, not much for Xs and Os, and more about managing people. A playoff spot was never in serious jeopardy, but we had won only six of the last 19 when Bill was fired by [Jack] Kelley with nine games to go, and replaced by assistant coach Don Blackburn."[103]

Bill Dineen was kicked upstairs to serve as the Whalers director of scouting before returning to minor league coaching in the 1980s, working for the Detroit Red Wings farm team in the AHL. During those years, Dineen became the only head coach in the history of hockey to coach both an Avco Cup winner and a Calder Cup winner.

Throughout the 1980s, Dineen never got a head coaching offer from the NHL, a fact that still saddens him today. Despite his stellar coaching work in the WHA, Dineen didn't coach in the NHL until 1991, when he was hired by the Philadelphia Flyers, where he stayed for two years. Unfortunately, Dineen could not coax winning seasons from the team.

The only high point to his stay in Philadelphia was that he got to coach his son Kevin, who was a forward for the Flyers during those years. (Three of Dineen's sons – Gordon, Kevin, and Peter – played in the NHL, and Gordon and Kevin followed in their father's footsteps to become hockey coaches in their own right.)

Dineen was fired in 1993 and as of 2015 spends his time living in quiet retirement in upstate New York.

---

103 *Gordie Howe's Son*, Mark Howe with Jay Greenberg, p.104.

BRUCE "GABBY" BOUDREAU RANK #25

PLUS: 69
MINUS: 6
VALUE: +63
PEAK RANK: #25 in 2014/15
PEAK RATING: +63 in 2014/15

COACHING EXPERIENCE: Washington Capitals, 2007[104]–2011[105]; Anaheim Ducks, 2011[106]–present

REGULAR SEASON W–L–OL: 363–167–69
PLAYOFF W–L: 38–35

JACK ADAMS AWARD: 2007/08

PRESIDENT'S TROPHY: 2009/10
SOUTHEAST DIVISION TITLES: 2007/08–2010/11
PACIFIC DIVISION TITLES: 2012/13–2014/15
PLAYOFF APPEARANCES: 2007/08–2010/11, 2012/13–2014/15

"Being a head coach in the NHL means being the lead dog in a room of people who have spent their lives as the lead dog in their respective packs. You have to be tactically and technically proficient, but the ability to be lead dog is the X-factor that makes the difference between being successful or not. It's at the heart of the mystery of why some coaches make it and some fail. I don't know if it's even definable or explainable.

You have it. Or you don't."[107]

Bruce Boudreau

---

104 Boudreau coached the last 61 games of the 2007/08 season.

105 Boudreau coached the first 22 games of the 2011/12 season.

106 Boudreau coached the last 58 games of the 2011/12 season.

107 *Gabby: Confessions Of A Hockey Lifer*, Bruce Boudreau and Tim Leone, p. 149.

Bruce "Gabby" Boudreau was an undersized centre who excelled greatly in the minors but never achieved the same results in major league hockey. He was born and raised in Toronto and played for the Marlboros in the Ontario Hockey Association. In 1974 he was drafted by the Minnesota Fighting Saints in the WHA and the following year was drafted by the Toronto Maple Leafs in the NHL.

Boudreau opted for the Fighting Saints and played 30 games with them during their final season of existence (at the same time he had a bit part in the movie *Slap Shot*).

When the Fighting Saints folded, Boudreau jumped to the NHL and shuttled back and forth between Toronto and their minor league affiliate in Dallas, Texas. (Roger Neilson was his coach in Dallas and Randy Carlyle and Ron Wilson were teammates.)

Boudreau's playing career ended in 1992, and he immediately went into coaching, working first in the IHL and then later in the ECHL (where he won a championship in 1998/99).

From 1999 to 2007, Boudreau coached in the AHL with the Lowell Lock Monsters, the Manchester Monarchs, and the Hershey Bears (with whom he won the 2005/06 Calder Cup). If you applied my rating system to his AHL coaching record, his career value would be +58.

In 2007 he took over a struggling Caps franchise that had been becalmed since 2003, had entered the 2007/08 season with a 6–14–1 record, and got them to win the Southeast Division title (while winning the Jack Adams Award). Boudreau led the Caps to three more Southeast Divisional titles – more than any other coach in their franchise history.

In 2009/10 Boudreau outdid himself and all his coaching predecessors in Washington when he led the Capitals to their first President's Trophy.

Boudreau's Caps teams excelled in overall offence, power-play offence, and superb on-ice discipline; possessing prodigious firepower; featuring enormous individual talents such as Alexander Ovechkin, Mike Green, Jeff Schultz, Nicklas Backstrom, and Alexander Semin.

Ovechkin, in particular, was the mainstay of the Caps' success and is one of the greatest players in the NHL today. Ovechkin earned NHL All-Star honours four times and won one Ross Trophy and two Hart trophies under Boudreau.

In his memoir, *Gabby: Confessions of a Hockey Lifer*, Boudreau defines his winning approach:

> Our goal as a team is to be proactive. If we're going to make a mistake, we want the mistake on our terms. We want to make the mistake playing our game rather than make the mistake while reacting to the other team's game. Our game is applying pressure in every zone.
>
> Because we attack and don't sit back, critics think we're ignoring defence. Not true. It's really about taking time and space away from everybody anywhere on the ice so they can't make a play and creating a turnover. Pressure defence is what I call it. We apply pressure to create turnovers and then attack when we get the puck.[108]

Boudreau and the Caps earned individual honours aplenty, but the prize that eluded them most was the Stanley Cup.

Playoff futility has been the bane of Boudreau's coaching career (see "Heartbreak Coaches" in Part Four). In the 2009/10 playoffs, the Caps suffered a first-round elimination by the eighth-seeded Montreal Canadiens – a team ranked #19 in the NHL. The Caps had the Habs down 3–1 in the series, yet allowed them to come back to beat them in seven games.

In the 2010/11 playoffs, after winning the first round against the New York Rangers with a feisty performance, they were swept by a young, upstart Tampa Bay Lightning making their first playoff appearance in four years.

What's galling about both playoff defeats was that Washington was deemed to be *the* team to beat both times. Both years were seen to be the culminating moments for both Boudreau and the Caps, and yet the team failed signally to realize its greatness.

The fatal flaw in Boudreau's tactical strategy and the main reason for the Caps' lack of playoff success from 2007/08 to 2009/10 was their rather average performance on defence and still-weaker effort in penalty-killing.

In two of Boudreau's four seasons of coaching, the Caps finished near the bottom in penalty-killing. During the 2009/10 playoffs, they gave up power-play

108 Ibid. p. 119

goals in six of their seven games, and their goaltending from 2007/08 to 2009/10 was also far from superlative. Given these facts, the Caps' failure to reach the Stanley Cup finals becomes understandable, but their failure in 2010/11 cannot be explained or excused.

The Caps' management and Boudreau worked hard to correct the team's defensive flaws and got wonderful results in 2010/11. The team went from 17th to 4th in defence and 25th to 2nd in penalty-killing.

And yet 2010/11 was a stern test for the Caps because the same Lightning team that swept them in the playoffs also challenged them for the Southeast Division title. It took a late-season surge by the Caps to maintain their stranglehold not only on the divisional title but also on the number-one seed in the Eastern Conference. One would have thought the challenge by the Lightning would have fired up the team, made them work harder. Instead, it was the Lightning who outworked the Caps, capitalized on their scoring opportunities, and advanced in the playoffs.

The Caps were not like the Philadelphia Flyers, who were riddled with injuries during the playoffs, or the Detroit Red Wings, an aging team. The Caps were beaten by a team much younger and rawer than themselves – led by a coach who was just as young and raw as his players.

If it was not a failure of talent, then was it more a failure of will?

Or was it a failure by the team to mature when it should?

The 2011/12 season appeared to augur well for Boudreau and the Caps, winning the first seven games of the season, and then it happened . . .

Seemingly invincible after the first two weeks of the season, the team switched off and went to sleep in the Gurdjieffian sense. Their offence became non-existent. During one three-game stretch, the Caps were outscored 3 goals to 18 by their opponents. Even worse, the team was seething with turmoil. Boudreau, in one game, benched Alexander Ovechkin in a key power-play situation, a public move that sent shockwaves throughout the hockey world.

Washington went 5–9–1 before Caps general manager George McPhee pulled the trigger on Boudreau on November 28, 2012, citing his failure to get the team to respond.

It had all ended so quickly, and then more extraordinarily, although not surprisingly, Boudreau found new life when he was hired by the Anaheim Ducks to replace the fired Randy Carlyle.

The Ducks, like the Caps, were in free fall, inhabiting the Pacific Division basement while their divisional rivals played musical chairs for first place. The Anaheim Ducks were an aging team, struggling to replace its worn-out parts, a team that failed to make the playoffs two seasons before and endured a humiliating first-round playoff loss in 2010/11. When Boudreau took over on December 1, 2011, the team had ground to a halt under Carlyle's stern hand.

Boudreau coaxed Anaheim through a rough December before getting the Ducks back in the air; getting solid efforts from Corey Perry and goalie Jonas Hiller; going 17–5–4 from January 6 to February 26 to get Anaheim two games above .500% before petering out in the final 20 games of the season and failing to make the playoffs.

The following season, Boudreau's Ducks commenced one of the greatest turnarounds in NHL history: the season before, they had finished in last place, with a winning percentage of .488 and 80 team points. In 2013 the Ducks roared out of the blocks and swiftly became the second-best team in the Western Conference, with a winning percentage of .688, a team record (if you translate the .688 percentage for an 82-game schedule, the Ducks would have had a 32-point improvement).

Boudreau got the Ducks to improve all across the board. With forwards Ryan Getzlaf, Bobby Ryan, and Corey Perry supplying the offence, the Ducks improved offensively from 24th to 7th. On defence, Boudreau got solid work from blue-liners Francois Beauchemin and Sheldon Souray. Beauchemin for the first time in his career earned All-Star honours. Goalies Jonas Hiller and Viktor Fasth split the net-minding duties and performed well. The Ducks' defence improved from 20th to 9th. The Ducks' special teams improved, although not as a dramatically as they did in overall offence.

When the playoffs came, the Ducks faced off against the aging Detroit Red Wings. In what was probably *the* stunning upset of the 2012/13 playoffs, they fell to the Wings in seven hard-fought games (with four of the games going into overtime). The Ducks allowed the Wings to outgrind them in key situations. Their Game 2 loss to Detroit in overtime was a major blow (had the Ducks won then, they would have won the series in five games). Instead, the Wings hung on to win, even though they lost home-ice advantage when the Ducks won Game 3 in Detroit. Superb goaltending work from Wings goalie Jimmy Howard combined with the coaching genius of Mike Babcock and the collective playoff wisdom held by the Wings players conspired against Boudreau and the Ducks.

The Wings outworked the Ducks to win in seven.

It was Boudreau's fifth playoff loss without ever reaching the Stanley Cup finals, a heartbreaking feat.

Gabby refused to give in to despair. Marshalling his Ducks, he inspired them to greater efforts, setting Ducks franchise records in wins, team points, and winning percentage; again, winning the Pacific Division title and finishing as the top-seeded team in the Western Conference.

Boudreau got Anaheim through the first round by defeating Lindy Ruff's Dallas Stars in six games – with Anaheim showing pluck by beating Dallas at Dallas in Game 6 to clinch the series.

The Ducks again showed their pluck by rebounding from a 2–0 series deficit against Darryl Sutter's Los Angeles Kings by beating L.A. in Games 3 and 4 in Los Angeles and winning Game 5 at home to take a 3–2 series advantage.

The Kings rallied back to win Game 6 and then routed Anaheim in Game 7 to inflict Bruce Boudreau's sixth consecutive playoff defeat.

The Ducks won the Pacific Division again in 2014/15. During the playoffs Anaheim reached the Western Conference finals for the first time in Boudreau's NHL coaching career. The Ducks took a 3–2 series lead before allowing Chicago to win Games 6 and 7 to take the series. It was Gabby's seventh playoff defeat in eight seasons of coaching.

The challenge that awaits Bruce Boudreau is whether he can overcome the playoff jinx that shadows his coaching accomplishments and keeps him from ascending even higher in the NHL coaching pantheon.

PAT BURNS RANK #26

PLUS: **70**
MINUS: **8**
VALUE: **+62**
PEAK RANK: **#20 in 2002/03**
PEAK VALUE: **+62 in 2003/04**

COACHING EXPERIENCE: **Montreal Canadiens, 1988–1992; Toronto Maple Leafs, 1992–1996[109]; Boston Bruins, 1997–2000[110]; New Jersey Devils, 2002–2004**

REGULAR SEASON W–L–T–OL: **501–353–151–14**
PLAYOFF W–L: **78–71**

JACK ADAMS AWARD: **1988/89, 1992/93, 1997/98**

ADAMS DIVISION TITLES: **1988/89, 1991/92**
ATLANTIC DIVISION TITLE: **2002/03**

PLAYOFF APPEARANCES: **1988/89–1994/95, 1997/98–1998/99, 2002/03–2003/04**
STANLEY CUP FINALS: **1988/89, 2002/03**
STANLEY CUP VICTORY: **2002/03**

Pat Burns was the only NHL coach ever to win the Jack Adams Award three times (with three different teams) and was one of the finest defensive coaches of his era. In 14 seasons of coaching, Burns's teams either finished first or second in the NHL in defence seven times and were among the top ten in defence ten times. (Ironically, Burns resented being labelled a defensive coach.)

---

109 Burns coached the first 65 games of the 1995/96 season.

110 Burns coached the first 8 games of the 2000/01 season.

Burns had that rare coaching talent (like Scotty Bowman, Toe Blake, Punch Imlach, and Hap Day) and the incredible motivational skills that allowed him to secure stellar defensive efforts from *all* his players. As a hockey coach, Burns played the good cop, bad cop role to perfection. He could be profane, puckish, engaging, and infuriating. His temper was legendary, but his outward angry man exterior hid a slew of vulnerabilities and flaws brought on by a troubled childhood in which he was raised in a broken home, coping with abandonment by his father and a difficult relationship with his mother. Burns himself had failed marriages and relationships with his wives and children.

As biographer Rosie DiManno writes, "He'd claimed he never ran away from a fight. Actually he'd been a runner all his life. . . . None of this made him a bad man – far from it."[111]

His inner fire was his greatest strength and his biggest weakness: at first igniting and inspiring, then later devouring and destroying.

There was nothing complex in his tactics. Again, DiManno writes, "No long shifts; if you lose the puck, put yourself in a position to get it back; short and crisp passes; if out-numbered, dump it out of the zone or into the other team's end; never lose the puck between the blue lines."[112]

Former Bruins general manager Mike O'Connell later told DiManno, "It was a trap mentality. Pat liked big, bruising guys but his was not a style that forced the issue. It was more of a classic 'let's wait, get in our position, and wait, and wait, and then we counter.' It does enable teams without talent to win. It gives them a chance because of how it's structured."

Burns's systems required intense preparation. His practices were brief yet very up-tempo. The fundamentals were taught over and over again until his players developed muscle memories. His system demanded execution, which is why he kept his players going at a fever pitch.

In Todd Denault's book *A Season in Time,* he quotes a 1993 Pat Burns interview with Toronto *Globe and Mail* writer Al Strachan, in which Burns said:

---

111 *Coach: The Pat Burns Story*, Rosie DiManno, p. XIV

112 Ibid. p. 241

> When I came in I told the guys I separated our zone into four quarters. Our defensive set-up has everybody looking after a certain part. You don't go and do another guy's job. He doesn't come and do your job. The center is your support guy. He's busier than a one-legged man in an ass-kicking contest. He has to cover both sides. On defense, we never leave the front of the net open. We never have two defencemen in the same zone. The winger goes from his point man to the slot. That's all he does.[113]

One extension of the system was his teams' superb penalty-killing skills. Nine times in 13 seasons, Burns's teams finished in the top ten in killing penalties. DiManno writes, "Burns ordered his players not to rush the puck carrier or challenge aggressively against the point." Opponents were always thrown "off stride by this passive-aggressive technique."[114]

Against Burns's system, opponents were prevented from hitting the open man and instead were forced to make bad shots on goal.

Still, for Burns's defence to work, it needed rigorous on-ice discipline from his players. Much to his credit, that's what Burns got. His teams only finished in the top ten in team penalty minutes twice in 13 seasons. Usually his squads were near the bottom of the NHL in terms of team penalty minutes.

That is why under Burns's aegis, defencemen Chris Chelios and Scott Niedermayer each won the Norris Trophy, forwards Guy Carbonneau and Doug Gilmour won Selke trophies, and goalies Patrick Roy and Martin Brodeur won multiple Vezina and Jennings trophies.

Pat Burns grew up yearning to play NHL hockey but was thwarted in his quest, so he worked as a police officer and coached local hockey teams in his spare time. Burns's coaching skills were so good that during the 1980s he had to choose between policework and coaching. He opted for the latter and never looked back.

---

113 *A Season In Time*, Todd Denault, p. 116

114 *Coach: The Pat Burns Story*, Rosie DiManno, p. 96.

Wayne Gretzky played a major role in Burns's career when he hired him to coach the Hull Olympiques (a team Gretzky owned) in junior hockey in 1984. Under Gretzky's encouragement, Burns excelled and by 1987 was coaching in the minors for the Montreal Canadiens.

In 1988 the Habs asked Burns to become their head coach.

Since 1979 the Montreal Canadiens have only reached the Stanley Cup finals three times for three different coaches: Jean Perron in 1985/86, Jacques Demers in 1992/93, and Pat Burns in 1988/89, when he led the Habs to the finals in his rookie season as coach.

It was rough going at first. Burns imposed discipline from the start – which caused friction from the players. Some of his measures were necessary, but a few also drew concealed snickers from some of the players. Burns also had to ward off the press, which called for his head after the Habs got off to a slow start in 1988/89.

Still, Burns received moral support from the team's old guard: Bob Gainey and Larry Robinson.

Larry Robinson writes, "Pat realized that Bob and I could lend a great deal to a young team. . . . Bob and I would often be invited to sit with Pat in his office and talk about our ideas. . . . As two of the leaders on the club, I really thought that was important, and so did Pat."[115]

The team rallied and found its synergy. Burns coupled superb defensive work from Chris Chelios, Guy Carbonneau, and Patrick Roy with goalscorers Mats Naslund and Bobby Smith. Burns was also settling into his role with greater ease.

Larry Robinson writes, "Pat was a hard guy to read at first. He would scream and yell, swear like a sailor, break his stick over the crossbar of the net – you name it. And yet, there was another Pat: one who would sit in the dressing room, talking and laughing with the guys."[116]

The Habs went 16–3 in the first three rounds of the 1988/89 playoffs, holding their opponents to only 1.68 goals per game during those 19 games. In the conference finals against the Philadelphia Flyers, they held the Broadstreet Bullies to only eight goals in six games.

---

115 *The Great Defender*, Larry Robinson with Kevin Shea, pp. 128-129.

116 Ibid, p. 129.

Unfortunately, Burns's magic touch failed him in the finals when the Habs lost to the Calgary Flames in six games. Montreal had a 2–1 series lead but failed to generate any significant offence in the remaining three games, allowing Calgary to win the Stanley Cup.

Burns spent three more years in Montreal but never got the team past the second round in the playoffs. He resigned and immediately became the head coach of the Toronto Maple Leafs. (Pat Burns and Dick Irvin are the only men in NHL history who have coached both the Leafs and the Canadiens.)

Only five times since 1966/67 have the Maple Leafs appeared in the Stanley Cup conference finals. In 1992/93 Pat Burns came closer than any other Leafs coach in reaching the Stanley Cup finals when the Leafs led the Los Angeles Kings 3–2 going into Game 6 of the conference finals. However, a controversial Game 6 loss in overtime led to a 5–4 Game 7 loss. What's even more ironic is that if the Leafs had won the series, they would have faced the Canadiens in the finals – shades of 1966/67.

In 1993/94 Burns led the Leafs to the conference finals again, only to go down in five games to Pat Quinn's Vancouver Canucks.

Burns was fired in 1996 and by 1997 was coaching the Boston Bruins.

Boston was his most lacklustre coaching performance. Although he led the Bruins to winning seasons, their playoff performances were poor. Burns won his third and last Jack Adams Award in 1997/98, but by the fall of 2000 the Bruins fired him. (Burns was doomed from the start in Boston. He was the ultimate defensive coach serving under Harry Sinden, the ultimate guru of offensive hockey. Something had to give.)

He endured the longest layoff in his coaching career. Nothing substantive was forthcoming until the call came from the grimmest and grimiest of places: Northern New Jersey.

The New Jersey Devils were a cool, stable team that had made back-to-back Stanley Cup finals appearances, but their coaching situation was a mess.

Devils general manager Lou Lamoriello was seeking the right coach to give his team the razor-sharpness needed to win the Cup again – and he wondered if Pat Burns might be it?

On the surface Burns was the perfect man for the job: the ultimate defensive coach for the ultimate defensive team, but Lamoriello had doubts.

Burns biographer Rosie DiManno notes that in order for Burns to get the coaching job, he literally had to do a personality makeover: curb his temper (which was an extension of his considerable ego), be more positive and inspirational instead of critical and harsh, make sure the team played within itself, and avoid needless confrontation, which in turn caused consternation.[117]

Amazingly, Burns (his professional back against the metaphorical wall) agreed to do all these things and more . . .

And it worked.

Larry Robinson, who served as an assistant coach under Burns, writes, "Burnsie was a tough, hard-ass guy. He knew the game fairly well, but he wasn't an Xs-and-Os guy, and he relied on Bobby Carpenter and, later, Jacques Laperrière to do all that kind of stuff. Burns was the line-changer and the disciplinarian. He carried a big stick and he scared the crap out of a lot of guys. . . ."[118]

The Devils took the Atlantic Division title with the second greatest performance in their franchise history and went 16–8 in the playoffs.

Burns got his revenge on Boston by beating them and Tampa Bay in the first two rounds. In round three, the Devils had to go seven games to beat Jacques Martin's Ottawa Senators, and then in the finals Burns and the Devils were taken to the limit by Mike Babcock's Anaheim Ducks, but three shutout victories by Martin Brodeur against the Ducks gave Burns the Stanley Cup victory he so richly deserved.

Burns failed to repeat the following season, but it was then that he faced a more serious and dangerous challenge: cancer.

In 2005 Burns's struggles with the disease forced him to step down as head coach. He successfully battled colon and liver cancer, but in December 2009 word came that the cancer had spread to his lungs. Burns decided to forego further treatment. He persevered for 11 months before passing away on November 19, 2010.

In the wake of his untimely passing there began a movement building in hockey circles to enshrine Pat Burns in the Hockey Hall of Fame. It took four years, but in 2014 he was inducted into the Hockey Hall of Fame – a fitting memorial to a great coach.

---

117 Ibid. Rosie DiManno, pp. 253–255.

118 *The Great Defender*, Larry Robinson with Kevin Shea, p. 185.

DAN BYLSMA RANK #27

PLUS: 59
MINUS: 0
VALUE: +59
PEAK RANK: #26 in 2013/14
PEAK RATING: +59 in 2013/14

COACHING EXPERIENCE: Pittsburgh Penguins, 2009[119]–2014; Buffalo Sabres, 2015–present

REGULAR SEASON W–L–OL: 252–117–32
PLAYOFF W–L: 43–35

JACK ADAMS AWARD: 2010/11

ATLANTIC DIVISION TITLES: 2010/11, 2012/13
METROPOLITAN DIVISION TITLE: 2013/14

PLAYOFF APPEARANCES: 2008/09–2013/14
STANLEY CUP FINAL: 2008/09
STANLEY CUP VICTORY: 2008/09

Dan Bylsma is a member of two rare hockey clubs:

1. Since 1917, only 14 coaches have won the Stanley Cup in their rookie season of coaching. Bylsma became #14 when he led the Pittsburgh Penguins over Mike Babcock's defending Stanley Cup champion Detroit Red Wings in a hard-fought seven-game series in 2008/09.
2. Since 1917, only four interim coaches have ever won the Stanley Cup: Al MacNeil, who led the Canadiens to the 1970/71 Stanley Cup; Larry

119 Bylsma coached the last 25 games of the 2008/09 season.

Robinson, who led the New Jersey Devils to the 1999/00 Stanley Cup; Darryl Sutter, who led the Kings in 2011/12; and . . . Dan Bylsma.

The story of how Bylsma (pronounced *biles-mah*) got to be a member of both of those clubs is compelling in its swiftness. (And one example of that swiftness is the fact that in 2012/13 he became the fastest NHL coach ever to win 200 games.)

Dan Bylsma comes from Michigan (like Bob Johnson) and was a versatile athlete, excelling in a variety of sports in high school and playing collegiate hockey in the Central Collegiate Hockey Association (CCHA) at Bowling Green University in Ohio. Bylsma played right wing but was never a prolific scorer.

He was chosen by the Winnipeg Jets in the 1989 NHL draft but never played for them. Instead, he remained in the minors until the mid-1990s when the Los Angeles Kings called him up to the NHL. Bylsma played two full seasons and parts of two others with the Kings before being traded to the Mighty Ducks of Anaheim (where he played for Bryan Murray and Mike Babcock). Bylsma as a player was used mostly as a defensive forward in penalty-killing situations.

By 2004 his playing career had ended and Bylsma was working as an assistant coach in the AHL. In 2005 Bylsma worked for the New York Islanders, serving as an assistant coach to Steve Stirling and Brad Shaw during the 2005/06 season.

In 2007 Bylsma returned to minor league coaching in the Penguins farm system, working as an assistant coach to Todd Richards with the Wilkes-Barre/ Scranton Penguins in the AHL. In 2008 when Todd Richards left to work for the San Jose Sharks, Bylsma took over as head coach.

Bylsma headed a team that had lost the Calder Cup finals in 2008, but he immediately proved his mettle by maintaining the team's winning ways at a level that exceeded that of his predecessor, Todd Richards. After 54 games, Bylsma had a winning percentage of .676 (Todd Richard's winning percentage in 2007/08 was .631).

On February 15, 2009, Bylsma got the call to take over as head coach of the Pittsburgh Penguins, who (despite being the Eastern Conference champions of 2007/08) were playing barely above the .500 level.

Injuries had sapped the Penguins strength, and by mid-February the team was five points out of playoff contention. Pittsburgh general manager Ray Shero (one of the NHL's finest general managers) was convinced the team could do better and that the players were not showing the proper aggressive spark. The replacement of head coach Michel Therrien with Bylsma was part of a greater team shakeup. After suffering a shootout loss in his first game as an NHL coach, Bylsma got the Penguins to win nine of the next ten games and would finish with an 18–3–4 record during the regular season.

Bylsma later explained to the Associated Press, "With the strengths we have, we should be able to go into buildings and make teams deal with the quality of players we have at every position. . . . We need to be an aggressive group, and get focused on playing back to our strengths, and focus away from this situation the last while here."

Bylsma got extra offensive spark from his players. Under Michel Therrien, the Penguins were scoring 3.00 goals per game. Under Bylsma, they were scoring 3.72 goals per game.

But the greatest improvement came in the defensive realm. Under Therrien, the Penguins were allowing 3.07 goals per game. Under Bylsma, they tightened up considerably, allowing only 2.56 goals per game during the regular season. (In the playoffs, the Penguins defence only allowed 2.66 goals per game.)

The 2008/09 playoffs were a seesaw affair for the Penguins. They ripped the Flyers in six games but faced a stern challenge from the Washington Capitals. The Penguins lost the first two games but roared back to win four of the next five (with two of their wins coming in overtime) to win the series.

They swept the Carolina Hurricanes in the conference finals before facing the Detroit Red Wings for the Stanley Cup. Like the Caps, the Wings won Games 1 and 2, holding the Penguins to a single goal in both games. The Penguins regained their punch at home, winning Games 3 and 4. Game 4 was a disaster when the Wings stoned the Penguins 5–0. It was there that Bylsma, using his superb motivational skills, got the Penguins to reach deep inside and summon up the spirit and grit needed to win the Cup.

In Game 6, the Penguins had a two-goal lead and hung on determinedly to win 2–1 to force a Game 7 in Detroit. Game 7 was a straight replay. Again, the Penguins gained a two-goal lead on Detroit while they hung on doggedly, Penguins goalie Marc-Andre Fleury making save after save to win the game and the Stanley Cup.

After 2009, the Penguins continued to win and perform at a high level, but they never repeated as Stanley Cup champions, nor did they return to the finals under Dan Bylsma – a factor that contributed to his eventual ouster.

In 2009/10 the Penguins suffered an upset, second-round elimination at the hands of Jacques Martin's Montreal Canadiens.

In 2010/11 Bylsma's Penguins experienced a stunning first-round loss to the Tampa Bay Lightning and in 2011/12 suffered an even more stunning loss to the Philadelphia Flyers (the Penguins were a consensus choice of the hockey writers to win the Stanley Cup that season).

Despite all this, Bylsma continued to earn the respect of his peers in the NHL coaching fraternity and in the hockey press in general. During the 2010/11 NHL season, the Penguins endured a plethora of injuries to their key players and yet Bylsma kept the team performing at their usual fever pitch. His yeoman coaching efforts resulted in him being awarded the Jack Adams Award.

Dan Bylsma is similar to Mike Babcock in that he is more motivator than tactician. However, Byslma differs from Babcock in that his teams are offensive-oriented and chippy instead of Babcock's grinding defensive, disciplined style. (One of the reasons why Ray Shero hired Bylsma was because of his tactical emphasis on offence as opposed to Michel Therrien's defence-first strategy.)

During Bylsma's reign, Pittsburgh finished in the top five in offence four out of the last six seasons – leading the NHL in offence from 2011/12 to 2012/13.

Interestingly, in the beginning of Bylsma's reign, the Penguins power-play offence was rather average at best, but between 2011/12 to 2013/14 the Penguins vastly improved their power-play offence – thanks to the efforts of Chris Kuniz and James Neal.

In 2012/13 the Penguins again were supposed to be Stanley Cup contenders. Again, they were magnificent, second only to the Chicago Blackhawks, who won the

President's Trophy that year. And just when everyone thought the Penguins were already loaded with talent, Ray Shero went out and acquired venerable NHL greybeards Jarome Iginla and Brenden Morrow to make the team even more invincible.

Pittsburgh seemed destined to reach the finals once more.

And then it happened again. First, they allowed the New York Islanders – a team that had long occupied the Atlantic Division basement but was now rebuilding with bright, raw phenoms and veterans cast off from other teams – to make them look bad. They allowed the Islanders to steal home-ice advantage in Game 2 (chasing Marc-Andre Fleury from the nets for the remainder of the series), then they allowed the Islanders to even the series after four games.

The hockey world was stunned. Even though the Penguins rallied to win Games 5 and 6 to clinch the series, it required a Herculean effort to do so. (Had the Islanders been able to win the series, it would have been the greatest upset in the 2012/13 playoffs.)

The Penguins took round two against the Ottawa Senators in five games, and yet the Sens gave the Penguins a thorough shaking with their hard-hitting play.

The Penguins made their first conference final appearance since 2008/09 against Boston. Pittsburgh had the best offence in the Eastern Conference; Boston, the best defence. As always, it was the defence that won. Pittsburgh was not only defeated, but they were also humiliated. The Penguins were outscored 2–12 by the Bruins. Tuukka Rask stoned the Penguins twice in Games 1 and 4. It was the worst thrashing Bylsma ever experienced in the playoffs.

Some hockey pundits (notably NBC Sport's Mike Milbury) thought Bylsma should have been fired, alleging that he failed to properly prepare the team. Luckily, Ray Shero refused to listen to such nonsense, instead giving Bylsma the contract extension he so richly deserved.

Bylsma was not the only great NHL coach to suffer a sweep in the playoffs: Scotty Bowman was swept in three consecutive Stanley Cup finals; Dick Irvin and Punch Imlach endured sweeps as did Fred Shero and Don Cherry.

In 2013, by my calculations, Bylsma was the finest active NHL coach when it came to getting quality effort from his players. Firing him would have been an act of madness on Shero's part, and Shero was no madman. You do not fire a pre-eminent coach such as Bylsma unless you have someone better available to replace him. No such coach existed.

Bylsma's excellence was such that he was named to coach the U.S. Men's Hockey Team in the 2014 Winter Games at Sochi, Russia.

When the 2013/14 season began, Pittsburgh resumed its high-octane performance, vying with the Boston Bruins for the number-one seed in the Eastern Conference. Pittsburgh faced negligible opposition in its own division – winning the Metropolitan Division title by 13 points. Sidney Crosby was sterling gold on the ice, winning the Hart and Ross trophies. Chris Kunitz continued to be dangerous on the power-play.

The team was seemingly on a roll, but when the Olympic break came and went – Dan Bylsma's Team USA losing the bronze medal game to Team Finland – the Penguins picked the wrong time to go into a slump. Pittsburgh went 11–9–4 going into the playoffs.

The malaise continued even though the Penguins won the first round against Columbus. The Blue Jackets hung tough and matched Pittsburgh in the first four games before the Penguins rallied to win Games 5 and 6 to clinch the series.

In the second round, it was déjà vu all over again. Pittsburgh had a 3–1 series lead before allowing New York to out-hit and out-defend in the remaining three games to lose the series. Pittsburgh (which had ranked fifth in the NHL in team penalty-minutes) allowed the Rangers to outslug them in Games 5 and 6 in one of the major shocks of the 2013/14 playoffs.

This time there was no forgiveness from the Pittsburgh ownership. In the bloodletting that followed, general manager Ray Shero was let go first while Dan Bylsma was left dangling before the Penguins finally hired a general manager stupid enough to fire Bylsma despite all the great things he had done for the franchise since 2009. (When Bylsma was fired, he had the best Average Season Rating of all active NHL coaches and was the fourth-best coach of the 2010s.)

Throughout all of 2014/15 Dan Bylsma sat and waited for the inevitable phone call until finally, on May 28, 2015, the Buffalo Sabres (a team going through a major overhaul) hired Dan Bylsma to be their head coach. In 2009 Bylsma took over a powerhouse that needed a firm hand at the wheel. In 2015 Bylsma takes over a team that is starting from scratch: the ultimate challenge for one of the game's ultimate coaches.

PETER LAVIOLETTE RANK #28

PLUS: 66
MINUS: 9
VALUE: +56
PEAK RANK: #27 in 2011/12
PEAK VALUE: +56 in 2014/15

COACHING EXPERIENCE: New York Islanders, 2001–2003; Carolina Hurricanes, 2003[120]–2008[121]; Philadelphia Flyers, 2009[122]–2013[123]; Nashville Predators, 2014–present

REGULAR SEASON W–L–T–OL: 436–307–25–73
PLAYOFF W–L: 45–43

SOUTHEAST DIVISION TITLE: 2005/06
ATLANTIC DIVISION TITLE: 2010/11

PLAYOFF APPEARANCES: 200102–2002/03, 2005/06, 2009/10–2011/12, 2014/15
STANLEY CUP FINALS: 2005/06, 2009/10
STANLEY CUP VICTORY: 2005/06

When the Philadelphia Flyers organization announced on December 4, 2009, the firing of head coach John Stevens and the selection of former Carolina Hurricanes coach Peter Laviolette to replace him, the general consensus among Flyers fans and the Philadelphia sports press at the time was one of forlorn resignation and a symbolic writing off of the season.

---

120 Laviolette coached the last 52 games of the 2003/04 season.
121 Laviolette coached the first 25 games of the 2008/09 season.
122 Laviolette coached the 57 games of the 2009/10 season.
123 Laviolette coached the first 3 games of the 2013/14 season.

The Flyers, picked by hockey experts to contend for the Stanley Cup, had instead underachieved and were moribund offensively and emotionally. Most felt that Stevens had got a raw deal and that it was the players' collective fault.

No matter, though, Laviolette was chosen to replace Stevens. During the press conference at which he was introduced to the Philadelphia media, Laviolette told reporters that he wanted the Flyers to be "moving forward, I'd like to see a very aggressive brand of hockey. Aggressive in the offensive zone. Get our D activated, get our D moving. I think you have to be tough on players. I want players playing hard. I want them running out the door and to play the game hard in a system that attacks the puck in all three zones. If you can get a team that works hard and if you can get a team that's disciplined, not in the penalty box, but disciplined in their life, disciplined in the system you put on the ice. And if you can get a team that cares about each other, there's nothing you can't do."

The Flyers lost eight of the first ten games coached by Laviolette, and by Christmastime if anyone had suggested that the Flyers could actually finish with a winning record, let alone contend for the playoffs and, ultimately, the Stanley Cup itself, they would have been deemed insane. In truth, Flyers fans were already waiting for the 2010/11 season to begin.

Then the impossible happened: the Flyers won 18 of their next 26 games, playing the brand of hockey that Laviolette wanted them to play, playing with aggression, attitude, and violence that evoked memories of the 1970s Broad Street Bullies era.

One wonders whether the Flyers streak could have lasted longer if the two-week layoff due to the 2010 Winter Olympics had not taken place. The layoff caused the Flyers to deflate, and during the last month of the regular season, coupled with injuries to key players such as Simon Gagne, Ray Emery, and goalie Michael Leighton, they struggled to remain in playoff contention. It took a shootout win in the last game of the season to get there.

Even then the consensus among Flyers fans was that the Flyers would suffer a first-round playoff defeat like they had the previous season. This was buttressed by the fact that their first-round opponents, the New Jersey Devils, who had the best defence and the greatest goalie in the NHL, had long been the bane of the Flyers in the playoffs.

Instead, what followed was nearly two months of magic. Even though the Flyers fell two wins shy of winning the Stanley Cup, what they did on the ice was one of the most amazing displays of team effort and character in the annals of hockey history.

During the first three playoff rounds, they beat the Devils in five, the Bruins in seven (after being down 3–0 in the series), and the Canadiens in five to reach the Stanley Cup finals. They did so with good goaltending, tight defence, and intense physicality, but the most notable aspect of the Flyers playoff run was their ability to force the Devils, Bruins, and Habs to play undisciplined hockey.

This is vital because the Devils and the Canadiens were coached by Jacques Lemaire and Jacques Martin, respectively, two of the greatest teachers of on-ice discipline in NHL history. Claude Julien's Bruins also possessed strong on-ice discipline, yet they too repeatedly committed penalties that gave the Flyers power-play opportunities – which they converted ruthlessly (the Flyers finished second and third in the NHL in power-play offence and power-play percentage, respectively).

The second-round comeback against the Bruins after being down 3–0 in the series was another test of character. No one would have blamed the Flyers if they had collapsed in Game 4 and lost the series, but they didn't. They rallied and forced a Game 7. Even that game was a stern test. After six minutes of play, they were losing 3–0 to the Bruins. Laviolette's impeccable time-out call and pep talk to the team after Boston's third goal will stand forever in the collective memories of Flyers fans everywhere.

The Flyers demonstrated the work ethic that Laviolette demanded (and still demands) from his players; when the final buzzer sounded in the TD Banknorth Gardens in Boston, the Flyers had won the game (and the series) 4–3.

When it came time for the Flyers to play the Blackhawks for the Stanley Cup, it was obvious that the Hawks were by far the stronger team in all the major categories, save for the power play. One would have expected a four-game sweep of the Flyers like the Red Wings did to them in 1996/97 (the last time the Flyers had reached the Stanley Cup finals). The fact that they forced the Hawks to six games is again a testament to the team's character and desire. What's more amazing is that they were able to reduce the Hawk's enormous offensive firepower and make the series competitive.

Indeed, the Flyers had a chance to win the series but didn't because the breaks didn't fall their way.

The key turning points were Games 2 and 6. The Flyers lost both games because they failed to shoot high on (now former) Blackhawks goalie Antti Niemi but instead tried to force the puck down low – where Niemi is strongest.

If the Flyers had won Game 2, they would have played Game 6 in Philadelphia with a 3–2 game advantage, which would have made an enormous difference to the team psychologically.

Many hockey fans thought the Flyers playoff run a fluke, but to do so is erroneous. In truth, the Flyers fulfilled their pre-season prediction of Stanley Cup contention because they found the right coach to ignite the team to play at their full potential.

Laviolette did the job he was hired to do and that was no fluke. Yes, the Devils and Bruins were better in the regular season than the Flyers, but the mark of a great team is always to win the games that need winning. Obviously the Devils and Bruins (and the Canadiens) failed to do so – a far greater shame than the fact that the Flyers beat them.

When one looks at the background of Laviolette, it becomes obvious that the Flyers' decision to hire him was an inspired one. He is the second-greatest American-born coach in NHL history (behind John Tortorella). He led the Carolina Hurricanes to their only Stanley Cup final victory in 2005/06.

Laviolette comes from the greater Boston area and grew up a devoted Bruins fan (ironic, considering his defeat of the Bruins). He was a defenceman who played NCAA hockey and went undrafted by the NHL. He spent most of his playing career in the Rangers and Bruins farm systems – enjoying a brief cup of coffee with the Rangers during the 1988/89 season.

His highlight as a player was competing for the U.S. Men's Olympic Ice Hockey teams in the 1988 Calgary and 1994 Lillehammer Winter Olympics. (He would coach the U.S. Men's Ice Hockey team at the 2006 Turin Winter Olympics.)

In 1997 he quit playing and took up coaching, eventually coaching in the Bruins farm system, where he excelled, winning the 1998/99 Calder Cup with the Providence Bruins in one of the greatest team performances in AHL history. (Laviolette is the fourth of six hockey coaches who have led teams to both Calder Cup and Stanley Cup wins.)

During the 2000/01 season, he was an assistant coach for the Bruins, serving under Pat Burns and Mike Keenan. The following season saw him manning the helm of the New York Islanders, who had finished last in the Atlantic Division.

Laviolette wasted no time making his mark as a winning coach. He led the Islanders to a winning season, a 44-point improvement in team points, and their first playoff appearance since 1993/94. The following season Laviolette did it again but was fired by the Islanders.

Thirty games into the 2003/04 season he was hired by the Carolina Hurricanes to succeed long-time coach Paul Maurice. Laviolette played out the string and then had to wait for the 2004/05 NHL lockout to end.

When hockey play resumed, Laviolette led the Hurricanes to their greatest season in their franchise history. Getting an All-Star performance from Eric Staal and solid defensive work from veteran Rod Brind'Amour, the Hurricanes were the fourth-best team in the NHL. In the playoffs, Laviolette showed nerve and resolve by replacing veteran goalie Martin Gerber with rookie Cam Ward. Ward rewarded Laviolette's faith by winning the 2005/06 Conn Smythe Trophy and leading the 'Canes to Stanley Cup victory over the Edmonton Oilers.

In 2005/06 Laviolette took a team that had consistently underachieved and got them playing like champions (like he would later do for Philadelphia in 2009/10).

His 2005/06 Hurricanes team was far weaker in terms of overall talent than his 2009/10 Flyers team, yet he got them to excel – something that his predecessor, Paul Maurice, could not do when they were annihilated in the 2001/02 Stanley Cup finals.

Laviolette could not sustain his success, however. Despite posting two more winning seasons, the 'Canes failed to reach the playoffs.

When Carolina got off to a mediocre start in the 2008/09 season Laviolette was fired, replaced, ironically, by Paul Maurice. One year later, Laviolette became the Flyers head coach.

Having grown up in the greater Boston area, Peter Laviolette's tactics strongly resemble those from the classic Bruins teams of the late 1960s and 1970s.

Like the big bad Bruins, Laviolette's teams have always been strong in overall offence, stronger still on the power play, and adept at scoring in penalty-killing situations.

Interestingly, Laviolette is flexible when it comes to on-ice physicality. His Islanders were average when it came to team penalty minutes. His Hurricanes teams practised on-ice discipline really well; his Flyers teams regained their reputation as the bad boys of the NHL with a vengeance. But when Laviolette went to Nashville, the Predators were below average in terms of team penalty minutes.

His emphasis on the two-man forecheck has cost him defensively throughout his coaching career. As one long-time 'Canes hockey blogger, Bob Wage, observes, "The argument against him was that his system was weak defensively – watch the odd man rushes coming at you – and once the rest of the league figured it out, he did not have the ability to change it or adapt."

And yet Laviolette's system succeeded at first with the Flyers because his blueline corps was much stronger than the one he had with the Hurricanes.

Since 2010 Laviolette and the Flyers have sailed through uncertain waters. Although showing great strength in the regular season (they won the Atlantic Division title in 2010/11), the team suffered two consecutive second-round defeats in the playoffs. Furthermore, the team has endured injuries to key players (especially Chris Pronger), but the main weakness of Laviolette's Flyers has been their inability to find a solid goaltender.

Laviolette got away with alternating Bryan Boucher and Michael Leighton in 2009/10. Since then the team has suffered between the pipes. Rookie Sergei Bobrovsky showed promise but was dogged with inconsistency and was later traded to Columbus, where, ironically, he won the 2012/13 Vezina Trophy.

In 2011/12 the Flyers acquired free agent Ilya Bryzgalov from Phoenix. Bryzgalov was supposed to fill the void in the nets, but he, too, showed inconsistency. This weakness in the net is ironic because the acquisition, breeding, and nurturing of fine goaltending talent has always been a hallmark of the Philadelphia Flyers franchise.

Laviolette was further undermined by the permanent loss of Chris Pronger. Pronger is a future Hockey Hall of Fame inductee who anchored the Flyers blueline corps. His loss due to a severe eye injury and the after-effects of too many concussions has left a huge void in the Flyers' defence. Couple that with the failure of Flyers general manager Paul Holmgren to fill that void during the summer of 2012, which forced Laviolette to rely on raw youngsters such as Luke Schenn and Erik Gustafsson – players with promise but still a ways from reaching their full potential.

Also, the loss of free agent Jaromir Jagr compromised the Flyers offence and their locker-room synergy. Jagr brought his Hall of Fame work ethic to the team, inspired linemates Claude Giroux and Bryan Hartnell to dig even deeper into their collective talents, brought his magnificent point-generating skills to the Flyers arsenal, and made his team even greater. The Flyers badly needed his leadership skills in 2012/13, but Jagr was playing instead for Dallas and later for the Boston Bruins, where he helped them make it to the Stanley Cup finals.

The Flyers (highly favoured by experts to excel) stumbled out of the gate and failed to reach .500 until game 23 in a 48-game season; then they slumped again. The Flyers defence was pathetic, and the team lacked emotional leadership.

Ironically, it wasn't until the Flyers acquired goalie Steve Mason from Columbus that they tightened up defensively, were inspired by Mason's fierceness between the pipes (and his desperate need to regain the goaltending form that had won him the 2008/09 Calder Memorial Trophy), and rallied to finish with a winning season but fell short of a playoff berth.

Laviolette faced a lot of pressure from the Philadelphia media. There was talk on Philadelphia sports radio that Laviolette should be fired (a view I vehemently disagreed with as a Flyers fan).

And yet on October 7, 2013, Peter Laviolette was fired as head coach of the Philadelphia Flyers after going 0–3–0 at the start of the 2013/14 NHL season. The Flyers were lifeless and unresponsive on the ice. Laviolette was also suffering troubles off the ice. Laviolette and his wife filed a lawsuit against their bank, alleging poor advice that had led to financial losses. (When Laviolette was fired, he denied that his family's financial troubles had been a distraction.)

Laviolette licked his wounds but quickly found diversion by serving as an assistant coach to the U.S. Men's Olympic Ice Hockey team bound for Sochi, Russia, in 2014. It was there he met Nashville Predators general manager David Poile (who was serving as general manager of the U.S. Men's Hockey Team). Nashville had failed to reach the playoffs in 2012/13 under Barry Trotz and was on their way to another failure to reach the playoffs. Poile, deciding that a coaching change was needed, looked no further than Peter Laviolette.

On May 6, 2014, Laviolette was hired as the second head coach in Nashville Predators franchise history. Despite the setbacks of the last two seasons, Laviolette was simply too good a coach to be left rusticating in the backwaters of the hockey coaching world; his passion for the game and his ability to ignite a team and generate solid offence on the ice made him a priceless commodity in the NHL coaching market. Poile has always been one of the shrewdest judges of playing and coaching talent; when a man of Laviolette's talents became available, only a fool would ignore him. David Poile was not and is not a fool. He seized the opportunity and hired a good man.

In 2014/15 Peter Laviolette engineered a 16-point turnaround and, for a time, had the Predators vying for the President's Trophy before a 0–4–2 streak at regular season's end and an injury to Shea Weber led to a first round playoff defeat at the hands of Joel Quenneville's Chicago Blackhawks. Nevertheless, Peter Laviolette has re-established his credentials as a great NHL coach.

BRYAN MURRAY RANK #29

PLUS: 73
MINUS: 22
VALUE: +51
PEAK RANK: #21 in 2007/08
PEAK VALUE: +51 in 2007/08

COACHING EXPERIENCE: Washington Capitals, 1981[124]–1990[125]; Detroit Red Wings, 1990–1993; Florida Panthers, 1997/98[126]; Anaheim Ducks, 2001/02; Ottawa Senators, 2004–2007, 2008[127]

REGULAR SEASON W–L–T–OL: 620–465–131–23
PLAYOFF W–L: 52–60

JACK ADAMS AWARD: 1983/84

PATRICK DIVISION TITLE: 1988/89
NORRIS DIVISION TITLE: 1991/92
NORTHEAST DIVISION TITLE: 2005/06

PLAYOFF APPEARANCES: 1982/83–1988/89, 1990/91–1992/93, 2005/06–2007/08
STANLEY CUP FINAL: 2006/07

As of 2015, Murray is the general manager of the Ottawa Senators, but during his coaching days he was one of the finest coaches in the NHL (and remains the greatest coach in Washington Capitals franchise history).

---

124 Murray coached the last 66 games of the 1981/82 season.
125 Murray coached the first 46 games of the 1989/90 season.
126 Murray coached the last 59 games of the 1997/98 season.
127 Murray coached the last 18 games of the 2007/08 season.

Bryan Murray came into NHL coaching in a roundabout manner. Unlike his younger brother, Terry, a former Los Angeles Kings coach, Bryan never made it past junior hockey as a player. In a 2013 interview, he stated, "I could have signed a contract to play pro hockey but I decided to pursue teaching and coaching in junior instead." Terry states, "Bryan was always a natural leader. He was always coaching, always teaching, always leading."

Murray's teaching background is intrinsic to his coaching genius: his ability to impart hockey wisdom, emphasizing and re-emphasizing hockey fundamentals, dealing with young people and getting them to work within the systems he inculcated them, and the belief that even an ice rink can be a classroom where players could learn not only to play hockey but also to be leaders in their own right. He helped bring out that command presence that made him one of the greatest hockey coaches of all time.

Murray can also be seen as a trendsetter. Before, to earn an NHL coaching job you had to have playing or assistant coaching experience at the AHL or NHL level. Murray changed all that. His coaching experience at the minor-league level was relatively brief – but very good.

By making his mark in the NHL, Bryan Murray made it possible for other future great coaches such as Pat Burns and Mike Babcock to succeed as well.

Throughout the 1970s, Bryan Murray taught physical education and went into business as a motel owner – all the while never abandoning his love for hockey.

Not satisfied with being an entrepreneur, Murray entered hockey coaching in 1973 in the Central Junior Hockey League, serving a nice apprenticeship in junior before moving up to the minors as a head coach – with attendant success along the way.

Murray's opportunity came in 1981 when the Washington Capitals made him their eighth head coach in their eighth season of existence.

The Caps by then were still the most hapless franchise in the NHL; their debut season in 1974/75 remains the worst in NHL history. Washington had never posted a winning season or made it to the playoffs.

Bryan Murray and the Caps had nowhere to go but up.

He played out the string in 1981/82 and the following season began a 29-team-point turnaround, leading the Caps to their first winning season and setting a franchise record of 94 team points (which he later broke in 1983/84 and 1985/86).

His record of 107 team points in the 1985/86 season remained the Caps franchise record for 23 years. From 1982/83 to 1988/89, the Caps reached the playoffs. By 1988/89 they had won their first divisional title.

What was Murray's secret?

Murray states, "David Poile [the Caps GM] and I had a great relationship. Before he came along, Washington was always trading its draft picks for older players. David changed that. We kept our young talents. David was able to move those players who refused to buy into our system out and we got some great players in return. The new players we got [like Brian Engbloom] brought a great work ethic. We practised, talked, and encouraged the players constantly. Today [2013] teams tend to go overboard using video and computers to teach players how to play. Terry [Murray, his assistant when Bryan coached the Caps] and I did it all on the ice. We stressed on-ice drills. We prepared our team thoroughly and made sure they were fundamentally sound. Our practices would sometimes take four hours – which you can't do anymore. We established credibility. We established a defensive philosophy and told the players if you follow the rules then we were going to win and the players bought into that system."

Phil Myre (who was the goaltending coach with Murray in 1991/92 with the Detroit Red Wings) adds, "Bryan Murray's teams were more physical, and Bryan always demanded that his players finish their checks. He was a teacher who was very specific about how he wanted his players to play hockey. He wanted his players to play within the system. He expected his players to adapt to his systems.

"He wanted them to battle for the puck but also skate well when they didn't have the puck. He liked to keep one forward high and he wanted the players to put pressure on the puck at all times."

Murray's teams were well balanced tactically, but his greatest strength was his defence.

He got All-Star and Hall of Fame efforts from blue-liners Rod Langway and Scott Stevens. Langway won two Norris trophies, in 1982/83 and 1983/84. Defensive forward Doug Jarvis won a Selke Trophy in 1983/84.

Murray achieved very strong goaltending from Pat Riggin, Pete Peeters, and Al Jensen during the 1980s. Later, when Murray coached in Detroit, centre Sergei Fedorov and defenceman Nicklas Lidstrom were Calder Trophy runners-up in 1990/91 and 1991/92, respectively, and later became superb defensive players in the NHL.

In a 2013 interview, Murray stated, "I demanded defensive effort from my players at all times. We drilled them constantly on how to defend from the red-line back to using the entire rink. We demanded that the players be supportive and we wanted everyone contributing defensively. We were aggressive on the forecheck because we wanted to take time and space away from the opposition. We wanted to make the opposing team pass it more often, four times instead of two, because that gave us more of a chance to force turnovers."

When it came to offence, Murray added, "We had an organized way to attack. I wanted my players who didn't have the puck to always be in the right position so when the puck did come their way they were in the position to move the puck forward, pass, or shoot the puck. In the 1980s we carried the puck more, whereas today [2013] it's more chip and chase."

In terms of motivating his players, Murray explained, "I treated my players with respect. I played everyone. I was a four-line coach, whereas other coaches used two lines. I gave everyone the opportunity to use their specific talents on the ice. Everyone got their minutes."

Murray's style was popular with his players. Former Caps player Darren Veitch later told the *Ottawa Sun* in 2005: "I would call him a players' coach. He was fair. Respectful. That's the way it worked in our relationship. . . . If you came to play every night, he'd play you."

Phil Myre adds, perceptively, "Bryan Murray had a plan and he always went according to the plan. He was not a rah-rah type of coach; no big speeches like Jacques Demers [Murray's coaching predecessor in Detroit]. He was businesslike. He was an emotional guy who kept his emotions in check. Not as flexible though. He insisted that the players adapt to his systems and if certain players wouldn't adapt to his systems then he would change personnel in order to get players who were willing to play within his systems."

More significantly, Myre says, "Murray would challenge a player in the locker room."

Bryan Murray was cursed with a poor playoff record. What ruined Murray's stint with the Caps was that they never made it past the second round of the Stanley Cup playoffs (see "Heartbreak Coaches" in Part Four).

By 1990 Caps management lost patience with Murray and fired him – replacing him with his brother, Terry.

Murray made his way to Detroit. At this stage of his career, he was devoting his energies toward working in the front office as a general manager instead of working behind the bench. But when he took over at Detroit, he was doing double-duty as head coach and general manager.

By his second season, Murray got Detroit back on the winning track but still couldn't take the Red Wings to the Stanley Cup finals. He had brought his playoff futility streak with him to Detroit, and again this proved to be his undoing.

Jim Devellano (who was senior vice-president of the Red Wings at that time) chafed at Murray's inability to succeed in the playoffs, later telling Douglas Hunter, "It was almost like a sickness for Bryan."[128]

Hall of Fame defenceman Mark Howe suggests another reason for the Wings playoff futility, "There were a lot of good people on that team, but they went their own ways. . . . There were no arguments in the locker room, but when the entire bench stood to cheer Steve Yzerman's goals and only half rose when Fedorov scored . . . the atmosphere was not conducive to winning. . . . Murray had a positive outlook and seemed to think the locker room would take care of itself. . . . Players were not being held accountable for the team's success, which was a shame because our club was loaded with talent."[129]

In a 2013 interview, when Murray was asked about the poor playoff luck his teams endured, he said, "It's all about goaltending. We were always outgoaltended, especially during the early years when we played the Islanders. The Islanders had Billy Smith and he always found a way to shut the door on us. We never had a special goaltender like Billy Smith or a Patrick Roy who could help you win the Cup."

Devellano cast about for a coach with a championship background and settled on two choices: Al Arbour and Scotty Bowman. His first choice was Arbour

---

128 *Scotty Bowman: A Life In Hockey*, Douglas Hunter, p. 293.

129 *Gordie Howe's Son*, Mark Howe with Jay Greenberg, p. 227.

(Devellano had been a protegé of Bill Torrey), but Arbour's heart remained in Long Island. It was Bowman who got the nod and Bryan Murray who got the gate.

In 1994 Murray took over as general manager of the Florida Panthers, firing Roger Neilson as head coach in 1995. (Murray felt the team needed more offence.) By 1995/96 the Panthers made their only Stanley Cup finals appearance.

Afterwards, Murray briefly coached the Panthers, but he left in 2001 to go to Anaheim: first as their head coach and later as their general manager. His coaching stint with the Ducks was lacklustre, but as general manager he worked wonders, giving Mike Babcock his first NHL coaching job. Babcock rewarded Murray's faith by leading the Ducks to the 2002/03 Stanley Cup finals. If Murray had not left the Ducks to work in Ottawa, Babcock might still be coaching in Anaheim today.

Murray returned home to Ottawa in 2004, replacing Jacques Martin as head coach of the Senators. Ottawa had underachieved in the playoffs under Martin. It was Murray's duty to change that. Getting All-Star work from players Daniel Alfredsson, Dany Heatley, and Zdeno Chara, Murray led the Senators to a divisional title win in 2005/06 and their first Stanley Cup finals appearance in 2006/07 – falling to Randy Carlyle's Anaheim Ducks in five games.

(It was Murray's first and only Stanley Cup finals appearance as a coach, finally putting an end to his playoff curse.)

In 2007 Murray was made the general manager of the Senators and in 2008 stepped down as coach while continuing to work in the Senators' front office, where he remains today, slowly but surely rebuilding the Sens into a competitive team. The Senators have shown flashes of success but have not yet returned to the Stanley Cup finals. Still, in the process, not only has Bryan Murray has emerged as one of the game's greatest coaches but also developed a reputation for being one of the NHL's best general managers.

Today, Bryan Murray is fighting an even greater battle. On November 13, 2014, he announced that he had stage 4 colon cancer, which has now spread to his liver and his lungs. He is undergoing chemotherapy and applying the same dogged determination toward fighting his cancer as he has building NHL teams into winners.

ART ROSS RANK #30

PLUS: 98
MINUS: 48
VALUE: +50
PEAK RANK: #6 in 1938/39
PEAK VALUE: +50 in 1944/45

COACHING EXPERIENCE: Montreal Wanderers, 1917/18[130]; Hamilton Tigers, 1922/23; Boston Bruins, 1924–1928, 1929–1934, 1936–1939, 1941–1945

REGULAR SEASON W–L–T: 368–300–90
PLAYOFF W–L–T: 27–33–5

PRINCE OF WALES TROPHY: 1938/39

AMERICAN DIVISION TITLES: 1927/28, 1929/30–1930/31, 1932/33, 1937/38

PLAYOFF APPEARANCES: 1926/27–1930/31, 1932/33, 1936/37–1938/39, 1941/42–1942/43, 1944/45
STANLEY CUP FINALS: 1926/27, 1929/30, 1938/39, 1942/43
STANLEY CUP VICTORY: 1938/39

Who's the greatest Boston Bruins coach of all time? Harry Sinden? Don Cherry? Milt Schmidt? Claude Julien? Nope, not even close. In many ways it's a sad comment on the history of the Bruins franchise that the first man ever to coach the team still remains their greatest coach of all time: Art Ross.

The Art Ross Trophy is awarded annually to the highest-scoring player in the NHL. Some hockey wags joke that it's funny that the award is named after a low-scoring defenceman – which is what Ross was when he played professional

130 Ross coached only six games of the 1917/18 season before the team folded.

hockey. What the jokesters don't realize is that the Art Ross Trophy *is* aptly named because Ross was the greatest offensive coach during the 1930s and 1940s, which is in addition to the other remarkable contributions Ross made to the game itself. His reputation as a builder and innovator is matched only by Lester and Frank Patrick.

It was Ross who designed the B-shaped nets that were used by the NHL until 1984.

It was Ross who designed the hockey puck that is still being used today.

He also became the first NHL coach ever to pull the goaltender for an extra skater – thus revolutionizing hockey tactics forever. How many hockey games have been decided by that simple stratagem?

When Ross was chosen by owner Charles Adams to coach and manage the brand-new NHL franchise in Boston, he was the man who gave the Bruins their name before making them into the longest-existing American franchise in NHL history.

Ross was innovative in another way too. C. Michael Hiam writes that "Ross smuggled movie cameras into other NHL arenas to spy on potential opponents, and he also diligently filmed his own players so that their various flaws could be projected onto the big screen." This makes him one of the first (if not *the* first) NHL coach to use film as a coaching tool – thus anticipating Emile Francis and Roger Neilson by decades.[131]

He was also one of the first NHL coaches to emphasize on-ice discipline and avoiding the penalty box. From 1917 to the 1970s, the NHL's greatest teams usually racked up above-average numbers in team penalty minutes. Ross was part of a minority countertrend that, over time, would become standard practice among successful NHL coaches today.

His main strength was offence, but unlike Glen Sather or Marc Crawford, his teams were well balanced defensively. Five times Ross's Bruins led the NHL in defence. Indeed, his Bruins usually possessed great depth with their blue-liners and their goaltenders.

Before Ross got to Boston, he had already made hockey his entire life. He was one of the finest defencemen of the 1900s and 1910s, playing on two Stanley Cup winners in 1907 and 1908. He, like Frank and Lester Patrick, was a daring blue-liner, willing and eager to take the puck up the ice, setting up his teammates or shooting the puck himself.

---

131 *Eddie Shore And That Old Time Hockey*, C. Michael Hiam, p. 180.

Like Ted Lindsay in the 1950s, Ross was always alert against any attempts by team owners to exploit or reduce not only his earning potential but also the earning potential of his fellow players.

When the NHL formed in 1917, Ross played and was head coach of the Montreal Wanderers. Six games into the 1917/18 season, however, their arena burned down, the team folded, and Ross retired as a player. Ross then refereed in the NHL and had an abortive coaching stint with the Hamilton Tigers in 1922/23.

In 1924 he finally found his niche in Boston, and for the next 30 years he left his mark on the Bruins and the NHL. Charles Adams may have owned the Bruins, but it was Art Ross who ran the team. Ross served as coach until 1945 (with only three interruptions, when Ross allowed others to coach the team while he remained as general manager). He never surrendered the general manager position – remaining in that capacity until 1954.

In terms of leadership style, Ross was a study in contradictions. For the most part he could play the role of a cantankerous, chain-smoking, combative SOB rather well. (He carried on a lengthy feud with Toronto's Conn Smythe and once brawled with New York Americans owner Red Dutton at a league meeting.)

Hiam writes that Ross would walk into the dressing room with a fistful of railway timetables to all points in Canada, throwing them down on a table and stalking out.[132] And yet there were times when he could lead with great restraint and subtlety. Milt Schmidt would later tell Dick Irvin Jr. that if a player wasn't showing the proper alertness, Ross, between periods, would enter the dressing room, give each of his players a cold look (making them squirm), until his eyes settled upon the guilty party. Ross would then silently point a finger at the player's head, say laconically, "Use it," and then walk away.[133]

It took time to make the Bruins winners. He finished last in his first season in Boston. It wasn't until 1925/26 that the Bruins stopped hibernating. The collapse of the Western Hockey League resulted in the transfer of many of the league's brightest stars to the NHL.

Ross got an offensive boost from Frank Fredrickson and Harry Oliver (both former WHLers and future Hall of Fame inductees), but the biggest prize of all

---

132 Ibid, p. 180.

133 *Behind the Bench*, Dick Irvin, p. 29.

was a pugnacious blue-liner with magnificent offensive skills named Eddie Shore.

Shore was the greatest defenceman in the NHL's first quarter-century, and he became the Boston Bruins' first superstar. He was the rock upon which Ross built his church at the Boston Gardens.

Others followed. In 1928/29 goalie Tiny Thompson joined the Bruins and became a fixture in net until 1937/38 – a four-time Vezina Trophy and All-Star honours winner. Thompson, like Shore, is in the Hockey Hall of Fame.

Centre Cooney Weiland supplied enormous firepower from the forward line. Winger Dit Clapper was Weiland's linemate before becoming an All-Star defenceman later in his career. Until Gordie Howe came along, Clapper had the longest playing career in NHL history. Clapper, like Weiland, made it to the Hockey Hall of Fame.

Ross ranked among the top three coaches during the 1930s (to know where he ranked see "Decades" in Part Four), according to my rating system. Five times Ross's Bruins had the best regular-season record in the NHL during the 1930s. No other team had more. During the 1929/30 NHL season, Ross's Bruins had a winning percentage of .875, which remains the NHL record. (To equal Ross's record today, an NHL team would need to earn 144 points.)

Oddly though, despite being so dominant in the regular season, the Bruins earned only one Stanley Cup win for Ross as a coach. (The Bruins 1928/29 Stanley Cup–winning team was led by player-coach Cy Denneny, and their 1940/41 Cup-winning team was led by Cooney Weiland.)

One reason for this was the ridiculous playoff system the NHL used from 1929 to 1938. The two divisional title winners were required to play each other; the two second-place teams faced each other; and the two third-place teams faced each other. The surviving second- and third-place teams would then play each other. The winner of that series would compete against the surviving division title winner for the Stanley Cup. A lot of top-notch teams suffered premature elimination. Ross was victimized three times, in 1929/30, 1932/33, and 1937/38, by that playoff system.

There was a rough spot in the 1933/34 season when the Bruins faltered (Eddie Shore was suspended for 16 games because of the Ace Bailey incident), but when Ross returned to coach again in 1936, he brought with him some new talent: a Teutonic trio named Milt Schmidt, Woody Dumart, and Bobby Bauer, the Kraut Line. They became one of the greatest scoring lines of the NHL's pre-red-line era.

Complementing Eddie Shore on defence were Jack Crawford, Dit Clapper, and Jack Portland. Manning the pipes was the legendary goalie Frank Brimsek (winner of two Vezinas for Ross and another Hall of Fame inductee). These were the men who helped Ross win his only Stanley Cup title in 1938/39 when they beat the Toronto Maple Leafs by holding their potent offence to only six goals in five games.

Shortly before his death, Ross explained how they did this, "Our defence was so strong that we used to do something that would be suicidal today. I used to order my forwards to play outside when back-checking against the opposing wings. In other words, instead of driving the play to the outside, which is normal, I had them driving it inside, toward the goal and not away from it. That way, my forwards could be looking at their defencemen at all times and be ready for a pass or a loose puck. You had to have a great defense to play like that, and we had it."[134]

Ross later said that the 1938/39 Cup winners were his greatest team ever, and they certainly were.

The Second World War cost Boston and Ross dearly. The Kraut Line and Brimsek joined the military. Ross had to make do with what little remained. He led the Bruins to a four-game loss to the Red Wings in the 1942/43 finals but had mixed results after.

Ross finally stepped down for good as coach in 1945. That same year he was among the first charter inductees into the Hockey Hall of Fame. In 1947 he lent his name to the trophy given to the NHL's top scorer and by 1954 had stepped down as Bruins general manager.

He died in 1964.

---

134 *Eddie Shore And That Old Time Hockey*, C. Michael Hiam, p. 250.

JACQUES LEMAIRE RANK #31

PLUS: 82
MINUS: 33
VALUE: +49
PEAK RANK: #24 in 2009/10
PEAK VALUE: +51 in 2009/10

COACHING EXPERIENCE: Montreal Canadiens, 1984[135]–1985; New Jersey Devils, 1993–1998, 2009–2010, 2010/11[136]; Minnesota Wild, 2000–2009

REGULAR SEASON W–L–T–OL: 617–458–124–63
PLAYOFF W–L: 61–56

JACK ADAMS AWARD: 1993/94, 2002/03

ADAMS DIVISION TITLE: 1984/85
ATLANTIC DIVISION TITLES: 1996/97–1997/98, 2009/10
NORTHWEST DIVISION TITLE: 2007/08

PLAYOFF APPEARANCES: 1983/84–1984/85, 1993/94–1994/95, 1996/97–1997/98, 2002/03, 2006/07–2007/08, 2009/10

STANLEY CUP FINAL: 1994/95
STANLEY CUP VICTORY: 1994/95

They should erect a Jacques Lemaire statue at the Prudential Center in Newark, New Jersey, because he is the greatest coach in Devils franchise history. Three times he was summoned by the Devils to make winners out of the team, and three times he got the team to play better than they had ever played before, making himself one of the best defensive coaches of all time.

---

135 Lemaire coached the last 17 games of the 1983/84 season.

136 Lemaire coached the last 49 games of the 2010/11 season.

When Lemaire made the neutral-zone trap the *schwerpunkt* of the New Jersey Devils defence, he sparked a counter-revolution in hockey strategy. It was meant to offset the offensive explosion led by Glen Sather's Edmonton Oilers in the 1980s when they used the European transition game to fuel their high-octane offence. The neutral-zone trap levelled the ice and, until the 2004/05 NHL lockout, reduced scoring in the NHL dramatically – even threatening the popularity of the game itself in North America – thus forcing the NHL to revamp its rules to enhance scoring once more.

Lemaire did not invent the neutral-zone trap. Trapping defences have been a part of hockey strategy for decades and were the preferred brand of European defensive hockey.

Chris Nilan (who played for Lemaire in Montreal and later was an assistant coach under him in New Jersey) explains, "The principle of the neutral-zone trap was to force the puck-carrier to an area. It could be the boards or centre ice. What we did was cover both areas, force the turnover, and go into our transition game.

"We always wanted the opponent to dump the puck in such a way that gave us the best opportunity to retrieve it. The trap didn't require too much skating but it demanded teamwork. Lemaire demanded that everyone play as a team at all times."

What Lemaire did was to take his centre and make him the forechecker in the offensive zone. When the opposing team took the puck up the ice, the centre would be in a position to cut off the passing lanes, thus forcing the puck-carrier along the sideboards. The defensive wingers would be in position along the boards (at the red line) to challenge the puck-carrier, prevent the pass, or stop the puck carrier from breaking through.

The two defencemen would be positioned at the blue line to halt any entry into the defensive zone and to stall for time until the forwards could return.

Lemaire's Devils added extra elements to the trap by obstructing, hooking, clutching, and grabbing their opponents. Also, for the trap to work, teams had to have good on-ice discipline and avoid drawing penalties that could reduce the number of defenders and thus create gaps in the trap.

During the 1980s and early 1990s, the neutral zone had become an area of offensive creativity in which teams with the puck could create scoring opportunities.

The neutral-zone trap now took away those opportunities, turning the neutral zone into a Sargasso Sea where opponents were becalmed, unable to navigate through the opposition and create scoring opportunities.

Scoring plummeted, and it took rule changes in 2004 to open up the game again. Referees were now obliged to call penalties for obstruction, and the red line was eliminated to open up passing.

Just as Freddie Shero's rough-house tactics of the 1970s drew heavy criticism from hockey purists, so, too, did Lemaire's use of the trap. Critics scorned the stratagem, but the results were extraordinary.

It helped the New Jersey Devils win three Stanley Cups from 1994/95 to 2002/03. It allowed Martin Brodeur to break Terry Sawchuk's record of 103 career shutouts and become the greatest NHL goalie in the game today. It inspired other coaches to imitate Lemaire, thus giving similar NHL teams a fighting chance to contend for the Stanley Cup and allowing coaches such as Jacques Martin to make names for themselves as well.

The irony of all this is that as a player Jacques Lemaire was a high-scoring centre for the Montreal Canadiens from 1967 to 1979 – playing on eight Stanley Cup winners in 12 seasons – and a clutch player. It was Lemaire's drop pass that set up Guy Lafleur's game-tying goal (which in turn led to Montreal's subsequent overtime victory) in Game 7 of the 1978/79 Stanley Cup semifinals.

He retired as a player in 1979 and went to Switzerland to take up coaching for two seasons (while absorbing European tactics and training methods).

By 1981 he was coaching in Canadian junior hockey before joining the Canadiens' front office. (The Canadiens have remained Lemaire's home away from home. Whenever he wasn't coaching the Devils or the Minnesota Wild, Lemaire would always return to the Canadiens organization in an advisory capacity.)

When Habs coach Bob Berry was fired in 1984, Lemaire took over, with mixed results: a conference final elimination in 1983/84 and a second round loss in 1984/85.

Despite this, Lemaire made a great impression with his players. Chris Nilan states, "He was the best coach I ever played for. He understood the game. He knew every position and he worked with every individual player to make sure they knew how to play their position and play within his systems. He was a teacher and a tactician."

Lemaire was not afraid to provide a player with extensive, individual hands-on instruction to improve their game. When Chris Nilan joined the Canadiens, his style of play was the antithesis of what Lemaire wanted. Jacques counselled Nilan to stop brawling, drilling him constantly to improve his foot speed and his transition game, all the while treating Nilan (along with the other players) with great respect and in the process making him a complete hockey player with a career that lasted 13 seasons.

Lemaire returned to the Canadiens' front office in 1985, where he remained for eight years.

In 1993 Lemaire was hired by the Devils to be their head coach.

For years the Devils franchise had been the laughingstock of the NHL, making only six playoff appearances in 19 seasons – never making it past the second round. Lemaire inherited a team with average productivity. He had his work cut out for him.

Lemaire instantly gained the respect of his players. In Stan Fischler's book *Coaches*, Devils goalie Chris Terreri told Fischler, "He gained the instant respect of everyone . . . but beyond that, it's his approach. He's upfront with everybody. He's honest. He tells you exactly what he expects of you. And if you don't do it, you don't play. It's not, 'This is the way I want you to play.' It's, 'This is the way we're going to play.' It's that simple."[137]

Lemaire's tactics produced All-Star and Hall of Fame work from defenceman Scott Stevens; when injuries thinned his goaltending ranks, Lemaire started a raw rookie named Martin Brodeur. Brodeur responded by winning the 1993/94 Calder Trophy and two Jennings trophies in 1996/97 and 1997/98. (Ironically, Lemaire, despite his reputation as a defensive genius, never ever coached a Vezina, Norris, or Selke Trophy winner.)

The Devils reached the conference finals in 1993/94 for the first time in their history, only to be beaten by Mike Keenan's New York Rangers. The following season they made Rutherford, New Jersey, the hockey capital of the NHL when they swept Scotty Bowman's Detroit Red Wings to win the 1994/95 Stanley Cup.

It was Lemaire's only Stanley Cup victory in his coaching career.

---

137 *Coaches*, Stan Fischler, p. 172.

Sadly, his luck changed. The Devils failed to retain the Cup, and by 1998 Lemaire resigned as the Devils coach.

In 2000 he returned to coaching to lead the expansion Minnesota Wild.

Again, Lemaire worked wonders. By 2002/03 the Wild made their only Stanley Cup conference final appearance, from 2002/03 to 2006/07 they were among the top five teams in overall defence – leading the NHL in defence in 2006/07 – by 2007/08 they had won their only divisional title, and by 2008/09 they had six consecutive winning seasons.

To achieve coaching greatness, Lemaire got his teams to overcome grave weaknesses in overall, power-play, and short-handed offence.

His teams' strengths came not only in overall defence but also in penalty-killing, on-ice discipline, and line matchups. Lemaire was the best teacher of penalty-killing in the NHL.

Chris Nilan states, "Lemaire worked a lot on teaching us how to play 2-on-1s in the areas on the ice where they usually take place."

When it came to on-ice discipline, Lemaire was one of the best in getting his players to avoid the penalty box. With regards to line matchups, Lemaire was renowned for the fluidity of his line assignments, a trait learned from his coach and mentor Scotty Bowman, who once said that a coach's most important job is "to get the right players on the ice."

In 2009 a new challenge emerged for Lemaire. The Devils had underachieved in the playoffs during the past two seasons. To regain their championship form they asked Jacques Lemaire to return. Lemaire resigned from the Wild and returned to New Jersey. In what he thought would be his last season of coaching, Lemaire and the Devils pitchforked their opponents with the best defence in the NHL – winning the Atlantic Division title. Unfortunately the Devils lost in the first round of the 2009/10 playoffs to the Philadelphia Flyers. Lemaire immediately announced his retirement as head coach.

When the 2010/11 season began, the Devils literally went to hell, swiftly becoming the worst team in the NHL. On December 23, 2010, the Devils fired John MacLean and asked Lemaire to return once more as head coach.

What followed must be seen as a personal triumph for Lemaire.

Even though the New Jersey Devils failed to have a winning season or reach the playoffs, Lemaire performed one of the greatest interim coaching jobs in NHL history. After losing seven of the first eight games he coached, Lemaire got the Devils playing at a fever pitch that astounded the rest of the hockey world. From January 9 to March 15, the Devils won 23 of their next 28 games, suffering only three defeats and two overtime losses.

By the Ides of March, the Devils had a winning record and a shot at the playoffs. Lemaire demanded (and got) the Devils to play at the level of excellence they were supposed to play at but had not reached under MacLean.

The turnaround was astonishing: under MacLean, the Devils were only scoring 1.79 goals per game while allowing 3.12 goals; under Lemaire, the Devils averaged 2.34 goals scored on offence while allowing only 2.16 goals on defence.

The Ides of March bode ill for Lemaire and the Devils. They lost 8 of their last 13 games and finished in fourth place in the Atlantic Division: 12 points out of playoff competition. Considering the amazing turnaround Lemaire wrought, it begs the inevitable question: What if Devils general manager Lou Lamoriello had fired John MacLean two or three weeks sooner?

When the regular season ended, Lemaire once again announced his resignation as head coach of the New Jersey Devils.

Although the team had failed to gain a winning season and a playoff slot, what they accomplished was a magnificent reaffirmation of Jacques Lemaire's excellence as a hockey coach. Only a true coaching genius could make a last-place team play like champions even though they did not win the championship.

And that is what Jacques Lemaire is: a true coaching genius.

TERRY MURRAY RANK #32

PLUS: 58
MINUS: 11
VALUE: +47
PEAK RANK: #21 in 1996/97
PEAK VALUE: +47 in 2011/12

COACHING EXPERIENCE: Washington Capitals, 1990[138]–1994[139]; Philadelphia Flyers, 1994–1997; Florida Panthers, 1998–2000[140]; Los Angeles Kings, 2008–2011[141]

REGULAR SEASON W–L–T–OL: 486–371–89–37
PLAYOFF W–L: 50–51

ATLANTIC DIVISION TITLES: 1994/95–1995/96

PLAYOFF APPEARANCES: 1989/90–1992/93, 1994/95–1996/97, 1999/00, 2009/10–2010/11
STANLEY CUP FINAL: 1996/97

Terry Murray is the younger brother of Bryan Murray. He ranked among the top three NHL coaches during the 1990s (see "Decades" in Part Four), always leading his teams with a cool, low-key approach.

The secret to Murray's coaching genius is his ability to adjust to the skills and talents of his players. In this way he's different from Bryan because Bryan (as mentioned earlier) insisted that his players conform to his systems.

138 Murray coached the last 34 games of the 1989/90 season.
139 Murray coached the first 47 games of the 1993/94 season.
140 Murray coached the first 36 games of the 2000/01 season.
141 Murray coached the first 29 games of the 2011/12 season.

Terry Murray, though, states, "Coaching is about adjustments; being able to change and adjust your philosophy to the times; to different generations of players."

Tactically, Murray always had a different look with the teams he coached. His Washington teams were slightly above average on offence and defence, but his special teams were balanced and quite good. Only in the 1993/94 season did the Caps decline tactically.

His Flyer teams were stronger in overall offence, but their special teams were not as good, not as well balanced as Murray's Caps teams were. His Flyer teams were adept at penalty-killing, but their power play failed to match up.

Terry's Panthers teams were very weak offensively and mediocre defensively.

When he coached the Los Angeles Kings, the Kings were anemic on offence but were developing one of the finest defences in the NHL by the time he was fired as head coach. His Kings teams had superb goaltending and a very good blue-line corps.

Terry was a journeyman defenceman who bounced around the NHL, playing variously with the hapless California Golden Seals, two stints with the Philadelphia Flyers (the first under Fred Shero and the second under Pat Quinn), and a brief stay with the Detroit Red Wings before finishing his playing career with the Washington Capitals (coached by his brother, Bryan).

By his own admission, Murray never contemplated a coaching career until he started playing with the Flyers. Murray states, "It was chaos playing for the California Seals because you didn't know whether the team was going to move or going to fold and the situation there was very chaotic and unsettling for me."

His two stints with the Flyers made an enormous impression. In a 2013 interview, he related, "It was incredibly enlightening to join the Flyers. Fred Shero was a tremendous influence for me. Going from the Seals to the Flyers was like going from chaos to structure. The Flyers team had great communal spirit. The whole team was one big family!" (The Flyers remained Murray's home away from home throughout much of his hockey career. Murray worked variously in the Flyers organization as a player, head coach, assistant coach, and head coach of their AHL affiliate – with a dedication forged in iron. As of June 2015, Murray is now an assistant coach for the Buffalo Sabres, whose general manager is his nephew, Tim.)

Playing for a winning team with a championship tradition opened Murray's eyes and gave him the impetus to contemplate a coaching career, "a chance to give back to the game," as Murray puts it poignantly.

When his playing career ended in 1982, Murray immediately became Bryan's assistant coach (making them the first-ever brother combo in NHL coaching history). Terry states that "I got the call from David Poile [the Caps GM] three weeks before training camp if I would be willing to work as an assistant coach with Bryan."

Terry was responsible for coaching the defencemen for five seasons. (The Caps finished in the top five in defence four of the five seasons and in penalty-killing three of the five seasons he coached the blue-line corps.)

In 1988 he became head coach of the Caps AHL affiliate, and in 1990 he took over as the Caps head coach when his brother, Bryan, was fired after a poor start to the 1989/90 season. Terry states, "It was difficult taking over from Bryan. I got a call from David Poile and he told me 'Terry, you need to know this. The change has already been made. Do you want to be head coach or not?'" After thinking it over (and getting strong urging from Bryan), Terry agreed to accept the job.

Terry got the Caps back on course and led them to their first Stanley Cup playoff conference final in franchise history (only to be swept by the Boston Bruins), which was the apex of his coaching stint in Washington. The Caps never reached that level again, which led to his being fired in 1994. (Terry, for a time, shared his brother's penchant for playoff futility. See "Heartbreak Coaches" in Part Four.)

He coached in the Florida Panthers farm system and made a good impression with Panthers general manager Bobby Clarke.

When Clarke left Florida to become (once more) the general manager of the struggling Philadelphia Flyers (who hadn't enjoyed a winning season since 1987/88), he took Murray with him and made him the head coach of the Flyers.

Murray's stint with the Flyers was the high point of his coaching career, in what he called, "an awesome experience! The team really came together and played extremely confident."

Murray described his motivational approach with his Flyers teams as "maintaining that emotional balance by emphasizing structure, continuity, playing within the systems I set up."

During his three seasons in Philadelphia, he led the Flyers to two Atlantic Division titles (the only ones he's ever won), three playoff appearances, and in 1996/97 the Flyers' first Stanley Cup finals appearance since 1986/87.

The Flyers emphasized offence. It was Murray who formed the Legion of Doom Line of John LeClair, Eric Lindros, and Mikael Renberg and got the most out of Lindros during his tumultuous career with the Flyers.

Supplementing the Legion of Doom Line were centre Rod Brind'Amour, defenceman Eric Desjardins (acquired from the Montreal Canadiens), and Flyers legend Ron Hextall (who was traded back to the Flyers from the New York Islanders in 1994). Murray singles out Desjardins as a key team leader during those glory years, stating, "He was a quiet player who really stabilized the defence. He helped me and he helped the players all the time."

Murray's first divisional title win in 1994/95 was marred when the Flyers lost to the New Jersey Devils (who won the Stanley Cup that year) in the conference finals of the playoffs. The following season the Flyers repeated as divisional champions but fared worse in the playoffs, losing to Florida (a team managed by his brother, Bryan) in the second round.

The third time was the charm for Murray and the Flyers. Although they lost the divisional title to New Jersey by one point, they were the fourth-best team in the NHL and had the third-best offence in the league (despite the fact that Eric Lindros missed 30 games due to injuries that season).

The Flyers swept through the first three playoff rounds with a 12–3 record and had to face the Detroit Red Wings for the Stanley Cup.

As a Flyers fan, I remember the euphoria and expectant hope of the team once more hoisting the Stanley Cup. I also recall the shock and humiliation of seeing my Flyers being swept by a Red Wings team that held them to six goals in four games.

It was during those finals that Murray talked himself out of his job when he referred to the Flyers 6–1 Game 3 defeat as "a choking situation." Needless to say, the Flyers players, management, and fans were outraged. The Flyers predictably lost Game 4 and Murray was fired.

Was it a choke?

In retrospect, no, it wasn't. A choke is when a great team loses to a team it has no business losing to, a team they would dominate normally. The Flyers (and their fans) didn't know it, but they were facing a franchise that would win four Stanley Cups in six tries during a 14-year span. (No other NHL franchise has done so well.)

The Flyers were facing a Red Wings team that had lost the 1994/95 Cup to New Jersey and had set an NHL record in team wins the following season.

The Wings were a team that hadn't won the Stanley Cup since 1954/55 and were led by a coach (Scotty Bowman) who had six Stanley Cup titles under his belt.

The Flyers had the better season record and had scored more goals, but the Wings had the superior defence and better goaltending. The teams the Flyers had beaten earlier in the playoffs did not use trapping defences. In fact, throughout the 1990s, the Flyers always did poorly against teams that used the trap. For many of the Flyers (including Terry Murray), this was their first Stanley Cup final. Indeed, Murray's Flyers were a relatively young team sprinkled with veterans (such as Ron Hextall) who were in the third period of their playing careers.

The Wings had greater experience and playoff maturity. The Red Wings already had one Cup finals appearance . . . and they were hungry.

Simply put, the Flyers didn't choke; they were outclassed. If the Flyers had beaten the Wings for the Stanley Cup, then that would have been a choke . . . for the Red Wings.

CLAUDE "PITON" RUEL RANK #33

PLUS: 48
MINUS: 2
VALUE: +46
PEAK RANK: #18 in 1968/69
PEAK VALUE: +46 in 1980/81

COACHING EXPERIENCE: Montreal Canadiens, 1968–1970[142], 1979[143]–1981

REGULAR SEASON W–L–T: 172–82–51
PLAYOFF W–L: 18–9

EAST DIVISION TITLE: 1968/69
NORRIS DIVISION TITLES: 1979/80–1980/81

PLAYOFF APPEARANCES: 1968/69, 1979/80–1980/81
STANLEY CUP FINALS: 1968/69
STANLEY CUP VICTORY: 1968/69

Claude "Piton" Ruel was the ultimate company man who devoted his entire career to the Habs, serving in all capacities: minor league coach, head coach, scout, and director of player development. He was selfless, dedicated, and had a keen eye for hockey talent.

It was Ruel who convinced a skeptical Sam Pollock to draft Larry Robinson and Bob Gainey in the 1971 and 1973 NHL Drafts, respectively. At the time, both draft picks looked like risky gambles, but eventually they both paid off handsomely. Robinson and Gainey played vital roles in the Habs dynasty teams of 1975/76 to 1978/79. Indeed, Ruel almost pulled off a trifecta when in 1977 he tried to convince Pollock to draft future New York Islanders immortal Mike Bossy. Unfortunately, Pollock took a pass on Bossy and chose Mark Napier instead.

---

142 Ruel coached the first 23 games of the 1970/71 season.

143 Ruel coached the last 50 games of the 1979/80 season.

Ruel (along with Al MacNeil) was part of the three-year interregnum that separated the Toe Blake era from the Scotty Bowman era. Both men coached the Habs during that span. Both men won Stanley Cups, yet in the end both men gave way to Scotty Bowman, who would take the Canadiens further than they had ever gone before.

Of the two, it was Ruel who did better, earning a higher rating in only five seasons of coaching (two of them were partial seasons). Furthermore, Ruel's debut season as an NHL coach was the third best in NHL history – only Toe Blake and David Gill exceeded him.

Today, Ruel still has the fifth-best winning percentage of any NHL coach who has coached a minimum of five seasons or more.

Ruel was a player who came out of the vast Canadiens farm system only to have his career cut short by a freak eye injury. He turned to coaching and during the early 1960s led the Montreal Junior Canadiens (which had future Habs greats Jacques Laperrière and Yvan Cournoyer on their roster).

After 1963 he left coaching and became a scout, working for Sam Pollock, who later succeeded the late Frank Selke Sr. as Montreal general manager. In time, Ruel became director of player development. When Toe Blake stepped down as head coach of the Canadiens in 1968, Pollock (to the surprise of many, including Ruel himself) chose Ruel to replace him.

At first there was nothing wrong with the move. The Habs continued their domination of the NHL, winning the Stanley Cup handily in a four-game sweep of the St. Louis Blues. Then the following season the bottom fell out (at least in the eyes of Canadiens fans).

The team, despite a winning season and a .605 winning percentage, finished in fifth place in the East Division – edged out by the New York Rangers – thus failing to make the playoffs for the first time since 1947/48.

If it were any other team, no fuss would have been made, but in Montreal it was heresy. When the Canadiens got off to a slow start in the 1970/71 season, Ruel stepped down as coach and went back to being director of player development while Al MacNeil replaced him.

What did in Ruel? A variety of factors played a hand in his brief reign. His previous lack of experience as an NHL coach was one reason. This lack of experience was compounded by Ruel's personality.

Douglas Hunter writes, "Ruel was an excitable yeller by nature, and at the beginning of the 1969/70 season he had begun to holler at defencemen like [Terry] Harper, [J. C.] Tremblay, and [Serge] Savard, who he felt weren't doing their jobs behind the blueline."[144]

Another factor was that Ruel had a Falstaffian quality to him that did not engender much respect or fear from the veteran players. In his book *The Game,* Ken Dryden describes Ruel as "a squat, dwarf-like figure" and likened him to a substitute teacher to whom no one paid any attention.[145]

Yvan Cournoyer would later tell Dick Irvin Jr., "Don't tell me Claude Ruel was a good coach. He was a good teacher but he was not a good coach. But we managed to win the Stanley Cup just the same."[146]

Jean Beliveau (who respected Ruel) in his memoir *My Life In Hockey* writes, "Claude's major problem was communication. We were a veteran team and we understood that he knew the game, but sometimes he'd go to the blackboard and simply fail to make his intentions clear. It took a while for us to realize that Claude was equally frustrated by his poor delivery and lack of presence, and that he wanted to do something about these shortcomings."[147]

A fourth factor was that Ruel was a francophone on a bilingual team. This worsened communications between him and the anglophone contingent of the Canadiens. (His successor, Al MacNeil, had the same problem in reverse, in that he was an anglophone who was at odds with the francophone contingent of the team. The problem was resolved when Scotty Bowman – who was bilingual – took over.)

But the biggest factor that tipped the scales against Ruel was the simple fact that Ruel was never happy serving as head coach of the Canadiens; the pressure-cooker atmosphere that existed while leading the Canadiens; the onerous and insatiable minimal acceptable standard that he should consistently produce Stanley Cup champions (like Toe Blake did), consumed and crushed Ruel. Throughout his first coaching term with the team, he repeatedly asked Sam Pollock to replace him as head coach, only to be talked out of it.

---

144 *Champions*, Douglas Hunter, p. 129

145 *The Game*, Ken Dryden, p. 12.

146 *The Habs*, Dick Irvin, p. 279.

147 *My Life in Hockey*, Jean Beliveau, p. 187.

Ruel happily returned to being director of player development for the remainder of the 1970s, and when he wasn't evaluating Canadian draft prospects, he was also assisting Scotty Bowman in superintending team practice sessions. During league games he would sometimes serve as an eye in the sky for Bowman, noting the opposing team's tactical dispositions and potential weaknesses.

Roger Neilson later told Kathy Blumenstock in 1980, "When Scotty was in Montreal, sometimes he had Claude Ruel . . . in the press box, and they'd talk on the phone between periods."[148]

Ruel remained as director of player development until 1979 when the Habs, struggling under Bernie Geoffrion, asked Ruel to take over as coach.

And so it was Ruel who presided over the ending of the Canadiens' dynastic reign on April 27, 1980, when they were eliminated by the Minnesota North Stars in the second round of the playoffs.

Ruel remained as coach for another season before giving way to Bob Berry, thus returning once more as director of player development.

When his career ended he lived in quiet retirement, battling ill health before passing away on February 9, 2015.

Claude Ruel will always remain an unsung hero of a time in the 1970s when the Canadiens were the most dominant franchise in the NHL.

---

148 "Read You, Roger, Wilco and Out," Kathy Blumenstock, *Sports Illustrated*, April 21, 1980.

BOB HARTLEY RANK #34

PLUS: 59
MINUS: 14
VALUE: +45
PEAK RANK: #22 in 2001/02
PEAK VALUE: +49 in 2006/07

COACHING EXPERIENCE: Colorado Avalanche, 1998–2002[149]; Atlanta Thrashers, 2003[150]–2007[151]; Calgary Flames, 2012–present

REGULAR SEASON W–L–T–OL: 428–321–61–52
PLAYOFF W–L: 54–41

JACK ADAMS AWARD: 2014/15

PRESIDENT'S TROPHY: 2000/01

NORTHWEST DIVISION TITLES: 1998/99–2001/02
SOUTHEAST DIVISION TITLE: 2006/07

PLAYOFF APPEARANCES: 1998/99–2001/02, 2006/07, 2014/15
STANLEY CUP FINAL: 2000/01
STANLEY CUP VICTORY: 2000/01

During the late 1990s and the early 2000s, Bob Hartley was one of the finest offensive hockey coaches in the NHL, winning games with an aggressive offence and exceptional power-play capability.

Hartley never played in the NHL, yet he became a successful NHL coach after

149 Hartley coached the first 31 games of the 2002/03 season.

150 Hartley coached the last 39 games of the 2002/03 season.

151 Hartley coached the first 6 games of the 2007/08 season.

serving a long coaching apprenticeship in Canadian junior hockey and the minors. Eventually Hartley found work in the Quebec Nordiques farm system, where he had great success. In 1996/97 he led the Hershey Bears to a Calder Cup win (which makes Hartley another one of the six hockey coaches who have led teams to a Calder Cup and a Stanley Cup win).

When Colorado Avalanche head coach Marc Crawford resigned in 1998, Hartley got the job.

Bob Hartley brought to the bench a throwback style of pugnacious hockey generated through intense preparation (Hartley's practices lasted around 90 minutes or more in length) and an even more intense personality. He demanded aggressive hockey, and if a player wasn't showing the necessary moxie, then that player would hear about it.

Hartley inherited a veteran team that had won the 1995/96 Stanley Cup. The Avalanche had All-Stars Peter Forsberg, Joe Sakic, and Patrick Roy on their roster. (Later they acquired Hall of Fame defenceman Raymond Bourque.)

Although he himself never played a minute in the NHL, Hartley was unafraid to shake the tree: changing lines; readjusting ice time even to the point of benching veteran players (one time Patrick Roy in a fit of rage smashed video equipment in Hartley's office).[152]

His hard-nosed approach didn't win him any friends (he was never a beloved figure in the eyes of his players), but it got results. Hartley led Colorado to four consecutive Northwest Divisional titles as well as four consecutive conference final appearances in the Stanley Cup playoffs – the first coach since 1968 to do so in his first four seasons of NHL coaching and (as of 2015) also the last NHL coach to do so.

His greatest season was in 2000/01, when he led the Avalanche to a franchise record 52 victories and 118 points – good enough to win the President's Trophy. Joe Sakic had a career season in which he won the Hart and Lady Byng trophies.

The 2000/01 playoffs were topsy-turvy for Hartley and the Avalanche. They swept the Canucks, got a bad seven-game scare from the Los Angeles Kings, and brushed aside the St. Louis Blues before facing the defending champion New

---

152 "Inside the NHL," Kostya Kennedy, *Sports Illustrated*, February 15, 1999.

Jersey Devils in the Stanley Cup finals. The matchup was a true clash of the titans that went the full seven games.

The Devils had a 3–2 series lead going into Game 6, but Avalanche goalie Patrick Roy put on the goaltending performance of his life, holding the Devils to one goal in two games.

Roy stoned the Devils in New Jersey in Game 6, clinching the Cup in Colorado in Game 7 while earning the Conn Smythe Trophy. The Stanley Cup finals also saw Raymond Bourque end his 22-season career by hoisting the Stanley Cup for the first and last time in his playing career.

Winning the Stanley Cup should have made Hartley a fixture in Colorado, but in December 18, 2002, he was fired by the Avalanche after getting off to a mediocre start – which wasn't the first time that had happened.

During his entire NHL coaching career, Hartley's teams had a disconcerting habit of starting out of the gate slowly. This happened six times out of eleven season starts in his coaching career (especially during his debut season in 1998/99). However, it must be noted that when his teams did start slowly, they would then get very hot by January, finish their seasons on a very strong note, and enter the playoffs with great momentum.

Also by 2002 the team was getting tired of Hartley's pressure-cooker leadership style. Colorado winger Mike Keane told Daniel Habib, "Bob was old school; he came across hard. You made a bad pass, and when you came back to the bench, you heard about it for five minutes."[153]

By 2002 the Avalanche front office had lost patience with Hartley and fired him. Since then, Colorado has not made it to the conference finals of the Stanley Cup playoffs.

On January 14, 2003, the Atlanta Thrashers (today the Winnipeg Jets) hired Hartley. They were still playing like an expansion team making its NHL debut, but the arrival of Hartley changed all that. He set new franchise records in season wins three straight years in a row, gave the Thrashers their first two winning seasons in franchise history, and led them to their sole divisional title and playoff appearance in 2006/07 while becoming the best coach the Thrashers ever had.

Sadly for Hartley, what led to his downfall in Colorado happened to him again

---

153 "Inside the NHL," Daniel G. Habib, *Sports Illustrated*, December 30, 2002.

in Atlanta. In the 2007/08 season, the Thrashers got off to a poor start and Hartley was fired for their 0–6 record.

After being fired, Hartley served as a hockey analyst for the RDS channel (the French-language channel on Canadian TV). Hartley's ancestry (like Toe Blake's) is Franco-Ontarian and he is a francophone.

In 2011 he went to Switzerland to become head coach of the ZSC Lions team based in Zurich. Despite the four-year layoff, Hartley hadn't lost his championship touch, leading the Lions to the Swiss League title. Even as he was abroad, Bob Hartley's name was bandied about from time to time during the 2011/12 NHL season as a possible coaching replacement for various teams, but it wasn't until the regular season was over that Hartley began to emerge as a potential NHL coaching candidate.

On May 31, 2012, Hartley was hired by the Calgary Flames to become their new head coach, replacing Brent Sutter, who had failed to get the Flames into the playoffs despite posting three consecutive winning seasons with the club. Hartley's hiring marked the end of the Sutter family era with the Flames. Throughout the 21st century, the Sutters had a powerful stake in the Flames franchise, with brothers Brian, Darryl, and Brent all taking turns coaching the team while Darryl served as general manager from 2004 to 2010. But when Jay Feaster took over as Flames general manager, it was obvious that a new era was now taking hold in Calgary.

The hiring of Bob Hartley was no surprise. Hartley's relationship with Feaster had always been close (Hartley is godfather to Jay Feaster's son, Ryan). But friendship aside, Hartley remained one of the finest coaches in the history of hockey, and the hockey gods gave him another great challenge, one particularly worthy of his talents: making the underachieving Calgary Flames playoff contenders and, it was hoped, Stanley Cup champions.

By 2012, the Flames had become hell with the fire out. They hadn't had a playoff appearance since 2008/09. They hadn't won a divisional title since 2005/06 and they hadn't reached the Stanley Cup finals since 2003/04. Hartley had his work cut out for him.

Unfortunately his first two seasons in Calgary proved to be a trial by fire. The Flames suffered two losing seasons and twice failed to reach the playoffs. Hartley lost six points off his career value and fell nine places in rank – a long fall.

Hartley struggled to rebuild the Flames. The team was deficient tactically both offensively and defensively; their special teams were equally impotent. The only good that came from those two losing seasons was the fact that Flames general manager Jay Feaster gave Hartley three number-one draft picks (forwards Sean Monahan, Emile Poirier, and Morgan Klimchuk) in the 2014 NHL amateur draft. All three men are shooters and scorers. Poirier, as a power forward, will bring muscle to the mix as well. It took Hartley three seasons to make the Thrashers winners. When Bob Hartley began his third season at the helm of the Calgary Flames, his men were ready.

The Flames started off slowly. Although never leading their division they always remained in playoff contention. There was a flutter in December when the Flames lost eight games in a row; but when 2015 dawned the Flames were back into playoff competition.

Calgary had engineered a 20-point turnaround in team points and earned its first playoff berth since 2008/09. Going up against the Vancouver Canucks, the Flames showed its offensive strength and muscle, stealing home-ice advantage in Game 1 and taking a 3–1 series lead before Vancouver won Game 5. In Game 6 at Calgary, the Flames allowed Vancouver take a 3–0 lead in the first nine minutes. Calgary refused to panic, persistently pecking away at the Vancouver lead before tying the game five minutes into the second period. Even when the Canucks regained the lead midway through the second period Calgary refused to be discouraged; when the third period began the Flames roasted Vancouver with goals by Jiri Hudler and Matt Stajan. Vancouver tried to force overtime but got stung by two empty net goals in the closing seconds of the game.

It was Calgary's first playoff series win since 2003/04.

When the Flames tried to roast the Anaheim Ducks the magic was gone and Calgary went down in five games but in the end Bob Hartley had re-established his credentials as one of the NHL's finest coaches. The Hockey press recognized his brilliant rebuilding efforts by awarding him the Jack Adams Award for being the NHL's best coach in 2014/15.

JACQUES MARTIN RANK #35

PLUS: 64
MINUS: 19
VALUE: +45
PEAK RANK: #28 in 2010/11
PEAK VALUE: +45 in 2010/11

COACHING EXPERIENCE: St. Louis Blues, 1986–1988; Ottawa Senators, 1996[154]–2004; Florida Panthers, 2005–2008; Montreal Canadiens, 2009–2011[155]

REGULAR SEASON W–L–T–OL: 613–481–119–81
PLAYOFF W–L: 50–61

JACK ADAMS AWARD: 1998/99

PRESIDENT'S TROPHY: 2002/03

NORRIS DIVISION TITLE: 1986/87
NORTHEAST DIVISION TITLES: 1998/99, 2000/01, 2002/03

PLAYOFF APPEARANCES: 1986/87–1987/88, 1996/97–2003/04, 2009/10–2010/11

Jacques Martin remains the greatest coach in the history of the Florida Panthers and Ottawa Senators franchises. (Ken Hitchcock and Jacques Lemaire are the only other NHL coaches who can also make the claim of being the greatest coach for two NHL franchises.)

He also is a product of the Roger Neilson coaching tree.

---

154 Martin coached the last 38 games of the 1995/96 season.

155 Martin coached the first 32 of the 2011/12 season.

Neilson biographer Wayne Scanlan writes, "Martin was one of several NHL coaches to have been nurtured by Roger in some way, somewhere along the line. In Martin's case, he had stayed at Neilson's house while he was first finding his way in the game, having abandoned a teaching career to coach full time – first in the Central Junior Hockey League, then as an assistant to Dick Todd in Peterborough in 1984."[156] (Dick Todd was a leading disciple of Roger Neilson.)

Martin never played in the NHL. He was a goalie for St. Lawrence University in New York and began his coaching career at the Canadian collegiate level in 1976. By the 1980s he was coaching junior hockey before being hired to coach the St. Louis Blues.

On the surface, Martin didn't do too badly. He led the Blues to a Norris Division title in his rookie season, but the Norris Division back then was the weakest division in the NHL. The Blues won with a losing record and were promptly eliminated in the first round. He failed to repeat as divisional champion and was fired by the Blues in 1988.

For the next seven years Martin bounced around the NHL doing assistant coaching work: first with Mike Keenan at Chicago before joining the Quebec Nordiques in 1990 as an associate coach. Martin remained with the Nordiques for five years, eventually joining up with Marc Crawford and Joel Quenneville to form a potent coaching troika. Crawford was the head coach while Martin and Quenneville were his assistants – with substantial responsibilities.

The team's revival attracted the attention of the fledgling Ottawa Senators expansion franchise, which was still performing terribly since its NHL debut in 1992. Martin left Colorado in January 1996 to become Senators head coach.

He wasted no time. Helped by 1995/96 NHL rookie of the year Daniel Alfredsson, Martin turned the Senators into a viable NHL team.

By 1996/97 the Senators made their first playoff appearance, by 1997/98 they had their first winning season, by 1998/99 they won the first of three Northeast division titles for Martin (which earned him the 1998/99 Jack Adams Award), and by 2002/03 they won the President's Trophy as the NHL's best team.

The 2002/03 season was when Martin came closest to reaching the Stanley Cup finals. Facing Pat Burns's New Jersey Devils, the Sens overcame a 3–1

---

156 *Roger's World*, Wayne Scanlan, p. 182.

deficit to force a Game 7 at home – only to lose by the score 3–2 in a tense, hard-fought contest.

Martin's undoing in Ottawa was his poor performance in the playoffs. The Senators were eliminated in the first round five times and the second round twice in eight years. (Playoff futility was the cross that Martin had to bear throughout his NHL coaching career. See "Heartbreak Coaches" in Part Four.)

In 2004 the Senators fired Martin, who immediately went to the Florida Panthers, who had fallen on hard times. Martin served as head coach (and in 2006 became their general manager) and turned the Panthers around, leading them to three straight winning seasons but was unable to get them into the playoffs. In 2008 Martin stepped down as coach but remained as general manager. In 2009 Martin left the Panthers to become the head coach of the Montreal Canadiens.

Like his mentor, Roger Neilson, Martin was a defensive specialist who relied heavily on the neutral-zone trap. His record on defence, although slightly above average, was never worthy of superlatives.

One could argue that coaching the expansion Senators and a weak Panthers team excuses his weak credentials. But that argument fails to hold up when you consider what Roger Neilson or Jacques Lemaire did in Florida and Minnesota, respectively. Both men took over brand-new expansion franchises and quickly got their teams playing at a high level of defensive excellence. Martin could never make that claim. Martin never coached a Vezina, Jennings, Selke, or Norris Trophy winner. His defensive record with Ottawa was respectable, yet his records with St. Louis and Florida were rather poor.

His one true skill is in getting his teams to play well-disciplined hockey. Martin's teams during the 1990s were the best with regards to on-ice discipline. He excelled in coaching and developing young hockey talent. Five times a Jacques Martin player earned NHL All-Rookie Team honours.

Phil Myre (who was the goalie coach for the Florida Panthers while Martin served as head coach) explains, "Organization was everything for Jacques Martin; from the way the pens were arranged on his desk to the type of practices we conducted throughout the season. He always made sure everyone knew what they had to do and he always explained how the things they were doing fit into the overall plan. He always had a solution for every problem that occurred. He never panicked. There was always a backup plan if something went wrong.

"We always followed our game plan. Martin was a teacher [like Bryan Murray] and the locker room was very much like a classroom. There was a methodology in Jacques's approach."

Another factor in the on-ice discipline was that Martin kept his teams on an emotional plateau. Myre adds, "There were no ups and downs with Jacques. No emotions. And the team reflected that and that's why we didn't draw that many penalties."

When dealing with his players, Martin was always tactful, preferring to discipline or instruct privately instead of challenging a player publicly.

Although his coaching personality was that of a dour technician, Martin should be remembered for a supremely noble gesture he did on behalf of a coaching colleague.

In 2000 Neilson had lost his head coaching job with the Philadelphia Flyers and was fighting the cancer that would eventually kill him. Jacques Martin (coaching the Ottawa Senators) needed a new assistant coach.

To repay a debt he owed to the man who mentored him, Martin offered the job to Neilson, who accepted. During the 2001/02 season, Neilson was losing his long fight with cancer. Martin went to the NHL and asked the league to allow Neilson to take the helm of the Senators for two games so he could become the ninth man to coach 1,000 NHL games. Permission was granted, and Neilson reached his milestone.

Martin's performance in the 2009/10 playoffs was his supreme moment as a coach. He took the eighth-seeded Habs and led them to astonishing upset victories over the Washington Capitals (who won the President's Trophy that season) and the defending Stanley Cup champion Pittsburgh Penguins.

The victory over the Caps is astonishing because the Caps had a 3–1 series lead and had the best offence in the NHL, yet the Habs, showing a magnificent ensemble effort (and great goaltending by Jaroslav Halak), held the Capitals to three goals in the last three games to win the series.

The second-round victory over Pittsburgh was another personal triumph for Martin. The Penguins had a 3–2 series lead over the Canadiens and yet they couldn't close the deal. They allowed the Habs to out-hit and outscore them in Games 6 and 7. In Game 7 the Canadiens got two power-play goals and one short-handed goal to clinch the game and the series.

What was amazing about the Canadiens' playoff run was the fact that they had made their first conference finals appearance since 1992/93 (when they won the Stanley Cup). The city of Montreal was in a state of ecstasy, and it was amazing to see the crowd dynamics at the Bell Centre. The Montreal fans were the seventh man on the ice, which helped fuel the psychic fires of the Canadiens.

Sadly, the clock struck midnight for Martin and the Canadiens in the third round when they lost to the Philadelphia Flyers in five games, but Martin's playoff coaching performance in 2009/10 was the apex of his coaching stay with Montreal. Afterwards, Martin's and the team's fortunes declined dramatically, which led to him being fired in 2011.

In 2013/14, Jacques Martin worked as an assistant coach for the Pittsburgh Penguins (then Penguins general manager Ray Shero had worked with him when Martin was with Ottawa), but in the aftermath of the firings of Ray Shero and Dan Byslma, Martin was promoted to senior adviser of hockey operations, where he remains today.

DON "GRAPES" CHERRY RANK #36

PLUS: 53
MINUS: 10
VALUE: +43
PEAK RANK: #15 in 1978/79
PEAK VALUE: +53 in 1978/79

COACHING EXPERIENCE: Boston Bruins, 1974–1979; Colorado Rockies, 1979/80

REGULAR SEASON W–L–T: 250–153–77
PLAYOFF W–L: 31–24

JACK ADAMS AWARD: 1975/76

ADAMS DIVISION TITLES: 1975/76–1978/79

PLAYOFF APPEARANCES: 1974/75–1978/79
STANLEY CUP FINALS: 1976/77–1977/78

I always thought actor Frank Bonner (who played the character Herb Tarlek in the TV series *WKRP in Cincinnati*) wore the loudest clothes in TV history, but it's former NHL coach and current *Hockey Night in Canada* (*HNIC*) commentator Don "Grapes" Cherry who owns the most cacophonous wardrobe on TV today. Cherry's clothing shrieks volumes about the man himself.

Since 1980 Cherry has become a household name in Canada because of his work for *HNIC*. No other Canadian sportscaster generates as much excitement and outrage as Cherry does. Bruce Dowbiggin tells Scott Burnside, "It's like if you took John Madden and overlaid him with Rush Limbaugh. It's become larger than life. I don't think there's any position in the U.S. that equates to it."[157]

But this is not a discussion about Don Cherry the commentator. This is a

157 http://sports.espn.go.com/espn/eticket/story?page=doncherry

discussion about Don Cherry the hockey coach. When you strip away the garish garb and the political incorrectness, what's left is an impressive legacy of an all-too-brief coaching career in the NHL.

Cherry was a career minor league defenceman (he played only one game with the Boston Bruins in 1954/55) who played all over North America. (His travels and travails are well documented in the numerous books he has written in his lifetime. Cherry's greatest promoter will always be himself.)

Cherry began his coaching career with the Rochester Americans in the AHL in 1971 and made the team winners before he took over the head coaching job in Boston in 1974. For the next five seasons, Grapes led the Bruins to five straight playoff appearances, four division titles, and two Stanley Cup finals appearances (while barely missing a third in 1978/79). He did all this while coping with the departures of Bruins icons Bobby Orr and Phil Esposito.

The Bruins were a well-balanced team, but their true strength was in their offence. The Bruins always finished in the top five in the NHL in offence during Cherry's reign. What's amazing is that after the departure of Orr and Esposito from the Bruins in 1975, the Bruins still continued to dominate offensively on the ice.

A lesser team and a lesser coach would have faltered in the face of losing two legendary talents like Orr and Esposito. Instead, the Bruins and Cherry maintained their winning ways.

Shorn of the twin pillars of Orr and Espo, Cherry resorted to goalscoring by committee. His 1977/78 Bruins had 11 players who scored 20 or more goals on the roster – which still remains an NHL record. That is a testament to the talent and resiliency of both the Bruins players and Cherry.

Tactically, Grapes eschewed the Xs and Os, which led to some conflicting views about Cherry among his players.

Bobby Orr in his memoir *Orr* writes, "Don allowed his players to play the game their way if that would benefit the team. . . . Don was smart enough to avoid putting a harness on his players, and instead expected us to get up ice and be creative. He understood there would be mistakes as a result of that style of play. He saw the potential downside, but obviously must have liked the potential upside, too."[158]

---

158 *Orr: My Story*, Bobby Orr, p. 170

However, Phil Esposito in his memoir *Thunder And Lightning* demurs, "I didn't particularly like Don Cherry's coaching style. We called him 'rap-it-around-the-board-and-get-it-in-deep Don.' That wasn't my style of play, and it wasn't Bobby Orr's either. Bobby could do whatever he wanted, and I suppose I could too, but the rest of the guys were told, 'Throw it in deep and go in and forecheck.' Our players were used to carrying the puck and making plays. But Don would say, 'Don't even look for the pass down the middle.' God forbid you did that. 'Just rap it around the . . . boards. And you better be there.' It was very difficult to make plays, but that's what Don wanted. . . ."[159]

Still, Don Cherry was no tactical dummy. Grapes possessed a keen, discerning eye for the ebb and flow for the game and could decipher an opposing team's weaknesses like the great coach that he was. One example came in the 1976 Canada Cup series, which featured teams from six countries: Canada, Czechoslovakia, Finland, the Soviet Union, Sweden, and the United States.

Cherry was an assistant coach to Scotty Bowman, who headed Team Canada. In the round-robin tournament, the Canada Cup finals featured Team Canada versus Czechoslovakia. In the deciding third game of the final, it was Don Cherry who helped Team Canada win the game and the series when he noticed a fatal flaw in the Czech goalie Vladimir Dzurilla.

Dzurilla (who had been brilliant in goal throughout the series) had a tendency of coming way out of his net to cut down the angle on the opposing shooters. Cherry told the Team Canada players to fake, lure Dzurilla out of position, then go by him to make the shot. Sure enough, Darryl Sittler, doing exactly what Cherry recommended, scored the winning goal to win the Canada Cup series.

Cherry's real strength was in motivating his teams by using a variety of philosophical, psychological, comedic, and sometimes shamanistic (to this writer at least) methods.

Grapes in his first book told Stan Fischler:

159 *Thunder and Lightning*, Phil Esposito and Peter Golenbock, p. 130.

> Reporters liked to ask me what I wanted in a hockey player. The answer was simple: to play on my team he had to have guts, otherwise there was no room for him. . . . A lot of coaches will take players as long as they can score goals, even if they are gutless. If you can have one guy who is willing to go into the corners and get his brains bashed in, why shouldn't some other guy go into the corner as well? That was my philosophy in putting together a successful team. Once the guts requirement was fulfilled, I then looked for skating ability, and hockey sense. A lot of players can shoot well, skate and stickhandle but they don't have hockey sense, which is essentially intuition on the ice.[160]

Wayne Cashman told Dick Irvin Jr., "He was a great coach who made the game fun. He made you work hard but he made you work hard for each other. He made you realize it's a team sport. He used to tell us to sit in the dressing room and look at each other because that was who you were playing for, your teammates."[161]

Hockey literature is filled with scores of stories (most of them told by Cherry himself – he is one of hockey's great raconteurs) about how Cherry motivated his Bruins teams during his glory ride. Grapes's wizardry was the font that sustained the Bruins during the waning years of the 1970s. Even though he never coached a Stanley Cup winner, he was one of the finest coaches in the history of hockey in getting optimum performance from his teams (see "Average Season Rating" in Part Four).

Cherry's misfortune was in coaching the Bruins during the reign of the Montreal Canadiens dynasty led by Scotty Bowman. Simply put, the Bruins were the second-best team in the NHL. The Bruins lost to Montreal in the 1976/77 and 1977/78 Stanley Cup finals.

(As of 2015, Cherry remains the last NHL head coach to lose two consecutive Stanley Cup finals.)

Still, no other NHL team came closer to ending the Canadiens' dynastic reign than when the Bruins faced the Habs in the 1978/79 semifinals. In that series, the Bruins took the Canadiens to the brink of defeat when they led Montreal in Game 7,

---

160 *Grapes*, Don Cherry with Stan Fischler, p. 150.

161 *Behind the Bench*, Dick Irvin, p. 305.

4–3, late in the third period. A costly Boston bench penalty in having too many men on the ice allowed Montreal to convert on the power-play opportunity, thus forcing an eventual Boston defeat in overtime.

That defeat was a defining moment in Cherry's career. He would later write about the loss: "I died on May 10, 1979; at 11:10 p.m. to be exact. Two shots killed me. The first, which left me critically wounded, was fired by Guy Lafleur. The one that wiped me out came from the stick of Yvon Lambert. Had I survived these attacks I have no doubt that I would still be coach of the Boston Bruins today and, quite likely, governor of Massachusetts."[162]

The truth behind Boston's loss in that game is that it wasn't a fluke occurrence. Guy Lafleur's game-tying goal was the exploitation of two fatal flaws on the Bruins team:

1. By 1978/79 the Bruins' power-play offence had declined dramatically, whereas Montreal had the best penalty-killing unit in the NHL.
2. The 1978/79 Bruins were ranked 14th (in a 17-team league) in penalty-killing, whereas the Habs were ranked fifth in power-play offence and second in power-play percentage.

When Boston committed that bench penalty late in the seventh game, it opened a door to a team that was brilliant at exploiting such opportunities.

That coaching mistake cost him dearly.

What also cost Cherry dearly was his own hard-hat personality. In military parlance, Cherry could never act like an officer and a gentleman. At heart he was an NCO who was too blunt, too honest, and too tactless to achieve the longevity that Scotty Bowman, Al Arbour, and Lindy Ruff achieved. That NCO spirit was what endeared him to his players, but it played havoc with his relations with his general managers and other members of the hockey establishment. (In his many books, Cherry has made a cottage industry of ripping former Bruins general manager Harry Sinden, describing in hilarious detail his internecine struggles with Sinden.)

Grapes became his own worst enemy because he always did the right thing for his players in the worst possible manner. He fought for his players and would not

---

162 *Grapes*, Don Cherry with Stan Fischler, p. 1.

back down in defending his team and his prerogatives as a coach. It is that proletarian spirit that endeared him to his players back then and what endears him to his fans today. Political correctness be damned, Grapes represents the innate conservatism and traditionalism of the common weal and the common hockey fan, a throwback to a sterner, leaner, more homogenous past (Cherry has always been a notorious hockey xenophobe).

He was fired by Boston general manager Harry Sinden and immediately became head coach of the expansion Colorado Rockies.

Cherry coached his only losing season in the NHL and was fired by the Rockies, whereupon destiny intervened when he was hired by *HNIC*, and the rest is history (or infamy, considering whose side you're on).

EMILE "THE CAT" FRANCIS RANK #37

PLUS: 56
MINUS: 13
VALUE: +43
PEAK RANK: #15 in 1973/74
PEAK VALUE: +44 in 1975/76

COACHING EXPERIENCE: New York Rangers, 1965[163]–1975; St. Louis Blues, 1976/77, 1981[164]–1983[165]

REGULAR SEASON W–L–T: 388–273–117
PLAYOFF W–L: 39–50

SMYTHE DIVISION TITLE: 1976/77

PLAYOFF APPEARANCES: 1966/67–1974/75, 1976/77, 1981/82
STANLEY CUP FINAL: 1971/72

"He was a gentleman and very understanding. He was very good to work for and a lot of us guys from that team always feel bad because of all the guys that should have had a Stanley Cup ring, it should have been a guy like Emile. He treated us so well and put his heart and soul into the Rangers. He was a good guy to play for."

Ted Irvine

"You have to get up very early in the morning to outfox the Cat."[166]

Vic Hadfield

---

163 Francis coached the last 50 games of the 1965/66 season.

164 Francis coached the last 12 games of the 1981/82 season.

165 Francis coached the first 32 games of the 1982/83 season.

166 *Vic Hadfield's Diary*, Vic Hadfield with Tim Moriarty, p. 81.

Emile Francis is the greatest coach in New York Rangers history. Scrappy, cerebral, inventive, innovative, insightful, and determined, Francis brought life and light back to the eyes to Rangers fans from 1965 to 1975 and helped keep NHL hockey in St. Louis during an extremely difficult period in Blues franchise history.

Francis played goalie for the Chicago Blackhawks and New York Rangers during the 1940s and 1950s. It was Francis (who played multiple sports in his youth) who got the idea of combining a first-baseman's baseball glove with a hockey glove. The end result is the catcher's glove that goalies all over the world use today. (Francis never thought to patent his invention.)

When his playing career ended, Francis worked in the Rangers farm system, coaching the Guelph Royals. Many of the prospects he signed would later play key roles when he coached the Rangers. He became the Rangers general manager in 1964, but by 1965 he was doubling as their head coach too.

The Rangers had been in the doldrums since the end of the Second World War, making only six playoff appearances since 1941/42. Their last Stanley Cup final had been in 1949/50, when Francis was still a reserve goalie for Chuck Rayner.

Francis said in a 2009 interview that he made comprehensive changes in the Rangers organization, not just with personnel but also with the team's facilities. Instead of using the inadequate practice rink at the old Madison Square Garden, Francis had a brand-new practice facility built in Long Island. Vic Hadfield writes in his diary of the 1972/73 season that Francis made sure that the travelling and hotel conditions were "first class."[167]

Francis states that he expanded the team's scouting corps and he wanted to beef up the offence, saying, "I believed in speed; people who could skate, win 60 percent of faceoffs. I kept track of everything: giveaways, takeaways . . . using films as a coaching tool."

It wasn't just speed that Francis emphasized. It was physicality too. Francis's philosophy was "play the man," saying, "the more hits you had the more shots on goal you could get. I wanted my teams to have a minimum forty hits per game."

To encourage contact, Francis had a bounty system of $5 per hit. (Back then, with low player salaries, $5 was a lot of money, and Francis would later say with a

---

167 Ibid. p. 17

chuckle that there were considerable arguments among the Rangers players about who got the most hits after each game.)

His changes paid off when the Rangers made it to the 1966/67 Stanley Cup playoffs. Although they were swept by Montreal ("We didn't have the depth!" Francis laments), all four games were hotly contested affairs.

Francis says, "Year by year, we kept getting better."

Indeed, offensively, from 1969/70 to 1973/74, the Rangers were always among the top four teams in goals scored and power-play offence. Defensively, from 1968/69 to 1973/74, the Rangers were always among the top five in defence and penalty-killing.

Former Rangers winger Ted Irvine tells George Grimm, "The beauty of that hockey club was that every guy on that team knew what each other's job was. So if we held a team to no goals, a guy like Jean Ratelle would tell us how great we played even though he might have gotten a hat trick. So we really respected each other and our jobs and it made it very easy to play in New York because we all knew what out roles were."

Another key aspect of Francis's Rangers was their on-ice discipline. Yes, he wanted his players to be aggressive and physical, but he didn't want them playing stupid hockey, committing unnecessary penalties. Once the NHL expanded in 1967, Francis's Rangers began reducing their time spent in the penalty box and by the 1970s were always near the bottom of the NHL in team penalty minutes.

Francis coached and/or developed many of the greatest players in New York Rangers history: Rod Gilbert, Jean Ratelle, Brad Park, Eddie Giacomin, and Harry Howell all earned Hall of Fame honours after playing for Francis. Gilbert remains the all-time Rangers goalscorer and was a two-time NHL All-Star. Jean Ratelle was a two-time Lady Byng Trophy winner. Blue-liner Harry Howell won the only Norris Trophy of his career in 1966/67 under Francis. Brad Park became a four-time Norris Trophy runner-up and a five-time NHL All-Star defenceman. Park and Bobby Orr were the two greatest defencemen of the NHL's first expansion era, from 1967 to 1979, under Emile Francis.

Francis's biggest coup was goalie Eddie Giacomin. There was great skepticism in hockey circles when the Rangers signed Giacomin and made him a starter. But Francis says that he saw Giacomin's determination and courage between the pipes, that Giacomin (despite playing for sub-par minor league teams) never gave up as a player.

Francis harnessed Giacomin's competitive drive and put solid defensive talent in front of him. Giacomin, in return, justified Francis's faith in him by being the 1966/67 Hart Trophy runner-up and winning the 1970/71 Vezina Trophy with goaltending partner Gilles Villemure.

Still, it's not enough to acquire and retain talent. A great coach has to mould and combine the talent until it jells, coalesces, and hardens into a singular entity that can skate, shoot, and defend intuitively, instinctively, and aggressively.

Again, Ted Irvine tells hockey writer George Grimm, "Emile was very good at designing the kind of hockey club he wanted. There was the Ratelle line that scored goals and you had the (Bill) Fairbairn, (Steve) Vickers and (Walt) Tkaczuk line that was kind of a checking and scoring line. Then he put (Pete) Stemkowski, (Bruce) MacGregor and I together as a pure checking line."

In many ways, Emile Francis was way ahead of the curve among his fellow hockey coaches and general managers. When the present NHL Players' Association began in 1967, Francis (unlike Punch Imlach of Toronto) saw the writing on the wall and dealt honestly and fairly with the new union, maintaining peace and harmony with his players.

When the WHA in 1972 made inroads on the NHL, luring away top players with huge salary offers, Francis (unlike Milt Schmidt and Harry Sinden of Boston) promptly renegotiated his contracts with his prime players, thus preventing any major defections to the new league.

Sadly, despite his efforts, Francis never won the Stanley Cup. The Rangers did make four consecutive Stanley Cup semifinal appearances from 1970/71 to 1973/74 (no other Rangers coach has done so since); and in 1971/72 they made it all the way to the Stanley Cup finals only to be beaten in six games by the Boston Bruins.

The following season saw the Rangers get their revenge on the Bruins when they beat Boston in the first round of the 1972/73 playoffs. The Bruins were the defending Stanley Cup champions, yet the Rangers held Boston to only 11 goals in five games – with Bobby Orr only scoring one goal throughout the entire series.

How did New York shut down the big, bad Bruins? What happened bore all the hallmarks of Emile Francis's tactical hockey genius; his keen eye for discerning weaknesses in his opponents through extensive film analysis; his willingness to take calculated risks in order to steal victories not only in single games but in whole series as well.

The stratagem Francis devised not only led to the Rangers winning the series, but it also inspired Philadelphia Flyers head coach Fred Shero (himself a keen film analyzer) to use the same tactic to beat the Bruins in the 1973/74 Stanley Cup finals.

Vic Haldfield (who chronicled the 1972/73 season in a diary) writes,

> We watched films of our last two regular season games against the Bruins and we came up with a plan to reduce Bobby's effectiveness. Have you ever noticed how Orr likes to take the puck behind his own net and then move out? In the past he used to be a threat to go all the way to the other team's blue line before passing. But his bad knees caused him to change his style. He might still give you one or two moves like that during a game, but most of the time he looks to pass off.
>
> Emile decided that on those occasions when Orr led the attack we would watch which route he takes – it's usually the right side – and then flood that area. Two men would encircle him, make him work harder, and put added pressure on him and his weak knees. The third forward on our attacking line would then act like a free safety in football. His job was to anticipate the pass and move in front of the likely receiver. There was some risk involved here because it left an open man on the other side, but we relied on the defense to back us up.
>
> Orr had trouble spotting that open man anyway because of our two forecheckers. And when he tried to pass to the other side, our free safety was there to intercept or knock the receiver off the puck.[168]

That tactic shut down the Bruins' offence. They also exploited a chink in the Boston defence when they noticed that Bruins blue-liner Don Awrey liked to rush up to attack the opposing team's puck handlers, leaving Orr by himself in the Boston zone.

---

168 *Vic Hadfield's Diary*, Vic Hadfield with Tim Moriarty, p. 124.

The Cat told his centres to hit the right wing with a pass behind Awrey or else dump the puck deep into the corner of the Boston zone – thus generating more scoring chances for the Rangers offence.[169]

The strategy worked. New York outscored the Bruins 22–11 in five games to get revenge, but sadly the Rangers lost the semifinals to Billy Reay's Chicago Blackhawks in five games. The Rangers offence deserted them, scoring only three goals in the last three games of the series.

In 1973/74 they came within an ace of making it to the finals again but were edged out by the Philadelphia Flyers (in my opinion, the Rangers gave the Flyers a sterner test than the Bruins did that year).

When new ownership took over the Rangers in 1974 and began interfering with Francis's leadership, he endured it for one season before getting fired and moving on to the St. Louis Blues.

The Cat left the frying pan and landed into the fire. Francis as general manager, coach, and part-owner of the Blues waged a desperate eight-year struggle to keep the Blues franchise operating. The reason why the Blues remain in St. Louis today is because of Francis's unstinting efforts.

After 1983, Francis left the Blues and became general manager of the Hartford Whalers until 1989.

As of 2015, he lives in retirement in Florida and remains a keen observer of hockey today and an invaluable looking-glass into the NHL's glorious past. His insights and analyses of the game are penetrating and magnificent. He truly and richly deserved his 1982 induction into the Hockey Hall of Fame as a builder.

169 Ibid, p. 125.

TODD MCLELLAN RANK #38

PLUS: 44
MINUS: 2
VALUE: +42
PEAK RATING: #38 in 2013/14
PEAK VALUE: +42 in 2013/14

COACHING EXPERIENCE: San Jose Sharks, 2008–2015; Edmonton Oilers, 2015–present

REGULAR SEASON W–L–OL: 311–163–66
PLAYOFF W–L: 30–32

PRESIDENT'S TROPHY: 2008/09

PACIFIC DIVISION TITLES: 2008/09–2010/11

PLAYOFF APPEARANCES: 2008/09–2013/14

Before he resigned as the San Jose Sharks head coach in 2015, Todd McLellan had been an NHL coach in a hurry. After seven seasons of coaching, he brought himself (and the San Jose Sharks) to the brink of greatness. In 2012/13 he became the winningest coach in San Jose Sharks history when he surpassed Ron Wilson in wins.

Todd McLellan is a product of the Mike Babcock coaching tree. A mark of a top-notch coach is their ability to inspire others to pursue coaching careers – especially if they can excel at coaching as their mentor did. McLellan, who served as an assistant coach under Babcock, roared out of the blocks when he became head coach of the Sharks.

McLellan was drafted by the New York Islanders in 1986 but played only briefly for them. Most of his professional playing career was spent in the minors, where he was an injury-prone centre.

In 1989 McLellan played hockey in Europe for three years before hanging up the skates for good. It was in Europe that he had his first coaching experience working as a player-coach for a team in the Netherlands.

Todd McLellan started coaching full-time in 1993 in junior hockey in Saskatchewan and later in the WHL, where he did very well.

When the 21st century dawned, McLellan was coaching in the Minnesota Wild farm system, first in the IHL and later the AHL – where he won the Calder Cup in 2002/03.

(If Todd McLellan ever coaches a Stanley Cup winner, he will become only the seventh coach in hockey history to coach both a Calder and a Stanley Cup winner.)

When Mike Babcock took over as head coach of the Detroit Red Wings, he hired McLellan as an assistant coach, making him responsible for coaching the team's forwards, managing the Wing's power-play offence, and performing overall player evaluations.

McLellan excelled in his role, helping the Wings finish among the top three in power-play offence and power-play percentage twice in three years. During their 2007/08 Stanley Cup win, the Red Wings scored 20 power-play goals in 22 playoff games.

It was time for McLellan to chart his own course. When the San Jose Sharks fired Ron Wilson as their head coach, they replaced him with McLellan.

Todd McLellan made his name right away when he led the Sharks to their first President's Trophy win as a franchise. Their performance in 2008/09 remains a team record in wins, team points, and winning percentage. In the process, McLellan became only the third person ever to win the President's Trophy in his rookie season as an NHL coach (the first two were Terry Crisp in 1987/88 and Mike Milbury in 1989/90).

McLellan won three consecutive Pacific Division titles and twice led the Sharks to the Western Conference finals. Unfortunately, McLellan suffers from the same malady of playoff futility that afflicts Dave Tippett and Bruce Boudreau (see "Heartbreak Coaches" in Part Four). Sadly for McLellan, four of his six playoff defeats have come at the hands of the team that eventually won the Stanley Cup.

That failure to reach the Stanley Cup finals (let alone win the Cup) has cost McLellan in terms of plus points and enhancing his coaching value. It is the main reason why McLellan does not rank higher in the top 50, whereas other coaches like Dan Bylsma and Claude Julien have surpassed him simply because they could take their teams to the Stanley Cup finals and win the Cup.

What was Todd McLellan's formula for success?

In his first two seasons, McLellan had a well-balanced team, finishing in the top ten in offence, defence, power-play offence, penalty-killing, and short-handed offence.

Then, from 2010 to 2012, the Sharks slipped up on defence, penalty-killing, and in short-handed offence. The team was rebuilding, and the process altered the Sharks' tactical balance for a time.

Todd McLellan patiently filled in the gaps in his roster and by 2013/14 had restored the team's two-way strength on offence and defence.

McLellan's strength derived from his enormous depth at the centre position: Patrick Marleau (who also plays left wing), Logan Couture, Joe Thornton, and Joe Pavelski are all first-rate point producers. Couture is emerging as a bright young star on the Sharks and has shown great skill on the power play, while Pavelski earned All-Star honours in 2013/14.

Defensively, the Sharks' strength was derived from veteran blue-liner Dan Boyle (who earned All-Star honors under McLellan in 2008/09 before leaving the Sharks in 2014) and goalie Antti Niemi, whom the Sharks stole from the Stanley Cup champion Blackhawks via free agency. Defencemen Brent Burns, Justin Braun, Jason Demers, and Marc-Edouard Vlasic also provide quality efforts to the Sharks.

The 2012/13 season was McLellan's sternest test yet as a head coach. After going unbeaten in their first eight games, the Sharks endured a horrible slump, going 5–10–5 into springtime.

There was talk in hockey circles that McLellan's job was in jeopardy, but in a great display of his coaching genius, McLellan rallied the team. The Sharks went on a 13–6–1 surge to clinch the sixth-seed berth in the Western Conference playoffs. (Considering the fact that the Sharks have been an aging team in transition since 2010, their late-season rally really was an affirmation of McLellan's coaching skill.)

For a brief, shining moment, the Sharks appeared ready to shake off their mantle of playoff futility. Their sweep of the Vancouver Canucks was a dazzling display of their offensive strength. Seven of the 15 goals they scored against Vancouver came on the power play. Defensively, they held the Canucks to only eight goals. (It was the first playoff sweep win in McLellan's NHL coaching career.)

In 2013/14 McLellan led the Sharks to triple digits in team points and were the fifth-best team in the NHL, but, again, McLellan's lack of playoff luck returned with a vengeance when the Sharks blew a 3–0 series lead to lose to the Los Angeles Kings in the first round of the playoffs.

The humiliating loss spilt over into the following season. The Sharks stumbled out the gate, had a brief spurt in December but went 22–21–5 for the remainder of the season. It was the first time in McLellan's NHL coaching career that his team failed to make the playoffs. On April 20, 2015, he and the Sharks parted ways.

McLellan was not unemployed for very long. On May 29, 2015, he was hired by the Edmonton Oilers to be their head coach. Edmonton is a team long on young offensive lions like Taylor Hall, Ryan Nugent-Hopkins, and Nail Yakupov but are woefully deficient in defence and goal-tending. The Oilers have won the 2015 NHL draft lottery which means they will get to draft *wunderkind* centre Connor McDavid who has burned up the Ontario Hockey League with his exceptional shooting and playmaking skills.

In 2008, Todd McLellan took over a veteran team in San Jose that was set in its ways and was transitioning with great difficulty. In 2015, Todd McLellan takes over a very young team that possesses talent that needs to be sculpted, molded, refined, and taught to become winners, playoff contenders, and, hopefully, future Stanley Cup champions.

MARC CRAWFORD RANK #39

PLUS: 78
MINUS: 36
VALUE: +42
PEAK RANK: #19 in 1997/98
PEAK RATING: +60 in 2003/04

COACHING EXPERIENCE: Quebec Nordiques, 1994/95; Colorado Avalanche, 1995–1998; Vancouver Canucks, 1998[170]–2006; Los Angeles Kings, 2006–2008; Dallas Stars, 2009–2011

REGULAR SEASON W–L–T–OL: 549–421–103–78
PLAYOFF W–L: 43–40
JACK ADAMS AWARD: 1994/95

PRESIDENT'S TROPHY: 1996/97

NORTHEAST DIVISION TITLE: 1994/95
PACIFIC DIVISION TITLES: 1995–1998
NORTHWEST DIVISION TITLE: 2003/04

PLAYOFF APPEARANCES: 1994/95–1997/98, 1999/00, 2001/02–2003/04
STANLEY CUP FINAL: 1995/96
STANLEY CUP VICTORY: 1995/96

Marc Crawford is the third-youngest NHL coach ever to win the Stanley Cup and was one of the best offensive hockey coaches of his time. Crawford's teams finished in the top ten in offence eight times, in power-play offence twelve times, and in short-handed offence ten times. Still, it's interesting to note

170 Crawford coached the last 37 games of the 1998/99 season.

that despite his reputation as an offensive genius, Crawford never coached a Ross Trophy winner.

The only time Crawford achieved the tactical balance needed to win championships was when he was leading the Colorado Avalanche. There, he had combined strength in offence and defence while possessing equal strength with his special teams. It was after he left Colorado that his teams were strong offensively but below average in defence and penalty-killing – with the inevitable result that his teams were never competitive in the playoffs.

Marc Crawford was a high-scoring winger in junior hockey and was drafted in 1980 by the Vancouver Canucks. He spent his entire NHL playing career in Vancouver but never achieved the same level of productivity with the Canucks as he did in junior. From 1981 to 1987, Crawford constantly shuttled back and forth between Vancouver and the minors. He was on the roster, though, when Roger Neilson led the Canucks to the 1981/82 Stanley Cup finals.

When his playing career ended in 1988, Crawford went immediately into coaching, but it wasn't until the 1991/92 season that he made a name for himself as a coach working in the Toronto farm system. It was there he linked up with Joel Quenneville and began a coaching partnership.

In 1994 the Quebec Nordiques (who had fallen on hard times) hired Crawford to be their head coach. Crawford (along with Quenneville) joined Jacques Martin to forge one of the greatest coaching staffs in NHL history.

Crawford is renowned for always hiring high-powered assistant coaches. In the book *Simply the Best*, Crawford explains to authors Mike Johnston and Ryan Walter that "I'm a delegator, there's no doubt about that. When Jacques Martin was my assistant in Colorado he told me that one of my best qualities was delegating really well. I have realized that it's important to have people around me who have very strong organizational skills, because I don't."[171]

Crawford wasted no time making his presence felt in the NHL. Behind the great play of Calder Trophy winner Peter Forsberg, Crawford's Nordiques were

171 *Simply the Best*, Mike Johnston and Ryan Walter, p. 66.

the second-best team in the NHL, and Crawford became the only NHL coach ever to win the Jack Adams Award in his rookie season as a coach. Crawford had enormous scoring talent in Forsberg and Joe Sakic, while blue-liner Sandis Ozolinsh and goalie Patrick Roy shored up the defence.

In his sophomore year, he shepherded his players through a franchise shift from Quebec to Colorado, where the Avalanche once again were the second-best team in the NHL. This time, in 1995/96, Crawford would not be denied. The Avs went 16–6 in the playoffs (beating Scotty Bowman's Red Wings in the conference finals in the process).

The team faced the expansion Florida Panthers in their only Stanley Cup finals appearance ever. It was no contest: Colorado declawed the Panthers – holding them to five goals in a four-game sweep.

The Avalanche won the President's Trophy in 1996/97 but could not repeat as Stanley Cup champions. After Colorado failed to make the Stanley Cup conference finals in 1997/98, Crawford resigned as head coach and was given a new challenge when Vancouver hired him to replace Mike Keenan. Crawford spent seven seasons in Vancouver but never reached the same heights with the Canucks as he did in Colorado. (As mentioned, it was because Crawford never got the same defensive performance from his Canucks, Kings, and Stars teams that he did with the Avalanche.) Crawford did, however, produce All-Star performances from Markus Naslund and Todd Bertuzzi and did become (until the arrival of Alain Vigneault) the greatest coach in Canucks history.

After 2004, Crawford's coaching stock declined sharply. In 2006 he was fired by the Canucks and went to Los Angeles but failed to make any progress there. He was let go by the Kings in 2008 and was unemployed until the beginning of the 2009/10 season when the Dallas Stars hired him to replace the departed Dave Tippett.

Marc Crawford spent two years with Dallas and coaxed winning seasons out of the team but failed to make the playoffs both years – which is why he was fired in April 2011 and has not returned to NHL coaching since.

ROGER NEILSON RANK #40

PLUS: 59
MINUS: 17
VALUE: +42
PEAK RANK: #26 in 1999/00
PEAK RATING: +42 in 1999/00

COACHING EXPERIENCE: Toronto Maple Leafs, 1977–1979; Buffalo Sabres, 1980/81; Vancouver Canucks, 1982[172]–1984[173]; Los Angeles Kings, 1984[174]; New York Rangers, 1989–1993[175]; Florida Panthers, 1993–1995; Philadelphia Flyers, 1998[176]–2000; Ottawa Senators, 2002[177]

REGULAR SEASON W–L–T–OL: 460–378–159–3
PLAYOFF W–L: 51–55

PRESIDENT'S TROPHY: 1991/92

ADAMS DIVISION TITLE: 1980/81
PATRICK DIVISION TITLES: 1989/90, 1991/92
ATLANTIC DIVISION TITLE: 1999/00

PLAYOFF APPEARANCES: 1977/78–1982/83, 1989/90–1991/92, 1998/99–1999/00
STANLEY CUP FINAL: 1981/82

172 Neilson coached the last 5 games of the 1981/82 season.
173 Neilson coached the first 48 games of the 1983/84 season.
174 Neilson coached the last 28 games of the 1983/84 season.
175 Neilson coached the first 40 games of the 1992/93 season.
176 Neilson coached the last 21 games of the 1997/98 season.
177 Neilson coached the last 2 games of the 2001/02 season.

"Roger Neilson . . . was extremely influential in my evolution as a hockey player and coach. Roger had the brightest hockey mind I've ever encountered. The man was brilliant, innovative, visionary."[178]

Bruce Boudreau

Roger Neilson loved life, he loved his God, he loved people, he loved hockey, and he loved coaching.

It didn't matter whether he was coaching in midget, junior, the minors, or the NHL.

It didn't matter whether he was a head coach, associate coach, or assistant coach.

It didn't matter whether he was working with players or with videotape.

It didn't matter what city he was working in.

No other NHL coach was hired (and fired) as much as Neilson was.

None of that mattered because he loved doing what he was doing, and by doing what he loved doing he touched the lives of so many people that his influence endures today, a decade after his death, and will continue to do so for years to come.

Neilson lived 69 years and five days in chronological terms, but he packed more living, more work, and more human outreach in those 69 years and five days than most people do in 100 years.

Several of Neilson's players who learned hockey at his knee later went on to become great players in the NHL: Doug Jarvis, Rick Macleish, Craig Ramsay, and Bob Gainey, to name a few.

And even more significantly, Neilson's scholarly approach to hockey inspired so many of his acolytes to become superb coaches in their own right. Many of those featured in this book – Jacques Martin, Marc Crawford, Lindy Ruff, Bruce Boudreau, Joel Quenneville, Randy Carlyle, and Ron Wilson – either played for or were guided by Neilson. All could be seen as products of the Roger Neilson coaching tree.

Another example of how Neilson's legacy endures today is the fact that the former coach of the Edmonton Oilers, Dallas Eakins, played for Neilson when he was coaching the Peterborough Petes and became a lifelong friend. Eakins became a hockey coach and performed well at the minor league level before finally entering the NHL coaching ranks in 2013.

---

178 *Gabby: Confessions Of A Hockey Lifer*, Bruce Boudreau and Tim Leone, p. 31.

Each of these men carries with them the ethics and spirit of Roger Neilson, and by teaching others (like Neilson taught them), they perpetuate his memory and enhance his long-term influence on the sport of hockey.

Roger Neilson never played in the NHL. He began his coaching career right after he finished his schooling. Neilson was the forerunner for other coaches, such as Pat Burns, Bryan Murray, Mike Babcock, and Bob Hartley, who, unable to play in the NHL themselves, pursued their love of hockey by coaching, working at all levels and capacities before reaching the NHL and achieving success and stature there.

During the 1950s, 1960s, and 1970s, Neilson coached bantam, junior, and minor league hockey (while doing some scouting on the side for Scotty Bowman – the start of a long and complex relationship with him).

Neilson was multifaceted. He was born into an intensely religious household yet never flaunted his faith. He rendered unto hockey the things that belonged to hockey, but he also rendered unto God the things that belonged to God. (Leafs legend Ron Ellis writes in his memoir *Over The Boards* that one factor in his returning to play hockey after a two-year retirement was because Roger Neilson was a Christian, like he was.)[179]

Yes, Roger Neilson was a born-again Christian, and yet he could be quite the trickster when he had to be.

He had an encyclopedic knowledge of the rulebook and devised tactics to exploit any loopholes he could find. This led to major rule changes to stop him. Neilson wasn't cheating. If the rules did not specifically prohibit a certain action on the ice, then Neilson would exploit that loophole until the league closed it. (This trait led to the creation of Neilson's legendary moniker, "Rulebook Roger.")

He was tireless and a workaholic, capable of staying up for days breaking down videotape and yet dozing off in the middle of conversations with coaches, players, parents, and friends while at his desk or behind the wheel of his car.

Neilson was innovative and industrious, earning another nickname, "Captain Video," because he extensively used videotape as a coaching tool. His use of

---

179 *Over the Boards: The Ron Ellis Story*, Ron Ellis with Kevin Shea, p. 162.

modern conditioning methods during training camp and the off-season for his players is now standard procedure for all hockey teams. He was the man who invented the term *scoring chances* because he thought shots-on-goal was a meaningless statistic. Today *scoring chances* is now a widely used statistic and a part of coaching nomenclature.

When he was an associate coach with the Buffalo Sabres, he prevailed upon the Motorola Company to devise wireless radio headsets so he could relay information in real time to assistant coach Jim Roberts, who then fed the data for Scotty Bowman to use during games. (Neilson had to apply to the U.S. Federal Communications Commission to get a licence to do this and amazingly he got one).[180]

Neilson could be maddeningly brilliant and also the absent-minded professor, intensely focused and yet lost at sea (literally, as his boating mishaps could be as bad as his driving mishaps).

Opera bouffe and bathos were always intrinsic to the life of Roger Neilson.

In 1977 Roger Neilson became the head coach of the struggling Toronto Maple Leafs. In his rookie season, he led the Leafs to their first Stanley Cup semifinal appearance since 1967 – losing to the Montreal Canadiens in four games.

Neilson was an inspiration to the Leafs players. Tiger Williams (who played for Neilson in Toronto and Vancouver) writes, "He built his reputation . . . with disciplined teams who were always willing to goon it up in a tight situation. . . . No one ever watched more video, poured himself more fully into the technicalities of the game; but at the end of the day, he never lost sight of the fact that the most vital component of a consistently winning team is character – and the ability to impose real physical strength."[181]

It was Neilson's misfortune to coach in Toronto during the Harold Ballard era. Like so many others, Neilson suffered under Ballard's antics before he was fired in 1979.

---

180 "Read You, Roger, Wilco and Out", Kathy Blumenstock, *Sports Illustrated*, April, 21, 1980.

181 *Tiger: A Hockey Story*, Tiger Williams with James Lawton, p. 103.

Neilson won with defence and penalty-killing. In their book *Simply the Best*, Neilson told authors Mike Johnston and Ryan Walter, "I've always felt that if a team has reasonable talent, in other words they are in the ballpark, and are sound defensively because that's something every team can be; then you are going to be in most games. You can't always be great offensively, because that depends on your talent. The foundation is to be sound defensively."[182]

Chris Nilan (who played with Neilson in New York) discusses one of Neilson's motivational approaches: "Before a game, Neilson, at practice, would have a sheet of paper with the names of every player on the opposing team with a brief quote beside each player's name listing their strengths and weaknesses. Sometimes the quotes were really funny like 'this guy is too fat and he can't skate' or something goofy like that. He was the only coach I knew who would do that for every opposing player. Roger demanded accountability, hard work, and focus from every player. I liked him. He was a great guy, a fair guy, loved video, understood players and was up-to-date on everything in the game."

Another Neilson facet was the power play. Offensively, his teams were always average, but in power-play situations, they were among the best in hockey.

Significantly, Neilson created a system of hockey that did not demand sterling talent but instead could elevate players with marginal skills into accomplishing more on the ice as long as they adhered to his systems. As Bob Pulford puts it, "Roger Neilson had the ability to get his players to play above their talent."

Roger Neilson went to the Buffalo Sabres as an associate coach to Scotty Bowman. When Bowman decided to focus solely on his general manager duties, Neilson became head coach, leading the Sabres to the Adams Division title in the 1980/81 season (and a second-round playoff elimination). A dispute with Bowman led to Neilson's firing from Buffalo, whereupon he became an associate coach to Harry Neale in Vancouver – and had an impending date with fame.

By 1981 the Canucks had underachieved for 11 seasons. The 1981/82 season appeared to be no different. The Canucks had a losing season and finished a

182 *Simply the Best*, Mike Johnston and Ryan Walter, p. 276.

distant second (34 points) behind the Edmonton Oilers in the Smythe Division. When Harry Neale was suspended for eight games after getting into an altercation with a fan, Neilson was tapped to finish the regular season and lead the Canucks into the playoffs.

That's when a funny thing happened on the way to the PNE Coliseum in Vancouver. Over the course of five regular-season and 13 playoff games, Neilson led the Canucks to a 15–2–1 record and their first Stanley Cup finals appearance in franchise history (someone could make a very entertaining movie about the Canucks playoff run in 1981/82).

Neilson later told Dick Irvin Jr. in his book *Behind the Bench*, "That year in the playoffs was one of those situations where all of a sudden a team with not a great amount of talent goes on a roll. Our goalkeeper Richard Brodeur was unbelievable, and it seemed everyone on the team played the best hockey of their career for a period of twenty-five games."[183]

The question is: How did it happen?

Despite their losing record, Neilson led a team that had the fourth-best defence in the NHL and, more significantly, had the best defence of any team in the Campbell Conference.

The Canucks were the fourth seed in the conference playoffs but got a huge break when the top three seeds were all eliminated in the first round. The surviving teams were weaker and fell accordingly. Lastly, as Neilson said, goalie Richard Brodeur played the greatest hockey of his career and would have been a shoe-in for the Conn Smythe Trophy if the Canucks had won the Cup.

Neilson showed his tactical wizardry throughout. During the semifinals against Chicago, Neilson knew that the only way they could win was to shut down Blackhawks sharpshooter Denis Savard. After losing Game 2 against Chicago (where Savard scored two goals), he did so by assigning a checking line of Gerry Minor, Tiger Williams, and Lars Molin to shadow Savard on the ice. Savard scored only one goal in the last three games of the series.

Opposing coaches damned Vancouver's defensive prowess. Al Arbour derided it as "Clutch, grab, tackle. Holding onto sweaters. Dump it out, dump it out. That's

---

183 *Behind the Bench*, Dick Irvin, p. 217.

the way they play. They try to frustrate you and they'll use the same tactics the whole series."[184]

And what angered opposing coaches most of all was that it worked (at least until the Stanley Cup finals).

It was also during that amazing stretch that Neilson became a part of hockey folklore when he performed the legendary towel-waving incident as a protest against the poor officiating that took place during Game 2 of the semifinals against Chicago. Towel-waving during playoff time is now de rigueur for hockey fans all over the NHL.

During the Stanley Cup finals against the New York Islanders, the Canucks were swept – Games 1 and 2 were close defeats, but as Neilson later told Irvin, "We had nothing left. We just didn't have any offence at all. The legs were gone."[185]

It was the only time Neilson reached the Stanley Cup finals.

He bounced around the NHL, working in Vancouver, Edmonton, Los Angeles, and Chicago before getting the New York Rangers' head coaching job in 1989. Neilson worked wonders with the Rangers, leading them to two divisional titles and winning the President's Trophy in 1991/92 as the NHL's best team. But it was Neilson's misfortune that he was there when Mark Messier joined the Rangers in 1991.

Messier was a player with Hall of Fame talent . . . and a superstar ego to match. He was there to help the Rangers end their long Stanley Cup drought. When it didn't happen, it was Messier who stayed and Neilson who had to leave New York in 1993.

In 1993 the Florida Panthers chose Neilson to be their first head coach (Lindy Ruff was one of his assistants). Blessed with a strong expansion and amateur draft, Neilson led the Panthers to a league-record 83 team points. No other NHL expansion team has done as well in its debut season. Unless the NHL plans to expand again, Neilson's record will likely never be broken.

Neilson's Panthers won with defence. The Panthers were weak offensively but ranked fourth in the NHL in defence – an astounding record for an expansion team. Neilson lasted two seasons in Florida but was ousted when Panthers general manager Bryan Murray wanted to go in a different direction.

---

184 "A Great Awakening in Vancouver", E.M. Swift, *Sports Illustrated*, May 17, 1982.

185 *Behind the Bench*, Dick Irvin, p. 218.

Neilson worked as an assistant coach for Mike Keenan in St. Louis before being lured to the Philadelphia Flyers. Neilson, despite the onset of the cancer that eventually killed him, led the Flyers to three playoff appearances, a divisional title, and the third and last Stanley Cup conference final appearance of his career in 1999/00 – losing to the New Jersey Devils in seven games.

His struggle with cancer led to Neilson being replaced as the Flyers' head coach. He wound up as an assistant coach to Jacques Martin in Ottawa. In 2002 he was allowed to lead the Senators for two games, thus becoming the ninth man to coach 1,000 NHL games.

He was rightfully elected to the Hockey Hall of Fame as a builder that same year, and he was decorated by his country when he was awarded the Order of Canada.

On June 21, 2003, he died, and all of hockey mourned.

Roger Neilson's body lies in his grave, but his hockey coaching legacy goes skating on.

DAVE TIPPETT RANK #41

PLUS: 57
MINUS: 16
VALUE: +41
PEAK RANK: #25 in 2011/12
PEAK VALUE: +51 in 2011/12

COACHING EXPERIENCE: Dallas Stars, 2002–2009; Phoenix Coyotes, 2009–2014; Arizona Coyotes, 2014–present

REGULAR SEASON W–L–T–OL: 488–332–28–102
PLAYOFF W–L: 33–41

JACK ADAMS AWARD: 2009/10

PACIFIC DIVISION TITLES: 2002/03, 2005/06, 2011/12
PLAYOFF APPEARANCES: 2002/03–2007/08, 2009/10–2011/12

Dave Tippett's stock as a coach has declined drastically in recent years. In 2011/12 he reached his peak rank in terms of coaching value, but three consecutive seasons of failing to reach the playoffs has resulted in him falling sixteen steps in rank in terms of coaching value. In 2011/12 he was the sixth best active coach. As of 2014/15 Tippett is the eleventh best active coach in the NHL based on career value, according to my rating system.

His NHL coaching career can be summed up in two terms: *rebuilding projects* and *playoff futility*.

From 2002 to 2012, Tippett rebuilt two teams, making them winners and playoff competitors. Although he has shown dazzling prowess behind the bench during the regular season, his team's failure to excel in the playoffs has thus far prevented Tippett from achieving even greater glory as an NHL coach. His teams have never reached the Stanley Cup finals, and it is that signal failing that has kept Tippett from standing even higher in the pantheon of hockey coaches today (see "Heartbreak Coaches" in Part Four).

Dave Tippett was a left winger from Saskatchewan who grew up playing junior hockey there before playing two years of National Collegiate Athletic Association (NCAA) hockey at the University of North Dakota (where they won the 1982 NCAA Title).

Twice he played on the Canadian Olympic hockey team, in 1984 and 1992. (Tippett states that his Olympic coach, Dave King, influenced his own coaching style with regards to tactics.)

Tippett was drafted by the Hartford Whalers and spent most of his playing career there until the 1990s, when he bounced around with the Washington Capitals, Pittsburgh Penguins, and Philadelphia Flyers before ending his playing career in the minors in 1995.

He immediately took up coaching in the International Hockey League (IHL) and did well, winning the IHL championship in 1998/99. He then served three seasons as an assistant coach to Andy Murray with the Los Angeles Kings.

When the Dallas Stars needed a new head coach in 2002, they chose Dave Tippett. Again, Tippett did not disappoint, leading the Stars through a stellar run and in 2006/07 becoming only the seventh NHL coach ever to lead a team to two consecutive 50-win seasons.

Tippett's winning formula has been a defence-first strategy. In 12 seasons of coaching, his teams have finished in the top ten in defence seven times and in penalty-killing five times. Tippett states aphoristically that "bad penalty-killing can lose you a game more than the power-play can win you a game."

His hockey is up-tempo and pressure-based, but Tippett believes that "your tactics are based on the hand you're dealt with in terms of playing talent. The skill level of your players governs the tactics you use to win."

In a 2013 interview Tippett maintains that his early Dallas teams (before the 2004/05 lockout) possessed greater skilled players than his latter Stars teams did. When asked to compare his Stars teams with his Coyote teams, Tippett states that the "Coyotes right now are at the middle of the pack" in terms of their skill-levels. Analyzing the stats of his two teams bears this out. His Dallas teams were consistently stronger defensively than his Phoenix teams. His Coyote teams have been inconsistent in terms of overall defence and in penalty-killing.

Offensively, his teams have been average in their goal production, weak on the power play, and weaker still in short-handed offence. His Dallas and Phoenix teams were roughly equivalent in overall offence, but his Dallas teams were much better in power-play offence than his Phoenix teams. The main weakness of his Coyote squads has been their sub-par record with regards to power-play offence.

Where his Dallas and Phoenix teams differed the most was in their on-ice play. Tippett's Dallas teams were chippier on the ice, whereas his Coyote teams showed very good on-ice discipline, scrupulously avoiding the penalty box.

His idyll in Dallas ended in 2008/09 when the Stars failed to reach the playoffs for the only time in Tippett's NHL coaching career. Plagued with injuries and the emotional aftershocks of the Sean Avery soap opera (in December 2008, Avery was suspended indefinitely – later shortened to six games – by the NHL for conduct detrimental to the league and the game for remarks he made about two of his Stars teammates dating two of his former lovers, actress Elisha Cuthbert and model Rachel Hunter), the Stars barely broke above the .500 level that season, which gave Stars general manager Joe Nieuwendyk the perfect excuse to remove Tippett.

It was a big mistake. Once Tippett left, the Stars finished in the Pacific Division basement three out of the next four seasons.

When Dave Tippett was given the head coaching job of the Phoenix Coyotes one week before the 2009/10 regular season started, he was jumping from the frying pan into the fire.

The Coyotes were on a precipice, having filed for bankruptcy in May 2009, thus forcing the NHL to take over the franchise. All the while, the team had to cope with rumours of the team moving to Hamilton, Ontario.

All great coaches revel in the opportunity to salvage losing teams, but even this situation appeared on the surface too much for Tippett to handle. Franchise survival alone outweighed all other considerations.

Amazingly, Tippett defied the odds and everyone's expectations with a coaching performance that earned him the 2009/10 Jack Adams Award as the NHL coach of the year. The Coyotes won a record 50 wins and broke the 100-team-point mark for the first time in their franchise history. Phoenix was the fourth-best team in the Western Conference and made its first playoff appearance since 2001/02. Thanks to the All-Star goaltending work of Ilya Bryzgalov, the Coyotes had the third-best defence in the NHL and were sixth in penalty-killing.

Tippett believes that the one paramount quality a great hockey coach must possess is "honesty with yourself and with the players you're coaching."

Even more importantly, Tippett made his players *believers*. This is borne out by what defenceman Ed Jovanovski told Craig Custance of *The Sporting News* in 2010, "He's given each guy a role and explained his role, and each guy is doing it. He's got that calming influence about him and doesn't get rattled behind the bench. When something needs to be said, he says it loudly and clearly."

And forward Lee Stempniak, "I came over [in a trade from Toronto] and I was impressed. He has a structure that everybody sticks to, but at the same time you're skating, you can be aggressive, play and trust your instincts. He keeps everyone on the same page but allows you to keep that aggressive style of play. Everything is communication."

Tippett states that "you have to sense where the players are at: mentally and physically. You want to maintain an even keel. If you sense the players are drained then you need to give them a boost but if they're too high then you need to bring them down . . . the greatest challenge is maintaining consistency in how we play and in what we do."

In that sense, Tippett is a cool study in terms of coaching personality as opposed to someone such as Mike Keenan, who brings psychodrama to the locker room.

Sadly for Tippett and the Coyotes, they were beaten in the first round of the 2010 playoffs by the Red Wings, but they have continued to persevere (and remain, for the time being, in Arizona).

In 2011/12, the team won its first division title in Coyotes franchise history behind the All-Star work of winger Ray Whitney, while goalie Mike Smith was dazzling throughout the regular season and the early playoff rounds before losing in the Western Conference final.

Things slipped a bit after the lockout ended in 2013. Tippett explains, "We wanted to go into the off-season with a good mindset and good momentum, but the lockout took it away."

The Coyotes stumbled out of the gate, never advancing far above .500 before enduring an eight-game winless streak in March. That streak killed the Coyotes playoff hopes: although they rallied to finish above .500, they still failed to make the playoffs.

It was also the end of Tippett's coaching contract with Phoenix, and there were rumours that he might go to the Rangers. There was the possibility that the Coyotes might move to Seattle too (and the possibility that Tippett might not accompany the team to Seattle).

In the end, Tippett was given a well-deserved contract extension by the Coyotes, and the team got new owners who are committed to keeping the franchise in Arizona.

The 2013/14 started well for Tippett and the Coyotes. The team roared out of the blocks with a 14–4–3 record going into mid-November, then suddenly and mysteriously they went into a tailspin, going 15–19–8 throughout the winter until it finally stopped in early March.

Phoenix rallied at first to get back into playoff contention, but when the Coyotes went 1–4–3 in the last eight games of the season, it meant another season without a playoff berth (Phoenix finished two points behind the eighth-seeded Dallas Stars).

Dave Tippett is at the crossroads of his coaching career, and either he can help Arizona move forward and recover the lost ground from the past three seasons or else sink farther and see his reputation and NHL coaching future shrivel and die in the unrelenting heat of the Arizona desert.

LINDY RUFF RANK #42

PLUS: **59**
MINUS: **19**
VALUE: **+40**
PEAK RANK: **#37 in 2009/10**
PEAK RATING: **+41 in 2010/11**

COACHING EXPERIENCE: **Buffalo Sabres, 1997–2013[186]; Dallas Stars, 2013–present**

REGULAR SEASON W–L–T–OL: **652–494–78–105**
PLAYOFF W–L: **59–48**

JACK ADAMS AWARD: **2005/06**

PRESIDENT'S TROPHY: **2006/07**

NORTHEAST DIVISIONAL TITLES: **2006/07, 2009/10**

PLAYOFF APPEARANCES: **1997/98–2000/01, 2005/06–2006/07, 2009/10–2010/11, 2013/14**
STANLEY CUP FINAL: **1998/99**

Until he was fired on February 20, 2013, Lindy Ruff was the longest-tenured active coach in the NHL.

Before that day of reckoning, almost his entire hockey career as a player and head coach (with two exceptions) was devoted to the Buffalo Sabres.

Just as baseball's Tommy Lasorda used to say that he bled Dodger blue, I suspect that if you had cut Ruff's veins you would have found that he bled midnight blue and gold – the colours of the Buffalo Sabres.

186 Ruff coached the first 17 games of the 2012/13 season.

(Even after his firing by the Sabres, Ruff remains supportive of the franchise with the exception of when his Stars play the Sabres in league game competition).

He was drafted by Buffalo in 1979 and spent nine seasons there (during the Scotty Bowman era) as a solid if not spectacular blue-liner and occasional forward before being traded to the New York Rangers in 1988. Ruff developed his leadership skills in Buffalo. In 1986 he succeeded Sabres immortal Gilbert Perreault as team captain.

When his playing career ended in 1993, he became an assistant coach for the Florida Panthers (serving under Roger Neilson and Doug Maclean) before getting the Buffalo head coaching job in 1997.

Ruff's coaching record in Buffalo was a reflection of his playing career: solid, consistent, steady, unspectacular, and occasionally pugnacious. Twice Ruff has been fined by the NHL for complaining about officiating and also using "questionable" tactics in league games.

Not surprisingly (since he was a defenceman), his emphasis was on defensive hockey during the early years of his stay in Buffalo. He got career years from Dominik Hasek in goal.

When Hasek was with Buffalo, he won a Hart Trophy (only the second NHL goalie to do so), three Vezinas, and a Jennings Trophy.

Later, after Hasek left, Ruff got solid goaltending from Martin Biron and Ryan Miller. (Miller won the 2009/10 Vezina under Ruff's aegis.)

Despite his early successes, Ruff never won the Stanley Cup. The closest he came was in 1998/99 when the Sabres made it to the Stanley Cup finals only to lose to Ken Hitchcock's Dallas Stars in six games (victimized in the process by the controversial "no goal" scored by Brett Hull in triple overtime of Game 6 – a goal still considered one of the most controversial calls in Stanley Cup playoff history).

What's sobering is that Buffalo started that series on a promising note: stealing home-ice advantage from Dallas with a Game 1 win. But it went downhill from there. Buffalo allowed Dallas to regain home-ice advantage when they lost Game 3 at home against Dallas. The Stars' defence was too much for Buffalo – holding them to three goals total in Games 2 and 3. Also, Buffalo's offence was flawed with a weak power play. The Sabres only scored three power-play goals in six games.

Even though Buffalo rallied to win Game 4 to even the series, the Sabres' offence had lost its edge. In Games 5 and 6, the Sabres scored only one goal. Still, that Stanley Cup finals appearance was only the second time in Sabres franchise history they had gotten that far – the other was in 1974/75.

Ruff's coaching stint with Buffalo suffered its first downturn between 2001/02 and 2003/04 when the Sabres franchise nearly suffered financial collapse and the subsequent ouster and imprisonment of its owner, John Rigas, as a result of the Adelphia Communications scandal.

Ruff endured his first losing season in 2002/03, although it was during that season he became the greatest coach in Sabres franchise history (which is not bad, considering that Scotty Bowman and Punch Imlach also coached the Sabres).

After the NHL lockout ended, Ruff rebounded with a vengeance in the 2005/06 and 2006/07 seasons, setting new franchise records in team wins while winning the Jack Adams Award in 2005/06 as the league's best coach and the President's Trophy in 2006/07 as the league's best team (only to face elimination in the conference finals in both seasons).

After 2007 Ruff's career became inconsistent. Until the year he got fired, the Sabres kept winning, but their ability to excel was uneven. In the last five full seasons of his coaching career in Buffalo, Ruff earned only two playoff berths and was eliminated in the first round both times. He did win the Northeast Division title in 2009/10, but that was his last hurrah in Buffalo.

In 2011 Terry Pegula purchased the Sabres and promptly informed its fans that "Starting today, the Buffalo Sabres reason for existence, will be to win the Stanley Cup." Unfortunately for Ruff, he failed to do so in 2010/11 and failed to even reach the playoffs in 2011/12.

When the Sabres started off the 2012/13 season in the Northeast Division basement, Pegula through Darcy Regier pulled the trigger on Ruff. In truth, the team was in free fall tactically. Offensive and defensive productivity had declined drastically. The Sabres' special teams were equally bad. (Although the team rallied to finish at .500, they still finished last in the Northeast Division.)

When Ruff was fired, I was convinced that his NHL coaching career was at an end. Ruff's coaching value had declined from +41 in 2010/11 back down to +37 in 2012/13. He was being surpassed by his peers, and one got the impression that perhaps his time had come and passed.

And yet, amazingly, he was reborn on June 21, 2013, when, ironically, the Dallas Stars hired him to become their new head coach. The Stars had cleaned house, firing general manager Joe Nieuwendyk and replacing him with long-time Red Wings assistant general manager Jim Nill.

A new era had begun in Dallas and Nill (at the press conference announcing Ruff's hiring) proclaimed, "One of the trademarks of successful organizations is their ability to have continuity and stability for an extended period of time. It is clear from Lindy's record, and from our conversations, that we have found the right person to provide that stability and lead this club to the next level. His steady hand and experience will prove invaluable in returning our team as a top-tier contender in the NHL."

Dallas had been in free fall ever since 2007/08, undergoing three coaching changes and three last-place finishes in the Pacific Division in five years.

But for Lindy Ruff, life began anew, and this time he was facing an even greater coaching challenge than he did when he took the head coaching job in Buffalo.

In 1997 he inherited a team that had won the division title the season before. In 2013 he was inheriting a team that finished in the Pacific Division basement and under realignment would be forced to compete in a more densely crowded and highly competitive division.

His place among the top 50 was literally hanging in the balance. If he led the Stars to another last-place finish, he would have been knocked out of the top 50 altogether, according to my rating system. It wasn't solely his career that was at risk; his standing in the annals of NHL coaching history was at risk too.

Did Lindy Ruff have the right stuff to regain the lost ground?

It was slow going at first. Dallas hovered at .500 at the start before going on a burst that took them to eight games above .500 by New Year's Eve 2013. The Stars dimmed for three weeks in January, with the team dragging at 21–20–8. During the final stretch run, the team began putting wins in the bank, going 19–11–3 to clinch the eighth seed in the Western Conference.

The Stars did not dominate in any of the team stats. Mostly they won due to the shooting of Tyler Seguin (acquired from the Boston Bruins) and the goaltending of Kari Lehtonen.

Dallas was brave in the first round, keeping the series even in the first four games before allowing Anaheim to win Game 5 in Anaheim and steal a Game 6 victory in overtime in Dallas.

Lindy Ruff regained three points in career value but remained stagnant at 42nd place in the top 50 ranks. It was a nice beginning in Big D.

Sadly, for Lindy Ruff, he brought the inconsistency that dogged his final years in Buffalo with him. In 2014/15, the Stars were mediocre, vying with the Colorado Avalanche for last place in the Central Division. Despite a surge at the end, the Stars failed to reach the playoffs, finishing sixth, five points away from playoff contention.

JIMMY SKINNER RANK #43

PLUS: 39
MINUS: 0
VALUE: +39
PEAK RATING: +39 in 1956/57
PEAK RANK: #10 in 1956/57

COACHING EXPERIENCE: Detroit Red Wings, 1954–1958[187]

REGULAR SEASON W–L–T: 123–78–46
PLAYOFF W–L: 14–12

PRINCE OF WALES TROPHIES: 1954/55, 1956/57

PLAYOFF APPEARANCES: 1954/55–1956/57
STANLEY CUP FINALS: 1954/55–1955/56
STANLEY CUP VICTORY: 1954/55

When Tommy Ivan left the Detroit Red Wings in 1954 to work for the Chicago Blackhawks, Wings general manager Jack Adams didn't have to look very far for his replacement. The man he chose, Jimmy Skinner, had already devoted more than a decade of his hockey career to serving the Red Wings franchise (as a player and minor league coach). Even though his coaching reign with the Wings lasted only three and a half seasons, Skinner continued to work for the Red Wings in various capacities (chief scout and farm director, director of player personnel, and general manager) until his retirement.

He was born and raised in Manitoba and played hockey there, where he attracted the attention of the New York Rangers and was offered a contract to play for their organization (an offer he turned down because they didn't offer enough money in his eyes). The Rangers' loss proved to be a gain for the Detroit Red Wings.

---

187 Skinner coached the first 37 games of the 1957/58 season.

Skinner caught the eye of Jack Adams, who signed him and sent him to the Wings' minor league affiliates in Indianapolis and later Omaha, Nebraska (where for a season he was a teammate of Gordie Howe). Skinner was an injury-prone defenceman who had great speed and checking ability on the ice, but when injuries curtailed his playing career, Adams prevailed upon Skinner to become a coach.

He coached junior teams in Windsor and Hamilton, Ontario, developing future Red Wings stars such as Glenn Hall, Johnny Wilson, Glen Skov, and Al Arbour. His big moment came in 1954 when Tommy Ivan (tired of Jack Adams's bovine interference and eager to carve his own niche in the NHL) left the Red Wings.

Adams, casting about for Ivan's replacement, had the choice of either Skinner or the late Bud Poile. In the end, he chose Skinner.

Douglas Hunter writes that "[Skinner's] promotion to the Red Wings came as a surprise to those who thought Bud Poile would have been chosen – Poile was a former NHLer, after all, and he was behind the bench of the WHL's Edmonton Flyers, which was a more senior coaching rung than Junior A. But Skinner was experienced, knew the Red Wings lineup intimately and was well respected as a player's coach."[188]

Skinner would later tell Terry Sawchuk biographer David Dupuis, "It took me two or three times to believe Jack when he said I was the next coach of the Red Wings. I took a plane down there the next day for a press conference. But I was green as the dickens. I didn't know what to think of it all."[189]

The reaction to Skinner's accession among the Wings players was mixed. Ted Lindsay told Gordie Howe biographer Roy MacSkimming that "Adams was looking for a yes-man, and Skinner was a good yes-man. He wouldn't have known a hockey player if he had a uniform on. He was a door opener."[190]

To David Dupuis, Lindsay stated, "Everybody on that Wing team and most players in the NHL were professionals. We were all the best at what we did. By the time we got to that level, a coach couldn't teach us anything else. We were all self-taught. The game wasn't that complicated; we could almost change the line ourselves."[191]

---

188 *Champions*, Douglas Hunter, pp. 70–71.

189 *Sawchuk*, David Dupuis, p. 92.

190 *Gordie: A Hockey Legend*, Roy MacSkimming, p. 132.

191 *Sawchuk*, David Dupuis, p. 93.

But among the younger players (especially those who had played for Skinner in junior), there were no doubts. They saw him as being a player's coach.

Very few NHL coaches have the rare privilege of inheriting a team like the Detroit Red Wings in 1954. The Wings were at the apex of their dynastic reign. They had just beaten the Montreal Canadiens in what is probably the greatest Stanley Cup finals performance in NHL history. They were young (only two members of the roster were over 30) and immensely talented (six future Hall of Famers were on the roster – and that's not counting Keith Allen, who was inducted as a builder).

They had the Production Line of Gordie Howe, Ted Lindsay, and Alex Delvecchio. Red Kelly was one of the greatest defencemen of the Original Six era. Terry Sawchuk was the greatest goalie in the NHL since 1950. This was a Wings team that dominated the regular-season standings since 1948/49 and had won three Stanley Cups in 1949/50, 1951/52, and 1953/54 in five tries.

Not only was their NHL roster solid from top to bottom, but their minor league talent was just as great. This was a Red Wings franchise that had the rights to John Bucyk, Bronco Horvath, Norm Ullman, Al Arbour, and Glenn Hall. All of these men save for Horvath would earn Hall of Fame honours. All of these men were proven talents, eager to earn a slot on the Wings roster.

During his rookie season as an NHL coach, Skinner had the best vantage point of any diehard NHL fan. Every game night he watched his players display a masterful artistry on the ice that brought joy and ecstasy to Detroit fans and true hockey fans around North America. Every night he watched men who were the glory of their times play with a confidence, efficiency, and dedication that overwhelmed their opponents.

Although the final standings for the 1954/55 season show that the Red Wings won the Prince of Wales Trophy by only two points over the Montreal Canadiens, what the standings do not show was the awe-inspiring way the Red Wings earned that honour. During the last 17 games of the regular season, the Wings were 13–1–3, going unbeaten in their last 12 games, with nine consecutive wins to their credit (two of which were against the Canadiens) when the regular season ended.

The Wings' dominance continued, winning six consecutive playoff games and, ultimately, the Stanley Cup. Winning the league championship had its blessings for the Red Wings because it gave them home-ice advantage throughout the 1954/55 playoffs.

That came in handy when they faced the Habs in the finals. During that seven-game series, the home team always won, which meant the Wings earned their fourth Stanley Cup title in six years.

Gordie Howe put on the greatest playoff performance of his career, scoring an NHL record 20 points. Howe, Lindsay, and Delvecchio finished 1–2–3, respectively, in the playoff scoring standings. Terry Sawchuk was superlative in goal, holding his opponents to only one goal in five of his eight wins.

When Skinner kissed the Stanley Cup in the dressing room of the Olympia that night in April 1955, he must have imagined that his future (and that of the team) would be forever golden.

It was not to be.

Jack Adams was not called "Trader Jack" for nothing. All throughout his 35-year reign as Wings general manager, Adams had engineered blockbuster deals. As long as he had burgeoning minor league talent waiting in the wings, then he could get away with his penchant for constant turnover with his NHL roster.

But in 1955 Adams's revolving door became a one-way street. Great talent was leaving Detroit and the Wings were getting nothing in return. Adams sent Glen Skov, Johnny Wilson, Benny Woit, and Tony Leswick to the Chicago Blackhawks (solid reserves and defensive stalwarts all), while getting no one of comparable value. Adams compromised Detroit's defence even further by sending the legendary Terry Sawchuk and Vic Stasiuk to Boston without getting anyone of comparable value.

In two broad strokes Adams had sacrificed the depth, the bench strength, and the defensive strength on the forward lines that made the Detroit Red Wings four-time Stanley Cup champions.

Still, at the time, it looked like Adams would get away with it because to replace a future Hall of Fame goalie like Sawchuk he had another future Hall of Fame goalie ready: Glenn Hall.

Hall played for Skinner in junior, and Skinner had the infinite wisdom not to alter Hall's innovative butterfly goaltending technique. When it came time for Hall to man the pipes with the Red Wings, Skinner was the perfect man to lead Hall through his rookie season, providing excellent moral support. Hall would later tell biographer Tom Adrahtas, "I really liked Jimmy. He taught us a lot about being prepared. He set a great example. Before and after a game he was loose and relaxed.

But during a game he was focused. He had that 'rah-rah' college mentality and he was very positive."[192]

In short, Skinner was doing in the 1950s what Bob Johnson would do in Calgary and Pittsburgh during the 1980s and 1990s.

Hall repaid Skinner in full, winning the Calder Trophy as the NHL rookie of the year during the 1955/56 season and leading the Red Wings to the 1955/56 Stanley Cup finals (only to lose to the Canadiens in five games).

The 1956/57 season brought out the worst in Jack Adams. Incensed at Ted Lindsay's ill-fated attempt at organizing an NHL Players' Association, in the blood purge that followed, Adams exiled Lindsay and Hall to the Blackhawks (Adams's favourite dumping ground for any player who dared displease him).

When the 1957/58 season began, only eight men were left on the roster from the Wings team that won the 1954/55 Stanley Cup. All the rest, including much of Detroit's minor league prospects, were playing (and starring) for other teams. Even worse, the team that had once had the greatest offence and defence in the NHL was now near the bottom of the league in both categories.

As the Wings declined, the tensions between Adams, Skinner, and the team increased. In the end, the pressure was compromising Skinner's health. He later told David Dupuis, "I began to get these awful migraine headaches, had trouble driving, sleeping. Jack Adams made me have an eye exam but my eyes were fine. I stepped aside and recommended Sid Abel who was around town doing TV telecasts, and I stayed on in the Wing organization handling the farm system."[193]

On New Year's Day 1958, Skinner coached his last NHL game and quit as head coach (never to work behind the bench again).

The once-proud Red Wings franchise was only a shadow of its former self. Skinner continued to work for the Wings until the late 1980s when he finally retired.

He died in 2007.

---

192 *Glenn Hall: The Man They Call Mr. Goalie*, Tom Adrahtas, p. 27.

193 *Sawchuk*, David Dupuis, p. 131.

TOM "TOMCAT" JOHNSON RANK #44

PLUS: 36
MINUS: 0
VALUE: +36
PEAK RATING: #15 in 1972/73
PEAK VALUE: +36 in 1972/73

COACHING EXPERIENCE: Boston Bruins, 1970–1973[194]

REGULAR SEASON W–L–T: 142–43–23
PLAYOFF W–L: 15–7

EASTERN DIVISION TITLES: 1970/71–1971/72

PLAYOFF APPEARANCES: 1970/71–1971/72
STANLEY CUP FINAL: 1971/72
STANLEY CUP VICTORY: 1971/72

Tom "Tomcat" Johnson's coaching reign with the Boston Bruins was brief but glorious. Inheriting the coaching position after Harry Sinden's angry departure from the Bruins in 1970, Johnson maintained the Bruins' regular-season dominance and became the last Bruins coach to lead the team to a Stanley Cup title until Claude Julien did it in 2010/11.

But Johnson didn't need to coach the Boston Bruins to make a name for himself. When he arrived in Boston in 1963, his name and reputation had already been made. From 1950 to 1963, Johnson (along with the immortal Doug Harvey and Jean-Guy Talbot) formed one of the greatest defensive combos in NHL history for the Montreal Canadiens. He was an integral part of the Habs teams that made ten consecutive Stanley Cup finals appearances from 1950/51 to 1959/60 while winning six Cups.

---

194 Johnson coached the first 52 games of the 1972/73 season.

Johnson was the antithesis to Doug Harvey, preferring to stay behind the blue line, delivering crushing checks (in the legendary photo of the Barilko goal in Game 5 of the 1950/51 Stanley Cup finals, you can see Johnson behind the Montreal net crunching Toronto's Howie Meeker against the boards), forcing turnovers, and setting up Montreal's great transition game.

Although toiling in Harvey's illustrious shadow, Johnson shone brightly during the 1958/59 season when he won the Norris Trophy – breaking Doug Harvey's four-season Norris Trophy winning streak. (Harvey was injured for most of that season.)

In 1963 after suffering a major facial injury, Johnson was placed on waivers and claimed by the Boston Bruins – metaphorically going from first to worst. The Bruins (before the arrival of Bobby Orr) were at the nadir of their existence, alternating occupancy of the NHL cellar with the New York Rangers.

Johnson alone could not alter the Bruins' circumstances, but he elevated the team in other ways by bringing enormous character and leadership to the Bruins locker room and inspiring his teammates to never give up in the face of adversity.

Goalie Eddie Johnston in a 2008 interview said that Johnson (along with John Bucyk) "was another guy who was not afraid to get on your case if you weren't giving 100% on the ice."

Before 1967, other teams may have outscored the Bruins but not before they got the physical beating of their lives in the process. And Johnson was there for two seasons delivering those beatings.

In 1965 his playing career ended suddenly when he collided with Chico Maki of the Chicago Blackhawks and Maki's skate severed the tendon on the back of Johnson's leg. (For the rest of his life, Johnson walked with difficulty.)

Johnson immediately got a job working in the Bruins' front office, ultimately becoming assistant general manager of the team behind Milt Schmidt.

In 1966 the Bruins signed Bobby Orr, and the revival of the Bruins franchise began. According to Harry Sinden, Johnson played a key role in advising the Bruins to acquire Phil Esposito in 1967 (one of the greatest one-sided trades in NHL history) when Bruins general manager Milt Schmidt expressed reservations about Espo. In 1969/70 the Bruins ended their 29-year Stanley Cup drought by winning the Cup, only to lose head coach Harry Sinden in the process.

Johnson was tapped to replace him, and he inherited a team that possessed enormous firepower on offence and special teams.

The years 1970/71 to 1971/72 were the glory seasons of the big bad Bruins. Stars Bobby Orr, Phil Esposito, and Gerry Cheevers were at the peak of their powers. In Johnson's rookie year as a coach, Espo scored an NHL record of 76 goals in a season. At the same time, Bobby Orr set an NHL record (which will likely never be broken) of having a stupendous plus–minus rating of +124.

The Bruins were the best regular-season team in the NHL from 1970/71 to 1971/72 with a winning percentage of .769 because they had the best offence, the best power-play offence, and the best short-handed offence in the NHL. Their penalty-killing ability was at its peak, and their defence was solid.

On paper the Bruins looked invincible, but during the 1970/71 Stanley Cup playoffs they got the shock of their lives when they were beaten by the Montreal Canadiens in the first round. Seen by many hockey historians as one of the greatest playoff contests of all-time, the Bruins looked like sure winners when they won the first game of the series behind the solid goaltending of Gerry Cheevers. It was Game 2 at home at the Boston Gardens where the Bruins faltered.

Throughout the regular season, Johnson practised a strict goalie rotation strategy of alternating Cheevers and Eddie Johnston in net. Cheevers played 40 games to Johnston's 38, with a combined GAA of 2.63 (third in the NHL in 1970/71). Going into the playoffs, Johnson saw no reason to change that strategy. When Game 2 began, Eddie Johnston started for Boston and, going into the third period, enjoyed a 5–2 lead over the Habs.

What followed was one of the greatest comebacks in Stanley Cup playoff history. Montreal, led by Jean Beliveau (playing in his last season), roared back with five unanswered goals against Eddie Johnston. Beliveau himself had two goals and one assist. John Ferguson (also playing in his final season) contributed one goal and two assists. Only one of Montreal's five goals came on the power play; the rest were at even strength. When the buzzer sounded, the Canadiens won the game 7–5.

Afterwards, Johnson would forever be second-guessed for his decision to start Eddie Johnston in Game 2, but at the time the damage wasn't readily apparent. Johnson started Gerry Cheevers in goal for the remainder of the series, and Boston had a 3–2 series lead after five games but couldn't close the deal.

The Canadiens (blessed by the sturdy presence of rookie Ken Dryden in goal) played the series of their lives – winning Games 6 and 7 to win the series and eventually the Stanley Cup.

Bobby Orr biographer Stephen Brunt later recorded Orr's response to the defeat, telling the press: "Tom Johnson isn't to blame for this. He did a helluva job. He made all the right moves. There's nothing he did wrong, and don't let anybody blame him. A lot of people want to blame him. But they can't."[195]

Stung and enraged, Boston redoubled their efforts and regained their focus. The 1971/72 season was a glory ride for the Bruins – one of the greatest performances in their franchise history. Bobby Orr won the trifecta of hockey trophies: the Hart, the Norris, and the Conn Smythe. Phil Esposito led the NHL in goals, points, and power-play goals. Both Orr and Espo earned All-Star honours. But even more significantly, Johnson kept faith in his goalie rotation system. Gerry Cheevers played in 41 games and Eddie Johnston played in 38, with a combined GAA of 2.60 (fourth in the NHL in 1971/72).

Nor did Johnson second-guess himself with his goalie assignments during the 1971/72 Stanley Cup playoffs. Cheevers and Johnston manned the nets for eight and seven games respectively – with both men performing brilliantly. His decision to maintain his rotation system was a badly needed reaffirmation for both men, but especially for Eddie Johnston after the debacle of 1970/71.

The opposition never had a chance. Toronto went in five games, the St. Louis Blues (led by Al Arbour) were swept in four, and the New York Rangers (led by Emile Francis) went in six.

Triumphant and regnant once more, Boston was poised to dominate the NHL for the remainder of the decade. Only it was never meant to be.

After 1972, Bobby Orr was dogged with persistent knee injuries that sapped his effectiveness. The emergence of the WHA (and the Bruins' financial penury) cost the team Gerry Cheevers, Mike Walton, and Derek Sanderson. NHL expansion robbed the Bruins of key defensive forward Ed Westfall.

Shorn of their defensive strength between the pipes and on the forward lines, the Bruins declined slightly on defence while their offensive firepower remained as potent as ever. Still, the Bruins became more vulnerable, no longer dominating the NHL Eastern Division.

The Bruins appeared listless and out-of-shape. (The Bruins during this time period lived by the credo of playing hard on the ice and playing even harder off it.)

---

195 *Searching for Bobby Orr*, Stephen Brunt, p. 235.

Stephen Brunt writes, "What players realized soon enough was that, compared with Sinden, Johnson was a soft touch, more than happy to let this exceptionally talented bunch do pretty much as they pleased."[196]

Phil Esposito in his memoir *Thunder and Lightning* writes, "If you're a coach you want the guys going out for a beer after practice or a game. We did that. We were good on and off the ice. We partied, boy. We had a *good* time. If we had been more disciplined, it's possible we could have won four or five Stanley Cups in a row. We were that good. We were cocky, arrogant, but we backed it up."[197]

After New Year's Day 1973, the Bruins went 5–8–2 before new Bruins general manager Harry Sinden fired Johnson, kicking him upstairs to be his assistant general manager and appointing Bep Guidolin to take his place (the Bruins revived for the remainder of the regular season but were eliminated in the first round of the 1972/73 playoffs).

It would be 29 years before the Bruins would win another Stanley Cup.

Tom Johnson never coached in the NHL again, preferring instead to serve in the Bruins' front office, but during his brief reign he carved an impressive streak as an NHL coach.

---

196 Ibid, p. 229.

197 *Thunder and Lightning,* Phil Esposito and Peter Golenbock, p. 75.

BOB "BADGER BOB" JOHNSON RANK #45

PLUS: 36
MINUS: 1
VALUE: +35
PEAK RANK: #25 in 1990/91
PEAK RATING: +35 in 1990/91

COACHING EXPERIENCE: Calgary Flames, 1982–1987; Pittsburgh Penguins, 1990/91

REGULAR SEASON W–L–T: 234–188–58
PLAYOFF W–L: 41–35

PATRICK DIVISION TITLE: 1990/91

PLAYOFF APPEARANCES: 1982/83–1986/87, 1990/91
STANLEY CUP FINALS: 1985/86, 1990/91
STANLEY CUP VICTORY: 1990/91

Bob Johnson was a great coach. Bob had no system. The only thing he required was that you go out there and have some fun. What he wanted more than anything else was for his players to have a great attitude, to come to the rink ready to play. He wanted everyone to be positive, to play with exuberance. We would lose 6–1 and the only thing he'd talk about was how good a play was we made on the one goal we scored. He never worried about negatives, and he wasn't overly concerned about who we were playing. His practices didn't have any rhyme or reason but, boy, we'd come off the ice dead-tired. Bob Johnson was a unique fellow. He was very pro-Bryan Trottier, and I loved him for that.[198]

Bryan Trottier

198 *Behind the Bench*, Dick Irvin, p. 317.

Cancer has robbed hockey of some of its greatest coaching talent. It killed Dick Irvin, Fred Shero, Roger Neilson, and Pat Burns, and it also took the life of Bob Johnson – the winningest coach in Calgary Flames franchise history and the first Pittsburgh Penguins coach to win the Stanley Cup.

Johnson's coaching career was brief but brilliant. He coached only six seasons, but he made each one of them count. During those six seasons he made the Calgary Flames into Stanley Cup contenders and the Pittsburgh Penguins into Stanley Cup champions; and he placed himself among the 50 greatest hockey coaches of all time, according to my rating system.

He won games with offence and with his infectious positivism. During his years with Calgary, the Flames had the second-best offence in the NHL after Edmonton. His teams were slightly below average defensively and weaker still on penalty-killing.

Johnson's true strength came from his motivational skills. He was to hockey what Ernie Banks was to baseball: an incurable optimist.

His catchphrase, "It's a great day for hockey!" was his last will and testament. He expected his players to share the same passion and traded anyone who didn't. He was not a whip-cracker though. When coaching the Penguins, Johnson told the press: "There are a lot of ways to coach. You can coach from fear, when it's 'do it this way or you're gone tomorrow,' or you can develop pride in performance."

Bob Johnson was an American, born and raised in Minnesota, and played collegiate hockey at the University of Minnesota. He was a Korean War veteran and, after the war, finished his college education. He took up teaching and hockey coaching at high school and at the college level in 1963.

He began his NCAA coaching career at Colorado College before moving to the University of Wisconsin where he coached the Badger hockey team for 16 seasons from 1966 to 1982 (hence the nickname "Badger Bob"), making seven tournament appearances and winning three NCAA championships in 1972/73, 1976/77, and 1980/81, and was edged out by North Dakota in the 1981/82 final.

In 1976 he coached the U.S. Men's hockey team to a fourth-place finish at the 1976 Winter Olympics in Innsbruck, Austria (former Toronto Maple Leafs head coach Ron Wilson was one of his players on that team).

Johnson never coached in the minors. He went from the NCAA to the NHL in 1982 when he was hired to become the head coach of the Calgary Flames. The Flames had been in existence since 1973 when they were in Atlanta. The team moved to Calgary in 1980 and was in the midst of a major rebuilding campaign when Johnson was hired. Flames general manager Cliff Fletcher sought to re-energize the team by recruiting heavily from the U.S. collegiate hockey ranks and drafting European players.

Going from NCAA hockey to the NHL was quite a transition for Johnson. There were difficulties along the way.

Hockey writer Douglas Hunter notes:

> His initial coaching assignment in Calgary required considerable adjustment in his approach to players and game preparation. He was accustomed in college hockey to training four days a week and playing on two; and this ratio of practices was simply not possible in the NHL. He bemoaned the fact that professionals would not commit to a Russian-style dry-land training regimen in the off-season. . . . Johnson was laboring in his new hockey milieu. 'You try different things,' he said of his efforts to get his Flames to win in 1983. 'You praise some, you embarrass others. You bench them. I've chewed them out one-on-one in my room. I've tried everything to get the most out of them.' Johnson turned the Flames around, in part by turning himself around. He conceded that the NHL was not the U.S. college game. He backed off prioritizing practices over games, stopped what he himself admitted was over-coaching, and learned that a win is a win, no matter how ugly.[199]

It worked. Johnson led the Flames to playoff appearances all five seasons he was there. He got All-Star effort from veteran Lanny McDonald and defenceman Al MacInnis. Forward Joe Mullen and rookie blue-liner Gary Suter also had big years with Johnson.

The Flames during Johnson's stay became fierce rivals with their fellow Albertans, the Edmonton Oilers. During the Oilers dynastic run, the Flames were the most dogged of all the Oilers' opponents.

---

199 *Scotty Bowman: A Life in Hockey*, Douglas Hunter, p. 262.

Oilers coach Glen Sather would later tell Dick Irvin Jr. that "Because we played against Bob Johnson so much when he was in Calgary I always knew he was the kind of guy who, if we had won, would try and change his style to make it more difficult for you the next game. I had a lot of admiration for him because he was a guy that could change right in midstream. Not a lot of coaches do that."[200]

In 1985/86 Johnson's Flames ended the Oilers' two-year Stanley Cup–winning streak when they upset the Oilers in the second round of the playoffs. Johnson used a multipronged strategy to contain the vaunted Oilers' offence. Johnson told his players to flood the left side of the ice, where the Oilers loved to go to the most when on offence, and to avoid any fighting situations with the Oilers goons; and he used his best defensive players to hamstring the Oilers in key situations.

What followed was a seesaw battle that went the full seven games and ended on a fluke play when Oilers defenceman Steve Smith accidentally shot the puck off the skate of teammate goalie Grant Fuhr into his own net – which gave Calgary the lead, the game, and the series.

The Flames almost blew it when they were forced to the full seven games by Jacques Demers's St. Louis Blues but hung on to win the series and make their first Stanley Cup final appearance in Flames franchise history. Sadly for Johnson and the Flames, the magic ran out. Their opponents, the Montreal Canadiens led by Patrick Roy, were too much for them, downing the Flames in five games.

Johnson could not repeat his success the following season and resigned as head coach.

For the next three years, Johnson served as the president of USA Hockey until he was enticed back into the NHL as head coach of the Pittsburgh Penguins.

The Penguins were tailor-made for Johnson's tactical mindset, packing enormous firepower with Mario Lemieux, rookie Jaromir Jagr, and Mark Recchi. They won the Patrick Division title (the only divisional title in Johnson's career) and went 16–8 in the playoffs, beating New Jersey, Washington, Boston, and the Minnesota North Stars to win the Stanley Cup.

In so doing, Johnson became the only coach in hockey history to coach an NCAA championship winner and a Stanley Cup winner.

---

200 *Behind the Bench*, Dick Irvin, p. 191.

Two months after his Cup win, Bob Johnson was hospitalized with a brain aneurysm, which in turn led doctors to discover inoperable brain cancer. Three months later, Bob Johnson was dead.

His premature death begs the question: Where would he have ranked if he had not been taken from the hockey world so swiftly and so cruelly?

What would Johnson's value have been if he had been able to coach a normal lifespan as an NHL coach?

Johnson's average season rating was a strong 5.833. If he maintained that average and coached another five seasons, his value would have been +64 (which would have placed him as #23 on my top 50 list).

If Johnson had coached until 2001 while maintaining his average season rating, his value would have been +93 (which would have placed him as #8 on my top 50 list).

Let's consider another possibility. Johnson was 60 years old when he died of cancer. Let's assume that if Johnson had not died and had continued coaching the Penguins until the age of 65 (up to the end of the 1995/96 season) and had gotten the same results as his coaching successors did with the Penguins, then his success point total would have been even better: +85 (during that time period the Penguins had five winning seasons, three divisional titles, five playoff appearances, two conference final berths, and another Stanley Cup win in 1991/92); based on that, Johnson would have been tied for #13 on my top 50 list.

And yet who knows whether he would have retired at the age of 65. Scotty Bowman kept going until he was 68.

Given Bob Johnson's exuberance and passion for the game, and considering that the Penguins were a very powerful team during the 1990s, would the Penguins management have prevailed upon Johnson to stay a little longer?

If he had coached five more years and achieved the same results as the Penguins did from 1996/97 to 2000/01, his value would have reached a staggering +104 (which would have put him as #6 on my top 50 list).

Naturally, this is sheer speculation. We will never know whether Johnson would have achieved the same results or worse results or perhaps even better results. Coaches (like players) can decline in skill and effectiveness, but for Bob Johnson the potential for future greatness was there. His tragic premature death by cancer robbed him (and the hockey world) of a chance to see that greatness reach its glorious peak.

RANDY CARLYLE RANK #46

PLUS: 46
MINUS: 11
VALUE: +35
PEAK RANK: #39 in 2010/11
PEAK RATING: +39 in 2010/11

COACHING EXPERIENCE: Anaheim Ducks, 2005–2011[201]; Toronto Maple Leafs, 2012[202]–2015[203]

REGULAR SEASON W–L–OL: 364–260–80
PLAYOFF W–L: 39–30

PACIFIC DIVISION TITLE: 2006/07

PLAYOFF APPEARANCES: 2005/06–2008/09, 2010/11, 2012/13
STANLEY CUP FINAL: 2006/07
STANLEY CUP VICTORY: 2006/07

In 2005 Anaheim general manager Brian Burke took a big risk in making a lowball offer to Mike Babcock, thus losing him as head coach. In many ways, however, the risk paid off when he replaced Babcock with Randy Carlyle. Carlyle did what Babcock and earlier what Ron Wilson could not do: make the Anaheim Ducks Stanley Cup champions.

In only six seasons of coaching, Carlyle became the greatest coach in Ducks franchise history (which isn't bad, considering that NHL coaching greats Ron Wilson, Bryan Murray, and Mike Babcock also coached the Ducks).

---

201 Carlyle coached the first 24 games of the 2011/12 season.

202 Carlyle coached the last 18 games of the 2011/12 season.

203 Carlyle coached the first 40 games of the 2014/15 season.

Carlyle (along with Tom Johnson and Larry Robinson) also shares the unique honour of being the only NHL defencemen to win the Norris Trophy and later coach a Stanley Cup winner.

Carlyle was a scrappy defenceman who was drafted by the Toronto Maple Leafs in the NHL and the Cincinnati Stingers in the WHA in 1976. Carlyle opted for the Leafs and spent two seasons with them and their minor league affiliate in Dallas (where he played for Roger Neilson). In 1978 he was traded to the Pittsburgh Penguins, where he played for six seasons. It was during the 1980/81 season that he won the Norris Trophy and earned NHL All-Star honours (while playing for Eddie Johnston). Carlyle was later traded to the Winnipeg Jets, where he ended his playing career in 1993.

Carlyle took up coaching in 1995, first as an assistant coach with the Winnipeg Jets before moving to the minors, where he began a long relationship with the Manitoba Moose franchise in the IHL. In time Carlyle made the Moose winners and playoff contenders. The Moose were part of the Vancouver Canucks farm system, and Carlyle's work drew the attention of Canucks general manager Brian Burke.

From 2002 to 2004, Carlyle did assistant coaching work with the Washington Capitals, but he returned again to the Manitoba Moose in 2004. When Brian Burke took over as general manager of the Anaheim Ducks in 2005, he chose Carlyle to coach the team.

Anaheim had suffered a losing season before the lockout in 2004. Carlyle turned the team around and led the Ducks to the conference finals in the 2005/06 playoffs, only to fall to the Edmonton Oilers in five games.

The 2006/07 season was Carlyle's greatest performance as a coach and also the greatest performance in Ducks franchise history.

The team won the Pacific Division title – the first time the team had done so – and they were the third-best team in the NHL. Carlyle got All-Star efforts from defencemen Chris Pronger and Scott Niedermayer.

Niedermayer won the Conn Smythe Trophy while leading the Ducks to a 16–5 record in the 2006/07 playoffs. Their toughest stretch was during the conference finals when they had to beat Mike Babcock's Detroit Red Wings in six games to reach the Stanley Cup finals – with two of their wins coming in overtime.

The Ducks faced Bryan Murray's Ottawa Senators for the Cup and beat them in five games.

Randy Carlyle's Anaheim teams were well balanced tactically, although they were stronger defensively than offensively (the Ducks finished in the top ten in defence during the first three years of Carlyle's coaching reign). The strongest part of their arsenal was their power-play offence, with Teemu Selanne pulling the trigger more often than not.

But the Ducks' one key, dominating factor was that they were one of the nastiest NHL teams during Carlyle's reign. His squads were the bad boys of the NHL during the 2000s.

Things began to slip during the 2009/10 season. At the time, it was the worst performance in Carlyle's NHL coaching career and the first time he had failed to make the playoffs.

The Ducks rebounded the following season with a strong performance and a playoff berth thanks to the efforts of top goalscorer and Hart Trophy winner Corey Perry and All-Star defenceman Lubomir Visnovsky.

Indeed, it was this strong performance that has placed Carlyle among the top 50 hockey coaches of all time. Unfortunately for Carlyle and the Ducks, they suffered the indignity of being the first team to lose a playoff series to the Nashville Predators, in 2011.

It got worse the following season. After a 4–1–0 start, the Ducks went into a shocking 3–12–4 collapse before Carlyle finally got canned on November 30, 2011.

History repeated itself when Toronto Maple Leafs general manager Brian Burke reached out to Carlyle, asking him to take over the crumbling Leafs, who had shrivelled up under Ron Wilson, their playoff chances fading.

For Carlyle, the challenge of restoring Toronto to its former greatness meant everything: the fact that Brian Burke was a dear friend who had given him his first NHL coaching opportunity and the fact he would become the 17th former Maple Leaf to coach the team was too much to resist. He took over, but the team failed to respond (the Leafs' defence and goaltending were porous), and Toronto didn't make the playoffs for the seventh straight season in a row (a source of great anguish to all citizens of Leafs Nation).

Going into the 2012/13 season, Carlyle's standing in the top 50 ranks was in the balance. His coaching value was +32, but if he suffered a substandard season like his predecessor Ron Wilson, then he was in danger of losing his place among the top 50, according to my calculations.

The Leafs were in bad straits in terms of their defensive skills. They had finished 29th in defence and 28th in penalty-killing at the end of the 2011/12 season. Their goaltending was suspect. Their offence was Phil Kessel, period.

On top of that, Carlyle lost his good friend Brian Burke. Burke was fired as Leafs general manager in January 2013 (just before the season started).

When play resumed after the end of the lockout, the Leafs did not overwhelm. They limped out of the gate, and it took a four-game winning streak (their longest of the season) to get them above .500.

The Leafs were lucky in that other, more powerful teams like the Flyers and Devils were doing worse than the Leafs; also, the weakness of the teams in the Southeast Division gave Toronto enough cushion in which they could maintain a playoff berth even in the midst of their uneven play.

What fuelled the Leafs turnaround?

Caryle engineered major tactical improvements across the board. The addition of youngsters Nazem Kadri and James Van Riemsdyk augmented Phil Kessel's scoring touch. The Leafs' overall offence improved from tenth to sixth. On defence, Carlyle got solid efforts from blue-liner Mark Fraser, who complemented Dion Phaneuf well.

Even more significantly, Carlyle achieved solid work from his special teams, especially on the penalty-kill (where the Leafs improved from 29 to 2 in the NHL).

The Leafs penalty-killing unit got a lot of work because Carlyle brought his pugnacious style with him from the West Coast. The Leafs hit their opponents with abandon: beating them in the alley, as Conn Smythe put it. The Leafs led the NHL in team penalty minutes, with forwards Colton Orr, Frazer McLaren, and Mark Fraser doing the dirty work (with Orr leading the NHL).

Goalie James Riemer made his presence felt too: the previous season he had been bombarded and riddled with a GAA of 3.10 and a save percentage of .900. Now that he was getting the proper support he needed, he responded with his best season ever, lowering his GAA from 3.10 to 2.46 and improving his save percentage from .900 to .924.

When the playoffs came, the Leafs faced the Boston Bruins, and what followed afterwards speaks volumes about how Carlyle elevated the character of their play.

In Game 2, Toronto stole home-ice advantage from Boston with solid work from Joffrey Lupul, Kessel, and Van Riemsdyk. Interestingly, the Leafs played with great discipline, avoiding the penalty box.

Sadly for the Leafs, it was all for naught. They forgot what helped them win Game 2, playing undisciplined hockey in the process. They lost their home games in Toronto (the first ones since 2004) and were in the hole, 3–1, going back to Boston for Game 5.

The Leafs as a team (but especially James Reimer) reached deep into their souls and showed courage. Reimer faced 74 shots in two games and allowed only two to get past him, holding the Bruins to two goals in two games while winning Games 5 and 6 in the process.

It was back to Boston for Game 7. Again, the Leafs responded with a brave effort.

After yielding a Boston goal early in the first period, Toronto answered back with four goals against Tukka Rask. There was 14:31 left to play in the game and the Leafs were up 4–1. Even though they gave up a goal midway through the third period, they still had a 4–2 lead, the minutes were ticking off, and it seemed that Toronto was going to make it to the second round. There were 82 seconds left to go.

What followed next had all the elements of the supernatural.

At 18:38, the Bruins (who had pulled their goaltender) drew within one; then, agonizingly, 31 seconds later, Boston (their net still empty) scored to tie the game. There were only 51 seconds left, yet the Leafs could not hold.

When Boston scored the game-winning goal in overtime, it was the coup de grâce on a historic collapse.

But the fact that Randy Carlyle had got them that far and had pushed them to that height was a reaffirmation of his coaching greatness.

Sadly for Carlyle and the Maple Leafs, the 2013/14 season was a retro-gression. All the progress that was made the season before now was unmade.

The Leafs got off to a wonderful start, going 10–4–0 in October, but then the team became a slow-motion car wreck, coasting bit-by-bit to disaster. Centre Dave Bolland suffered a sliced tendon, which knocked him out for four months, thus compromising the Leafs' offence and depriving the team of Bolland's leadership in the locker room. Heralded free-agent power forward David Clarkson was supposed to inject some muscle into the Leafs forward line. Instead, Clarkson fizzled, drawing a ten-game suspension at season's start and failing to live up to his salary throughout the season. By early January, the team was barely above the .500 level.

Toronto surged back, however, and going into the Olympic break in 2014 they were 31–22–6, seemingly in playoff contention.

But when play resumed, what followed was a collapse that left Leafs fans confused, furious, and deprived. The Leafs went 7–14–2 in the final stretch – the team losing eight straight games at one point, with their opponents outscoring the Leafs 32–19 during the losing streak.

Goalie James Reimer was shell-shocked between the pipes. In the end the Maple Leafs finished at 38–36–8, nine points out of playoff contention – a choke of epic proportions.

New Leafs president Brendan Shanahan sent a stern message to Randy Carlyle by firing all of his assistants while retaining Carlyle for the 2014/15 season.

His neck firmly secured in the guillotine, Carlyle still managed to coax the withered Maple Leafs to a 21–16–3 record before Brendan Shanahan finally dropped the blade on January 6, 2015 (a move which clearly illustrates the vacillation and pusillanamity of Brendan Shanahan's leadership of the Toronto Maple Leafs rather than any criticism of Randy Carlyle's coaching abilities).

KEN MACKENZIE RANK #47

PLUS: 43
MINUS: 9
VALUE: +34
PEAK RANK: #3 in 1925/26
PEAK RATING: +34 in 1925/26

WCHL/WHL COACHING EXPERIENCE: Edmonton Eskimos, 1921–1926

REGULAR SEASON W–L–T: 78–58–6
PLAYOFF W–L–T: 1–4–3

WCHL LEAGUE CHAMPIONSHIP: 1922/23

PLAYOFF APPEARANCES: 1921/22–1922/23, 1925/26
STANLEY CUP FINAL: 1922/23

Ken Mackenzie was the most successful manager and head coach in the five-year history of the Western Canada Hockey League/Western Hockey League. He was the only head coach to last all five years of the league's existence, leading the Edmonton Eskimos franchise to a league championship, three Stanley Cup playoff appearances, and one Stanley Cup finals appearance.

Using my rating system retroactively, Mackenzie at the end of the five-year span of the WCHL/WHL emerged as one of the best hockey coaches of his time. By 1926 he was among the top five coaches (see "Decades" and "The Progressive Chart" in Part Four). He remained in the top ten until 1935/36 and was among the top 20 until 1975/76.

The WCHL was founded in 1921 and vied with the NHL, which dominated Eastern Canada (and later the northeastern United States) and the PCHA (which controlled hockey along the west coast of Canada and the Pacific Northwest). The league had four teams, in Edmonton, Calgary, Regina, and Saskatoon (although during the first season the Saskatoon team transferred to Moose Jaw).

The Edmonton Eskimos swiftly became the flagship franchise of the new league: three times finishing first in the regular-season standings, three times competing in the league playoffs, and winning the league championship in 1922/23.

Mackenzie's Eskimos won with offence, leading the league in goals scored from 1921/22 to 1922/23 and finishing second in offence from 1923/24 to 1925/26.

Overall, Mackenzie was the finest offensive coach in the WCHL/WHL, averaging 3.42 goals per game. No other WCHL/WHL coach came close to that figure.

Mackenzie accomplished this due to the efforts of centre Duke Keats and right winger Art Gagne. Keats led the WCHL in scoring in 1921/22, and Gagne followed in 1922/23.

Keats' and Gagne's efforts were augmented by the talented play of defenceman Joe Simpson. Simpson was a splendid blue-liner with great scoring ability. All of these men, save for Gagne, were inducted into the Hockey Hall of Fame.

But Mackenzie's greatest player was a defenceman from Fort Qu'Appelle, Saskatchewan, named Eddie Shore.

Before he became a fixture with the Boston Bruins, Shore showed his dazzling skills in the WHL, earning All-Star honours during the 1925/26 season and helping Edmonton finish in first place.

Ken Mackenzie had three shots at the Stanley Cup. In the 1921/22 Stanley Cup playoffs, the Eskimos lost to the Regina Capitals in the series that determined which WCHL team would face the PCHA and NHL winners for the Cup. The following season, Mackenzie got his revenge on the Capitals when the Eskimos won the series against them.

Mackenzie competed for the Stanley Cup against the original Ottawa Senators coached by Pete Green. The Eskimos lost both games of the finals in a best-of-three series. Both games were tense one-goal affairs, with a badly wounded Senators team playing on their last legs eking out the victories with superior defence and clutch goaltending.

It was the closest Mackenzie came to greatness. The next two seasons in the WCHL were dismal, with the Eskimos finishing last in 1923/24 (his worst season) and fourth in 1924/25.

It took the presence of Eddie Shore to restore Edmonton back to primacy. Although Edmonton finished in first place, they lost to Lester Patrick's Victoria Cougars in a two-game total goals playoff series during the 1925/26 Stanley Cup playoffs.

That same year the WHL folded, and Ken Mackenzie would never coach major league hockey again.

MICHEL "BULLDOG" THERRIEN RANK #48

PLUS: 52
MINUS: 18
VALUE: +34
PEAK RATING: #48 in 2014/15
PEAK VALUE: +34 in 2014/15

COACHING EXPERIENCE: Montreal Canadiens, 2000[204]–2003[205], 2012–present; Pittsburgh Penguins, 2005[206]–2009[207]

W–L–T–OL: 337–246–23–68
PLAYOFF W–L: 38–33

ATLANTIC DIVISION TITLES: 2007/08, 2014/15
NORTHEAST DIVISION TITLE: 2012/13

PLAYOFF APPEARANCES: 2001/02, 2006/07–2007/08, 2012/13–2014/15
STANLEY CUP FINAL: 2007/08

After reaching the Eastern Conference finals in 2009/10, the Montreal Canadiens' fall from grace took only two years. They had followed up their conference final appearance with a first-round elimination in the 2010/11 playoffs, followed by a lacklustre 13–12–7 start during the 2011/12 season. Montreal general manager Pierre Gauthier, losing patience and perhaps sensing his own inevitable end, did the predictable: he fired head coach Jacques Martin in mid-December. Martin's replacement, Randy Cunneyworth, laboured under the handicap of being an anglophone head coach in a city that

204 Therrien coached the last 62 games of the 2000/01 season.
205 Therrien coached the first 46 games of the 2002/03 season.
206 Therrien coached the last 51 games of the 2005/06 season.
207 Therrien coached the first 57 games of the 2008/09 season.

demanded minimally that the head coach of the city's most beloved sports team be bilingual.

Although the team never fell below .400, the team failed to escape the Northeast Division basement. It was Montreal's first last-place finish in 11 years. The team ownership, having lost patience with its head coach, Jacques Martin, now lost patience with Pierre Gauthier, casting him into the darkness (as well as special team adviser Bob Gainey). It was a blood purge and the augury of a new era, but who was the team going to turn to for leadership behind the bench?

There was speculation that Canadiens icon Patrick Roy would become head coach and general manager of the team. Instead, St. Patrick opted to become head coach and vice-president of hockey operations with the Colorado Avalanche.

It took a month for Montreal to hire a new general manager (Marc Bergevin), and it took Bergevin another month to select a new head coach. The man he chose was not the dawn of a new era but a flashback to the team's not-so-distant and not-so glorious past.

Michel "Bulldog" Therrien was born and raised in Montreal. When he was 15 he began playing midget hockey for two years as a defenceman before moving up to the Quebec Major Junior Hockey League (QMJHL), where he spent three seasons.

As a player, Therrien was a stay-at-home type of defenceman, more adept at hitting and checking. He was never drafted by the NHL but instead spent the remainder of his playing career in the AHL. He was a member of the Sherbrooke Canadiens team that won the Calder Cup in 1984/85 (Patrick Roy was a teammate of his).

In 1990 his playing career ended and he went immediately into coaching, returning to the QMJHL, coaching first in Laval and later Granby. Therrien excelled as a coach, leading his teams to the league finals three times and winning the Memorial Cup in 1995/96 (the first time in 35 years a team from Quebec had done so).

The Habs tapped Therrien to coach their AHL affiliate in Fredericton and later in Quebec City. His record in the AHL was decent but not spectacular (if you applied my rating system to his AHL coaching career during that time period, his value was +12).

Still, in 2000 he was called up to coach the Canadiens (succeeding Alain Vigneault). The Habs were moribund, wallowing in last place in the Northeast Division. Therrien played out the string. The following season Therrien engineered a 16-team point improvement with the team, leading them into the playoffs for the first time since 1997/98. The team was anchored in net by goalie Jose Theodore, who had a career year, winning the Vezina and Hart trophies. (Theodore had been Therrien's prize pupil during the latter's AHL coaching stint.)

Therrien coaxed the Habs past Robbie Ftorek's Boston Bruins in the first round, with Theodore holding the Bruins to two goals in the last two games. Montreal lost the second round to the Carolina Hurricanes, who went on to win the Eastern Conference title.

Bulldog couldn't sustain his success, going from the penthouse to the doghouse. The Canadiens were mediocre the following season, and midway through 2002/03 the Habs fired Therrien (Claude Julien was his replacement).

Therrien was not unemployed for very long. He was hired by the Pittsburgh Penguins to coach their AHL affiliate at Wilkes-Barre/Scranton. His second AHL coaching stint was much better, earning a +16 rating for his years at Wilkes-Barre/Scranton, reaching the Calder Cup finals in 2003/04.

Twenty-five games into the 2005/06 AHL season (with Therrien's Wilkes-Barre/Scranton Penguins possessing a white-hot winning percentage of .900), Therrien returned to NHL coaching when he was asked to replace Ed Olczyk as head coach of the Pittsburgh Penguins.

The Penguins were in the last year of their quadrennial residency in the Atlantic Division basement, but the team was rebuilding. Therrien was soon surrounded by a plethora of bright young hockey talents. After playing out the string, the Penguins emerged from their long hibernation and began a resurgence that has not stopped until 2014/15.

Pittsburgh recaptured their glory years with a high-octane offence (led by Sidney Crosby), an even deadlier power play (featuring Evgeni Malkin, Petr Sykora, and Mark Recchi), and a chippy on-ice attitude with Jarkko Ruutu and Georges Laraque spearheading the violence. Pittsburgh was opportunistic when it came to scoring, showing great ability to force turnovers in penalty-killing situations and create scoring chances (Jordan Staal and Maxime Talbot excelled at that particular skill).

Pittsburgh suffered a first-round elimination in 2006/07 but rebounded with a solid regular-season performance, the Atlantic Division title, and a dazzling playoff run that culminated in the Penguins reaching the Stanley Cup finals for the first time since 1991/92.

Therrien led his troops through the first three rounds, going 12–2, with Pittsburgh outscoring their opponents 51 to 26 (nearly a 2-to-1 goal ratio) and goalie Marc-Andre Fleury shutting out the opposition three times during that span.

It would take an opponent with super-human ability and confidence to knock off the Penguins, and that's exactly the team they encountered in the 2007/08 Stanley Cup finals: the Detroit Red Wings (led by Mike Babcock) at the peak of their power.

Wings goalie Chris Osgood shut the door on the Penguins offence, holding Pittsburgh scoreless in Games 1 and 2. Even though the Penguins eked out a narrow victory in Game 3, Detroit retaliated with a Game 4 win (in Pittsburgh), holding the Penguins to only one goal. Therrien got the Penguins to delay the inevitable by beating Detroit in triple overtime (in Detroit), but when the action returned to Pittsburgh for Game 6, Detroit returned the favour by controlling Pittsburgh in Game 6. Even though the final score was 3–2, the Wings were in control all the way, winning the Stanley Cup in Pittsburgh.

That playoff series represents the farthest Therrien has ever gone in Stanley Cup playoff competition.

Still, the defeat obviously took something from Therrien and the Penguins. The following season, Pittsburgh was inconsistent, waxing hot and cold, their defence and power play declining rapidly. The team was not playing up to its enormous potential, and Penguins general manager Ray Shero was bridling at Therrien's conservative style of play (Shero is a maven of offensive hockey).

On February 15, 2009, Shero pulled the trigger on Therrien, giving the job to Dan Bylsma and watching him do what Therrien couldn't do: win the 2008/09 Stanley Cup against the same Detroit Red Wings team that defeated them in 2007/08 (and in Detroit too!).

Therrien hibernated for three years before he returned to his roots and accepted the head coaching job at Montreal. There was a lot of skepticism about Therrien's return. But he quieted the skeptics by leading the Habs through a glittering comeback. During a truncated season, Montreal was the second-best team in the Eastern

Conference, toppling Boston from their plinth atop the Northeast Division. It was Montreal's first division title since 2007/08.

How did he do it?

Therrien revamped the Habs' offence. The season before, they were 19th in offence. Under Therrien, they were third in the NHL. No one player stood out offensively. Instead, Therrien resorted to an ensemble offensive effort, with Max Pacioretty, Brendan Gallagher, Tomas Plekanec, and Brian Gionta supplying the firepower. (Gallagher was runner-up in the Calder Memorial Trophy stakes.)

Their power-play offence improved from 23rd to third under Therrien. Norris Trophy winner P. K. Subban and Andrei Markov were deadly when Montreal had the man-advantage. Furthermore, Therrien got the team to play with greater ferocity than before, with Brandon Prust providing the muscle on the ice.

A solid team, yes, but were they good enough to go all the way?

The answer was no, and their first-round loss to the upstart Ottawa Senators exposed the flaws in the Habs tactical makeup. The Canadiens had not experienced an equal improvement in their defence and penalty-killing. Their defence remained stagnant and their penalty-killing ability dropped from second to 23rd. These were flaws that could be exploited, and they were.

The Senators were far superior in defence, goaltending, and penalty-killing; and it showed in their beating of Montreal. The Habs scored only three power-play goals in five games as opposed to Ottawa's six.

After splitting the first two games with Montreal, Ottawa held the Canadiens to only four goals in the last three games while winning the battle of intimidation on the ice.

Although Montreal failed to win the Atlantic Division title in 2013/14, the team advanced farther in the playoffs than the season before. One reason for this was their vastly improved defensive play. In 2012/13 the Habs were 13th in defence. In 2013/14 they were sixth in the NHL. The prime reason for this was goalie Carey Price, who finally grew into his pads and had a first-rate season between the pipes, finishing among the top five in save percentage and shutouts.

In the playoffs, the Habs showed off their defensive prowess by sweeping the Tampa Bay Lightning in the first round; outperforming Tampa 17–10 in goals scored. It was in the second round that Montreal showed its capability at giant-killing: slaying the President's Trophy winning Boston Bruins in a tense series that went the full seven.

The Habs stole home-ice advantage when they beat Boston in double overtime in Game 1. However, Boston regained it when they upset Montreal 1–0 in Game 4, then put Montreal's backs to the wall with a Game 5 victory in Boston.

It was here that Montreal (and especially Carey Price) showed character, toughness, and resilience, holding the vaunted Bruins offence to only one goal scored in six periods of play while scoring seven goals of their own against the Vezina Trophy–winning Tuukka Rask. When Boston tried to brawl with the Habs in Games 6 and 7, the Canadiens held their own, scoring clutch power-play goals in both games.

Montreal's victory was a quantum jump in terms of the team's maturity and confidence but, sadly, they could not sustain their drive, allowing the New York Rangers to upset them in the conference finals.

In 2014/15, Michel Therrien led the Habs to their best regular season performance since 1988/89 (it was also Therrien's best regular season performance in his entire NHL coaching career). Montreal withstood the Tampa Bay Lightning to win the Atlantic Division title. Carey Price had a career year where he won the Hart, Vezina, Jennings, and Ted Lindsey trophies. The Habs' stellar effort finally lifted Michel Therrien into the top 50 ranks. In the playoffs, Montreal took a 3–0 series lead, allowing Ottawa to win Games 4 and 5 before icing the series in 6. The second round against an upstart Tampa Bay Lightning team was déjà vu all over again, only in reverse. Montreal allowed a team which had the 11th best defence in the league to beat them at their own game. Tampa's defence only allowed four games in the first three games while taking a 3–0 series lead. Montreal rallied to win Games 4 and 5, but lost badly to Tampa in Game 6 to lose the series. It was a sad, shocking end to a breakthrough season for the Canadiens and Michel Therrien.

RALPH "COONEY" WEILAND RANK #49

PLUS: 31
MINUS: 0
VALUE: +31
PEAK RANK: #9 in 1940/41
PEAK RATING: +31 in 1940/41

COACHING EXPERIENCE: Boston Bruins, 1939–1941

REGULAR SEASON W–L–T: 58–20–18
PLAYOFF W–L: 10–7

PRINCE OF WALES TROPHIES: 1939/40–1940/41

PLAYOFF APPEARANCES: 1939/40–1940/41
STANLEY CUP FINAL: 1940/41
STANLEY CUP VICTORY: 1940/41

Ralph "Cooney" Weiland was a bright shooting star during the first quarter-century of the NHL's existence (1917–1942). Although diminutive by today's standards (Weiland was a five-foot-seven and 150-pound centre, whereas today's NHL centres are usually over six feet and weigh more than 190 pounds), Weiland was a master stick-handler, shooter, and two-way player who anchored the Dynamite Line (along with Dit Clapper and Dutch Gainor) that provided the offensive firepower for the Boston Bruins from 1929 to 1932.

C. Michael Hiam writes that "as a youth, Weiland had honed his hockey skills on the frozen ponds of Seaforth, Ontario, using cow pats as pucks. At only 150 pounds, Weiland was a giant in action, if not in size, using his extra-long hockey stick to poke or hook the puck away from opposing players. 'Little' Cooney Weiland was not only a defensive wonder, but shifty on the attack, baffling to the enemy, and great at making pretty dashes."[208]

---

208 *Eddie Shore and That Old Time Hockey*, C. Michael Hiam, pp. 154–155.

In his sophomore year in the NHL (1929/30), Weiland took advantage of the rule changes that allowed increased passing on the ice (to promote scoring) and gave one of the most sensational scoring performances in NHL history. Although his 43 goals and 30 assists are modest by today's standards, when you adjust his scoring totals to today's 82-game season, his totals would be an astounding 70 goals, 98 assists, for a total of 168 adjusted points. Based on that figure, Weiland's performance that season is the third-greatest individual offensive effort in NHL history.

Weiland (he got his nickname "Cooney" in childhood) was a phenom who played for the Minneapolis Millers in the minors, where he caught the attention of Art Ross. Cooney played on the Bruins team that won the Stanley Cup in 1928/29 but failed to defend the Cup in the 1929/30 finals against Cecil Hart's Montreal Canadiens.

A dispute with Art Ross led to Weiland being traded first to the original Ottawa Senators in 1932 and then to the Detroit Red Wings in 1933. Weiland was a mainstay for both teams, leading the Red Wings to a 1933/34 Stanley Cup finals loss against the Chicago Blackhawks.

Weiland returned to Boston for good in 1935, but during the final years of his playing career he was no longer a starting centre, instead backing up the Kraut Line of Milt Schmidt, Woody Dumart, and Bobby Bauer, providing experience to bolster the Kraut Line's youthful presence.

Cooney was the team captain of the 1938/39 Bruins team that won the Stanley Cup for Art Ross. When Ross retired from coaching (or so he thought at the time), he gave the keys to the Bruins' kingdom to Weiland, who had retired as a player.

The selection of Weiland was inspired. Although he coached only two seasons in the NHL, Weiland blasted through the league in his usual dynamite fashion. The Bruins were the best regular-season team from 1939/40 to 1940/41 (with a winning percentage of .698 during that two-year period). They had the best offence and the second-best defence in the NHL. They had the best scoring combo in the Kraut Line, along with other great scorers such as Bill Cowley and Herb Cain. They had a potent blue-line corps led by Hall of Famers Dit Clapper and Eddie Shore (who was in the twilight of his playing career); and they had goalie Frank Brimsek, who was at the peak of his Hall of Fame career.

Weiland's Bruins failed to defend their Stanley Cup title in 1939/40, falling to the New York Rangers in the semifinal round, but the following season they would not be denied, exploding through the regular season but facing a stern challenge from Hap Day's Toronto Maple Leafs in the semifinal round. Toronto had a 3–2 series lead before Boston rallied to win Games 6 and 7 and the series.

The 1940/41 Stanley Cup final against Jack Adams's Detroit Red Wings was an anticlimactic affair.

The Bruins held the Wings to only six goals in four games (although Games 1 and 2 were won by only one-goal margins). The Bruins were always in control. It looked as if the Bruins would be the dynasty of the 1940s, but the Second World War changed all that.

The war took away the heart of the team: the Kraut Line and Frank Brimsek were drafted en masse into the armed forces, and Weiland had to yield the coaching reins back to Art Ross.

Bruins fans didn't realize it, but they were entering a long drought that would see Boston being denied the Stanley Cup for next 29 years.

Weiland spent the next five years coaching in the AHL and continued to show brilliant coaching ability, leading the Hershey Bears to two Calder Cup finals appearances in 1941/42 and 1944/45 (but failing to win) and in the process becoming the first hockey coach ever to attempt to win both the Stanley Cup and the Calder Cup in a coaching career – which only six hockey coaches have ever done.

Weiland, in the minors, developed future NHLers such as Frank Eddolls, Gaye Stewart, and Bob Goldham. If you combined Weiland's AHL work with his NHL coaching record, his coaching value is an impressive +66.

Weiland stopped coaching in the AHL in 1946, but his coaching career wasn't over yet. In 1950 Harvard University asked Weiland to coach their hockey team and during the next 21 years he led the Crimson as their head coach, earning honours and the respect of fans, writers, and his players alike.

In 1971 he won the Lester Patrick Trophy (which is awarded for making significant contributions to American ice hockey). That same year he was elected into the Hockey Hall of Fame as a player, but when you look at how sterling and sublime his coaching career was at the NHL, AHL, and collegiate levels, Weiland was also worthy of induction as a builder.

Cooney Weiland died in 1985.

GERRY CHEEVERS RANK #50

PLUS: 31
MINUS: 0
VALUE: +31
PEAK RANK: #25 in 1983/84
PEAK RATING: +31 in 1984/85

COACHING EXPERIENCE: Boston Bruins, 1980–1985[209]

REGULAR SEASON W–L–T: 204–126–46
PLAYOFF W–L: 15–19

ADAMS DIVISION TITLES: 1982–1984
PLAYOFF APPEARANCES: 1981–1984

Gerry Cheevers was Eddie Johnston's goaltending partner with the Boston Bruins from 1965 to 1972. Although he never won the Vezina Trophy, Cheevers was one of the greatest clutch goalies in NHL history, earning the respect of his peers not only in the NHL but also around the world. Opponents might score three, four, or even five goals against him during a game, but Cheevers would somehow get the win.

While he was still playing, Cheevers never had coaching aspirations. In a recent interview, Cheevers stated, "I had no inkling whatsoever that I would become a coach. There are guys you play with who you think are going to become coaches but they don't and there are players you see who you think will never become coaches but they do. I was one of the latter ones."

In 1980 Cheevers was facing major knee surgery and contemplating the end of his playing career when Bruins general manager Harry Sinden prevailed upon Gerry to become head coach of the Bruins, replacing Dave Creighton, who had been fired the previous season.

---

209 Cheevers coached the first 56 games of the 1984/85 season.

For Cheevers, this was a major challenge. He was being asked to become the head coach of the oldest American franchise in the NHL (with no prior coaching experience in the NHL or the minors). He was going to follow in the wake of other Bruins coaching luminaries such as Art Ross, Harry Sinden, Tom Johnson, and Don Cherry while trying to maintain the Bruins' winning and playoff-contender status – a daunting task by any stint of the imagination.

Nevertheless, Cheevers took the plunge and from 1980/81 to 1983/84 did a solid, commendable job, leading the Bruins to four winning seasons, two Adams Division titles, and four playoff appearances. During the 1982/83 season, Cheever's Bruins had the best regular-season record in the NHL – not bad, considering he was playing against Al Arbour's New York Islanders and Glen Sather's Edmonton Oilers dynasty teams. (During the same time period, Cheever's teams outperformed those of his former goaltending partner, Eddie Johnston.)

How did he do it?

As a player, Cheevers had played for Punch Imlach, Harry Sinden, Tom Johnson, and Don Cherry. As a youth, he had played under the legendary Father David Bauer, and in the minors he had played for Joe Crozier.

Cheevers says that he took key elements from each of these fine coaches and incorporated them into his own coaching style. He balanced Punch Imlach's cold, calculating style with Harry Sinden's sense of propriety, approachability, and tactical preparedness; then added Don Cherry's ability to make hockey fun and also take pressure off his players' backs.

Cheevers's motivational approach was to rely on his veteran players (many of whom had been his teammates) to provide leadership. Cheever says, "Leadership comes from the room," and he was blessed with stalwart players such as Wayne Cashman, Rick Middleton, Jean Ratelle, and Brad Park – holdovers from the glory years of the 1970s.

Tactically, Cheevers (by his own admission) patterned himself after Father David Bauer. Bauer emphasized heavy forechecking and being able to outshoot your opponents.

Considering his legacy as a great goaltender, it's not surprising that Cheevers got solid defensive work from his players. The Bruins were always in the top tier in defence and penalty-killing. Bruins legend Raymond Bourque was a five-time NHL All-Star during Cheever's coaching reign. Cheevers also got All-Star efforts from forwards Rick Middleton (who won the 1981/82 Lady Byng Trophy), Barry Pederson, and goalie Pete Peeters.

Peeters won the 1982/83 Vezina Trophy, and Bruins forward Steve Kasper won the 1981/82 Selke Trophy while playing for Cheevers.

Despite four consecutive playoff appearances, Cheever's Bruins never reached the Stanley Cup finals. The closest they came was in 1982/83 when they were eliminated in six games in the conference finals by the New York Islanders.

After suffering a first-round elimination sweep by Montreal in the 1983/84 Stanley Cup playoffs, things began to slip for Cheevers. During the 1984/85 season, the Bruins were barely playing above .500; the team was getting old and Cheevers had the onerous task of being the man who had to bench his former teammates. Cheevers says, "It was the toughest aspect of being an NHL coach."

With 24 games left in the season, Harry Sinden fired Cheevers as head coach.

After 1985, he never coached again, either in the NHL or the minors. Instead, he took up broadcasting work for the Hartford Whalers and later the Boston Bruins while simultaneously engaging in thoroughbred horse-breeding.

It's a pity that Gerry Cheevers never coached again in the NHL. He was a very good one.

PART THREE

HONOURABLE MENTION

HONOURABLE MENTION

This part is devoted to eight former hockey coaches who once ranked among the top 50 hockey coaches of all time (according to my rating system) but have been displaced in recent years.

The standard I used for selecting these coaches was as follows:

1. They had a value of +20 or better.
2. They coached a minimum of five seasons at the major league level.
3. They had a significant impact on the game during their coaching career.

Even though they no longer occupy the elite ranks of the top 50, their collective impact on the game merits special attention. Each of these coaches made a contribution to the game and were superb coaches in their own right.

ROBBIE FTOREK RANK #51

PLUS: 31
MINUS: 1
VALUE: +30
PEAK RANK: #38 in 2002/03
PEAK RATING: +30 in 2002/03

COACHING EXPERIENCE: Los Angeles Kings, 1987[210]–1989; New Jersey Devils, 1998–2000[211]; Boston Bruins, 2001–2003[212]

REGULAR SEASON W–L–T–OL: 229–152–44–18
PLAYOFF W–L: 10–19

ATLANTIC DIVISION TITLE: 1998/99
NORTHEAST DIVISION TITLE: 2001/02

PLAYOFF APPEARANCES: 1987/88–1988/89, 1998/99, 2001/02

"He who controls others may be powerful but he who has mastered himself is mightier still."

Lao Tzu

For 13 years, from 2000/01 to 2013/14, Robbie Ftorek ranked among the top 50 hockey coaches of all time until he was displaced by Michel Therrien in 2014/15. Robbie Ftorek's ranking came as a big surprise to me. Considering the vicissitudes of his NHL coaching career, the controversies he was involved in, and the rather embarrassing denouement of his career, it surprised me that Ftorek had been able to make the cut and once ranked among the top 50 hockey coaches of all time.

Given what happened (and also what didn't happen) during his brief coaching

210 Ftorek coached the last 52 games of the 1987/88 season.

211 Ftorek coached the first 74 games of the 1999/00 season.

212 Ftorek coached the first 73 games of the 2002/03 season.

skein, Ftorek's story should be seen as a cautionary tale for those who aspire to coach in the NHL some day.

Ftorek is a story of unfulfilled coaching promise, of potential unrealized not because of external forces but because of what lay within himself. He's an example of the difference in having the skills to obtain an NHL coaching job and having the requisite skills for *keeping* an NHL coaching job.

Robbie Ftorek was one of the finest American hockey players in the 1970s. A Massachusetts native, he was a member of the 1972 U.S. Olympic Ice Hockey team that won silver at the Winter Olympics in Sapporo, Japan. Ftorek was drafted by the New England Whalers in the WHA in 1972 but opted instead to play for the Detroit Red Wings.

Unfortunately, Ftorek's small size (he was five-foot-ten and 155 pounds) worked against him, and he only played briefly in the NHL, spending most of his time in the minors. In 1974 he jumped to the WHA and played for the Phoenix Roadrunners, becoming an instant star in the rival league.

Ftorek compensated for his size by using great speed and dazzling moves to advance and pass the puck. When the Roadrunners folded in 1977, he joined the Cincinnati Stingers and remained with them until the WHA folded in 1979. During the last four years of the WHA's existence, Ftorek was a perennial All-Star and was always among the league's top ten in points scored. During the 1976/77 season, Ftorek was named the league MVP. In the league's last season in 1978/79, he led the league in assists and was runner-up in points scored. Ftorek ended up as the sixth-greatest scorer in the history of the WHA. When the World Hockey Association Hall of Fame was opened in 2010, Ftorek was among the inaugural inductees that year.

When the WHA folded in 1979, Ftorek was drafted by the Quebec Nordiques. In 1981 he was traded to the New York Rangers, but his best years were behind him. He retired as a player in 1985.

Ftorek immediately took up coaching in the AHL with the New Haven Nighthawks in the Los Angeles Kings farm system. His performance there was so-so. (His AHL coaching value while there was only +3 after three seasons of coaching – not particularly great.)

By 1988 Ftorek became head coach of the Los Angeles Kings and led them to the playoffs (despite having a losing season). The following season he had the honour of coaching Wayne Gretzky when the Great One came over in the now infamous trade from Edmonton. The Kings made it to the second round of the playoffs (the only time Ftorek ever got that far as an NHL coach) before falling to the Calgary Flames.

On the surface all looked well, but in truth the team was seething internally. There were rumours swirling in the Los Angeles press about conflicts between Ftorek and his players (including Gretzky), some of which were true.

Gretzky in his memoir *Gretzky* (written in 1990) sums up his time with Robbie Ftorek:

> Robbie did some . . . odd things. He had some talented guys . . . whom I know could play, guys like Doug Crossman, who made the 1987 Canada Cup team. But as the season unfolded, Crossman didn't play. Robbie decided to let Brian Maxwell, his assistant coach, handle the defence lock, stock, and barrel. Whatever Brian said, went. Brian didn't play Crossman. Nobody could figure it out.
>
> On the other hand, Robbie was a great teacher of the game and he was great with young players. He loves the underdog. Robbie wasn't afraid to give kids . . . a chance. The problem was he'd do it to a fault.
>
> I admire Robbie's compassion for young guys, but I'm not sure loving the underdog is a trait that gets you points in the NHL. Clearly we needed a coach who could handle veterans, a coach's coach. Robbie wasn't that guy. And since he hated dealing with the press, the press hated him back. Pretty soon, their game was, 'let's get Robbie fired.' And they succeeded. . . . People want to make Robbie and me out to be blood enemies. We weren't. We were friends.[213]

Ftorek spent the next two years with the Nordiques organization, head coaching their AHL affiliate and then working as an assistant coach with the Nordiques themselves.

---

213 *Gretzky: An Autobiography*, Wayne Gretzy with Rick Reilly, p. 204.

In 1991 he switched to the New Jersey Devils: first serving as an assistant coach to Tom McVie during the 1991/92 season, then becoming the head coach of the Devils' AHL affiliate team in Utica, New York (the following season they moved to Albany to become the Albany River Rats).

His work in Albany rehabilitated his coaching reputation. He led the River Rats to three straight winning seasons and playoff appearances; each year their winning percentage improved greatly. In 1994/95 the River Rats won the Calder Cup. (Ftorek's AHL coaching value during the 1990s was a solid +35.)

The following year, Ftorek returned to the NHL to serve as an assistant coach to Jacques Lemaire, with the New Jersey Devils. When Lemaire resigned as head coach in 1998, Ftorek was tapped to replace him.

At first he did quite well, winning a divisional title in 1998/99. Late in the 1999/00 season, Ftorek was coaching a team that had the talent to go all the way to the Stanley Cup finals when (with eight games to go in the regular season) he was fired as head coach and replaced by assistant coach Larry Robinson. Robinson led the Devils to the Stanley Cup.

Again, Ftorek was his own worst enemy. He had lost in the first round of the 1998/99 playoffs due to poor coaching (the Devils had a 3–2 series lead but lost the last two games). The team in 1999/00, although vying for the Atlantic Division title, had been slumping and appeared shaky.

Ftorek was estranged from the team, the media, and management while assistant coach Larry Robinson was acting as a buffer between Ftorek and the players (and the media) to maintain harmony. Devils general manager Lou Lamoriello, knowing his team's Cup-winning potential, pulled the trigger.

Writing after the firing, Joe Lapointe of *The New York Times* stated that "Ftorek was curiously, strangely aloof. He needlessly alienated players and staffers with unexplained benchings and petty indignities, like the time he ordered a bus to leave after practice in San Jose, stranding his aides. He picked fights with referees and treated the news media coldly, with thinly disguised contempt."[214]

Larry Robinson writes, "I had the utmost admiration and respect for Robbie, and appreciated that Robbie had given me a chance to coach during the lock-out.

---

214 "Ftorek Did Not Bend, Causing Devil Breakup", Joe Lapointe, *New York Times*, March 25, 2000

But I also knew where some of his shortcomings lay. He treated the stars a little bit differently than his muckers and grinders, and when guys who don't get all the notoriety see that, you don't get the most out of them."[215]

Pat Burns biographer Rosie DiManno writes, "As a franchise, the Devils had their own way of doing things, which wasn't flashy or histrionic. Psychologically, they were outliers, marching to a monotonous drum beat, anonymous and controversy-free. Except for their devotion to a defensive doctrine, Jersey was . . . even-keeled, almost anal."[216]

Lamoriello (one of the greatest general managers in NHL history) expected the same even strain from his coaches. Indeed, a coach like Punch Imlach, Don Cherry, or Mike Keenan would never have been allowed to coach the Devils as long Lamoriello was general manager.

Ftorek's melodramatics, his oscillating moods, and the needless confrontationalism of his nature were all violations of Lamoriello's team ethic. Following his lights as he saw them, convinced that the team had Stanley Cup title potential (as it eventually did), Lamoriello had no choice but to fire Ftorek.

In 2001/02 Robbie Ftorek went to Boston and was able to coax the Bruins to their first divisional title win (and best team performance) since 1993. Ftorek got solid work from Bill Guerin and Joe Thornton, but again Ftorek suffered another first-round defeat.

The following season Boston could not get untracked, playing listlessly and inconsistently (with nine games to go in the season). Ftorek was fired by the Bruins. (He remains the only NHL coach ever to be fired so close to the playoffs twice during an NHL coaching career.)

After 2003, Ftorek never coached in the NHL again, preferring instead to coach in the AHL, where he worked once more with the Albany River Rats (later to become the Lowell Devils) and performed atrociously, leading the River Rats to

---

215 *The Great Defender*, Larry Robinson with Kevin Shea, p. 174.

216 *Coach: The Pat Burns Story*, Rosie DiManno, p. 253.

three consecutive last-place finishes and earning an AHL coaching value of -27 during those three seasons.

In 2007 he tried his hand at coaching junior hockey in the OHL, leading the Erie Otters for six seasons, where his work was inconsistent: three winning seasons and playoff appearances sandwiched by two last-place finishes. During the 2012/13 season, the Otters were again in the basement when Ftorek was fired as head coach in November 2012.

On August 7, 2013, the Calgary Flames hired him to serve as assistant coach to its AHL affiliate, the Abbotsford Heat.

The sad part about the story of Robbie Ftorek is that despite his failure to properly lead his players at the NHL level, he still ranks among the top 50 hockey coaches of all time. He was able to get solid offensive productivity from his teams (in six seasons of NHL coaching, his teams always finished in the top seven in offence).

It was Ftorek who formed the A Line of Jason Arnott, Patrik Elias, and Petr Sykora that powered the New Jersey Devils' offence from 1999 to 2002. Although his Kings and Bruins teams were weak defensively, they played gritty, tough hockey. Furthermore, Ftorek had a regular-season winning percentage of .587 during his NHL coaching career (better than Randy Carlyle, Alain Vigneault, Peter Laviolette, Emile Francis, and Pat Burns, to name a few).

Despite his leadership flaws, Ftorek still achieved good, solid, decent results from his teams – which makes his saga all the more tragic.

And yet Robbie Ftorek could not master himself.

His negativity and volatility lowered his stature in the eyes of his players. (Ftorek once threw a wooden bench onto the ice during a Devils–Red Wings game in a January 2000 game to protest what he thought was poor officiating, drawing a one-game suspension from the NHL in the process. That faux pas is still shone in NHL highlight clips today)

His flaws denied him the opportunity to add at least 13 plus points to his coaching value (the 12 points the Devils earned during the 1999/00 playoffs and the one point the Bruins earned in the 2002/03 playoffs), which would have made him rank even higher in the NHL coaching pantheon.

Hockey coaches have to deal with a lot of external pressures and threats: the players, the fans, management, the media. But the greatest test all coaches must face is the internal pressure a coach places upon himself. Most are able to handle that particular adversity, but when a coach fails to handle himself then the results can be fatal, professionally speaking.

So it was for Robbie Ftorek. He had the potential and the skills for greatness, but he was undone by himself.

PETE MULDOON RANK #52

PLUS: 46
MINUS: 17
VALUE: +29
PEAK RANK: #3 in 1919/20
PEAK VALUE: +32 in 1923/24

PCHA COACHING EXPERIENCE: Portland Rosebuds, 1914/15, 1917/18; Seattle Metropolitans, 1915–1917, 1918–1924

PCHA REGULAR SEASON W–L–T: 117–109–2
PCHA PLAYOFF W–L–T: 10–12–2
PCHA LEAGUE CHAMPIONSHIPS: 1916/17, 1918/19–1919/20
PCHA PLAYOFF APPEARANCES: 1918/19–1921/22, 1923/24

WHL COACHING EXPERIENCE: Portland Rosebuds, 1925/26

WHL REGULAR SEASON W–L–T: 12–16–2

NHL COACHING EXPERIENCE: Chicago Blackhawks, 1926/27

NHL REGULAR SEASON W–L–T: 19–22–3
NHL PLAYOFF W–L–T: 0–1–1

NHL PLAYOFF APPEARANCE: 1926/27
STANLEY CUP FINALS: 1916/17, 1918/19–1919/20
STANLEY CUP VICTORY: 1916/17

Pete Muldoon is remembered mainly for a curse he allegedly placed upon the Chicago Blackhawks after he left as their head coach in 1927. Muldoon reputedly claimed that the Hawks would never finish first in the NHL – and for 40 years after his departure they didn't, until 1966/67 when they won the league championship and put the curse to bed forever.

In truth, Muldoon never placed a curse upon the Blackhawks. The so-called curse was a media concoction invented decades later to explain why the Blackhawks always underachieved in the NHL. In many ways, associating Muldoon's name with this fictitious curse dulls his lustre because he was one of the finest hockey coaches of his era.

He was born Linton Muldoon Treacy in 1881. Like most other Canadian hockey figures, he was a versatile athlete not only in hockey but also in boxing, lacrosse, and ice dancing. (He would entertain crowds by figure skating or playing hockey while on stilts.)

It was during his days as a middleweight and light-heavyweight boxer that he changed his name to Pete Muldoon because, as hockey author Morey Holzman explains, "Muldoon was born with the surname of Treacy but changed it because pursuing a career in professional sports was frowned upon in his native Ontario." To this day, his descendants use the surname Treacy.[217]

Muldoon made his way to the Pacific Northwest and struck up a fortuitous friendship with Frank Patrick, who, along with his brother, Lester, was running the Pacific Coast Hockey Association.

Muldoon became the second-greatest coach in the 13-season history of the PCHA. He and Frank Patrick were the only PCHA coaches ever to win the Stanley Cup (when you add the years Muldoon coached from 1914/15 to 1916/17, his coaching value is an impressive +54).

The PCHA was already three years old when Muldoon became head coach of the new Portland Rosebuds franchise, which had joined the league in 1914.

After helping the Rosebuds bloom with a second-place finish in the 1914/15 season, Muldoon moved on to head the Seattle Metropolitans franchise, where, again, he led them to a second-place finish.

It was the following season that Muldoon made the Mets a power to be reckoned with when they finished first in the PCHA and challenged the Montreal Canadiens for the Stanley Cup in 1916/17. It was to be the last time the PCHA would challenge the National Hockey Association for the Cup.

---

217 Holzman, Morey. "Blackhawks: Cursed or Concoction?" *The New York Times*, Sunday May 30, 2010.

After suffering a first-game defeat, Muldoon's Mets swept the next three games to win the Stanley Cup – the first time an American hockey team ever did so. In the process, Muldoon became the youngest man ever to coach a Stanley Cup winner.

He briefly yielded the coaching reins to Lester Patrick in order to coach the Portland Rosebuds through their last season in the PCHA in 1917/18 before returning to Seattle in 1918.

Muldoon's presence was a tonic for the Mets. They made two more Stanley Cup finals appearances, in 1918/19 and 1919/20.

The 1918/19 Cup is remembered because of the Spanish Influenza outbreak that forced the cancellation of the remaining games without determining a winner, but what's not remembered is that Seattle had the series lead but was denied victory in Game 4 due to a scoreless tie that lasted five periods before the game was called by the officials.

In Game 5, the Mets were winning 3–0 after two periods but allowed two quick goals early in the third period. They were still leading the game 3–2 when Newsy Lalonde of Montreal scored the tying goal with 2:52 left in the game to force an overtime, which the Canadiens eventually won – resulting in the series ending in a tie when the epidemic broke out.

Had Seattle been able to hang on to win Game 5, the Stanley Cup would have been theirs, epidemic or no epidemic. (Montreal Canadiens manager George Kennedy – sick in the hospital – offered to forfeit the Stanley Cup to Muldoon. Muldoon, demonstrating a rare and wonderful chivalry, refused the offer.)

In 1919/20 Seattle lost to Pete Green's original Ottawa Senators dynasty in another tense, hard-fought Stanley Cup final that went the full five games. The Senators won the first two games, but the Mets rallied to win Games 3 and 4 to force a Game 5.

Game 5 was tied at one after two periods before the Senators erupted to score five in the third period to win the game and the Stanley Cup.

What made Pete Muldoon such a great coach?

His Seattle Metropolitans were the most well-balanced team in the PCHA, and Muldoon was the greatest defensive coach in the history of the league.

During the last seven seasons of the league's existence, Seattle finished second in offence to Frank Patrick's Vancouver teams seven times.

Muldoon's Metropolitans boasted scoring talent like centre Frank Foyston, one of the greatest sharpshooters of his era and a perennial scoring title contender. He led the PCHA in goals scored from 1919/20 to 1920/21 and was a solid shooter in the clutch. Foyston scored nine goals in the 1918/19 Stanley Cup finals.

Bernie Morris was another top gun on offence, leading the league in goals scored in 1915/16, points in 1916/17, and assists in 1917/18. Morris led all scorers in the 1916/17 Stanley Cup finals, with 14 goals in only four games (including six goals in the fourth and final game). Had there been a Conn Smythe Trophy in those days, Morris would have earned it.

Jack Walker was one of the toughest defensive forwards in the game during the 1910s and 1920s. He was a fierce hook and back-checker, providing the muscle on the Metropolitans forward line, as did winger Cully Wilson, who was also a superb defensive forward who led the PCHA in penalty minutes during the 1918/19 season.

Foyston, Walker, and Morris together were one of the greatest scoring lines in PCHA history.

Muldoon's defensive talent featured not only Walker and Wilson on the forward lines but also goalie Hap Holmes and defenceman Bobby Rowe.

Rowe is an example of how Muldoon could be a shrewd chess master when harnessing the skills of his players. Before Rowe joined the Seattle Metropolitans in 1915, he had played as a defensive forward for two other teams. Muldoon, already flush with talent on his forward line, took advantage of Rowe's first-rate checking skills and shifted him to defence.

Rowe became one of the hardest-hitting defencemen in the game, earning PCHA All-Star honours in 1917/18 and 1918/19 and leading the league in penalty minutes during the 1922/23 season.

Hap Holmes was one of the greatest goalies of the game, playing on four Stanley Cup champions. He is the only goaltender ever to play on three Stanley Cup–winning teams representing three different leagues: Seattle in the PCHA in 1916/17, the Toronto Arenas in the NHL in 1917/18, and the Victoria Cougars in the WCHL in 1924/25.

Due to their efforts, Seattle led the PCHA in defence four times.

All of the above-mentioned players were PCHA All-Stars and all (with the exception of Morris and Rowe) would later earn induction into the Hockey Hall of Fame.

Muldoon guided, developed, and focused this talent into one of the finest hockey teams of all time from 1914/15 to 1916/17 and from 1918/19 to 1923/24, leading his players with a gentle, firm hand. Jack Walker later paid Muldoon the ultimate compliment a player can make about his coach when he said, "No hockey player, no man in fact, ever had a better friend than Pete Muldoon."[218]

Muldoon remained competitive until the PCHA collapsed in 1924. He returned to Portland and worked a concessions business at the local Portland racetrack.

In 1925 he became head coach of the new Portland Rosebuds franchise in the Western Hockey League but finished a lacklustre fourth place. When the WHL folded in 1926, Muldoon and his players moved to Chicago, where they became the Chicago Blackhawks in the NHL.

It was Muldoon's misfortune that he had to serve under Hawks owner and general manager Major Frederic McLaughlin.

McLaughlin was the Harold Ballard of his era, interfering constantly with Muldoon. The Hawks, despite having the best offence in the NHL, finished a poor third and were eliminated in the first round of the playoffs.

Morey Holzman writes, "Muldoon was an experienced coach and a good teacher; 8 of the 16 men who played for his Blackhawks eventually coached, including Dick Irvin . . . but Muldoon tired of the interference from . . . Frederic McLaughlin and gave two weeks' notice with 14 days left in the season."[219]

Holzman quotes Muldoon saying after his departure "our worthy President wanted to run the club, the players, the referees, etc. He learned the game very quickly. In fact, after seeing his first game, he wrote me a letter telling me what players should and should not do."[220]

(During the first 26 years of the Blackhawks existence, 18 different men served as head coach of the team. If there was a curse placed on this team, it wasn't the curse of Muldoon – it was the curse of Major Frederic McLaughlin – but somehow the phrase *the curse of McLaughlin* doesn't sound quite as lyrical or poetic as *the curse of Muldoon*.)

---

218 Harrison, Cliff. "Honest Pete Muldoon Gone." *Seattle Star.* March 14, 1929.

219 Holzman, Morey. "Blackhawks: Cursed or Concoction?" *The New York Times,* Sunday May 30, 2010.

220 Ibid.

Muldoon returned to Portland and resumed his work as a concessionaire, maintaining his friendship with Frank Patrick and helping him to resurrect West Coast hockey (albeit at the minor league level).

On March 13, 1929 Muldoon was in Tacoma, Washington, with his business partners, inspecting land in order to build a future indoor arena. After viewing a promising plot and obtaining the contact info of owners, the men experienced something tragic.

Morey Holzman and Joseph Nieforth write poignantly, "[Nate] Druxman later said that he heard Muldoon breathe oddly and then saw his head fall forward, his chin resting upon his chest. 'I thought he was jesting at first, then I saw his face become discolored,' he told the Tacoma *Spokesman-Review*. 'I knew something was wrong, thinking perhaps that Muldoon had suffered an epileptic attack.' His companions lifted him from the car and attempted to revive him on the grass, but in vain."[221]

It was not an epileptic seizure but a heart attack. Pete Muldoon was dead at the age of 47. His best friend and colleague, Frank Patrick, was devastated by his death. (One wonders if the trauma of Muldoon's sudden passing may have been a contributing factor in Patrick's own personal and emotional decline in the decades that followed.)

Patrick eulogized Muldoon this way: "Nothing has ever affected me like this. Pete was like a brother to me. In eighteen years of association with Pete. I have never had one cross word with him. Not one. He was always smiling and happy and well liked by everyone. He had not an enemy."[222]

---

221 *Deceptions and Doublecross*, Morey Holzman and Joseph Nieforth, p. 294.

222 Ibid.

BOB PULFORD RANK #53

PLUS: **37**
MINUS: **8**
VALUE: **+29**
PEAK RANK: **#26 in 1985/86**
PEAK RATING: **+31 in 1985/86**

COACHING EXPERIENCE: **Los Angeles Kings, 1972–1977; Chicago Blackhawks, 1977–1979, 1981/82[223], 1985[224]–1987, 1999/00[225]**

REGULAR SEASON W–L–T: **363–330–136**
PLAYOFF W–L: **28–43**

JACK ADAMS AWARD: **1974/75**

SMYTHE DIVISION TITLES: **1977/78–1978/79**

PLAYOFF APPEARANCES: **1973/74–1978/79, 1981/82, 1984/85–1986/87**

A recurring theme in sports is of the long-serving team executive who is deemed responsible for a winning team's decline and fall, or its long-term failure to win a championship, destined to become damned forever in the eyes of that team's fans. M. Donald Grant of the New York Mets is one example. Harold Ballard of the Toronto Maple Leafs is another.

And then there's Bob Pulford . . .

The Chicago Blackhawks failed to win the Stanley Cup from 1961/62 to 2008/09, the longest Cup drought in recent times. For many long-suffering Blackhawks fans, the man responsible for perpetuating that drought is Bob

---

223 Pulford coached the last 28 games of the 1981/82 season.

224 Pulford coached the last 27 games of the 1984/85 season.

225 Pulford coached the last 58 games of the 1999/00 season.

Pulford. Pulford was a fixture with the Hawks for 30 years as a coach, general manager, and éminence grise to the late William Wirtz.

Pulford, as a player, was a key member of Punch Imlach's Toronto Maple Leafs dynasty teams that won four Stanley Cups from 1961/62 to 1966/67. He was a solid, gritty two-way forward. (Former Ranger Earl Ingarfield Sr. said in a 2008 interview that he considered Pulford one of the toughest defensive forwards he ever faced.)

Long before he became head coach of the Blackhawks, Pulford was a thorn in the side of Chicago, scoring a hat trick in an 8–4 slugfest against the Blackhawks in Game 5 of the 1961/62 Stanley Cup finals, then five years later setting up goals by Pete Stemkowski and Jim Pappin in the third period of a clutch 4–2 win in Game 5 of the 1966/67 Stanley Cup semifinals.

Pulford ended his playing career in 1972 with the Los Angeles Kings and took over as head coach of the team the following season. After a last-place finish in his coaching debut, Pulford led the Kings to five consecutive playoff appearances and three straight winning seasons (the first ever in Kings franchise history) while setting a franchise record of winning 105 team points in the 1974/75 season (which earned him the Jack Adams Award).

Pulford's Kings played a very tight, well-disciplined defensive brand of hockey featuring the talents of goalie Rogie Vachon and veteran blue-liners Terry Harper and Gilles Marotte.

Bob Pulford states, "I emphasized the defensive part of the game. You can teach a person how to play defence but you really cannot teach a player how to play offence. I gave my players a system. I taught them how to react in certain situations: how to play a 3-on-2; how to play in the defensive zone."

It wasn't until the Kings bagged free agent Marcel Dionne that they got a solid offensive star, but it's interesting to note that when they got him, Pulford insisted that Dionne cease his centre-ice wanderings and adapt to Pulford's defensive systems – which Dionne did to perfection, though it took a bit of prodding from Pulford.

Pulford relates, "When Marcel came right away I made him do everything like the other players. When he did his first skate he wasn't skating hard enough so I hit him in the behind with my stick and I told him if he didn't skate harder, I was going to hit him again. He laughed and became a part of the team."

Pulford was much like his old coach, Punch Imlach, in terms of coaching personality. Stan Fischler in his book *Coaches* quoted Darryl Sutter (who played for Pulford in Chicago): "Pulford was [demanding] too, when I first came to Chicago. I mean I was scared of him because of his intensity but, by the same token, I liked him. Pulford made me a better player."[226]

Jeremy Roenick echoed those sentiments in his memoir, *J.R.*, "Pulford never seemed like he was having a good day. He was always mumbling and complaining under his breath. Pully was a stubborn cuss, but he was mostly good to me. I viewed him as a lovable curmudgeon. But it could be painful to talk to him."[227]

By his own admission, Pulford was a rigorous disciplinarian. He stated in a 2013 interview, "I consider discipline to be the essential element to coaching. I demanded discipline from my players and I enforced it. There were rules and I expected the rules to be followed. When I was coaching in Los Angeles, I spent a lot of time with UCLA basketball coach John Wooden and we would spend hours talking about coaching. Wooden believed that enforcing discipline was essential to winning."

Pulford related that he would use one of his players as a symbolic whipping boy to send a message to the team. During the early part of his coaching career in Los Angeles, Pulford had an arrangement with winger Dan Maloney whereby Pulford would rail against Maloney at a team meeting, but Maloney never took offence to the criticism because he knew Pulford was only using him as an example and that the criticism was directed at the whole team.

Despite the turnaround, however, the Kings were always eliminated in the early rounds of the playoffs. Still, Pulford's success in making the Kings a winning team drew the attention of Blackhawks owner William Wirtz. Long-time Hawks coach Billy Reay was gone, and the team had suffered their first losing season in 17 years.

In 1977 Wirtz lured Pulford to Chicago, making him the head coach and general manager of the team, and for the next 30 years Pulford made his presence felt.

At first he worked wonders: getting Chicago back on the winning track in his first season and winning two consecutive Smythe Division titles (his only ones).

---

226 *Coaches*, Stan Fischler, pp. 125–126.

227 *J.R.*, Jeremy Roenick with Kevin Allen, p. 92.

But looks can be deceiving. In his second season Pulford won the Smythe Division title with a losing record (the Smythe Division was the weakest in the entire NHL), and both years the Hawks were swept in the first round.

After 1979, Pulford moved to the front office, yielding the bench to a succession of coaches who led teams that were borderline successful.

Twice, in 1981/82 and in 1984/85, Pulford returned to the Chicago bench as interim coach while leading the team to conference final losses in the playoffs. Pulford's 1981/82 defeat came at the hands of the red-hot Vancouver Canucks, led by Roger Neilson. The Canucks won in five games. Ironically, the Hawks' sole win in that series also resulted in Neilson's legendary towel-waving moment.

The defeat rankles Pulford today. As he puts it, "I believe we were the better team that year but [Roger] Neilson got Vancouver to play above themselves and that's why we lost."

Pulford's 1984/85 defeat came at the hand of the Edmonton Oilers, who won the Stanley Cup that year. The Hawks never had a chance against the relentless cannonade of the Oilers.

From 1985 to 1987, Pulford did double duty as head coach and general manager with uneven results: both seasons his teams endured early playoff elimination.

His record of playoff futility is a major reason why he no longer ranks among the top 50. Had he made at least one Stanley Cup finals appearance (forget about winning the Cup) as a coach, he would still rank among the top 50 today (see "Heartbreak Coaches" in Part Four).

After 1987, Pulford withdrew to the front office, not returning to coaching until the 1999/00 season, where, once again, he served as an interim coach.

In retrospect, when Pulford went to Chicago, he crossed a metaphorical Rubicon. The lustre Pulford acquired while coaching the Kings was tarnished by his reign in Chicago.

Pulford was the best coach in Los Angeles Kings franchise history (and would remain so until Andy Murray came along). His partnership with William Wirtz became an unholy marriage that brought out, enabled, and compounded the worst professional and business instincts of both men.

During the 30-year psychological Valley Forge for Chicago Blackhawks fans, Pulford became the face of the team's underachievements and the cynosure of their growing anger.

It took the death of William Wirtz in 2007 to topple Pulford from his plinth. After Bob Pulford retired, the Blackhawks resurged with a vengeance, ending their long Stanley Cup drought and asserting their presence as one of the strongest NHL teams of the 2010s.

HARRY SINDEN RANK #54

PLUS: 35
MINUS: 10
VALUE: +25
PEAK RANK: #29 in 1979/80
PEAK RATING: +25 in 1984/85

COACHING EXPERIENCE: Boston Bruins, 1966–1970, 1980[228], 1985[229]

REGULAR SEASON W–L–T: 153–116–58
PLAYOFF W–L: 24–19

PLAYOFF APPEARANCES: 1967/68–1969/70, 1979/80, 1984/85
STANLEY CUP FINAL: 1969/70
STANLEY CUP VICTORY: 1969/70

"Harry Sinden was a coach you'd go through walls for. He complimented you, or knocked you, in subtle ways. He'd put the numbers on the blackboard of the players who didn't have to practice the next day. If you weren't playing well your name was never on the vacation list. . . . I think the job Harry did with Team Canada in 1972 was the finest coaching in the history of the game. They tried to force him to use the superstar concept, but in the end he did it his way. I think he saved face for the nation with that one."[230]

Derek Sanderson

228 Sinden coached the last 7 games of the 1979/80 season.

229 Sinden coached the last 24 games of the 1984/85 season.

230 *Behind the Bench*, Dick Irvin, p. 318-319

Hockey purists will ask by now: Why isn't Harry Sinden ranked among the top 50?

My answer is that he was (according to my rating system), starting from 1979/80 until the end of the 2010/11 season when he (along with several other coaches) was displaced by new arrivals Bruce Boudreau, Dan Bylsma, Claude Julien, and Todd McLellan.

Several factors played a part in his displacement:

1. 1) The brevity of his coaching career. Sinden coached only six seasons in the NHL. His decision to leave the Bruins after 1970 (just as the Bruins were reaching their full potential as a team) cost him, according to my rating system. Had he remained and achieved the same results as his successor, Tom Johnson, Sinden would still rank among the top 50.
2. His rookie season in 1966/67 (where he earned all ten of his minus points) cost him dearly in the long run with regards to his coaching value. According to my rating system, Sinden started off in a terrible hole and had to spend the rest of his coaching career getting himself out of it. If Sinden had been able to earn a fifth-place finish and keep the Bruins above the .400 level during his rookie season, he would still rank among the top 50 today.
3. Sinden missed chances to enhance his coaching value because he failed to win the Eastern Division title during the 1968/69 and 1969/70 NHL seasons. In the former season, the Bruins finished three points behind the first-place Montreal Canadiens. In the latter season, the Bruins were tied with the Chicago Blackhawks in team points, but Chicago won the title because they had more wins than the Bruins. The failure to dominate the Eastern Division standings cost Sinden a chance to add points to his coaching value.

Even though according to my rating system, Sinden no longer ranks among the top 50, this should not be seen as a disparagement of his illustrious hockey career.

Harry Sinden's greatness is self-evident. His Hall of Fame legacy as a coach and general manager endures forever in the annals of hockey history.

Harry Sinden presided over two signal events in hockey history: he was the head coach of the Boston Bruins when they broke their 29-year Stanley Cup drought in 1969/70, and he was the head coach of Team Canada during the legendary 1972 Summit Series against the Soviet Union – rallying Team Canada from a 3–1–1 deficit to win the series 4–3–1.

As mentioned, what's amazing about Sinden is the sheer brevity of his coaching career – only four complete seasons with two interim coaching stints in the 1980s – yet he compiled a record impressive enough to rank him (for a time) among the all-time greats.

Not only did Sinden rank among the greatest hockey coaches of all time, but he also remains one of the most successful general managers in NHL history, serving as Bruins general manager from 1972 to 2000 and presiding over 30 consecutive playoff appearances – an NHL record. (Only Art Ross served longer as Bruins general manager than Sinden.) Indeed, Harry Sinden must be considered one of the top ten NHL general managers of all time.

Another Sinden legacy is that he passed along his coaching excellence among his players: Eddie Johnston, Glen Sather, and Gerry Cheevers not only played for Sinden in the NHL and the minors but also achieved coaching success in their own right.

Furthermore, Sinden can be seen as the spiritual godfather of the offensive explosion in the NHL from 1979 to 1994, in which Wayne Gretzky and Mario Lemieux (coached by Sather and Johnston, respectively) rewrote the NHL record book with their scoring skills. Tactics and styles that Sinden created were later synthesized by Sather and Johnston both to create a new brand of offensive hockey.

Sinden never played in the NHL. He was, in his own words, "a play-making defenceman who never came close to making it in the NHL." During the 1960s Sinden was playing in the minors, where he drew the attention of Bruins general manager Lynn Patrick (son of Lester Patrick).

In a 2010 interview, Sinden said that they used to commute back and forth on the same train: "He and I had built up a good relationship and our views on hockey were the same."

Impressed with Sinden's acumen, Patrick shrewdly guided him toward coaching. Sinden spent the 1960s serving as a player-coach for various minor league teams in the Bruins farm system – winning the championship in the Central Hockey League in 1965/66.

When Boston needed a new head coach, again it was Lynn Patrick who helped Sinden by touting him to Bruins owner Weston Adams. Impressed with Patrick's recommendation, and as Sinden adds laughingly, "I came cheap," Adams reached out to Sinden personally and hired him.

At age 34, Sinden was the youngest head coach in the NHL and he was taking over a team that had been in free fall since 1959.

It was a daunting task for any coach, but more so for Sinden, considering his lack of NHL playing and coaching experience. Goalie Eddie Johnston would later state in a 2008 interview that there was some initial skepticism among the older players about Sinden's inexperience.

Sinden overcame the doubts by impressing upon the Bruins his feisty, burning will to win, his sincerity, and his demand that his players receive the proper physical and tactical training. Furthermore, he was determined to establish an identity with the Bruins, which he felt the team had lacked for quite some time.

The Bruins were an extremely physical team long before Sinden ever arrived. During their dark period, from 1959 to 1966, it was well known that other teams may outscore the Bruins but they could never out-hit them. Sinden took that dynamic and changed it from being a reaction against losing all the time into a proactive part of the Bruins' tactical makeup. Under Sinden, the Bruins became the meanest team in the NHL during the first three years of the first expansion era (1967–1979), leading the NHL in team penalty minutes from 1967 to 1970.

Sinden stated in a 2010 interview that "coaches that overlook offence generally can't win. Hockey cannot be separated like football into offence and defence."

He wanted the Bruins to emphasize puck control and passing on the attack, and to make that happen he wanted the Bruins to use their innate team aggressiveness on the forecheck and back-check, to work hard on winning faceoffs (which he considered part of the checking game), and to force turnovers and transition immediately into the attack. Sinden stressed that "the teams that go to the puck carrier end up being the best teams."

To make that system successful, Sinden needed players, in his words, "who were creative, intelligent, had good hockey sense, and were well-rounded and not one-dimensional."

In 1966 Sinden found a player who embodied all those qualities and then some . . . and then some more: an 18-year-old crew-cut defenceman from Parry Sound, Ontario, named Bobby Orr.

Orr became a catalyst of Sinden's system. His offensive greatness was self-evident and overwhelming from the start, yet Orr's ability to block shots, force turnovers, gain puck possession, and play the transition game added that extra spark to the Bruins' strategy.

In 1967 Orr was joined by acquisition Phil Esposito, the other prime catalyst of the Bruins.

Esposito writes in his memoirs: "Harry Sinden was the greatest coach I ever played for. He saw something in me that I didn't even know I had: scoring potential. . . . Harry would say to me, 'Park yourself in front of the net. That's where you're going to play, and we'll get you the puck. You're going to be our scorer.'"[231]

Esposito supplied physical and emotional grit both on and off the ice and a ruthlessly dogged determination to score. Esposito, hovering in the slot, was perfectly placed to blunt any opposing line rush or to be set up for any pass that came his way.

Teamed with Wayne Cashman and Ken Hodge (whose selfless work in the corners helped set up many an Espo goal), Esposito raised the scoring bar to new levels.

Orr and Espo were the reasons why from 1967 to 1970 the Bruins led the NHL in overall offence and short-handed offence three straight times and in power-play offence twice.

Interestingly, despite the presence of Bobby Orr, Gerry Cheevers, and Eddie Johnston, Sinden's Bruins teams never dominated defensively. Their defensive performance was, at best, average, and that must be seen as a key factor as to why the Bruins only won two Stanley Cups between 1968 and 1979, their glory period.

---

231 *Thunder and Lightning*, Phil Esposito and Peter Golenbock, p. 64.

The big bad Bruins were a powerful, intimidating team, but they were not invincible. In 1970/71, 1972/73, and 1973/74, they lost in the playoffs to teams with superior defensive skills.

Still, when the Bruins competed in the 1969/70 playoffs, the full panoply of their hockey talents was showcased: outscoring their opponents by a 2–1 ratio, winning ten consecutive playoff games, and going unbeaten in the last two rounds (with only four of their 14 games ending in one-goal margins). Individually, the Bruins dominated the top three slots in goals, assists, and total points (with Espo and Orr accounting for one-third of the Bruins offence).

Still, it took Harry Sinden's coaching genius to make the difference in the deciding game that clinched the Stanley Cup.

Derek Sanderson writes in his memoirs:

> Just before the overtime period began, Harry shocked us. 'I'm going to start Sanderson, Westfall, and Carleton,' [the Bruins checking line] he said. 'Orr and Awrey on the blue line.' We all fully expected that Phil's line would be called. It was Harry who contended that overtimes were usually won and lost in the first minute. He used to insist that we not get scored on in the first or last shift. Get us into the period and get us out of the period and we'll score in the 14 to 16 minutes in between. He said, 'I don't want them scoring on us right away, so Derek, you start.' That was his logic.[232]

Forty seconds into the overtime period, it was Derek Sanderson's pass to Bobby Orr that set up one of the most memorable moments in Bruins (and NHL) history: the winning goal that won the 1969/70 Stanley Cup for Boston, their first in 29 years; Bobby Orr: airborne, exultant, transcendent, glorious, never to be forgotten.

After winning the Stanley Cup, Sinden would have felt atop the world, one would think, but shortly after winning the Cup he abruptly and angrily resigned as Bruins

232 *Crossing the Line*. Derek Sanderson with Kevin Shea, pp. 141–142.

head coach, claiming later that he felt that the Bruins organization did not appreciate what he had done for the team by not rewarding him properly.

Sinden went into a two-year limbo, first trying his hand at private business. He ignored coaching offers from the St. Louis Blues and the Toronto Maple Leafs, even turning down an offer to be the first head coach of the expansion New York Islanders (if he had accepted any of those offers, it would have made for a great hockey what-if scenario).

Then came the 1972 Summit Series win against the Russians, resuscitating Sinden's hockey career. Boston coaxed him back by making him their general manager, and he has remained with the Bruins ever since.

Twice, in 1979/80 and 1984/85, he did brief interim coaching stints, replacing Dave Creighton and Gerry Cheevers, respectively, as head coach when he felt that the team wasn't performing up to standard.

In many ways it's a shame that Sinden left full-time coaching behind after 1970 because Boston (and the NHL) was denied the services of a great coach.

Indeed, when you look at Boston's record from 1967 to 1979, it is one of sustained excellence, and Harry Sinden was a prime reason for it.

If Sinden had remained at the helm of the Bruins during those years (and achieved the same results they had achieved under Tom Johnson, Bep Guidolin, and Don Cherry), he would have had a value of +121 as a coach and would have ranked #5 on my top 50 list. If he had continued up to 1984/85 (when Fred Creighton and Gerry Cheevers were coaching), his rating would have been +159 and he would have ranked #4 on my top 50 list.

EDDIE JOHNSTON RANK #55

PLUS: 37
MINUS: 12
VALUE: +25
PEAK RANK: #41 in 1996/97
PEAK RATING: +25 in 1996/97

COACHING EXPERIENCE: Chicago Black Hawks, 1979/80; Pittsburgh Penguins, 1981–1983, 1993–1997[233]

REGULAR SEASON W–L–T–OL: 266–251–79
PLAYOFF W–L: 25–28

SMYTHE DIVISION TITLE: 1979/80
NORTHEAST DIVISION TITLES: 1993/94, 1995/96

PLAYOFF APPEARANCES: 1979/80–1981/82, 1993/94–1995/96

Eddie Johnston is very much a company man. With a brief exception in the late 1980s, Johnston has been a fixture with the Pittsburgh Penguins since 1981 – serving variously as an assistant coach, head coach, general manager, and assistant general manager. When he was a head coach, he ranked among the top 50 greatest head coaches of all time from 1995/96 until the end of the 2010/11 season.

Before he took up coaching, Johnston played 15 seasons in the NHL as a goaltender. He was a solid but unspectacular net-minder who has gone down in history as being the last NHL goaltender to play every minute of every game during an entire season. During the 1963/64 season, Johnston played all 4,200 minutes – and he did so without a facemask. When asked in a 2008 interview how he was able to tend goal without a mask, he answered with self-deprecating terseness: "Stupidity."

---

233 Johnston coached the first 62 games of the 1996/97 season.

In truth, he was courageous and tough. In one game against the Detroit Red Wings, he was hit in the head with the puck and knocked comatose for several days. In a game against the Chicago Blackhawks, he was hit high atop his forehead by a Bobby Hull slapshot, resulting in blood and stitches. He later said that if the shot had struck him any lower, he would have been killed. Nevertheless, he came back and resumed his net-minding duties, not donning a facemask until the late 1960s.

Johnston tended goal for the Boston Bruins during their lean years, from 1962/63 to 1966/67, before being paired with Gerry Cheevers during their glory years, from 1967/68 to 1972/73. Johnston was a staunch presence for the Bruins, serving as mentor to the rookie Bobby Orr and other young players while helping the Bruins win two Stanley Cups, in 1969/70 and 1971/72.

After 1973, Johnston was traded from Boston and spent the last five seasons of his career bouncing between the Toronto Maple Leafs, St. Louis Blues, and the Chicago Blackhawks before retiring as a player in 1978.

Johnston went into coaching immediately, leading the Hawks' AHL farm team, where he did quite well. When Hawks coach and general manager Bob Pulford decided to yield the coaching reins (for the time being) to focus on his general manager duties, he picked Johnston to succeed him – the first of 14 head coaches to serve under Pulford during his infamous reign in Chicago.

Again, Johnston excelled, leading the Hawks to a winning season and a division title in his NHL coaching debut and taking the Hawks farther in the playoffs (leading the team to a second-round elimination) than Pulford had done in his first two seasons as coach.

Despite all this, Johnston was let go by the Hawks.

As Johnston put it tersely in a 2013 interview, "Within 48 hours I went from a lifetime contract with the Black Hawks to getting fired. I was never told by management. I found out from the media."

It was then that he began his long-standing relationship with the Pittsburgh Penguins when he became their head coach in 1980. Johnston's first coaching stint with the Penguins was the roughest spot of his coaching career; suffering three straight losing seasons, including a last-place finish in 1982/83.

Despite this, he was promoted to be the Penguins general manager – a post he held until 1988. The Penguins' fortunes did not improve, which proved to be a blessing in disguise.

On June 9, 1984, Eddie Johnston chose Mario Lemieux as the number-one draft pick in the NHL draft. Decades later Johnston would tell the *Pittsburgh Post-Gazette* that "We were getting a guy who comes along once in a lifetime. Mellon Arena would be a parking lot now if not for Mario. There would be no hockey in Pittsburgh."

Despite Lemieux's greatness, the Penguins remained moribund, and in 1989 Johnston became the general manager of the Hartford Whalers. His three-year stint there was undistinguished, but in many ways Johnston's heart was still in Pittsburgh because it was his trade of Ron Francis and Ulf Samuelsson to Pittsburgh that helped the Penguins win their first two Stanley Cups in franchise history, in 1990/91 and 1991/92.

To this day the trade is damned by hockey experts as being one of the great bonehead transactions in NHL history. It also marked the beginning of the end for the struggling Whalers franchise. In 1997 they moved to Raleigh, North Carolina.

When Scotty Bowman left the Penguins to coach the Detroit Red Wings, Eddie Johnston was chosen to succeed him. This time he did much better as Penguins head coach, leading the team to three winning seasons, two divisional titles, and a conference final elimination in seven games by the Florida Panthers in the 1995/96 playoffs – the closest Johnston ever came to coaching a team to the Stanley Cup finals. Johnston notes sadly, "We out-shot the Panthers but John Vanbiesbrouck played out of his tree in goal."

If the Penguins had won that series against Florida, Johnston would still rank among the top 50 today.

What were the main strengths of Eddie Johnston's teams?

Ironically (considering he was a former goalie), his teams were stronger offensively than they were defensively (especially in the 1990s when he coached Mario Lemieux and Jaromir Jagr). The only time Johnston coached a team that finished in the top five in defence was in his first season with Chicago. Thanks to an All-Star effort by the legendary Tony Esposito, Johnston's Hawks finished fifth in defence. After that, Johnston's teams usually brought up the rear in defence and penalty-killing.

Johnston's teams' greatest asset was their power-play goal production. When it came to generating power-play offence, Johnston was probably the greatest of all time in getting optimum effort from his team's power-play unit. His teams were averaging 1.039 power-play goals per game. No other hockey coach who served since 1960 has ever exceeded that figure.

Johnston's teams had the best power-play offence of the 1980s and 1990s. Naturally, one could say that this was due to having Mario Lemieux and Jaromir Jagr on his teams. And it certainly was the case during Johnston's second coaching stint with the Penguins, but even during his first stint in the 1980s, the Penguins were superlative on the power play.

From 1980/81 to 1982/83, the Penguins always finished in the top five in the NHL in power-play offence, finishing second in 1980/81, and leading the league during the 1981/82 season.

Rick Kehoe, Paul Gardner, and Pat Boutette were Johnston's big guns on the power play during that time. How did he get such stellar power-play work from his players?

Johnston states that he taught his players to constantly run picks while on the power play. He claims he got the idea from former Boston Celtics head coach Tommy Heinsohn, who coached the Celtics in the NBA from 1969 to 1978. The idea was to draw the opposing defence wide, screen off the defenders, and create an odd-man rush up the middle. To get the offence to work, it demanded deception and quick reflexes from the power-play unit. Still, it was risky. If the player setting the pick wasn't quick or careful enough, then he could be called for interference.

The Penguins were so dazzling on the power play that Scotty Bowman once asked Johnston for pointers on how to run their style of power-play offence.

Johnston states roguishly, "Bowman asked me for pointers on how to run the picks on the power-play but I told him 'I'm not running any picks.'"

When it came to team penalty minutes, Johnston's teams in the 1980s were near the top of the NHL, but during the 1990s (when on-ice discipline was coming to the fore as an essential team strategy) his teams' penalty minute totals declined somewhat. Obviously Johnston was going with the flow in that category.

When it came to motivating his players, Johnston states, "I always stayed positive. I accentuated the positive. If you keep being negative the players just tune you out."

In 1997 Johnston yielded the coaching duties to become Penguins assistant general manager to Craig Patrick and later Ray Shero. Since 2009, Eddie Johnston has semi-retired, but he still has offices at the Penguins organization – which is only fitting since he helped make the Penguins a championship franchise and an enduring presence in the Pittsburgh sports scene.

LEO DANDURAND RANK #56

PLUS: 37
MINUS: 13
VALUE: +24
PEAK RANK: #3 in 1924/25
PEAK VALUE: +34 in 1924/25

COACHING EXPERIENCE: Montreal Canadiens, 1922[234]–1926, 1935[235]

REGULAR SEASON W–L–T: 78–76–9
PLAYOFF W–L: 10–6

PLAYOFF APPEARANCES: 1922/23–1924/25, 1934/35
STANLEY CUP FINALS: 1923/24–1924/25
STANLEY CUP VICTORY: 1923/24

Leo Dandurand was elected to the Hockey Hall of Fame in 1963 as a builder, and rightfully so. Like Art Ross, he dedicated himself to hockey, serving in many capacities: referee, owner, general manager, and head coach. But Dandurand was not only a hockey maven as his involvement in the Montreal sports scene was vast and deep. His influence extended to horse-racing, boxing, wrestling, and football (he was a founder of the Montreal Alouettes franchise in the Canadian Football League).

Although born in America, Dandurand's ancestors hailed from Quebec. When he was a teenager, he had moved to Montreal, where he remained for the rest of his life: completing his education, competing in sports, and getting started as a businessman (his wealth derived from selling real estate, tobacco wholesaling, horse-racing, and owning restaurants).

---

234 Dandurand coached the last 17 games of the 1921/22 season.

235 Dandurand coached the last 32 games of the 1934/35 season.

In time he became quite prosperous, but while he was making money he never stopped his involvement in sports: organizing, sponsoring, and managing baseball and lacrosse teams. Even more importantly, he played a key role in the creation of the Canadian Amateur Hockey Association (CAHA) in 1914. CAHA became the governing body that controlled amateur hockey in Canada until 1994, when it merged with the Canadian Hockey Association to become Hockey Canada.

In 1921 Dandurand (along with two partners) was able to purchase the Montreal Canadiens franchise from the estate of George Kennedy for only $11,000. (Today, the Canadiens franchise is worth more than $575 million.)

He was not a man who worked in the background. Dandurand made his presence felt early when he fired the popular Newsy Lalonde as Canadiens head coach and installed himself in Lalonde's place.

Montreal Canadiens historian D'Arcy Jenish writes that Dandurand "was a talker and a backslapper" and "an advocate of fitness and conditioning.

"The players began their days with a brisk run. . . . They practiced late in the morning and were back on the ice in mid-afternoon. Dandurand directed the drills himself, and he gave the players Sunday off so they could attend Mass and have lunch in Niagara Falls."[236]

Using the skills of his trusty assistant, Cecil Hart, Dandurand signed new talent, acquiring future Hall of Famers Howie Morenz, Aurel Joliat, and Sylvio Mantha and shrewdly mixing the youngsters with such veteran holdovers from the team's NHA days as goalie Georges Vezina and the Cleghorn brothers, Odie and Sprague (all Hall of Famers in their own right).

By 1922/23 the Canadians were playoff contenders.

It was during the 1923/24 NHL season that Dandurand put it all together. Using Georges Vezina's superb goaltending and the intense physical play of his players, the Canadiens ended the original Ottawa Senators' dynastic run by beating them in the NHL playoffs, defended the NHL's honour by beating PCHA champion Vancouver in the interleague playoffs, and then defeated the WCHL champion Calgary Tigers for the 1923/24 Stanley Cup – all the while going undefeated in six playoff games and allowing their opponents only six goals scored in the process.

---

236 *The Montreal Canadiens*, D'Arcy Jenish, p. 57.

The team's triumph marked their first Stanley Cup win since 1915/16.

Dandurand led the Habs to a return engagement in the 1924/25 Stanley Cup finals. The Canadiens possessed the best offence and defence in the NHL but were humbled by Lester Patrick's WCHL champion Victoria Cougars. (It was in this series that Patrick introduced the concept of line changes to keep his players fresh while Dandurand kept the same six Canadiens players on the ice – standard practice at the time – which only resulted in the Habs flagging and faltering in the finals.)

Despite the loss, Dandurand was at the apex of his coaching career, but his stay on the summit would be brief. The Habs collapsed, finishing last in the NHL during the 1925/26 season (the death of Georges Vezina seriously compromised the Canadiens defensively).

Dandurand wisely decided to yield the coaching reins to Cecil Hart while remaining as Canadiens general manager. The team righted itself and for the next six years resumed its dominance of the NHL. (Leo Dandurand still remains one of the greatest general managers in NHL history.)

It was in 1932 that things began to slip for Dandurand and the Canadiens. As noted earlier, his relationship with Cecil Hart became acrimonious. After Hart quit as head coach, Dandurand replaced him with Newsy Lalonde, but the team failed to respond, playing indifferently under Lalonde's regime. Dandurand repeated history by firing Lalonde and taking over the team himself, but the team was growing old and creaky and Dandurand failed to replenish its roster. Attendance was flagging in the face of the Great Depression and the decline in the team's fortunes. The franchise was losing money. In 1935 Leo Dandurand sold his interests in the team and never looked back. He remained a prosperous businessman and continued to add to his economic interests while remaining a force in Montreal civic and athletic affairs.

His election to the Hockey Hall of Fame was the icing on the cake of a glorious life.

He died in 1964.

FLOYD SMITH RANK #57

PLUS: 28
MINUS: 6
VALUE: +22
PEAK RANK: #27 in 1976/77
PEAK RATING: +23 in 1976/77

NHL COACHING EXPERIENCE: Buffalo Sabres, 1972[237], 1974–1977; Toronto Maple Leafs, 1979/80[238]

NHL REGULAR SEASON W–L–T: 173–95–41
NHL PLAYOFF W–L: 16–16

WHA COACHING EXPERIENCE: Cincinnati Stingers, 1978/79

WHA REGULAR SEASON W–L–T: 33–41–6
WHA PLAYOFF W–L: 1–2

WHA PLAYOFF APPEARANCE: 1978/79

ADAMS DIVISION TITLE: 1974/75

STANLEY CUP PLAYOFF APPEARANCES: 1974/75–1976/77
STANLEY CUP FINAL: 1974/75

Floyd Smith's presence in this part may be surprising to some, but during the 1970s Smith carved a solid swath as a hockey coach both in the AHL and in the NHL. (If you combined his AHL coaching value with the figures you see above, his value would be a splendid +49.)

---

237 Smith coached 1 game of the 1971/72 season.

238 Smith coached the first 68 games of the 1979/80 season.

His major league coaching career was relatively brief, like Don Cherry's, in that he coached only six seasons in the NHL and WHA. Smith never reached the same apex as Cherry did, but what he did accomplish with the young, expansion Buffalo Sabres remains impressive. He led the Sabres to new heights that still remain unsurpassed, and he became only the fifth head coach in hockey history to attempt to win both the Calder Cup and the Stanley Cup.

Smith played right wing and bounced between the NHL and AHL during the 1950s – with brief stints with the Boston Bruins and the New York Rangers but spending most of the time with their AHL affiliates.

Smith played with the Springfield Indians AHL dynasty teams (owned by the legendary Eddie Shore) that won three consecutive Calder Cups, from 1958/59 to 1960/61 (the only AHL team ever to do so).

Smith's playing fortunes improved even further when he was claimed by Detroit in the intra-league draft in 1962. He spent the next five seasons playing for the Wings, helping them make three Stanley Cup finals appearances, in 1962/63, 1963/64, and 1965/66. Smith was a good second-liner, adept at shooting and setting up his linemates. In the 1965/66 Stanley Cup playoffs he scored five goals in 12 games, including the game-winning goal in Game 1 of the finals. It was Smith who got the game-tying goal in Game 6, which set up their eventual loss in overtime.

Smith later went to the Toronto Maple Leafs in a legendary trade that included Paul Henderson and Norm Ullman in exchange for Frank Mahovlich, Pete Stemkowski, Garry Unger, and the rights to Carl Brewer.

While playing at Toronto, Smith drew the attention and respect of Punch Imlach. When Imlach was fired by Toronto and eventually helped create the Buffalo Sabres franchise in 1970, Imlach acquired Smith in a trade and promptly named him the Sabres' first captain.

Smith finished his playing career and did a one-game interim coaching stint with the Sabres after Imlach stepped down as head coach to focus solely on his managerial duties.

When asked why he took up coaching, Smith is both modest and a bit self-deprecating about his decision. He states, "I fell into coaching because of Punch Imlach. I didn't particularly like coaching. At times I asked myself, 'Who the hell am I to tell someone how to play hockey?'"

Smith's modesty notwithstanding, it's obvious that Imlach saw potential in Smith.

Tactically, Smith drew inspiration from his years of playing under the late Sid Abel and Punch Imlach. Smith emphasized offence like Abel's Detroit Red Wings teams did in the 1960s. Imlach also influenced Smith's concepts on the power play in that Punch always demanded great speed in moving the puck up the ice on the power play.

Still, Smith was different than Punch when it came to motivating his players. Whereas Imlach was intensity personified, Smith was easygoing (like Sid Abel was in Detroit). Smith says, "I wanted honest effort from my players. I treated them fairly and tried to make sure the right players were always on the ice. I tried to look at my playing talent and utilize it to the fullest extent; making sure that I never asked a player to do something he wasn't capable of doing."

Floyd Smith became head coach of the Sabres' AHL affiliate, the Cincinnati Swords, during the 1971/72 AHL season and played out the string. The 1972/73 AHL season marked the beginning of a remarkable five-year coaching run for Smith.

In his first full season as the Swords head coach, he led the team to the 1972/73 Calder Cup title, beating Al MacNeil's Nova Scotia Voyageurs (who had been the defending AHL champions). The Swords failed to repeat as AHL champions, although they did make the playoffs. Still, Smith's excellent coaching effort drew the attention of Punch Imlach. In 1974 Smith became the head coach of the Buffalo Sabres.

Smith inherited a young team filled with many bright talents: the French Connection Line of Rick Martin, Gilbert Perreault, and Rene Robert, who would occupy three of the top ten scoring slots during the 1974/75 NHL season. (All three men earned All-Star honours for their sterling work during Smith's coaching reign in Buffalo.)

Centre Don Luce was a solid forward who (along with teammate Craig Ramsay) excelled in penalty-killing situations, taking advantage of turnovers and scoring short-handed goals. Rick Dudley (who played for Smith in the AHL) was a tough power forward. Defencemen Jerry Korab and Jim Schoenfeld were crushing hitters who provided the muscle for the Sabres.

Sharpened and honed to a keen edge, the Sabres fenced their way through the NHL. Smith's debut season still remains the greatest single-season performance in Sabres franchise history. The team won their first division title with a record-winning percentage of .706. (During Lindy Ruff's season in which he led the Sabres to the President's Trophy in 2006/07, the Sabres' winning percentage was only .689.) The divisional race wasn't even close. Smith's Sabres led the second-place Bruins (led by Don Cherry) by 19 points.

Smith's Sabres were a well-balanced team, but their main strength was in the offensive sphere, especially on the power play. When asked why the Sabres had such a great power-play offence, Smith states that "Gilbert Perreault was the key because he was so unselfish. He knew how to set up his teammates on the powerplay and Rick Martin was a sniper who knew how to get the puck into the net." (Rick Martin was second only to Phil Esposito in power-play goals scored that season.)

The Sabres were strong with their defensive special teams too. They were among the top five in penalty-killing and were dangerous in short-handed situations, leading the NHL in short-handed goals scored in 1974/75.

During their 1974/75 Stanley Cup playoff run, the Sabres showed courage and determination throughout the entire stretch: holding the Chicago Blackhawks to only ten goals in five games in round one, bouncing back from two blowouts by the Canadiens in Games 3 and 4 by grinding down the Habs with two wins by one-goal margins in Games 5 and 6 to win the series, and reaching the Stanley Cup finals for the first time in their five-season history.

The 1974/75 Stanley Cup final was the first time two expansion teams that had entered the league after 1967 faced each other. The Philadelphia Flyers were the defending Stanley Cup champions and luxuriated in their Broad Street Bully image. To win, the Sabres needed to maintain the potent offence that had got them to the finals (the team was averaging 3.72 goals per game when they reached the finals).

It was not to be. Led by Conn Smythe Trophy–winner Bernie Parent, the Flyers held the Sabres to 12 goals in six games (the Sabres scored only one goal in Games 1, 2, and 5, and were stoned in Game 6).

Smith would never come that close again. Although the Sabres continued to win and reach the playoffs, they failed to repeat as Adams Division champions and never made it past the first round of the playoffs.

By 1977 Smith was fired as Sabres head coach, and it wasn't until 1978 that he returned as head coach of the Cincinnati Stingers in the WHA. Although the Stingers had a losing season and backed into the playoffs, they still displayed a potent offence led by Robbie Ftorek and Rick Dudley. Even in the WHA, Smith's teams exhibited great strength on the power play, leading the WHA in power-play goals scored.

The Stingers fell in the preliminary round of the WHA playoffs, and with that the team (and eventually the league) folded.

By 1979 Punch Imlach had returned as Toronto Maple Leafs general manager, and he hired Floyd Smith to be their head coach in the hopes of recapturing the magic from the 1960s.

Sadly, it was not to be. The Leafs – torn and bleeding by the buffoonery of Harold Ballard and seething with strife because of Imlach's feuding with Leafs star Darryl Sittler – underachieved, playing barely below the .500 level. With 12 games to go in the regular season, Smith was literally knocked out of the season when he was involved in a severe automobile accident that resulted in two fatalities. Smith was hospitalized for a lengthy period of time while first Dick Duff and later Punch Imlach (with help from Joe Crozier) led the Leafs for the remainder of the season.

Smith never coached in the NHL again, but he did remain with the Leafs, working first as a scout, then a chief scout, before ending as Leafs general manager from 1989 to 1991 (a time in which the Leafs performed inconsistently).

Still, for a brief, shining moment in the mid- to late 1970s, Floyd Smith ranked among the coaching greats of the game. According to my rating system, even though his coaching career ended in 1980, he remained among the top 50 greatest hockey coaches of all time until 2007, when he was supplanted by Randy Carlyle, Ron Wilson, Lindy Ruff, and Mike Babcock.

RON WILSON RANK #58

PLUS: 66
MINUS: 44
VALUE: +22
PEAK RANK: #38 in 2007/08
PEAK RATING: +34 in 2007/08

COACHING EXPERIENCE: Anaheim Ducks, 1993–1997; Washington Capitals, 1997–2002; San Jose Sharks, 2002[239]–2008; Toronto Maple Leafs, 2008–2012[240]

REGULAR SEASON W–L–T–OL: 648–561–101–91
PLAYOFF W–L: 47–48

SOUTHEAST DIVISION TITLES: 1999/00–2000/01
PACIFIC DIVISION TITLES: 2003/04, 2007/08

PLAYOFF APPEARANCES: 1996/97–1997/98, 1999/00–2000/01, 2003/04–2007/08
STANLEY CUP FINAL: 1997/98

In Greek mythology, Sisyphus was compelled by the gods to roll a huge rock up a steep hill, but before he could reach the top of the hill, the rock would always roll back down, forcing him to begin again. It's an apt metaphor to describe the coaching career of Ron Wilson.

Until he was fired by the Leafs, Wilson had coached in the NHL since 1993. He led three teams (the Ducks, Caps, and Sharks), turned them into winners and playoff contenders, taking them closer to the Stanley Cup than they had ever been before, only to be fired and forced to start all over again.

---

239 Wilson coached the last 57 games of the 2002/03 season.

240 Wilson coached the first 64 games of the 2011/12 season.

As of 2015, in eighth place on the all-time wins list for NHL coaches, Wilson has very good hockey genes. His father (the late Larry Wilson) and his uncle (the late Johnny Wilson) both played and coached in the NHL. Although born in Canada, Ron Wilson played NCAA hockey for Providence College and was drafted by the Toronto Maple Leafs in 1975.

Wilson had a nondescript playing career as a defenceman. He bounced between Toronto and the minors and played for a time in Europe before ending his playing career with the Minnesota North Stars in 1988.

He immediately took up coaching, working as an assistant coach in the minors and later under Bob McCammon and Pat Quinn for the Vancouver Canucks from 1990 to 1993.

Displaying the technological bent that would distinguish him in the coaching world, Wilson assumed responsibility of the Canucks' video and statistical analysis, converting data from video digitally while simultaneously using the data to improve internal preparation for the team's personnel and external preparation against the team's opponents.

In so doing, Wilson added a 21st-century touch to the Canucks in the 1990s and made a strong impression with Pat Quinn in the process.

When the Anaheim Ducks made their NHL franchise debut in 1993, Wilson was at the helm. The Ducks did well, finishing fourth in a six-team division, earning 71 team points while playing gritty hockey.

Wilson later told TSN's Jonas Siegel in March 2012: "I think part of the advantage we had is everybody laughed at us. That was our motivation. Every town we went into is 'Oh the Mighty Ducks are coming. It's a Mickey Mouse Disney production' and we just said 'well, let's use that for our motivation to prove everybody wrong' and it worked the first year, for sure."

Given his intellectual nature, Wilson's motivational approach was not surprisingly professorial, although as the years passed he strove to simplify his approach. Wilson explained to Jonas Siegel:

> You simplify as you get older. I think when you're younger you focus more on complicated things, like little details that might have been important to you when you played, but then you realize you've got to simplify. That's the art of coaching is to make something that's complicated that you've

> spent a lot of time [on] and you've got to simplify, you've got to get right down to basics . . . you break down the equation but you don't solve the problem. The players have to go out and solve the problem. But all your students are different. Some don't want your involvement at all and some want a lot of information so that's what you learn over time. You don't flood guys who don't want information with that information [or] you'll lose them fast. So you make it available somewhere else that they can see the information.[241]

Under Wilson's guidance, Paul Kariya developed into a franchise player and in 1996 the Ducks acquired Teemu Selanne. By 1997 the Ducks had their first winning season and playoff appearance.

Kariya won the Lady Byng Trophy and was the Hart Trophy runner-up while Selanne was runner-up to the Ross and Lady Byng trophies. Both men received NHL All-Star honours.

The Ducks won the first playoff round but were swept by the Red Wings in the second round. Wilson didn't do too badly, considering that the Ducks were in their fourth year of existence as a franchise. The Ducks' management saw otherwise.

After a dispute with the Ducks' management, Wilson was fired and was quickly hired by the Washington Capitals.

The Caps had fallen on hard times and by 1996/97 had failed to make a playoff appearance for the first time since 1981/82. Wilson's first season with the Caps was also the high point of his coaching career. He led the team to their first and only Stanley Cup finals appearance in Caps franchise history (and also Wilson's sole appearance in the Stanley Cup finals as a coach).

The 1997/98 Stanley Cup playoffs were déjà vu all over again. Like Terry Murray's Flyers did in 1996/97, the Caps were fortunate that six of the seven teams that finished better than the Caps that season suffered early elimination. Washington beat Boston, Ottawa, and Buffalo – all of whom had finished lower than the Caps in team points. Their first real test came in the Stanley Cup finals

---

241 http://www.tsn.ca/nhl/story/?id=390788 – March 19, 2012, Jonas Siegel story on Ron Wilson

against the defending champion Detroit Red Wings, led by Scotty Bowman. The Wings had swept the Flyers the year before in four games. They did so again against the Caps. It was no contest.

The Caps never got that close again, despite winning two divisional titles for Wilson. The boulder slipped again from Wilson's grasp when the Caps fired him in December 2002. He was immediately hired by the San Jose Sharks (to replace Darryl Sutter). In 2003/04 the Sharks made it to the conference finals for the first time in their franchise history.

Again, like he did with Washington, Wilson succeeded without any major stars on his roster. His best player was goalie Evgeni Nabokov. Wilson coaxed a 31-point improvement with the Sharks and made them the third-best team in the NHL. Ironically, though, the Sharks lost the third round of the playoffs to Darryl Sutter's Calgary Flames.

Like before, in Washington, Wilson's Sharks never reached those heights again, despite winning two divisional titles. Although Wilson became the greatest coach in Sharks history, in 2007/08 the boulder slipped from his grasp once more and he was fired.

He was at the apex of his coaching career and had finally entered the ranks of the top 50, according to my rating system, but he would never stand so high ever again.

In 2008 Wilson became the 20th coach to attempt to break the Toronto Maple Leafs' 44-year Stanley Cup drought, and he was also the 15th coach in Leafs franchise history to both play and coach for the Leafs. Unfortunately for Wilson, his coaching stint with Toronto proved to be his undoing. He endured two consecutive last-place finishes before finally coaxing the Leafs to a winning season. Even so, he could not get the Leafs into the playoffs. By 2011/12 Wilson was at war with the Toronto press, the fans were in full cry against him (actually, they were against Leafs general manager Brian Burke as well), and on March 2, 2012, he was fired as head coach.

He is one very good season away from re-entering the top 50 ranks, but whether he can or will remains to be seen. No NHL team has rehired him, and it's likely he may never return to the NHL coaching ranks. Still, today Ron Wilson (along with Brian Burke) has resumed working with USAHockey, promoting the game of hockey with the youth of America.

PART FOUR

THE BEST OF THEIR TIMES

AVERAGE SEASON RATING

My rating method measures a hockey coach's value by the number of times a coach can get his team to reach certain levels of success during a season. Obviously, the more success levels a team reaches can serve as a strong indicator of a coach's ability to get optimum performance from that team.

My coaching value rating represents one way of determining a coach's excellence, but is there an additional way to determine coaching excellence?

Is there another way to measure coaching quality, regardless of how long the coach in question was able to coach in major league hockey?

Not every coach can last 30 seasons like Scotty Bowman did. Bowman's amazing longevity is a key factor as to why his coaching value exceeds all other coaches.

But was Bowman truly the best when it comes to getting optimum performance from his players?

Can a rating method be created that can measure a coach's ability to excel in any given season, regardless of how long he coached in the NHL, WHA, PCHA, or WCHL/WHL?

The average season rating (ASR) is my solution. The ASR is calculated quite simply: you take a coach's value and divide it by the number of seasons he coached in the NHL, WHA, PCHA, or WCHL/WHL to get the figure.

For example, former Toronto Maple Leafs head coach Ron Wilson has a coaching value of +22. If you divide his +22 by the number of seasons he coached (18), then his ASR is a rather munificent +1.222. (If you didn't count the years he coached in Toronto, Wilson's ASR is +2.429.)

Another example is former Edmonton Oilers head coach Tom Renney. Renney's coaching value is a -17, and when you divide his -17 by the number of seasons he coached (9), his ASR is a -1.889.

Like coaching value, the ASR fluctuates by the results a coach achieves each season he coaches. If a coach can get his team to perform (and maintain) a consistently high level of excellence, then his ASR will also be high. In my rating system, perfection is +21.00: how close a coach's average season can get to that figure serves as powerful evidence of his ability to get the most out of his team.

When a coach shows inconsistent results, then that will show in his ASR.

What coaching value does is measure the *quantity* of a coach's success over the course of his career.

What the ASR does is measure the *quality* of that success. It levels the coaching field and allows people to compare coaching ability irrespective of how long they coached.

What follows is a list of 121 hockey coaches who coached a minimum of five seasons in the NHL, PCHA, WCHL/WHL, and the WHA and how they ranked according to their ASR. (I chose a five-season minimum because my calculations show that that is the length of the average coaching career in the NHL.)

Whenever two or more coaches were tied in their ASRs, I resorted to the following tie-breakers:

1. The coach who has the higher coaching value gets the nod.
2. If the coaches are tied in coaching value, then the coach with the higher winning percentage gets the nod.

All the coaches who made my top 50 list are featured here, with the exception of Tom Johnson and Cooney Weiland, who did not coach the five-season minimum. If you're curious about what their average season ratings are, however, their numbers were as follows:

1. Cooney Weiland had an ASR of +15.50 in only two seasons of NHL coaching (no one rated higher). If you applied my rating method to Weiland's AHL coaching record, his coaching value is +35. When you combine it with his NHL record of +31, his professional hockey coaching value is +66; divide this by seven seasons of professional coaching and his ASR is a more realistic (but still awesome) +9.428.

2. Tom Johnson had an ASR of +12.00 in only three seasons of NHL coaching.

Here's how the coaches who qualified rated (*italic* names indicate they are active coaches as of 2015):

1.	Toe Blake	+15.00
2.	Pete Green	+13.67
3.	Tommy Ivan	+10.56
4.	Scotty Bowman	+10.30
5.	Dan Bylsma	+9.833
6.	Claude Ruel	+9.200
7.	Hap Day	+8.700
8.	Cecil Hart	+8.556
9.	Fred Shero	+8.300
10.	*Mike Babcock*	+7.917

In my entry on Toe Blake, I proclaimed him the greatest hockey coach ever, even though Scotty Bowman's coaching value was greater than Blake's. This is my evidence to support it. Blake's teams averaged a +15.00 rating out of a possible +21.00 during his 13 seasons of NHL coaching. Compare that with Bowman's +10.30.

Even during the lean years, from 1961 to 1964, when the Habs failed to win the Stanley Cup, the team was still playing at a fever pitch of excellence. Even when the team was in transition and rebuilding, Blake never allowed his players to fall short of his expectations, the team's expectations, and the fan's expectations.

What Blake accomplished at Montreal is as close to perfection as a hockey coach can ever get – never to be equalled or surpassed by any hockey coach before or since.

At the end of Blake's fifth season (in 1960), his ASR was +19.60. By 1964 it had fallen to +14.56 (and yet it was still the best of all time). When Blake's coaching career ended in 1968, it had risen again to its present level.

At all stages of his magnificent coaching career, Toe Blake was the best at getting the utmost from his players.

Before the advent of Tommy Ivan and Toe Blake, it was Pete Green who had the greatest ASR of all time. In fact, if you take away Green's final season of NHL coaching (which was sub-par), his ASR is +16.40 (the best of all time).

Tommy Ivan finished third behind Toe Blake and Pete Green for one reason: his two losing seasons of coaching the Chicago Blackhawks, which cost him dearly. His ASR when he left the Red Wings in 1954 was a devastating +15.57.

Had he not returned to active coaching in Chicago, Ivan would have had the greatest ASR of all time.

Scotty Bowman's ASR was +8.250 when he left the St. Louis Blues in 1971. When he left Montreal in 1979, it was +13.33. When he left Buffalo in 1987, it had fallen to +9.368. When he left Pittsburgh in 1993, it rose slightly, to +9.619. When Bowman finally retired in 2002, it rose to the figure you see above. It was Bowman's years in Buffalo that really served as a drag to his ASR.

Before he was fired in 2014, Dan Bylsma was leading all active NHL coaches in ASR. Ever since his debut in 2009, he had been gaining on Mike Babcock in the ASR stakes, surpassing him in 2013. Even though he failed to repeat his 2009 Stanley Cup success, Bylsma's high ASR stands as compelling evidence of the quality of his coaching genius.

It's amazing that Claude Ruel ranks sixth even though he was reluctant to coach and was ill-suited for the job. It begs the obvious question: If Ruel had got his coaching act together, what more could he have accomplished?

Cynics will ask: Why is Hap Day ranked behind Claude Ruel? Despite the fact that Day coached five Stanley Cup winners, his Leafs teams of the 1940s failed to dominate the regular-season standings and never had exceptionally high winning percentages. That lack of regular-season dominance served to lower Day's ASR.

When Cecil Hart resigned as head coach of the Montreal Canadiens in 1932, his ASR was +11.33 (second only to Pete Green). It was his second coaching stint with Montreal during the lean years of the 1930s that lowered his rating to its present level. Still, despite the fact that Hart's ASR declined in his latter years, he still ranks among the top ten.

Again, it begs the obvious question: Why isn't Cecil Hart in the Hockey Hall of Fame?

Fred Shero's ASR further reinforces his image as a coaching genius, regardless of the aesthetic brutality of the Broad Street Bullies during the 1970s. Shero was a winner and a champion and his rating reflects that fact.

Mike Babcock's ASR has declined slowly because Detroit is no longer the dominant team they used to be in the 1990s and the 2000s. In 2011 Babcock's ASR was 9.625, today it is 7.917.

11.	*Bruce Boudreau*	+7.875
12.	Glen Sather	+7.750
13.	Bill Dineen	+7.333
14.	Don Cherry	+7.167
15.	Dick Irvin	+7.000
16.	Ken MacKenzie	+6.800
17.	*Joel Quenneville*	+6.778
18.	Frank Patrick	+6.364
19.	*Claude Julien*	+6.250
20.	Gerry Cheevers	+6.200

In 2013/14, Bruce Boudreau surpassed Don Cherry (for the time being) for having the best ASR without ever having coached a Stanley Cup winner. Gabby's ASR has risen sharply despite his lack of playoff success from +6.600 to +7.875.

Bill Dineen's ASR when the WHA folded in 1979 was +10.71 (good for third place on this list), but when he coached the Philadelphia Flyers during the early 1990s those two lacklustre seasons served to drag him down to his present level.

Those who scorn Don Cherry as a coach err grievously. As mentioned above, before Bruce Boudreau surpassed him in 2013/14, Cherry had the highest ASR for all non–Stanley Cup–winning coaches with a minimum five years' coaching experience (and if Boudreau ever does coach a Stanley Cup winner, then Cherry will regain that honour).

In terms of coaching quality, Don Cherry was one of the greatest hockey coaches never to have won the Stanley Cup.

Now having bandied that about, let's consider these scenarios:

1. Take away his one season of coaching the Colorado Rockies and Grapes's ASR is +10.60 (good for #3 on this list).
2. If Cherry had reached the 1979 Stanley Cup finals, his ASR would have been +8.000 (good for #10 on this list) and that's including his abortive

run with the Colorado Rockies. Take away the 1979/80 season and his ASR would be +11.60.

3. If Cherry had won the 1979 Stanley Cup, his ASR would have been +9.000 (good for #7 on this list) *and, again, that includes his abortive run with the Colorado Rockies*. But if you take away 1979/80 again then Cherry's ASR would be a stupendous +12.80 (good for #3 on this list).

Love Grapes or hate him, he was an awesome hockey coach.

Chicago's failure to repeat as Central Division and Stanley Cup champions in 2013/14 caused Joel Quenneville's ASR to dip slightly from +6.188 to +6.176 but when the Blackhawks reached the Stanley Cup finals in 2014/15 it jumped to +6.778.

Frank Patrick had a greater ASR than his brother, Lester.

Claude Julien's two appearances in the Stanley Cup finals coupled with his 2011 Stanley Cup win propelled his ASR skyward. Before 2011, it was +3.286; by 2013/14 he doubled it to +6.818 but Boston's failure to reach the playoffs in 2014/15 reduced it to +6.250.

21.	Punch Imlach	+6.143
22.	*Todd McLellan*	+6.000
23.	Bob Johnson	+5.833
24.	*Ken Hitchcock*	+5.667
25.	*Alain Vigneault*	+5.385
26.	*Darryl Sutter*	+5.333
27.	Robbie Ftorek	+5.000
28.	Billy Reay	+4.875
29.	Al Arbour	+4.565
30.	Pat Burns	+4.429

When Punch Imlach was fired by the Toronto Maple Leafs in 1969, his ASR was +8.364 (good for #9 on this list), but his seasons of coaching in Buffalo and later again in Toronto served to drag him down.

Todd McLellan's ASR was +10.00 after his third season; it declined to +8.250 after his fourth season, and now after seven seasons it has sunk further, to +6.000. Two major reasons for this decline are as follows:

1. McLellan's failure to coach a Stanley Cup winner
2. His inability to regain the Pacific Division title after winning it in his first three seasons as an NHL coach. That failure has helped reduce his ASR considerably.

In my entry on Bob Johnson, I did some hypothetical calculations of his coaching value had he coached the Penguins up to 1995/96 and up to 2000/01 based on how the Penguins really performed as a team during those years.

If I did the same thing with his ASR, the numbers would look like this:

1. If Johnson had coached to 1995/96, his ASR would have been +7.727 (good for #13 on this list).
2. If Johnson had coached to 2000/01, his ASR would have been +6.500 (good for #17 on this list).

Ever since he became head coach of the St. Louis Blues in 2011/12, Ken Hitchcock's ASR has risen from +5.000 to +5.667.

Darryl Sutter's second Stanley Cup win in 2013/14 was a boon to his ASR, causing it to ascend from +4.846 to +5.714. When the Kings failed to reach the playoffs in 2014/15 it fell to +5.333.

In 2008/9 Alain Vigneault's ASR was +1.000. Today, it has risen to +5.385 because he ranks among the top three coaches of the 2010s.

Take note of Robbie Ftorek's ASR. Experts may scoff at the fact that he used to rank among the top 50 in my book, but his high ASR stands as evidence of the untapped potential he possessed as coach, the untapped potential that was undermined by his leadership flaws.

Had Ftorek kept his head and achieved the same results as the men who replaced him as head coach in New Jersey in 1999/00 and Boston in 2002/03 then his ASR would have been at least +7.167.

That is the tragedy of Robbie Ftorek's coaching career.

If you're surprised to see how low Al Arbour's ASR is given the fact that he won four Stanley Cups, it's because of his return to coaching in 1989 and the relatively poor job the Islanders did during that second coaching stint. When Arbour retired in 1986, his ASR was a solid 7.563 (good for #13 on this list), but look where it ended up.

31. *Peter Laviolette* +4.308
32. Mike Keenan +4.250
33. Harry Sinden +4.167
34. Jack Adams +4.050
35. Lester Patrick +4.045
36. Leo Dandurand +4.000
37. Marc Boileau +3.800
38. *Bob Hartley* +3.750
39. Floyd Smith +3.667
40. Al MacNeil +3.600

Peter Laviolette's failure to make the playoffs in 2012/13 and his firing three games into the 2013/14 season reduced his ASR to +4.167, but his brilliant comeback with the Nashville Predators in 2014/15 has pushed him back up the ASR charts.

When Mike Keenan won the 1993/94 Stanley Cup, his ASR was +9.889 (good for #5 on this list). See where it is now and that shows you how poor the second part of his coaching career turned out to be. Harry Sinden's ASR is +4.167 for one reason: his NHL debut season of 1966/67, where the Bruins finished in last place. His ASR was a -10.00, and Sinden spent the remainder of his NHL coaching career climbing out of that hole. Take away the disastrous rookie season and his ASR would be +7.000 (it doesn't pay to start off a loser in the ASR stakes).

Lester Patrick's ASR is low because of the years he coached in the PCHA. His teams usually finished last in the league, especially from 1917 to 1924. Those losing seasons served to pull down his rating. From 1917 to 1926, Patrick's rating was only +0.444, whereas when he coached in the NHL from 1926 to 1939, his ASR was +6.538 (if you include the years he coached in the PCHA from 1912 to 1917, his ASR would be only +3.321).

Bob Hartley's decline is even worse. Before he became head coach of the Calgary Flames his ASR was +5.333, but two losing seasons reduced his ASR dramatically. In 2014/15 it rose back to +3.750.

Marc Boileau coached the Quebec Nordiques to their only Avco Cup title in 1976/77.

Floyd Smith and Al MacNeil both emerged suddenly and dramatically in the 1970s as hockey coaches both in the AHL and the NHL. Both men coached Calder Cup winners (MacNeil had three). Both men led their teams to the Stanley Cup finals (MacNeil in 1971 and Smith in 1975). MacNeil won the Cup, whereas Smith lost to the Flyers in six games. Both men were, for a brief time, ranked among the greatest coaches of the game, according to my rating system (see "The Progressive Chart"), but because of the brevity of their coaching careers, neither coach was able to remain on the charts. Smith's coaching career ended in 1979/80; MacNeil's in 1981/82 (with a brief interim stint in 2001/02).

41.	Randy Carlyle	+3.500
42.	*Dave Tippett*	+3.417
43.	Pat Quinn	+3.400
44.	*Michel Therrien*	+3.400
45.	Emile Francis	+3.308
46.	Pete Muldoon	+3.222
47.	Brent Sutter	+3.200
48.	Terry Murray	+3.133
49.	Eddie Johnston	+3.125
50.	Bryan Murray	+3.000

Coaching the Toronto Maple Leafs reduced Randy Carlyle's ASR from +6.500 to +3.500.

Dave Tippett's failure to reach the Stanley Cup playoffs from 2012/13 to 2014/15 has reduced his ASR from +5.667 to +3.417.

Pat Quinn, Emile Francis, and Pete Muldoon all had reduced ASRs because they coached bad teams at the tail end of their careers.

Michel Therrien's three superb seasons coaching the Montreal Canadiens has helped his ASR rise from +1.143 to +3.400.

51.	Jacques Lemaire	+2.882
52.	Marc Crawford	+2.800
53.	Bobby Kromm	+2.800
54.	Herb Gardiner	+2.800

55.	Art Ross	+2.778
56.	Rudy Pilous	+2.714
57.	Jacques Martin	+2.647
58.	Roger Neilson	+2.625
59.	Larry Robinson	+2.625
60.	Bob Pulford	+2.417

Although tied with Herb Gardiner and Bobby Kromm in ASRs, Marc Crawford ranks above Kromm and Gardiner because his coaching value is way higher than that of either man. Still, Crawford's ASR was not always this small. In 2003/04 his ASR was a solid +6.000, but during the last five seasons of his coaching career it plummeted to its present level. (Both Bobby Kromm and Herb Gardiner share the same coaching value of +14 and the same ASR of +2.800; however, Kromm ranks higher than Gardiner because he has a better winning percentage of .509 to Gardiner's .440.)

Kromm missed his chance for glory when he left the Winnipeg Jets to become head coach of the Detroit Red Wings. Had he stayed in Winnipeg and achieved the same results the Jets achieved under his successors (Larry Hillman and Tom McVie), then his ASR would have been an astonishing +11.80.

Herb Gardiner led the Calgary Tigers in the WCHL to the 1923/24 Stanley Cup finals against Leo Dandurand's Montreal Canadiens. Roger Neilson is ahead of Larry Robinson because Nielson's coaching value is better than Robinson's.

61.	*Lindy Ruff*	+2.353
62.	Tommy Gorman	+2.250
63.	John Tortorella	+1.929
64.	Ron Wilson	+1.222
65.	Bernie Geoffrion	+1.200
66.	Fred Creighton	+1.167
67.	Terry Crisp	+1.111
68.	Glen Sonmor	+1.100
69.	Michel Bergeron	+1.000
70.	Jim Schoenfeld	+1.000

Lindy Ruff's inconsistency has played havoc with his ASR. His final season with Buffalo cost him dearly. His ASR fell from +2.929 to +2.467, but his debut season coaching the Dallas Stars helped inch his ASR back up to +2.500. Then his failure to lead Dallas to the playoffs in 2014/15 reduced it to +2.353.

Tommy Gorman is the only man in NHL history to coach back-to-back Stanley Cup winners for two different teams. Gorman led the Chicago Blackhawks to the 1933/34 Stanley Cup but was fired by Major Frederic McLaughlin (another one of McLaughlin's victims) and was promptly hired by the Montreal Maroons. Gorman led the Maroons to the 1934/35 Stanley Cup title. He later became general manager of the Montreal Canadiens from 1940 to 1946.

John Tortorella is the sixth man to coach a Calder Cup and Stanley Cup winner. His failure to lead Vancouver to the playoffs in 2013/14 caused his ASR to fall from +2.077 to +1.929 and stands as evidence as to why he hasn't cracked the top 50 ranks yet after 13 seasons of NHL coaching. The inconsistency of his coaching record has kept him from making the great leap into the elite ranks of the NHL coaching pantheon.

As mentioned before, Ron Wilson's years with Toronto really caused his ASR to decline dramatically.

Terry Crisp's ASR after the first three years of his NHL coaching career with the Calgary Flames was a white-hot +13.67. But six seasons of coaching the expansion Tampa Bay Lightning undid all his great work in Calgary. Sometimes all the coaching skill in the world cannot reverse bad luck.

71.	John Muckler	+0.800
72.	Kevin Constantine	+0.714
73.	Brian Sutter	+0.692
74.	*Barry Trotz*	+0.563
75.	Craig MacTavish	+0.500
76.	Bob Gainey	+0.500
77.	Newsy Lalonde	+0.467
78.	Sid Abel	+0.438
79.	Bep Guidolin	+0.400
80.	Bob McCammon	+0.375

All of the ten coaches listed directly above had flashes of brilliance mixed with great disappointments in their careers. Of the ten, only three – Muckler, Lalonde, and Gerard – coached Stanley Cup winners.

The poor performance of the Nashville Predators in 2012/13 and 2013/14 dealt a mortal blow to Barry Trotz's standing as a coach. After the end of the 2011/12 season, I had Trotz on the cusp of greatness, with a +10 coaching value and an ASR of +0.769.

He started coaching in 1998, and by 2002/03 Trotz's coaching value was -26 and his ASR -5.200. Then Trotz began accumulating plus points, and his ASR between 2003 and 2012 was a respectable +4.500. His stock was rising slowly but surely. In 2012/13, Trotz lost seven points off his career value (which means he's no longer on the cusp of greatness), and his ASR was reduced significantly. In 2013/14 it fell to +0.200 and he lost his Predators coaching job. His first season with the Washington Capitols helped raise it back to +0.563.

When I first began doing research for this book, I was using the success points method I described in "Methodology." I wasn't calculating minus points at all. In my first draft, I had Abel ranking among the top 50, but when I began re-evaluating and improving my methods, which eventually evolved into their present form, I realized that Abel did not deserve to rank among the top 50 (even though he led the Detroit Red Wings to four Stanley Cup finals from 1960/61 to 1965/66).

In 16 seasons of NHL coaching, Abel had only five winning seasons and one first-place finish. On the debit side, he endured 10 losing seasons and his teams finished last four times. Those failures conspired to reduce his ASR to what it is now.

81.	Eddie Gerard	+0.364
82.	Jacques Demers	+0.333
83.	Herb Brooks	+0.286
84.	Lynn Patrick	+0.200
85.	Jack Gordon	+0.200
86.	John Stevens	+0.200
87.	Harry Neale	+0.154
88.	Red Kelly	-0.100
89.	Dave King	-0.167
90.	Andy Murray	-0.300

Harry Neale is in the same boat as Bobby Kromm. He had a solid coaching career in the WHA but failed to emulate that success when he jumped to the NHL in 1978.

91.	Bobby Francis	-0.400
92.	Terry Simpson	-0.500
93.	*Paul Maurice*	-0.529
94.	Mike Milbury	-0.667
95.	*Todd Richards*	-0.667
96.	Doug Maclean	-0.800
97.	Craig Hartsburg	-0.857
98.	Paul Thompson	-1.286
99.	John Paddock	-1.400
100.	Peter DeBoer	-1.429

Paul Maurice's return to the NHL coaching ranks in 2013/14 helped reduce his already mediocre ASR even further from -0.733 to -0.529.

Mike Milbury's first two seasons coaching in the NHL were splendid. His coaching value was +25 and his ASR was a hefty +12.50, but (like Terry Crisp) his years of coaching the New York Islanders destroyed whatever good he had accomplished.

Actually, Milbury was a worse general manager than he was a coach. If you applied my rating system to his managerial record, his value would be a horrific -42 and his ASR a -4.200.

Todd Richards' work with the Columbus Blue Jackets has improved his ASR from -1.750 to -0.667.

Even though Peter DeBoer has the same ASR as Joe Crozier, he ranks above Crozier because he has the better winning percentage.

101.	Joe Crozier	-1.429
102.	Ron Low	-1.714
103.	Tom Renney	-1.889
104.	Red Dutton	-2.000
105.	Pierre Page	-2.000

106. Frank Boucher -2.000
107. *Jack Capuano* -2.400
108. Phil Watson -2.444
109. Dan Maloney -3.000
110. Tom McVie -3.222

The further we move down the list, the greater the mediocrity and futility we see in the coaches listed directly above. Before he was fired in 2012, Tom Renney had the worst coaching value and the worst ASR among all the active coaches in the NHL. Frank Boucher suffered the same fate as Terry Crisp, only worse. After his first three seasons of coaching the New York Rangers, Boucher's coaching value was +30 and his ASR +10.00. What followed were eight seasons coaching a sinking ship – which is what the New York Rangers were during most of the Original Six era. The only bright spot in Boucher's later coaching career was that he led Team Canada to the gold medal in the 1948 Winter Olympic Games at St. Moritz, thus becoming the first man ever to coach a Stanley Cup winner and an Olympic gold medal–winning team.

Jack Capuano is a new arrival in the ASR stakes. Even though he ranks near the bottom, Capuano's ASR has actually improved in recent years. After his second season in 2011/12 his ASR was -7.000, but two winning seasons and two playoff appearances have helped improve his ASR to its present level.

111. *Ted Nolan* -3.333
112. Paul Holmgren -3.500
113. Johnny Wilson -3.556
114. Tom Watt -3.857
115. Jack Evans -4.000
116. Milt Schmidt -4.077
117. Red Sullivan -4.286
118. Larry Pleau -4.600
119. Doug Carpenter -5.000
120. Rick Bowness -6.333
121. Fred Glover -6.833

When Ted Nolan took over as head coach of the Sabres his ASR was 0.000 but leading the Sabres (who are in a major rebuilding mode and cleaning the Augean stables) to the Atlantic Division basement helped reduce it to -3.333 and his dismissal as head coach of the Sabres.

Most of the names you see directly above are featured prominently in "Losing Coaches" coming up.

Since -10.00 is the absolute bottom, it begs the question: Did any coach ever have an ASR of -10.00 in his career?

The answer is yes. Four coaches, each of whom had only two years' coaching experience in the NHL, earned that ignominious honour: Art Chapman, Ebbie Goodfellow, George Kingston, and Percy Thompson. Chapman coached the New York/Brooklyn Americans during the last two seasons of their miserable existence. Goodfellow coached two years with the Chicago Blackhawks when they were considered the Siberia of the NHL. Kingston is a living legend in Canadian collegiate hockey, but his two years of coaching the expansion San Jose Sharks were the nadir of his illustrious career. Thompson coached the Hamilton Tigers in the NHL during the early 1920s and was the worst coach of that decade.

DECADES

Another advantage of using my rating system is that we can determine not only which hockey coaches were the most successful overall but also which ones were the best in a certain decade. What follows is a listing of the top three most successful hockey coaches along with their success point totals for each decade from 1917 to 2015.

Since hockey seasons start near the end of one year and end in the spring of the following year, there is a question of how to benchmark a decade. The system I used is as follows. For the 1920s, I started with the 1919/20 season and ended with the 1928/29 season. For all subsequent decades I adhered to the same standard.

When determining which coaches were best at offence, defence, and other categories for a specific decade, I decided that any coach who coached a minimum of three complete seasons within the decade was eligible for statistical consideration.

1917–1926

1. Pete Green +82
2. Frank Patrick +57
3. Ken Mackenzie +34

WORST COACH: Art Ross
BEST OFFENSIVE COACH: Newsy Lalonde
BEST DEFENSIVE COACH: Leo Dandurand
MOST PENALIZED TEAMS: Eddie Gerard
LEAST PENALIZED TEAMS: Frank Patrick

The NHL was formed in 1917 as a successor to the National Hockey Association. The NHL was a four-team league (soon to become three) and vied with the PCHA and later the WCHL/WHL for the Stanley Cup. The Americanization of the game began with the formation of the Boston Bruins in 1924 and the New York Americans in 1925.

Newsy Lalonde's teams were averaging 3.93 goals scored per game during this era. Frank Patrick was second, with a 3.81 average.

Leo Dandurand was the head coach of the Montreal Canadiens from 1921/22 to 1925/26 (in addition to being their owner and manager). He led the Habs to two Stanley Cup finals appearances, in 1923/24 and 1924/25, winning the 1923/24 Cup. During this era his Canadiens teams had the best defence with a 2.58 GAA.

Eddie Gerard's teams averaged 13.39 penalty minutes per game during this time. The only coach who came near him was Leo Dandurand.

One reason why Art Ross didn't rank higher on my top 50 list is because of his poor performance during this time. Ross's coaching value was an appalling -28. He would spend the rest of his coaching career overcoming this deficit.

1920S

1. Pete Green +82
2. Frank Patrick +36
3. Lester Patrick +36

WORST COACH: Percy Thompson
BEST OFFENSIVE COACH: Pete Green
BEST DEFENSIVE COACH: Cecil Hart
MOST PENALIZED TEAMS: Eddie Gerard
LEAST PENALIZED TEAMS: Frank Patrick

Pete Green's dynastic run during the first part of the 1920s explains his domination of the decade. Lester Patrick dominated the latter half and would continue his winning ways into the 1930s.

Green was the best offensive coach of the decade because his original Ottawa Senators were averaging 3.72 goals per game from 1919/20 to 1924/1925.

Although Frank and Lester Patrick are tied in coaching value for the decade at +36, I've given Frank the nod for second place because his ASR for the decade is better than Lester's: +5.143 for Frank, whereas Lester's is +3.600. Frank earned his points during the first half of the decade. Lester earned his during the later part of the decade.

Despite that fact, he remained the best coach when it came to instilling on-ice discipline with his teams. His Vancouver teams averaged only 5.06 penalty minutes per game during the 1920s.

The restrictions placed on passing in the three zones led to a dramatic drop in offence in the NHL in the latter half of the 1920s. Indeed, several goaltending records you see in the NHL record book today were established during this time. From 1925/26 to 1928/29, Cecil Hart's Montreal Canadians were allowing only 1.20 goals per game.

Ottawa Senators head coach David Gill was the second-best defensive coach with a 1.46 GAA. (He had Hall of Famer Alec Connell as a goaltender and King Clancy as a defenceman.)

Eddie Gerard's Montreal Maroons were the bad boys in the NHL during the decade, averaging 14.07 penalty minutes per game, which was extraordinary for the time. Most hockey teams were averaging around eight to nine penalty minutes per game.

1930S

1. Dick Irvin +87
2. Art Ross +55
3. Lester Patrick +53

WORST COACH: George Boucher
BEST OFFENSIVE COACH: Art Ross
BEST DEFENSIVE COACH: Art Ross
MOST PENALIZED TEAMS: Eddie Gerard
LEAST PENALIZED TEAMS: Clem Loughlin

Even though he won only one Stanley Cup during the 1930s, Dick Irvin dominated the decade with his brilliant, consistent coaching.

Art Ross coached brilliantly too, despite winning only one Stanley Cup and missing two seasons when he yielded the bench to Frank Patrick.

Lester Patrick's appearances on the 1920s and 1930s rankings reflect his coaching career. His teams never really dominated the NHL, but they were always tough, competitive, and occasionally played championship hockey.

Art Ross dominated the offensive and defensive standings. Ross's Bruins averaged 2.92 goals scored per game. Dick Irvin was second, with a 2.80 average.

Ross was the best defensive coach, with a 2.12 GAA. Having Tiny Thompson and Eddie Brimsek in goal and Eddie Shore and Dit Clapper playing defence had a lot to do with that.

Eddie Gerard maintained his reputation for coaching nasty teams, but Dick Irvin wasn't too far behind. Gerard led the decade by averaging 10.23 penalty minutes per game, with Irvin finishing second with 10.15.

Clem Loughlin was a defenceman who had played for a long time with Lester Patrick in the PCHA and later in the WCHL/WHL. He was a member of the Victoria Cougars team that won the 1924/25 Stanley Cup. When the WHL folded in 1926, Loughlin played with the Detroit Red Wings and the Chicago Blackhawks in the NHL.

Loughlin coached the Chicago Blackhawks from 1934/35 to 1936/37. During that time, his teams were averaging only 7.55 penalty minutes per game – as opposed to Jack Adams's teams, which averaged 7.59 penalty minutes per game – which is why Loughlin is listed above.

George Boucher was the worst coach of the 1930s, with a coaching value of -17. He had the misfortune of coaching the original Ottawa Senators (later to become the St. Louis Eagles) when they were in their death throes.

1940S

1. Hap Day +84
2. Dick Irvin +73
3. Jack Adams +46

WORST COACH: Johnny Gottselig
BEST OFFENSIVE COACH: Art Ross
BEST DEFENSIVE COACH: Dick Irvin
MOST PENALIZED TEAMS: Dick Irvin
LEAST PENALIZED TEAMS: Art Ross

Hap Day dominated the decade with his five Stanley Cup wins. Dick Irvin again coached brilliantly, despite enduring three losing seasons during the decade. He made up for them by winning two Stanley Cups.

The 1940s were Jack Adams's best decade as a hockey coach.

I was surprised myself to see Art Ross as the best offensive coach of the 1940s, but when you look at the NHL team offensive stats for the 1940s you come across some big surprises. In four seasons of coaching in the 1940s, Ross had a goals scored average of 3.82. His nearest competition was Hap Day at 3.38 and Dick Irvin with a 3.23 goals scored average.

How does Dick Irvin rank third even though he had Rocket Richard? After 1946, Irvin's Habs teams' offensive output declined dramatically (the Canadiens were rebuilding). From 1946 to 1949, Irvin's teams finished fifth, sixth, and fourth in a six-team league, despite the presence of Rocket Richard and Elmer Lach. Also in the 1941/42 season, Irvin's Habs finished sixth in offence in a seven-team league.

Those poor finishes biased Irvin's offensive ratings during the decade.

When it came to penalty minutes, Irvin beat out Day. Irvin's teams averaged 9.77 penalty minutes per game. Day's teams were second, with 8.58.

Art Ross continued his penchant for on-ice discipline. During his coaching stint during the 1940s, his Bruins averaged 6.13 penalty minutes per game. Red Dutton, who coached the New York (later Brooklyn) Americans, was second, with only 6.21 penalty minutes per game.

I named Johnny Gottselig as the worst coach of the 1940s, even though he is tied with Frank Boucher with a decade coaching value of -21. I chose Gottselig over Boucher because Gottselig's decade ASR is far worse than Boucher's: -5.250 to Boucher's -2.100, which means Gottselig did a much worse job of leading his players than Boucher did.

Boucher coached the New York Rangers and Gottselig the Chicago Blackhawks: two teams that took turns occupying the NHL cellar.

1950S

1. Toe Blake +77
2. Tommy Ivan +69
3. Dick Irvin +39

WORST COACH: Ebbie Goodfellow
BEST OFFENSIVE COACH: Toe Blake
BEST DEFENSIVE COACH: King Clancy
MOST PENALIZED TEAMS: King Clancy
LEAST PENALIZED TEAMS: Lynn Patrick

Tommy Ivan dominated the first half of the 1950s while Toe Blake dominated the second half. Still, if Ivan had not coached the Chicago Blackhawks during the latter half of the decade, he would have trumped Blake as the best hockey coach of the 1950s.

Dick Irvin is the only coach to rank among the top three hockey coaches in three decades, according to my rating system.

Toe Blake overwhelmed the competition with regards to offence. His Canadiens teams from 1955 to 1959 were averaging 3.36 goals scored per game. No other coach was even close.

How does King Clancy emerge as the best defensive coach of the 1950s? King Clancy was head coach of the Toronto Maple Leafs from 1953 to 1956, and during those three seasons his Leaf teams finished first, second, and third in the NHL in defence (and the year he finished second in defence, he was only one goal behind the league leader).

Clancy's Leafs had Harry Lumley in goal and Tim Horton, Fern Flaman, and Leo Boivin on defence. Clancy's GAA for the 1950s was 2.13, which barely edges Toe Blake's 2.15 for the decade.

Clancy also had the nastiest team on the ice, averaging 14.59 penalty minutes per game. No other NHL coach during the 1950s came close to that average.

Lynn Patrick was head coach of the New York Rangers from 1948 to 1951 and the Boston Bruins from 1951 to 1954. Patrick's teams were consistently at or near the bottom in team penalty minutes, averaging 9.18 penalty minutes per game. Again, no other NHL coach came close to that figure.

Actually, Patrick's emphasis on on-ice discipline is not surprising, considering that he played for Frank Boucher during the 1940s. Boucher as New York Rangers head coach and general manager made on-ice discipline a cornerstone of his hockey philosophy, and it stuck with the majority of the players who served under him. With the exception of Phil Watson and Fred Shero, Boucher's players who later became head coaches themselves stressed on-ice discipline. Emile Francis was another devoted follower of Boucher's teachings.

As a player, Ebbie Goodfellow was a prize pupil of Jack Adams, but he failed as a hockey coach. He led the Blackhawks for two seasons and had a coaching value of -20.

1960S

1. Toe Blake +118
2. Punch Imlach +84
3. Billy Reay +30

WORST COACH: Milt Schmidt
BEST OFFENSIVE COACH: Harry Sinden
BEST DEFENSIVE COACH: Toe Blake
BEST POWER PLAY OFFENCE: Toe Blake
BEST PENALTY-KILLING: Toe Blake
BEST SHORT-HANDED OFFENCE: Billy Reay
MOST PENALIZED TEAMS: Harry Sinden
LEAST PENALIZED TEAMS: Red Sullivan

Despite a four-season Stanley Cup drought, Toe Blake continued his domination of the NHL. Blake, along with Punch Imlach, ruled the NHL. During the decade, only three coaches won Stanley Cups: Blake won five, Imlach won four, and Rudy Pilous of the Blackhawks won the other one.

Even though Harry Sinden coached only three seasons in the 1960s, he immediately made an impact when it came to offence and on-ice meanness. Sinden's Bruins, taking advantage of the offensive explosion that accompanied the league's expansion, were scoring 3.38 goals per game. Billy Reay was second, with 3.34 goals scored.

The Montreal Canadiens were always fantastic on the power play, and Toe Blake's teams were the best, averaging .7303 power-play goals per game. Billy Reay was a close second, with a .7279 average.

Another reason why Blake won four Stanley Cups in the 1960s was because he had the best penalty-killing unit in the NHL.

Sinden's teams set new records in team penalty minutes and presaged the goon squad mentality that had marred the 1970s. The only other NHL coach who came close to Sinden in team penalty minutes was Rudy Pilous, who coached the Chicago Blackhawks from 1958 to 1963. During the early 1960s, Pilous's Hawks were the most penalized team in the NHL, averaging 13.72 penalty minutes per game.

Sinden may have edged out Reay in overall offence, but Reay was the best at short-handed offence. His Blackhawks led the NHL in short-handed offence from 1963 to 1967.

Red Sullivan was one of the worst NHL head coaches of all time (see "Losing Coaches"), but if he had one virtue it is that his teams were seldom penalized on the ice. Again, Sullivan, who played with the New York Rangers before becoming their head coach, was a product of the Frank Boucher–Lynn Patrick school of on-ice discipline.

Milt Schmidt was the worst coach of the 1960s, with a coaching value of -49, the worst decade performance by any NHL coach, according to my rating system.

1970S

1. Scotty Bowman +142
2. Fred Shero +81
3. Bill Dineen +75

WORST COACH: Fred Glover
BEST OFFENSIVE COACH: Scotty Bowman
BEST DEFENSIVE COACH: Scotty Bowman
BEST POWER PLAY OFFENCE: Floyd Smith
BEST PENALTY-KILLING: Emile Francis
BEST SHORT-HANDED OFFENCE: Fred Shero
MOST PENALIZED TEAMS: Fred Shero
LEAST PENALIZED TEAMS: Scotty Bowman

Scotty Bowman's coaching value for the 1970s is a record, according to my rating system. No other coach did better during a decade. Bowman's excellence was made possible because his teams dominated the NHL in offence, defence, the power play, and avoiding the penalty box.

Fred Shero's second-place finish further reinforces his stature as a great hockey coach. Yes, his teams racked up the penalty minutes, but when their opponents had a man-advantage, it merely made the Flyers more dangerous, as you can see from Shero's excellence with regards to short-handed offence.

Harry Sinden's teams in the 1960s were averaging 14.03 penalty minutes per game. Shero blew everyone out of the water by averaging 20.55 penalty minutes per game. No one else came close.

The same can be said with regards to short-handed offence. Shero's Flyers were averaging .1624 short-handed goals per game. Interestingly, the second-best coach was Bill Dineen, who got his teams to average .1614 short-handed goals per game.

Dineen's presence on this list may surprise a few people, considering he coached in the WHA, but he was the greatest coach in the seven-year history of the league and did a magnificent job in making the Houston Aeros one of the strongest franchises in the WHA.

Are you wondering who the third-best NHL coach was during the 1970s? It was Billy Reay of Chicago, with a coaching value of +59.

It may surprise some people that Emile Francis had the best penalty-killing teams during the 1970s, but the stats bear it out: the Cat beat Scotty Bowman by a whisker.

Fred Glover's coaching value of -41 made him the worst coach of the 1970s. It is also the third-worst decade performance in hockey history, based on my calculations.

1980S

1. Glen Sather +118
2. Al Arbour +87
3. Mike Keenan +43

WORST COACH: Doug Carpenter
BEST OFFENSIVE COACH: Glen Sather
BEST DEFENSIVE COACH: Scotty Bowman
BEST POWER PLAY OFFENCE: Eddie Johnston
BEST PENALTY-KILLING: Scotty Bowman
BEST SHORT-HANDED OFFENCE: Glen Sather
MOST PENALIZED TEAMS: Mike Keenan
LEAST PENALIZED TEAMS: Scotty Bowman

Glen Sather came closer to equalling Scotty Bowman's decade coaching value of +146 than any other hockey coach, according to my rating system.

Al Arbour's score might have been higher if he had not retired as a coach in 1986.

Even though he didn't coach during the first half of the 1980s, Mike Keenan was still able to finish third in coaching value due to his sterling work with the Philadelphia Flyers.

Glen Sather was the greatest offensive coach ever, with his performance in the 1980s proving that claim because his Oilers were averaging 4.79 goals per game during the decade. Bob Johnson was next, with 4.17 goals scored average.

Scotty Bowman may not have won the Stanley Cup during the 1980s, but his Sabres had the best defence during the decade, allowing only 3.21 goals per game. He was able to achieve this because his teams were also the best in penalty-killing and in avoiding the penalty box.

The 1970s saw an enormous upsurge in on-ice violence, but that decade was nothing when compared with the 1980s. Fred Shero's teams were the most penalized in the 1970s by averaging 20.55 penalty minutes per game, but those numbers pale when you compare them with what Mike Keenan, Eddie Johnston, Pat Quinn, and Terry Crisp were doing in the 1980s.

Keenan's squads were averaging 25.63 penalty minutes per game; Johnston's were averaging 22.53; Pat Quinn's teams were averaging 25.53 penalty minutes. Terry Crisp coached only two years in the decade, which makes him ineligible for statistical consideration, but his Flames averaged 30.36 penalty minutes per game from 1987 to 1989!

The 1980s were the most violent decade in all of hockey.

There were other explosions in NHL hockey. Power-play offence spiked to its greatest peak in hockey history during this decade.

During the 1970s, Scotty Bowman's teams were averaging .864 power-play goals a game. In the 1980s several coaches dwarfed that figure. Eddie Johnston led the pack with 1.05 power-play goals a game. Bryan Murray, Mike Keenan, Roger Neilson, and Michel Bergeron followed in his wake with numbers that exceed what Bowman had done in the 1970s.

Since then, no other NHL coach has achieved those levels in power-play offence.

I selected Doug Carpenter as the worst coach of the 1980s, even though he is tied with Larry Pleau with a decade coaching value of -23. Carpenter's decade ASR was -5.750 compared with Pleau's ASR of -4.600. Carpenter set a record for futility while coaching the New Jersey Devils, whereas Larry Pleau beached himself as head coach of the Hartford Whalers.

1990S

1. Scotty Bowman +94
2. Mike Keenan +44
3. Terry Murray +41

WORST COACH: Rick Bowness
BEST OFFENSIVE COACH: Eddie Johnston
BEST DEFENSIVE COACH: Jacques Lemaire
BEST POWER-PLAY OFFENCE: Eddie Johnston
BEST PENALTY-KILLING: Marc Crawford
BEST SHORT-HANDED OFFENCE: Scotty Bowman
MOST PENALIZED TEAMS: Mike Keenan
LEAST PENALIZED TEAMS: Jacques Martin

Scotty Bowman and Toe Blake are the only hockey coaches to dominate two decades, according to my rating system.

Mike Keenan's coaching value was +52 by 1995, but for the remainder of the decade his value declined steadily. Keenan also continued his domination with regards to team penalty minutes. His teams were averaging 25.71 penalty minutes per game.

Terry Murray's presence may surprise some people, but he did solid coaching work from 1990 to 1997. If he hadn't done so poorly with the Florida Panthers, then he would have placed second in the decade.

It's not surprising that Eddie Johnston was the best offensive coach of the 1990s. When you're coaching Mario Lemieux and Jaromir Jagr at the peak of their respective careers, then you're going to rack up some serious numbers in overall offence and power-play offence. Johnston's Penguins were averaging 3.84 goals scored per game. Scotty Bowman was second, with 3.72

On the power play, Johnston continued his domination from the previous decade. His teams were averaging 1.03 power-play goals per game. Again, Bowman was second, with 1.01.

Bob Berry coached two seasons during the 1990s and put up impressive power-play figures, averaging 1.06 power-play goals per game, but since Berry failed to coach the three-season minimum, he is not rated the best.

Jacques Lemaire altered the game with his neutral-zone trap. During the decade, his Devils were allowing only 2.36 goals per game. Ken Hitchcock was the second-best defensive coach, with a 2.37 GAA.

Marc Crawford is renowned for being an offensive coach, but during the early years of his coaching career he was getting superb penalty-killing stats with his Avalanche and Canuck teams. Scotty Bowman was right behind him.

Even though Lemaire, Hitchcock, and Bowman were coaching in the 1990s, it was Jacques Martin who was the best when it came to on-ice discipline during this decade. That's a pretty solid achievement considering that Lemaire, Hitchcock, and Bowman were masters at reducing their team's penalty minute totals.

Rick Bowness's coaching value of -43 is the second-worst coaching performance during a decade in hockey history, according to my rating system.

2000S

1. Mike Babcock +61
2. Bob Hartley +41
3. Ken Hitchcock +41

WORST COACH: Curt Fraser
BEST OFFENSIVE COACH: Scotty Bowman
BEST DEFENSIVE COACH: Scotty Bowman
BEST POWER-PLAY OFFENCE: Randy Carlyle
BEST PENALTY-KILLING: Scotty Bowman
BEST SHORT-HANDED OFFENCE: Bryan Murray
MOST PENALIZED TEAMS: Randy Carlyle
LEAST PENALIZED TEAMS: Mike Babcock

Mike Babcock dominated the decade with his three Stanley Cup finals appearances and 2008 Stanley Cup title.

Although tied with each other in terms of coaching value, Bob Hartley trumps Ken Hitchcock for second place in the decade race because his decade ASR of +5.125 is superior to Hitchcock's decade ASR of +4.566.

Scotty Bowman coached only three seasons during the 2000s, yet he did well enough to finish as the best offensive and defensive coach of the decade. Bowman's Wings were scoring 3.18 goals per game and allowing only 2.44 goals per game. Bowman's teams were also the best at penalty-killing, with Jacques Lemaire finishing a close second.

Bryan Murray was the second-best offensive coach, but when it came to short-handed offence, he was the tops. His Senators teams were averaging .1969 short-handed goals per game. No other coach came close.

Randy Carlyle had the best power-play unit in the NHL during the decade. His Ducks were averaging .9421 power-play goals per game. His Ducks were also the meanest team on ice, averaging 17.75 penalty minutes per game. Darryl Sutter and Mike Keenan were tied for second in that category.

One of the main reasons why Mike Babcock's teams excelled during the decade was because of their on-ice discipline. Babcock's teams were averaging only 12.08 penalty minutes per game. Lindy Ruff was right behind him, with 12.22.

Curt Fraser was the worst coach of the 2000s because of his work with the expansion Atlanta Thrashers (now the Winnipeg Jets). Fraser was the first head coach in the franchise's history and had a coaching value of -27. Glen Hanlon was the second-worst coach, with a -24 value while coaching the Washington Capitals.

2010S

1. **Joel Quenneville** +74
2. **Alain Vigneault** +63
3. **Claude Julien** +55

WORST COACH: **Jack Capuano**
BEST OFFENSIVE COACH: **Dan Byslma**
BEST DEFENSIVE COACH: **Darryl Sutter**
BEST POWER-PLAY OFFENCE: **Todd McLellan**
BEST PENALTY-KILLING: **Dan Bylsma**
BEST SHORT-HANDED OFFENCE: **Peter DeBoer**
MOST PENALIZED TEAMS: **Randy Carlyle**
LEAST PENALIZED TEAMS: **Mike Babcock**

Joel Quenneville and Alain Vigneault have raced neck and neck throughout the decade but Quenneville's third Stanley Cup finals appearance in the 2010s has helped him leap ahead of Alain Vigneault.

Vigneault, who, despite failing to win the Stanley Cup in two tries, has remained close by having a better regular season record than Quenneville: .616% to Quenneville's .613% (as well as winning three President's Trophies in the 2010s); and by winning five divisional titles to Quenneville's two.

Claude Julien's failure to make the playoffs caused him to fall behind significantly in the decade sweepstakes. Before 2014/15, Julien was ahead of Quenneville and Vigneault both. Even though he was fired in 2014, Dan Bylsma remains the best offensive coach of the decade with an average of 3.168 goals scored per game with Joel Quenneville second with a 3.118 average.

Darryl Sutter is the best defensive coach of the 2010s. His teams have yielded only 2.333 goals per game (Claude Julien is second, with a 2.389 average).

The biggest surprise of this decade has been the decline in power-play goal production. Todd McLellan leads all NHL coaches, with a .7183 per game average. Contrast this with Randy Carlyle's decade leading average of .9421 in the 2000s. Most NHL coaches' power-play averages today range in the .6000 percentile, whereas last decade most coaches were in the .8000s.

Dan Bylsma's Penguins squads were the best at penalty-killing during the 2010s, edging out Ken Hitchcock's St. Louis Blues teams with an average of .8494 to Hitchcock's .8476.

Despite being fired in 2014/15, Randy Carlyle's teams have been the meanest squads in the NHL, averaging 13.78 penalty minutes per-game with Peter Laviolette's teams finishing second with a 13.52 average.

Mike Babcock eclipses Joel Quenneville with regards to on-ice discipline. Babcock's Red Wings have averaged only 8.734 penalty minutes per game, while Quenneville's teams have averaged 9.050.

Before he was fired in 2014/15, Peter DeBoer got superb short-handed offence from his New Jersey Devils with a .1141 average. Bob Hartley finished second with a .1132 average.

Jack Capuano has been head coach of the New York Islanders since 2010. As of 2014/15 his coaching value of -12 is the worst of the decade (thus far), but he may not remain the worst for long. Twice in the past three season he has led the Islanders to the playoffs, thus improving his standing.

RIVAL LEAGUES

This section lists the top head coaches for the three rival major hockey leagues that went toe-to-toe with the NHL from 1917 to 1979. The point totals you see for each coach are based on their seasonal records within the time frame specified.

PACIFIC COAST HOCKEY ASSOCIATION: 1911–1924

1.	Frank Patrick	+90
2.	Pete Muldoon	+57
3.	Edward Savage	+15
4.	Jimmy Gardner	+9
5.	Eddie Oatman	-1
6.	Lester Patrick	-24

WORST COACH: Lester Patrick
BEST OFFENSIVE COACH: Frank Patrick
BEST DEFENSIVE COACH: Pete Muldoon
MOST PENALIZED TEAMS: Ed Savage
LEAST PENALIZED TEAMS: Frank Patrick

Not surprisingly, Frank Patrick and Pete Muldoon finished first and second in coaching value while coaching in the PCHA.

Ed Savage was the head coach and manager of the Portland Rosebuds, which played in the PCHA from 1914/15 to 1917/18. Savage replaced Muldoon as head coach in 1915 and coached the team until 1917 (when Muldoon returned as head coach for the 1917/18 season). During those years, Savage's Rosebuds averaged 11.85 penalty minutes per game.

The Rosebuds were not a bad team at all. Hall of Famers Dick Irvin, Ernie "Moose" Johnson, and Tommy Dunderdale played for the Rosebuds. Savage led the Rosebuds to a Stanley Cup finals appearance in 1916 (the first American team ever to appear in the Stanley Cup finals), losing to Newsy Lalonde's Montreal Canadiens in five games.

Lester Patrick was the worst coach in the history of the PCHA simply because in a mostly three-team league someone has to finish in third place and it was usually Lester Patrick. His coaching value while coaching in the PCHA was -24.

WESTERN CANADA HOCKEY LEAGUE/WESTERN HOCKEY LEAGUE: 1921–1926

1.	Ken Mackenzie	+34
2.	Lester Patrick	+32
3.	Herb Gardiner	+22
4.	Wesley Champ	+8
5.	J. Lloyd Turner	+3
6.	Newsy Lalonde	-1
7.	Pete Muldoon	-3
8.	Robert Pinder	-10
9.	Frank Patrick	-13

WORST COACH: Frank Patrick
BEST OFFENSIVE COACH: Ken Mackenzie
BEST DEFENSIVE COACH: Lester Patrick
MOST PENALIZED TEAMS: Lester Patrick
LEAST PENALIZED TEAMS: Frank Patrick

As noted earlier, Ken Mackenzie was the best coach in the WCHL/WHL and the only man to coach throughout the league's five-year existence. Mackenzie made it to the Stanley Cup finals only one time in 1922/23, losing to the Ottawa Senators.

Herb Gardiner was a player-coach for the Calgary Tigers franchise and one of the best defencemen in the WCHL/WHL. He led the Tigers to the 1923/24 Stanley Cup finals against Montreal, losing in two games in a best-of-three series. When the league folded in 1926, Gardiner joined the Montreal Canadiens and won the 1926/27 Hart Trophy. He remains the second-oldest NHL player ever to win the trophy.

Lester Patrick only coached two seasons in the league's existence but very quickly became the best defensive coach in the league. His Cougars had a GAA of 2.00 during those two seasons. No other coach in the league came that close. The Cougars were not only stingy with regards to defence, but they were also tough and gritty. They led the league in team penalty minutes during their two-season stint, averaging 10.9 penalty minutes per game. Again, no other league coach came close to matching that figure. Lester Patrick was the only WCHL/WHL coach to make two Stanley Cup finals appearances.

Just like he did in the PCHA, Frank Patrick had the best on-ice discipline of any coach in the WCHL/WHL. Although the Vancouver Maroons fared poorly in the standings, Frank Patrick's teams averaged only 5.1 penalty minutes per game. The only other coach in the league who came close was Newsy Lalonde's Saskatoon teams. They averaged 6.83 penalty minutes per game.

WORLD HOCKEY ASSOCIATION: 1972–1979

1.	Bill Dineen	+75
2.	Bobby Kromm	+29
3.	Jack Kelley	+27

WORST COACH: Camille Henry
BEST OFFENSIVE COACH: Bobby Kromm
BEST DEFENSIVE COACH: Bill Dineen

BEST POWER-PLAY OFFENCE: **Bobby Kromm**
BEST PENALTY-KILLING: **Bill Dineen**
BEST SHORT-HANDED OFFENCE: **Bill Dineen**
MOST PENALIZED TEAMS: **Sandy Hucul**
LEAST PENALIZED TEAMS: **Bobby Hull**

As noted earlier, Bill Dineen annihilates his competition because he was the only WHA coach to serve all seven seasons. One of the reasons for Dineen's longevity in the WHA is because he was the best defensive coach in the league and had the best penalty-killing unit and the best short-handed offence. His Aeros had a strong blue-line corps and solid goaltending. In addition, people forget that Gordie Howe's presence on the ice was a double strength defensively because his two-way skills (which were transmitted to his sons Mike and Marty) were what made Howe the greatest to ever play the game.

As mentioned, Bobby Kromm's two solid seasons coaching the Winnipeg Jets helped him earn the #2 slot on this list.

John H. "Jack" Kelley had a lifelong association with the Boston University hockey program, first as a player and later as head coach. Kelley coached ten seasons at Boston University, leading his teams to two NCAA championships in 1970/71 and 1971/72 before accepting the head coaching job with the WHA's New England Whalers in 1972.

Kelley scored 21 of his 27 plus points in his first season, winning the first Avco Cup ever awarded against the Winnipeg Jets (and was named WHA coach of the year) in 1972/73. (This gives Kelley the unique honour of being the only head coach in hockey history to coach an NCAA champion and an Avco Cup champion.)

Kelley became the Whalers general manager the following season but returned to coaching in 1974/75 to finish out the regular season and lead the team to a first-round playoff defeat (thus earning seven more plus points in the process). Kelley stayed on as coach in 1975/76 but left the bench nearly midway through the regular season and never coached a major league hockey team again, preferring instead to serve in the front office (he was once the president of the Pittsburgh Penguins).

When it came to calculating which WHA coach was the best in the above-mentioned offensive and defensive categories, I rated only those coaches who served in the WHA for at least two complete seasons. The coaching turnover was so great in the WHA that only 13 coaches were eligible for consideration.

Bobby Kromm just barely emerges as the best offensive coach in the WHA for the simple reason that he coached the Hot Line of Bobby Hull, Ulf Nilsson, and Anders Hedberg during their glory years.

Kromm's Jets were averaging 4.416 goals per game. Kromm's closest competitor was Jean-Guy Gendron, who led the Quebec Nordiques and whose teams averaged 4.415 goals per game.

Sandy Hucul was the head coach of the Phoenix Roadrunners franchise in the WHA for two seasons, from 1974/75 to 1975/76 (he was named WHA coach of the year in 1974/75); during those two seasons the Roadrunners were averaging 22.44 penalty minutes per game. No other WHA coach comes close.

Bobby Hull's selection as the best WHA coach in terms of on-ice discipline may seem surprising to readers, but when you look at his background and where he learned his hockey from, it makes sense. Hull had played many seasons with Billy Reay in Chicago in the NHL, and Reay was an ardent practitioner of on-ice discipline. When the Golden Jet was doing his own coaching with the Winnipeg Jets, it seemed obvious that he would emulate Reay's disciplined approach to the game.

Camille Henry was the worst coach in WHA history (according to my rating system) because of his work with the New York Raiders (later known as the New York Golden Blades and after that the New Jersey Knights). The team finished last in the WHA East in its first two seasons before relocating to San Diego to become the San Diego Mariners.

Henry had a coaching value of -12. The next two worst coaches were Gilles Leger and Gerry Moore, who shared a -11 coaching value while coaching in the WHA.

HEARTBREAK COACHES

I would like to add a new term to the hockey lexicon: *heartbreak coach*.

If you were looking it up in a hockey dictionary, the definition would read as follows:

HEARTBREAK COACH, n. a hockey coach capable of leading teams to the Stanley Cup playoffs yet unable to get them to reach the Stanley Cup finals, let alone win the Stanley Cup itself.

I invented this term while conducting the research for this book. I noticed that certain NHL coaches who were able to lead their teams to the playoffs had the heartbreaking tendency of failing to reach the Stanley Cup finals. I became fascinated with this phenomenon and began to keep stats on the subject.

My research resulted in the following: From 1917 to 2015, only 14 NHL coaches have led their teams to the NHL playoffs five times or more without ever reaching the Stanley Cup finals. In addition, eight other hockey coaches were once members of the Heartbreak Coaches Club before finally breaking their playoff curses.

Those eight former members were renowned coaches in their own right (many of whom are already featured in this book).

Emile Francis was the first NHL coach ever to suffer five playoff defeats before finally reaching the Stanley Cup finals in 1971/72 – which therefore made him the greatest heartbreak coach of all time until his record was broken in 1974/75. (Before 1971/72, the record for playoff futility had been shared by Red Dutton and Phil Watson. Both men had earned four playoff spots without ever reaching the

Stanley Cup finals.) Harry Neale also suffered five WHA playoff defeats before finally reaching the Avco Cup finals in 1977/78. Al Arbour dealt with six straight playoff defeats from 1973/74 to 1978/79 before making his Stanley Cup finals debut in 1979/80. Terry Murray, too, endured six consecutive playoff defeats during the 1990s before ending his playoff curse in 1996/97.

Before ending his own curse in 2003/04, Darryl Sutter shouldered eight playoff defeats. Jacques Demers experienced playoff futility nine times before reaching the Stanley Cup finals in 1992/93 (and hoisting the Cup in the process).

Joel Quenneville waited a long time before he could lead his team to the big dance. In 2008/09 he suffered his tenth playoff loss when his Chicago Blackhawks lost the conference finals to Detroit, placing Quenneville in a first-place tie with another coach who will be discussed later in this section. The following year, Quenneville earned his reward by leading the Hawks to the 2009/10 Stanley Cup finals (and winning the first of his two Stanley Cups).

And lastly there is Bryan Murray.

Before he ended his Cup final drought in 2006/07, he was the greatest heartbreak coach of all time, enduring 11 playoff defeats before finally leading the Ottawa Senators to their first Stanley Cup finals appearance.

Luckily for Murray, another coach came along to break his record for playoff futility.

Being a heartbreak coach is not meant to cast aspersions on those coaches mentioned in this section, far from it. What this section discusses is how luck and fate can often play major roles in the playoff destiny of a hockey coach.

Being a Stanley Cup finalist doesn't always require hockey genius, but it does require having the requisite luck and the right personnel to make the difference. Many a great coach has fallen short of reaching the finals simply because he lacked these two elements. That's why the term *heartbreak coach* is an apt one because it can be heartbreaking for those who never experienced the thrill and honour of competing in the Stanley Cup finals.

This section examines those 14 coaches who repeatedly led their teams to the gates to the NHL's Promised Land – the Stanley Cup finals – but were never good enough (or lucky enough) to earn an invite to the big dance. Some of the coaches you will see listed here were (and are) some of the best and brightest members of the NHL coaching ranks. (The lists display the following: where the heartbreak coaches are ranked, their names, and the number of playoff appearances they have earned without reaching the Stanley Cup finals).

13. HERB BROOKS AND KEVIN CONSTANTINE 5

The late Herb Brooks's name lives forever more for what he did on that wondrous night of February 22, 1980, when he coached the U.S. Olympic Men's Hockey team to a victory against the defending Olympic champions from the former Soviet Union. The subsequent victory in the gold medal game against Finland was the icing on the most transcendental moment in U.S. hockey history.

Before 1980, Brooks had coached NCAA hockey at the University of Minnesota from 1972 to 1979, leading them to three NCAA titles in 1974, 1976, and 1979 while missing out on another in 1975. But in 1981 Brooks made his NHL coaching debut when he became head coach of the New York Rangers. His record with the Rangers was spotty. He had the misfortune of leading a team that shared the Patrick Division with the New York Islanders dynasty teams of 1980 to 1983. Even though Brooks became the first American-born head coach to win 100 games in Rangers history, he was unable to translate his Olympic success into Stanley Cup success.

The Islanders were Brooks's bane throughout his Rangers coaching stint: from 1981/82 to 1983/84 they stood in the way, defeating the Rangers three consecutive times in the Stanley Cup playoffs. Brooks was fired as Rangers head coach in 1985 and didn't return to NHL coaching until 1987/88 when he served a miserable one-season stint with the Minnesota North Stars, leading them to a last-place finish in the Norris Division.

It took four years before Brooks coached in the NHL again, this time with the New Jersey Devils. In 1992 the Devils were only just beginning to achieve a mild, uncertain respectability after being the laughing-stock of the NHL during the 1980s. The team was slowly building up but still lacked the right head coach who could elevate the Devils' game and take the team further than they'd gone before.

Sadly, Brooks could not get the Devils out of the bottomless pit. Even though they had a winning season and earned a playoff berth, the Devils lost in the first round to the Pittsburgh Penguins and Brooks was fired after only one season.

Ironically, Brooks later worked for the Penguins as a scout for the remainder of the 1990s, even doing an interim coaching stint for the team during the 1999/00 season.

Brooks led the Penguins to the second round and had a 2–0 series lead on the Philadelphia Flyers before losing the next four games (two of them in overtime) for his fifth and final NHL playoff loss.

He never coached in the NHL again, instead devoting himself to working in the Penguins front office before perishing in a tragic car accident in 2003. In 2006 Brooks was posthumously inducted into the Hockey Hall of Fame.

It's ironic that the man Herb Brooks replaced when he coached in Pittsburgh in 1999/00 is also the man who is tied with Brooks for the #11 spot in the heartbreak coaches list. Kevin Constantine, like Herb Brooks, led his teams to five NHL playoff appearances without reaching the Stanley Cup finals.

Constantine grew up as a goalie and was drafted by the Montreal Canadiens in the 1978 amateur draft. He played three seasons of NCAA hockey without ever playing in the minors or in the NHL. By the mid-1980s, Constantine took up coaching in the USHL and IHL, performing exceptionally in the latter league, leading the Kansas City Blades to the 1992 IHL championship.

This drew the attention of the fledgling San Jose Sharks, who hired him to be their second head coach in Sharks franchise history. Constantine demonstrated great promise, engineering a 58-team point upsurge and the Shark's first Stanley Cup playoff appearance in only their third season of existence.

The Sharks astounded the hockey world by upsetting the Detroit Red Wings in the first round of the 1993/94 playoffs. The Sharks continued to play with grit and toughness, taking a 3–2 series lead against the Toronto Maple Leafs before losing Games 6 and 7 to lose the second round.

It was Constantine's greatest moment as Sharks head coach. The following season, the team declined in the regular-season standings although earning another playoff berth. Even though the Sharks reached the second round again, they were annihilated in a rematch against the Red Wings.

The Sharks continued to decline and Constantine was fired. In 1997 he became head coach of the Pittsburgh Penguins. By the late 1990s the Penguins were slowly fading from their Stanley Cup dominance earlier in the decade. Although the Penguins continued to play exciting, high-octane hockey, the team was grinding imperceptibly to an impending halt.

Constantine led the Penguins to the Northeast Division title but suffered a first-round defeat to the Canadiens. The following season he and the Penguins did only slightly better, reaching the second round before falling to the Maple Leafs. Twenty-five games into the 1999/00 NHL season, with the Penguins losing, Constantine was fired as head coach.

His final attempt at Stanley Cup playoff glory came in 2002 when he took over the becalmed New Jersey Devils and got them into the playoffs. Sadly, though, the Devils suffered a first-round playoff loss to the Carolina Hurricanes, who made it to the Stanley Cup finals that year.

Like Herb Brooks, Kevin Constantine never reached the conference finals in five playoff attempts.

---

10. EDDIE JOHNSTON, JIM SCHOENFELD, AND TODD MCLELLAN 6

Three men are tied for tenth place in the NHL heartbreak coaching stakes, with six playoff stints but no Stanley Cup finals appearance.

Eddie Johnston's playing and coaching career has already been discussed. When he took up coaching in 1979, Johnston did well, winning the Smythe Division title and leading the Hawks to the playoffs. Johnston cleared the first round but was swept brutally by the Buffalo Sabres. Despite his success, Johnston became the first man (of many) to fall under Hawks general manager Bob Pulford's axe.

Johnston went to Pittsburgh (where he would serve for 25 years as head coach and general manager). During the next three years, Johnston suffered three losing seasons but was able to salvage two playoff appearances, losing in the first round both times. He stepped down as head coach to become general manager of the Penguins and the Hartford Whalers before returning to the NHL coaching ranks in 1993 to succeed Scotty Bowman as head coach of the Penguins.

Johnston got solid efforts from the Penguins (winning two divisional titles), but his playoff luck continued to run bad. In 1993/94 the Penguins lost in the first round to the Washington Capitals. The following year, they lost in the second round to the New Jersey Devils.

It was in 1995/96 that Johnston came closest to reaching the Promised Land. Helped by Mario Lemieux and Jaromir Jagr, the Penguins dominated the Northeast Division and cruised through the first two rounds of the 1995/96 playoffs, beating the Caps and the Rangers handily.

The Penguins faced the fledgling Florida Panthers in the conference finals. By all appearances the Penguins appeared destined to win; after all, they were a veteran Stanley Cup–winning team and the Panthers were in only their third season of existence. On paper it was a no-contest set-up, but on the ice it was different.

The Panthers, backed by the gritty goaltending of John Vanbiesbrouck, took a 2–1 series lead. Shocked, the Penguins rallied to win Games 4 and 5.

It was here that fate turned once more against Eddie Johnston and the Penguins.

The Panthers pounced again, holding firm in Game 6 with a tight 4–3 victory and then holding the Penguins to only one goal in Game 7 to win the series. It remains one of the greatest upsets in Stanley Cup playoff history.

Eddie Johnston stepped down as head coach the following season, never to coach again, never to experience the glory of coaching in the Stanley Cup finals.

Jim Schoenfeld, like Eddie Johnston, had a long, productive playing career with the Buffalo Sabres, Detroit Red Wings, and Boston Bruins. When his playing career ended in 1985, he got his first coaching stint immediately with the Sabres, spending one lacklustre season with them before being fired.

Schoenfeld's luck changed in January 1988 when he took over as head coach of the New Jersey Devils. The Devils were in their 14th season as an NHL franchise and had never had a winning season. They had endured two franchise shifts already and were still seen by many hockey fans as a boil on the buttocks of the NHL. Schoenfeld got the team to rally, end the season with a winning record, and earn only the second playoff half berth in their franchise history.

What followed was Schoenfeld's greatest effort as a coach in playoff competition. The Devils took on the New York Islanders (who, too, had seen better times) in a hard-fought series. Both teams were split at 2–2 before the Devils rallied to win the next two games.

There came a tougher nut to crack when they faced the resurgent Washington Capitals, led by Bryan Murray, an up-and-coming coach in NHL competition. Again, the second round was a seesaw battle that saw both teams at 2–2 midway through the series. What followed was another miracle, when the Devils took two of three from the Caps, beating them twice on the Caps home ice to improbably win the series. It was an astonishing upset, and now the Devils (and Jim Schoenfeld) were one step away from reaching the Stanley Cup finals.

Their opponents the Boston Bruins were powerful competitors in the 1980s and had shown great strength in beating the Sabres and the Canadiens during the 1987/88 playoffs. But New Jersey still had the Devil's luck, again extending their opponents to a 2–2 series tie midway through the series. One of their losses came at home, however, costing them the home-ice advantage they had gained when they had won Game 2 in Boston. The Bruins regained their home-ice advantage and maintained it during Games 5 through 7.

Schoenfeld never came that close to reaching the Stanley Cup finals again. Two seasons later he was fired by the Devils. In 1993/94 he replaced Terry Murray as head coach of the Washington Capitals and led them to three consecutive playoff appearances, only to suffer a second-round loss in 1993/94 and two first-round losses in 1994/95 and 1995/96.

In 1997 Schoenfeld left Washington to become head coach with the Phoenix Coyotes. Schoenfeld got the Coyotes to perform good enough to earn two first playoff defeats at the hands of the Red Wings and the St. Louis Blues in 1997/98 and 1998/99, respectively. Since then, Jim Schoenfeld has not coached in the NHL again.

In 2012/13 Todd McLellan of San Jose entered the heartbreak coaching ranks when he suffered his fifth consecutive playoff defeat without reaching the finals.

In his first six years of coaching the Sharks, he has always led them to the playoffs and twice reached the conference final round, only to lose at the hands of the Chicago Blackhawks in 2009/10 and the Vancouver Canucks in 2010/11.

In 2011/12 McLellan suffered a first-round defeat from the St. Louis Blues and in 2012/13 and 2013/14 his Sharks lost to the Los Angeles Kings. The former loss took place in the second round and the latter defeat came in the first round in a truly heartbreaking fashion. The Sharks had a 3–0 series lead over the Kings but allowed the Kings to sweep the next four games to lose the series.

7. MICHEL BERGERON, BOB BERRY, AND BRUCE BOUDREAU 7

Who's the winningest coach in Colorado Avalanche team history?

Marc Crawford? Bob Hartley?

Nope, it's Michel Bergeron, and he did it when the team was still called the Quebec Nordiques.

And not only that: Bergeron, the "*petit tigre*," led the Nordiques in what was their most productive stretch during their 16-year stay in Quebec as an NHL franchise.

The Nordiques played highly entertaining hockey that emphasized a two-fisted, high-octane offensive approach to the game. Bergeron was blessed with stalwart players such as Dale Hunter, Michel Goulet, and the Stastny brothers: Anton and Peter. During the 1980s the Nordiques were second only to the Edmonton Oilers in power-play offence.

Bergeron led the Nordiques to seven consecutive playoff appearances. Their first in 1980/81 ended with a first-round elimination, but in 1981/82 Bergeron and the Nordiques had a flashing chance at Stanley Cup finals bliss. The team barely eked out a winning season, but during playoff time they showed their mettle, going the full distance to beat the Canadiens and the Bruins in the first two rounds, respectively.

It was then that they faced the New York Islanders in the conference finals. Just as Herb Brooks' teams were done in by the Islanders dynasty teams, so, too, were

Bergeron's Nordiques. The Islanders held the Nordiques to only nine goals in four games to sweep the series.

Bergeron kept the Nordiques going with mixed results: losing in the first round in 1982/83 and the second round to the Canadiens in 1983/84 (the year of the infamous Good Friday brawl).

The 1984/85 Stanley Cup playoffs was the closest Quebec (and Bergeron) ever came to reaching the Stanley Cup finals. They repeated history by going the full distance in winning the first two rounds against Buffalo and Montreal, respectively. Beating Montreal was perfect revenge for last year's playoff loss.

The Nordiques were at their peak physically and offensively, but now they had to face an even more formidable opponent: Mike Keenan's Philadelphia Flyers. Keenan (making his NHL coaching debut) was a coaching *wunderkind* and had sparked the Flyers to new heights with a keenly balanced team that was highly capable on offence and defence.

Despite this, Bergeron made the series tough, keeping it at 2–2 before succumbing in Games 5 and 6. The Flyers asserted their superior defence and goaltending, holding the Nordiques' offensive cannonade to only one goal in two games.

The Nordiques and Bergeron never again came that close to reaching the Stanley Cup finals. It would take a franchise shift before the team would ever hoist the Stanley Cup.

Bob Berry never got as near to reaching the Stanley Cup finals as Michel Bergeron did. Although his NHL coaching career began before Bergeron's and lasted longer, Berry never got his teams to reach the same heights in the Stanley Cup playoffs as Bergeron's did.

Unlike Bergeron, Berry had played in the NHL, mostly with the Los Angeles Kings (where he learned his craft at the knee of Bob Pulford). When his playing career ended in 1978, Berry became head coach of the Los Angeles Kings, staying there for three erratic seasons (the Kings wavered from .500 to below .500 before surging strongly in the 1980/81 season). Berry led the Kings to three playoff appearances, but the team was always eliminated in the first round.

Berry drew the attention of the Montreal Canadiens, who made him their head coach in 1981. He did much better with the Habs during the regular season, winning the Adams Division title in 1981/82 (the only one in his coaching career), but his lack of playoff luck continued to dog him.

Again, Berry couldn't get his teams past the first round, losing to the Quebec Nordiques in 1981/82 and the Sabres in 1982/83.

The Habs floundered during the 1983/84 season and Berry was fired before the season's end. He coached unsuccessfully in Pittsburgh, suffering three losing seasons and no playoff appearances. Berry was fired in 1987 and worked as an assistant coach with the St. Louis Blues under Brian Sutter.

When Sutter was fired as Blues head coach, Berry took over the team in 1992 and led the Blues to two winning seasons and two playoff appearances. Interestingly, in 1992/93 Berry finally broke his first-round playoff jinx and reached the second round for the only time in his NHL coaching career, only to lose to Pat Burns' Toronto Maple Leafs despite possessing a 2–1 series lead.

The following season Berry's Blues suffered another first-round playoff defeat and he was fired, never to return as a head coach.

Bruce Boudreau is the second active coach in the heartbreak coaching ranks. He entered the same season that Todd McLellan did (2012/13) but his playoff luck was (until 2014/15) much worse. He suffered three first-round and three second round playoff defeats in his first six playoff appearances. Five times Boudreau's squads allowed their opponents to rally from series deficits to beat them in the playoffs (in 2008/09, 2009/10, 2012/13, 2013/14, and 2014/15). The 2014/15 loss was deeply crushing. It was Gabby's first conference finals appearance and his Ducks had a 3-2 series lead before allowing Joel Quenneville's Chicago Blackhawks to rally to win the series.

3. RED KELLY, BRIAN SUTTER, DAVE TIPPETT, AND BARRY TROTZ 8

When Red Kelly's Toronto Maple Leafs were swept by the Philadelphia Flyers in the 1974/75 Stanley Cup playoffs, it marked the first time in NHL history a head coach had earned six playoff appearances without ever making it to the Stanley Cup finals.

For Kelly (one of the game's true living legends), it was a dubious achievement to an otherwise glorious career in hockey. He had become the greatest heartbreak coach in NHL history and would retain that sad distinction until 1985/86.

When Kelly hung up his skates as a player after helping the Leafs win the Stanley Cup in 1966/67, he immediately went to the West Coast to become head coach of the expansion Los Angeles Kings.

In their inaugural season, the Kings placed second in their division, with Kelly leading them to a playoff berth against the Minnesota North Stars. The series was a seesaw affair, as the Kings held a 3–2 series lead, but an overtime loss in Game 6 led to an even greater disaster – a 9–4 drubbing at the hands of the North Stars at home in Los Angeles.

The following season saw the Kings play worse in the regular season but go farther in the playoffs. Kelly led the Kings past the ill-fated Oakland Seals in the first round before encountering the defending Western Conference champion St. Louis Blues.

The Blues possessed one of the finest defences in the Western Conference and had two legends in goal: Glenn Hall and Jacques Plante. Even though Hall was injured, Jake the Snake held the Kings to only five goals in a masterful four-game sweep.

Kelly left the Kings in 1969 to coach the Pittsburgh Penguins; despite finishing a weak second place, he led the Penguins to their first playoff appearance in their franchise history. Again, Kelly got his players to reach the second round, sweeping the Oakland Seals in four to face (once again) the defending Western Conference champion St. Louis Blues.

He got a better effort from his players this time around, but the results were no different. Despite evening up the series at 2–2, the Penguins lost Games 5 and 6 to lose the series.

It would take 21 years before the Penguins would ever get that close to the Stanley Cup again. Kelly would never again come that close to coaching a Stanley Cup finalist.

He stayed three more seasons with the Penguins but earned only one more playoff berth. In 1973 he returned to Toronto to serve as head coach and led the Leafs to four straight playoff appearances, only to earn one first-round and three second-round defeats.

All in all, Red Kelly's playoff coaching record is a heartbreaking side-story in an otherwise magnificent career.

As mentioned, Brian Sutter was the first of four Sutter brothers to enter the NHL coaching ranks. The moment he retired as a player in 1988 after 12 years of sterling service to the St. Louis Blues, he was offered the head coaching job.

Sutter wasted no time making his presence felt in the NHL. He led the Blues to three straight second-round defeats in the playoffs while steadily improving the team. During the 1991/92 season, Sutter was expected to lead the Blues to the Stanley Cup finals but instead suffered a first-round defeat at the hands of the Chicago Blackhawks, who went to the finals themselves.

This led to Sutter's firing, but the much-respected coach quickly received numerous offers and became head coach of the Boston Bruins. He led Boston to the Adams Division title only to suffer another first-round defeat. (It was Sutter's fifth defeat, which automatically placed him on the heartbreak coaches list.)

Sutter endured two more playoff losses before resigning as head coach of the Bruins. He returned to NHL coaching in 1997, but he would not return to the playoffs until 2001/02, when he led the Chicago Blackhawks to a first-round playoff defeat (his last one). His NHL coaching career ended in 2004.

Dave Tippett is the third of the four active head coaches to grace the heartbreak coaches list. In 2011/12 he tied Kelly and Sutter for third place on the heartbreak list when his Phoenix Coyotes lost the Western Conference finals to the Los

Angeles Kings. For Tippett, it marked the second time he had come so close to becoming a Stanley Cup finalist, only to be denied by the team that eventually won the Cup.

Being on the heartbreak coaches list is the only dubious distinction in Tippett's magnificent coaching career. He has been one of the finest NHL head coaches to emerge during the 21st century. His failure to reach the Stanley Cup finals has served to keep Tippett from standing among other 21st-century coaching greats such as Mike Babcock, Dan Bylsma, and Claude Julien.

As of 2015 Tippett has coached twelve seasons in the NHL for the Dallas Stars and the Phoenix Coyotes, earning eight playoff spots. The major reason why he has never been a Stanley Cup finalist can be summed up in one name: Mike Babcock.

Four times Babcock has beaten Tippett in playoff competition. In 2002/03 it was Babcock's Mighty Ducks of Anaheim that beat Tippett in the second round of the playoffs (Babcock reached the finals that year). In 2007/08 he lost the conference finals to Babcock's Detroit Red Wings (who won the Stanley Cup that year). It was the first time that Tippett had reached the conference finals. In 2009/10 and 2010/11 (after Tippett had been fired by Dallas to later become head coach of the Phoenix Coyotes), he lost to Babcock twice in the first round.

In a sense, that is why Tippett's third-round loss in 2011/12 is poignant, because Tippett (and the Coyotes) got a lucky break when Babcock's Red Wings lost in the first round to the Nashville Predators.

Freed from his bête noire, Tippett got his Coyotes to play the greatest playoff hockey in their franchise history. All that stood in their way were the Los Angeles Kings. Even though Phoenix had played great defence in the playoffs, the Kings were better. The Coyotes lost in five games, unable to solve the Kings' regal defensive style.

Barry Trotz is the last of the four active head coaches on the heartbreak coaches list. He was the first head coach in the Nashville Predators franchise history. He spent 15 seasons crafting this small-market franchise into a tough, competitive team in the Western Conference of the NHL.

It took the Predators six seasons to have their first winning season and first playoff appearance. It was the first of four consecutive playoff appearances and four consecutive first-round defeats at the hands of the Detroit Red Wings and the San Jose Sharks.

There was a one-season hiccup in 2008/09 when they failed to make the playoffs, but since then the Predators have grown in skill and playoff prowess. In 2009/10 they suffered a first-round loss to the Chicago Blackhawks, who won the Stanley Cup that year, but in 2010/11 and 2011/12 the Predators broke new ground by reaching the second round twice.

In 2010/11 they beat the Anaheim Ducks in six games but lost to the Vancouver Canucks in six games despite holding the Canucks (who had the best offence in the NHL that season) to only 14 goals in six games.

The following year, they did even better. They upset the Detroit Red Wings in only five games and faced the Phoenix Coyotes in the second round. Sadly, the Predators lost in five games, but again (like in 2010/11) they showed courage and character in defeat, holding the Coyotes to only 12 goals in five games – a splendid display of defensive grit. Three of the Predators' losses were by one-goal margins and one came in overtime.

Trotz's next playoff came after he was fired by the Nashville Predators and was hired by the Washington Capitals in 2014/15. He led the Caps to the second round of the playoffs and had a 3–1 series lead over the President's Trophy winning New York Rangers. Barry Trotz was poised to be a Giant Killer but instead the Giant squashed the Caps by rallying to win games five through seven to win the series and add to Trotz's miserable playoff record. Today Trotz and Dave Tippett lead all active coaches in playoff misery.

2. BOB PULFORD 10

Bob Pulford remains a controversial figure in Chicago Black Hawks history, a symbol of the 49-year Stanley Cup drought that plagued the Windy City.

His failure to win the Stanley Cup, coupled with his inability (or unwillingness, in the eyes of others) to build a team capable of competing for, let alone winning, the Cup, has made him odious in the eyes of innumerable Hawks fans.

His Hawks (and Los Angeles Kings) teams were always competitive, rarely exceptional, always profitable, yet in the end never capable of earning a ticket to the big dance.

Pulford's five years of coaching in Los Angeles earned him four playoff slots, resulting in two first-round defeats and two second-round defeats.

When he left Los Angeles to become head coach and general manager of the Black Hawks, the trend continued, enduring two consecutive first-round sweeps. After 1979 Pulford abandoned coaching to focus solely on being a general manager, but during the early to mid-1980s twice he was forced to return to the bench to attempt to light a fire in the Hawks' forlorn quest for the Cup; both times he reached the Conference final round.

His first attempt in 1981/82 was especially significant because he was facing the insurgent Vancouver Canucks, who had been dazzling ever since Roger Neilson had taken over as head coach during the suspension of Harry Neale.

The Canucks were the Cinderella team during the playoffs, and Pulford's Black Hawks were all that stood in their way to reaching the Stanley Cup finals.

Pulford's intensity proved to be no match for Neilson's wizardry. The Canucks stole Game 1 in Chicago, and although Chicago rallied to win Game 2 to even up the series, what transpired during that game has become a part of hockey iconography. Outraged at the officiating during the 4–1 loss, Neilson started waving a white towel atop a hockey stick in a mock act of surrender.

Even though the act earned him an ejection from the games, it lit a collective fire in the hearts and minds of Canucks players and their fans. Towel Power was born, and the Canucks went on to sweep the next three games to reach the finals.

In 1984/85 Pulford rallied the Hawks to the conference finals again but ran into the buzz-saw that was the Edmonton Oilers dynasty from 1984 to 1990. The Hawks never stood a chance. The Oilers out-shot them 44 goals to 25 in six games to win the series and, eventually, the Stanley Cup.

Bob Pulford never got that close again. His next two playoff appearances resulted in two first-round defeats. He was the greatest heartbreak coach in NHL history from 1985/86 to 2005/06 (until Bryan Murray broke his record) and then was the greatest again (when Murray ended his playoff curse in 2006/07) from 2007/08 to 2009/10.

1. JACQUES MARTIN 12

Jacques Martin's failure to reach the Stanley Cup finals, let alone win the Stanley Cup, is a major reason why he doesn't rank higher in the pantheon of NHL coaching. The fact that Martin was always coaching rebuilding projects in the NHL (Ottawa and Florida, for example) didn't help his cause either.

By the time Martin took over as head coach of the Ottawa Senators in 1996, he already had two playoff appearances under his belt from his St. Louis Blues coaching days. By the following year, Martin began a skein of eight consecutive playoff appearances – all doomed to fall short of the Stanley Cup finals. Five of them ended up in first-round eliminations; two were second-round eliminations.

The bane of Jacques Martin's playoff existence was the Toronto Maple Leafs. From 1999/00 to 2001/02, the Leafs denied Martin's Senators. In 1999/00 Martin's Sens lost in six games. In 2000/01 the Sens were swept by the Leafs in the first round (despite being the second seed in the Eastern Conference). In 2001/02 the Leafs edged out the Senators in seven games.

The 2002/03 season promised to be the Senators' year and it was (at first). They won the President's Trophy and then beat the New York Islanders and Philadelphia Flyers in the first two rounds to reach the conference finals for the first time in their franchise history.

All that stood between Martin's Senators and the Stanley Cup finals were the New Jersey Devils.

And then it happened . . .

New Jersey took away Ottawa's home-ice advantage when they beat the Sens in Game 2. After four games the Sens were down 3–1 in the series, but they rallied back to force a Game 7 at home in Ottawa. Sadly, it wasn't to be. The Sens saw a 1–0 lead evaporate before tying the game early in the third period. Overtime seemed imminent before New Jersey scored the winning goal with 2:14 left to play.

It would be four years before Ottawa reached the Stanley Cup finals (with a different coach at the helm).

After his tenth playoff elimination in 2003/04, Martin left Ottawa to coach the Florida Panthers (without any playoff success). By 2009 he was the head coach of the Montreal Canadiens and was ready for the headiest playoff ride of his career.

Martin's Habs were the eighth seed in the 2009/10 playoffs and didn't stand a chance against the Washington Capitals (who won the President's Trophy that year and were favoured to win the Cup).

What followed was a smashing comeback. Using a tight defence and strong, physical hockey the Habs rebounded from a 3–1 series deficit to beat the Caps in seven.

In the second round the Habs took on the defending Stanley Cup–champion Pittsburgh Penguins and, again, shocked the hockey world by fighting Pittsburgh to a standstill before beating the Penguins in Pittsburgh in Game 7.

All the while this was going on, the Montreal fans were in a state of delirium, playing their role of seventh man on the ice to perfection. For the first time since 1992/93, Montreal Canadiens fans were in the conference finals. Jacques Martin and the Habs had brought joy, life, and light back to the eyes of their fans.

Sadly, it was their misfortune to play another team that had defied the odds during their playoff run too. The Philadelphia Flyers had also played superb comeback hockey. Their defeat of the Boston Bruins after being down 3–0 in the series had sent shockwaves through the hockey world.

Something had to give, and for the Canadiens the clock struck midnight and the Habs' became pumpkins once more, going down in five games.

What was sad about this defeat was that this was Martin's 11th playoff failure, which made him the greatest heartbreak coach in NHL playoff history, surpassing Bob Pulford.

The following year, Martin added to his record with another playoff loss. Since 2011 he has not returned to NHL coaching.

In the end, being a heartbreak coach is worse than being incapable of winning the big one because to win the big one a coach was at least good enough to be in that position. Being a heartbreak coach means you are never good enough to be in that position, and that is truly heartbreaking.

PLAYOFF RIVALRIES

This section discusses how the coaches featured in this book fared against each other in Stanley Cup playoff competition. The coaches are listed alphabetically and thereunder by how they ranked against their peers.

The results are listed by playoff series won or lost and not by individual games.

The records listed below are not comprehensive. They do not list every single opponent each coach faced in Stanley Cup playoff competition but only those coaches who are featured in "The Top 50" and "Honourable Mention."

What this list shows is how the greatest fared against the greatest in playoff competition: the ultimate test for any head coach.

JACK ADAMS versus:	LESTER PATRICK	1–1
	DICK IRVIN	3–2
	CECIL HART	1–0
	ART ROSS	3–0
	COONEY WEILAND	0–1
	HAP DAY	1–3

Jack Adams's five playoff matchups against Dick Irvin made for the greatest playoff rivalry of the NHL's Expansion and Contraction Era (1926–1942). Adams won the first two in 1933/34 and 1935/36, but Irvin came back to win in 1938/39 and 1939/40 before Adams won the rubber match in 1941/42. All the series except for 1935/36 and 1941/42 were semifinals matchups. Adams's 1935/36 win was during the Stanley Cup finals, and his 1941/42 series win was a quarter-final matchup when Irvin was coaching the Montreal Canadiens.

AL ARBOUR versus:

TOM JOHNSON	0–1
EMILE FRANCIS	1–0
FRED SHERO	0–2
FLOYD SMITH	2–0
SCOTTY BOWMAN	2–2
ROGER NEILSON	1–2
BOB PULFORD	1–0
HARRY SINDEN	1–0
PAT QUINN	1–0
GLEN SATHER	2–1
EDDIE JOHNSTON	1–0
BRYAN MURRAY	3–1
GERRY CHEEVERS	1–0
JACQUES LEMAIRE	1–0
MIKE KEENAN	0–2
TERRY MURRAY	1–0

Al Arbour got into coaching at Scotty Bowman's behest and encouragement.

He faced off against his mentor four times, losing twice to Bowman in the 1970s when his Islanders faced Bowman's Habs dynasty, but Arbour got his revenge in the 1979/80 when he beat Bowman's Buffalo Sabres in the semifinal round and in 1992/93 when the Islanders upset Bowman's Pittsburgh Penguins in 1992/93.

MIKE BABCOCK versus:

DAVE TIPPETT	4–0
JACQUES LEMAIRE	1–0
PAT BURNS	0–1
RON WILSON	1–0
RANDY CARLYLE	1–1
JOEL QUENNEVILLE	2–1
MICHEL THERRIEN	1–0
KEN HITCHCOCK	1–0

DAN BYLSMA	0–1
TODD MCLELLAN	0–2
BRUCE BOUDREAU	1–0
CLAUDE JULIEN	0-1

Mike Babcock's losses to Pat Burns and Dan Bylsma took place during the 2002/03 and 2008/09 Stanley Cup finals, respectively.

TOE BLAKE versus:

SID ABEL	2–0
RUDY PILOUS	2–2
PUNCH IMLACH	4–3
BILLY REAY	2–0
EMILE FRANCIS	1–0
HARRY SINDEN	1–0
SCOTTY BOWMAN	1–0

Toe Blake's playoff rivalry with Punch Imlach is the greatest coaching rivalry in Stanley Cup playoff history. Blake won the first two against Imlach during the 1958/59 and 1959/60 Stanley Cup finals. Imlach got his revenge by beating Blake in the 1962/63 and 1963/64 semifinals. Blake retaliated in the 1964/65 and 1965/66 semifinals before losing the final (and most famous) matchup to Imlach in the 1966/67 Stanley Cup finals.

BRUCE BOUDREAU versus:

DAN BYLSMA	0–1
JACQUES MARTIN	0–1
MIKE BABCOCK	0–1
LINDY RUFF	1-0
DARRYL SUTTER	0-1
BOB HARTLEY	1-0
JOEL QUENNEVILLE	0-1

Bruce Boudreau's 2009/10 playoff loss to Jacques Martin was a humiliation. Boudreau's Caps had just won the President's Trophy but were eliminated by Martin's eighth-seeded Montreal Canadiens. Boudreau's playoff loss against Mike

Babcock in 2012/13 was his first as head coach of the Anaheim Ducks. His victory over Lindy Ruff and his loss to Darryl Sutter both took place during the 2013/14 playoffs.

SCOTTY BOWMAN versus:		
	TOE BLAKE	0–1
	CLAUDE RUEL	0–1
	HARRY SINDEN	0–1
	EMILE FRANCIS	1–2
	FLOYD SMITH	0–1
	FRED SHERO	3–0
	BILLY REAY	2–0
	AL ARBOUR	2–2
	DON CHERRY	3–0
	ROGER NEILSON	3–0
	EDDIE JOHNSTON	1–0
	GERRY CHEEVERS	0–2
	TERRY MURRAY	2–0
	MIKE KEENAN	2–0
	DARRYL SUTTER	1–0
	JACQUES LEMAIRE	0–1
	MARC CRAWFORD	2–1
	JOEL QUENNEVILLE	3–0
	RON WILSON	2–0
	KEN HITCHCOCK	1–0
	BOB HARTLEY	1–2

Scotty Bowman's playoff losses to Toe Blake, Claude Ruel, and Harry Sinden all took place when Bowman was coaching the St. Louis Blues and all came about during the Stanley Cup finals from 1967/68 to 1969/70.

When you look at Bowman's matchups with the other great coaches of his time, you notice the absence of three names: Pat Burns, Pat Quinn, and Glen Sather.

Burns's absence is explained further on in this section.

Bowman never faced Glen Sather in the playoffs because during the 1980s Bowman's Buffalo Sabres and Sather's Edmonton Oilers were in different conferences; therefore, the only way they could have met in playoff competition would have been in the Stanley Cup finals. But Buffalo never reached the finals under Bowman.

The same goes for Pat Quinn. During the 1980s, Quinn and Bowman were coaching in different conferences; however, they came closer to meeting each other than Glen Sather did. During the 1979/80 Stanley Cup playoffs, Bowman's Sabres lost to the New York Islanders in the semifinals. If Buffalo had won, then they would have faced Quinn's Philadelphia Flyers for the Stanley Cup.

Bowman had another opportunity in 1993/94 when he was coaching the Detroit Red Wings. During the 1993/94 playoffs, the Wings were upset in the first round by the San Jose Sharks while Quinn's Canucks won the first round. If the Red Wings hadn't lost, then they would have faced the Canucks in the second round.

Bowman missed a third chance at meeting Quinn in playoff competition in 2001/02 – his last playoff run. Quinn's Toronto Maple Leafs lost to the Carolina Hurricanes in the conference finals. If the Leafs had won, then they would have faced Bowman's Detroit Red Wings for the Stanley Cup.

Most intriguing are Bowman's losses to Emile Francis. Bowman suffered two first-round defeats to Francis in 1971/72 and 1973/74 when he was coaching the Canadiens. The Habs were a great team, but they hadn't yet reached dynastic status; also the second defeat took place during Ken Dryden's holdout in the 1973/74 season.

What's amazing about Bowman's record against the other great coaches is that he was able to repeatedly defeat them when the chips were down. Bowman was a perfect 3–0 against Fred Shero, Don Cherry, Roger Neilson, and Joel Quenneville, and a perfect 2–0 against Billy Reay, Mike Keenan, Ron Wilson, and Terry Murray.

His mastery transcended several eras of hockey history, and it was that mastery that made him the most successful hockey coach of all time.

PAT BURNS versus:

	BRYAN MURRAY	1–0
	DARRYL SUTTER	1–1
	PAT QUINN	0–1
	RON WILSON	0–1
	LINDY RUFF	0–1
	JACQUES MARTIN	1–0

MIKE BABCOCK	1–0
KEN HITCHCOCK	0–1

As stated above, Pat Burns never faced Scotty Bowman in playoff competition. Both men faced many of the greatest coaches of their time, but they never met each other in playoff competition.

The closest Burns ever came to a playoff matchup with Bowman took place in 1991/92. Burns's Canadiens lost to the Bruins in the second round of the playoffs. Had Burns and the Habs won, then they would have faced Bowman's Pittsburgh Penguins in the conference finals.

When Bowman later became head coach of the Detroit Red Wings (therefore moving to the Western Conference), any future playoff matchup was made even more difficult since Burns always coached in the Eastern Conference.

DAN BYLSMA versus:

BRUCE BOUDREAU	1–0
MIKE BABCOCK	1–0
JACQUES MARTIN	0–1
PETER LAVIOLETTE	0–1
CLAUDE JULIEN	0–1
ALAIN VIGNEAULT	0-1

Dan Bylsma's wins against Bruce Boudreau and Mike Babcock both took place during the 2008/09 playoffs.

His losses to Jacques Martin, Peter Laviolette, Claude Julien, and Alain Vigneault took place in 2009/10, 2011/12, 2012/13, and 2013/14 respectively.

RANDY CARLYLE versus:

DARRYL SUTTER	1–0
JOEL QUENNEVILLE	1–0
JACQUES LEMAIRE	1–0
ALAIN VIGNEAULT	1–0
MIKE BABCOCK	1–1
BRYAN MURRAY	1–0
DAVE TIPPETT	0–1
CLAUDE JULIEN	0–1

Randy Carlyle's victories over Jacques Lemaire, Alain Vigneault, Mike Babcock, and Bryan Murray all came during the 2006/07 playoffs when Carlyle's Anaheim Ducks won the Stanley Cup.

GERRY CHEEVERS versus:	SCOTTY BOWMAN	2–0
	AL ARBOUR	0–1
	JACQUES LEMAIRE	0–1

Gerry Cheevers is one of the three coaches who performed the rare feat of beating Scotty Bowman in playoff competition two years in a row. Indeed, Cheevers did it before his other two counterparts: in 1981/82 and 1982/83. (Michel Bergeron is one of the three, and you will know the name of the third man as you read farther along in this section.)

DON CHERRY versus:	BILLY REAY	0–1
	BOB PULFORD	3–0
	FRED SHERO	2–1
	SCOTTY BOWMAN	0–3
	PAT QUINN	1–0

What surprised me while compiling this list is how well Don Cherry outperformed Fred Shero in the playoffs: Cherry's Bruins beat Shero's Flyers in 1976/77 and 1977/78, costing the Flyers two more opportunities to appear in the Stanley Cup finals.

Even more ironic: If Cherry's Bruins had won the 1978/79 semifinals against Montreal, they would have faced Shero's New York Rangers. How would that matchup have ended? My money would have been on Grapes.

MARC CRAWFORD versus:	BOB HARTLEY	0–1
	SCOTTY BOWMAN	0–1
	JOEL QUENNEVILLE	1–0
	JACQUES LEMAIRE	0–1
	DARRYL SUTTER	0–1

Marc Crawford's loss to Bob Hartley (the man who succeeded him after he left the Avalanche) came in 2000/01. Crawford's win against Joel Quenneville came in the 2002/03 playoffs when his Vancouver Canucks beat Quenneville's St. Louis Blues in the first round. Crawford lost the second round to Jacques Lemaire's Minnesota Wild. Crawford's loss to Darryl Sutter came during the 2003/04 playoffs.

LEO DANDURAND versus:	PETE GREEN	1–1
	FRANK PATRICK	1–0
	LESTER PATRICK	0–2

Leo Dandurand lost the NHL finals to Pete Green in 1922/23 but avenged himself the following year. His victory over Frank Patrick came during the 1923/24 interleague playoffs, which determined which two teams would compete in the 1923/24 Stanley Cup finals.

Dandurand's losses to Lester Patrick came during the 1924/25 Stanley Cup finals (the only time the NHL ever lost in the Cup finals to a team from a rival league) and the 1934/35 playoffs when he lost in the first round to Patrick's New York Rangers.

HAP DAY versus:	COONEY WEILAND	0–1
	JACK ADAMS	3–1
	DICK IRVIN	2–1
	TOMMY IVAN	2–1

Hap Day's rivalry with Jack Adams was the greatest of the 1940s. Two of Day's wins were for the 1941/42 and 1944/45 Stanley Cups. The 1941/42 Cup win was the most sweet because the Leafs were down 3–0 in the series before coming back to win the next four games and the Cup – a feat repeated by Al Arbour in 1974/75, Peter Laviolette in 2009/10, and Darryl Sutter in 2013/14.

BILL DINEEN versus:	GLEN SATHER	1–0

Bill Dineen's playoff victory over Glen Sather came during the first round of the 1976/77 WHA playoffs. It was Sather's first playoff appearance as a coach.

EMILE FRANCIS versus:		
	TOE BLAKE	0–1
	BILLY REAY	1–3
	CLAUDE RUEL	0–1
	HARRY SINDEN	0–1
	SCOTTY BOWMAN	2–1
	TOM JOHNSON	0–1
	FRED SHERO	0–1
	AL ARBOUR	0–1
	BOB PULFORD	0–1

Emile Francis may have done well against Scotty Bowman in playoff competition, but the Cat's playoff bête noire was Billy Reay of Chicago. The Cat lost three lives against Reay in 1967/68, 1970/71, and 1972/73. The last two defeats were particularly galling because they denied Francis and the Rangers a berth in the Stanley Cup finals.

The third defeat is well chronicled in Vic Hadfield's diary of the 1972/73 NHL season. Despite upsetting the defending Stanley Cup champion Boston Bruins, the Rangers fell to Chicago because they were dogged by injuries and were incapable of generating any offence against the Blackhawks in Games 3 to 5 in the series.

ROBBIE FTOREK versus:		
	GLEN SATHER	1–0
	MICHEL THERRIEN	0–1

Robbie Ftorek's win against Glen Sather came in the first round of the 1988/89 Stanley Cup playoffs and ended the Oilers' chances of three-peating the Stanley Cup. Ftorek had Wayne Gretzky, and it was Gretzky's first playoff meeting with his old team.

PETE GREEN versus:		
	PETE MULDOON	1–0
	FRANK PATRICK	2–0
	LEO DANDURAND	1–1
	KEN MACKENZIE	1–0

Three of Pete Green's four playoff series victories came in the 1919/20, 1920/21, and 1922/23 Stanley Cup finals. His second playoff victory against Frank Patrick came in the preliminary round of the 1922/23 playoffs.

CECIL HART versus:		
	LESTER PATRICK	1–1
	ART ROSS	2–0
	DICK IRVIN	1–0
	JACK ADAMS	0–1

Hart's losses to Lester Patrick and Jack Adams both happened in the semifinal rounds of the 1931/32 and 1936/37 playoffs, respectively.

BOB HARTLEY versus:		
	DARRYL SUTTER	2–0
	SCOTTY BOWMAN	2–1
	KEN HITCHCOCK	0–2
	MARC CRAWFORD	1–0
	JOEL QUENNEVILLE	1–0
	BRUCE BOUDREAU	0-1

Bob Hartley is the last of the three coaches (Gerry Cheevers and Michel Bergeron being the others) to defeat Scotty Bowman in playoff competition in consecutive years. But Hartley's feat is far more remarkable than Cheevers's or Bergeron's because the latter two faced Bowman when he was coaching the Buffalo Sabres (the weakest team Bowman ever coached and the only team he failed to take to the Stanley Cup finals).

Hartley in 1998/99 and 1999/00 had to face Bowman's Detroit Red Wings – a team that dominated the NHL from 1994/95 to 2008/09. In fact, during the 1998/99 matchup, the Wings were the defending two-time Stanley Cup champions looking to three-peat.

Instead, Hartley's Avalanche beat the Wings in six games and in the following year added insult to injury by whipping the Wings in five games – a glorious coaching achievement by any stint of the imagination.

Even more interesting is the fact that Hartley had a combined 4–1 playoff record against Bowman and Darryl Sutter – two of the finest defensive coaches of that time period.

The only coach who had Hartley's number in playoff competition was Ken Hitchcock.

His loss to Bruce Boudreau took place during the 2014/15 playoffs.

KEN HITCHCOCK versus:		
	DARRYL SUTTER	2–2
	SCOTTY BOWMAN	0–1
	JOEL QUENNEVILLE	1–2
	BOB HARTLEY	2–0
	LINDY RUFF	1–1
	PAT QUINN	2–0
	JACQUES MARTIN	0–1
	PAT BURNS	1–0
	MIKE BABCOCK	0–1
	TODD MCLELLAN	1–0

Ken Hitchcock's 5–1 record against Bob Hartley, Joel Quenneville, and Pat Quinn combined (three offensive-minded coaches) is further proof of the old saw that in a battle between offence and defence, the defence usually wins.

PUNCH IMLACH versus:		
	TOE BLAKE	3–4
	BILLY REAY	1–0
	HARRY SINDEN	0–1

Punch Imlach's win over Billy Reay came during their legendary semifinals matchup in 1966/67.

DICK IRVIN versus:		
	LESTER PATRICK	2–2
	CECIL HART	0–1
	ART ROSS	2–2
	JACK ADAMS	2–3
	FRANK PATRICK	2–0
	HAP DAY	1–2
	TOMMY IVAN	1–3

In the 1930s Dick Irvin was the man you had to beat if you had any chance of winning the Stanley Cup. His teams were always strong, always feisty, and always competitive. To beat him, his opponents had to be the same (and then some).

Irvin's playoff rivalry with Lester Patrick was the greatest of the 1930s. All four of their matchups took place during the decade, with two of them taking place during the 1931/32 and 1932/33 Stanley Cup finals.

Jack Adams and Art Ross faced Irvin three times apiece during the 1930s, with Irvin holding a 2–1 advantage over Ross and a 1–2 deficit with Adams.

During the mid- to late-1940s, Irvin again became the man you had to beat to win the Stanley Cup. And from 1950/51 to 1954/55, Irvin continued to be that man.

TOMMY IVAN versus:		
	HAP DAY	1–2
	DICK IRVIN	3–1

Tommy Ivan's playoff rivalry with Irvin was one of the greatest in NHL history. Ivan scored a semifinal win in 1948/49. Irvin's sole victory took place in the 1950/51 semifinals, but Ivan retaliated with Stanley Cup final wins against Irvin in 1951/52 and 1953/54.

BOB JOHNSON versus:		
	ROGER NEILSON	1–0
	GLEN SATHER	1–2
	TERRY MURRAY	1–0

Bob Johnson's three playoff matchups against Glen Sather made for one of the great playoff rivalries of the 1980s. Johnson's sole series win came in 1985/86.

TOM JOHNSON versus:		
	AL ARBOUR	1–0
	EMILE FRANCIS	1–0

Al Arbour was coaching the St. Louis Blues when he lost to Tom Johnson in the 1971/72 playoffs.

EDDIE JOHNSTON versus:		
	SCOTTY BOWMAN	0–1
	AL ARBOUR	0–1
	JACQUES LEMAIRE	0–1

Eddie Johnston's loss to Scotty Bowman came in the second round of the 1979/80 playoffs when Johnston was coaching in Chicago.

His loss to Al Arbour came in the 1981/82 playoffs when Johnston was coaching the Penguins. His loss to Jacques Lemaire came in 1993/94 when the Penguins lost to the New Jersey Devils in the second round.

CLAUDE JULIEN versus:		
	LINDY RUFF	1–0
	PETER LAVIOLETTE	1–1
	JACQUES MARTIN	1–0
	ALAIN VIGNEAULT	1–0
	RANDY CARLYLE	1–0
	DAN BYLSMA	1–0
	JOEL QUENNEVILLE	0–1
	MIKE BABCOCK	1-0
	MICHEL THERRIEN	0-1

Claude Julien's loss to Peter Laviolette took place in the second round of the 2009/10 playoffs.

The Bruins had a 3–0 series lead before allowing the Flyers to win the next four games and the series. The following season Julien and the Bruins exacted their revenge by sweeping the Flyers four straight and, ultimately, winning the 2010/11 Stanley Cup.

His loss to Joel Quenneville took place during the 2012/13 Stanley Cup finals.

MIKE KEENAN versus:		
	AL ARBOUR	2–0
	GLEN SATHER	0–2
	BRYAN MURRAY	1–1
	SCOTTY BOWMAN	0–2
	JACQUES LEMAIRE	1–0
	PAT QUINN	1–0

RON WILSON	0–1
JOEL QUENNEVILLE	0–1

Mike Keenan's two playoff losses to his idol, Scotty Bowman, came in 1991/92 and 1995/96. The 1991/92 loss took place during the Stanley Cup finals when Keenan's Chicago Blackhawks lost to Bowman's Pittsburgh Penguins. The 1995/96 loss took place during the second round when his St. Louis Blues lost to Bowman's Detroit Red Wings.

PETER LAVIOLETTE versus:

PAT QUINN	0–1
JACQUES MARTIN	1–1
LINDY RUFF	2–0
JACQUES LEMAIRE	1–0
CLAUDE JULIEN	1–1
JOEL QUENNEVILLE	0–2
DAN BYLSMA	1–0

Peter Laviolette's losses to Pat Quinn and Jacques Martin came in 2001/02 and 2002/03, respectively, when Laviolette was head coach of the New York Islanders. His two losses to Joel Quenneville came during the 2009/10 Stanley Cup finals when Laviolette was coaching the Flyers and in 2014/15 in the first round when Laviolette was coaching in Nashville.

JACQUES LEMAIRE versus:

GERRY CHEEVERS	1–0
AL ARBOUR	0–1
HARRY SINDEN	1–0
MIKE KEENAN	0–1
EDDIE JOHNSTON	1–0
TERRY MURRAY	1–0
SCOTTY BOWMAN	1–0
JACQUES MARTIN	0–1
MARC CRAWFORD	1–0
MIKE BABCOCK	0–1
RANDY CARLYLE	0–1

JOEL QUENNEVILLE	0–1
PETER LAVIOLETTE	0–1

Of all Scotty Bowman's players who later became head coaches, Jacques Lemaire was his brightest pupil, and Lemaire proved it by beating Bowman in the 1994/95 Stanley Cup finals – the only time those two ever faced each other in playoff competition.

JACQUES MARTIN versus:

JACQUES LEMAIRE	1–0
RON WILSON	0–1
LINDY RUFF	0–1
PAT QUINN	0–4
PETER LAVIOLETTE	1–1
KEN HITCHCOCK	1–0
PAT BURNS	0–1
BRUCE BOUDREAU	1–0
DAN BYLSMA	1–0
CLAUDE JULIEN	0–1

Pat Quinn is the main reason why Jacques Martin is the ultimate heartbreak coach in hockey history. Martin suffered four defeats at the hands of Quinn's teams. What's striking is that despite Martin's reputation for being a great defensive coach, this was a rare instance where the offence was able to beat the defence.

KEN MACKENZIE versus:

PETE GREEN	0–1
LESTER PATRICK	0–1

Mackenzie's loss to Pete Green came in the 1922/23 Stanley Cup finals. The loss to Lester Patrick came in the 1925/26 WHL playoffs. Had Mackenzie won then he would have earned his second Stanley Cup finals appearance and added possibly 5 to 11 points to his coaching value.

TODD MCLELLAN versus:

RANDY CARLYLE	0–1
MIKE BABCOCK	2-0

JOEL QUENNEVILLE	0–1
TERRY MURRAY	1-0
ALAIN VIGNEAULT	1–1
KEN HITCHCOCK	0–1
DARRYL SUTTER	0–2

Todd McLellan is the first (and so far only) head coach to beat Mike Babcock twice in Stanley Cup playoff competition. His two losses to Darryl Sutter came in 2012/13 and 2013/14. The latter defeat the most galling of all. As noted before McLellan's Sharks had Sutter's Kings down 3–0 in the series and allowed the Kings to win the next four games, the series, and, eventually, the Stanley Cup.

PETE MULDOON versus:

FRANK PATRICK	2–3
ART ROSS	0–1

From 1919 to 1924, Pete Muldoon and Frank Patrick vied with each other five times for the honour of representing the PCHA in the Stanley Cup playoffs against the NHL. Indeed, this was the greatest playoff rivalry of the 1917–1926 era. Muldoon's loss to Art Ross in 1926/27 was his sole playoff appearance as an NHL coach.

BRYAN MURRAY versus:

AL ARBOUR	1–3
MIKE KEENAN	1–1
PAT BURNS	0–1
LINDY RUFF	1–1
MICHEL THERRIEN	1–1
RANDY CARLYLE	0–1

The Bryan Murray–Al Arbour playoff rivalry was the biggest (if not the best) of the 1980s. No other coaching tandem engaged in as many matchups during that decade.

TERRY MURRAY versus:

ROGER NEILSON	2–0
BOB JOHNSON	0–1

SCOTTY BOWMAN	0–2
AL ARBOUR	0–1
JACQUES LEMAIRE	0–1
ALAIN VIGNEAULT	0–1
TODD MCLELLAN	0–1

Murray's playoff wins against Roger Neilson came in 1989/90 and 1990/91. Terry Murray's clash with Scotty Bowman in the 1996/97 Stanley Cup finals wasn't the first time they had met in playoff competition. Bowman had beaten Terry Murray before in 1991/92 when Bowman's Pittsburgh Penguins beat Murray's Washington Capitals in the first round.

ROGER NEILSON versus:

AL ARBOUR	2–1
SCOTTY BOWMAN	0–3
BOB PULFORD	1–0
BOB JOHNSON	0–1
TERRY MURRAY	0–2
LINDY RUFF	1–1
PAT QUINN	0–1

Two of Roger Neilson's three playoff losses to Scotty Bowman came in 1977/78 and 1978/79 when Neilson was coaching the Toronto Maple Leafs against Bowman's Montreal Canadiens. The third came in 1991/92 when Neilson was coaching the New York Rangers and Bowman, the Pittsburgh Penguins. The first loss was tough because it was in the semifinal round. It was the first the Maple Leafs had come that close to the Stanley Cup finals since 1966/67. The second and third losses were both in the second round. All three times Bowman would go on to win the Stanley Cup.

FRANK PATRICK versus:

PETE MULDOON	3–2
PETE GREEN	0–2
LESTER PATRICK	2–0
LEO DANDURAND	0–1
DICK IRVIN	0–2

In 1917/18 and 1922/23 Frank Patrick faced his brother, Lester, in the PCHA playoffs to see who would represent the league in the Stanley Cup playoffs. They were the only times in Stanley Cup playoff history when two brother coaches faced each other in a playoff series. The Sutter brothers (Brian, Darryl, Brent, and Duane) never faced one another in playoff competition; neither did the Murray brothers (Bryan and Terry).

LESTER PATRICK versus:

FRANK PATRICK	0–2
KEN MACKENZIE	1–0
LEO DANDURAND	2–0
ART ROSS	1–2
CECIL HART	1–1
DICK IRVIN	2–3
JACK ADAMS	1–1

Lester Patrick avenged his 1929/30 playoff loss to Cecil Hart by beating him in the 1931/32 semifinal round, thus denying Hart a chance to three-peat as Stanley Cup champion.

BOB PULFORD versus:

BILLY REAY	0–1
DON CHERRY	0–3
AL ARBOUR	0–1
EMILE FRANCIS	1–0
ROGER NEILSON	0–1
GLEN SATHER	0–1

When you look at the film footage of Roger Neilson engaging in his legendary towel-waving mock surrender protest against the officials (during the Canucks Game 2 loss against the Chicago Blackhawks in the 1981/82 conference finals), you will notice a silver-haired man behind the Blackhawks bench with a stern look on his face (even though his team is winning the game handily). The silver-haired man is Bob Pulford.

JOEL QUENNEVILLE versus:

SCOTTY BOWMAN	0–3
KEN HITCHCOCK	2–1
DARRYL SUTTER	2–2
BOB HARTLEY	0–1
MARC CRAWFORD	0–1
DAVE TIPPETT	1–0
RANDY CARLYLE	0–1
JACQUES LEMAIRE	1–0
MIKE BABCOCK	1–2
MIKE KEENAN	1–0
ALAIN VIGNEAULT	2–1
PETER LAVIOLETTE	2–0
CLAUDE JULIEN	1–0
BRUCE BOUDREAU	1-0

Joel Quenneville's losses to Scotty Bowman came in 1996/97, 1997/98, and 2001/02 when he was coaching the St. Louis Blues. His two defeats at the hands of Mike Babcock came in 2007/08 and 2008/09: the former when he was coaching the Colorado Avalanche, and the latter when he was coaching the Chicago Blackhawks.

He lost to Darryl Sutter in 1998/99 but got his revenge in 1999/00 and beat Sutter again in 2012/13 but Sutter evened up the rivalry by beating Quenneville's Blackhawks in the 2013/14 Western Conference finals.

PAT QUINN versus:

FRED SHERO	1–1
GLEN SATHER	1–1
AL ARBOUR	0–1
PAT BURNS	1–0
MIKE KEENAN	0–1
MARC CRAWFORD	0–1
ROGER NEILSON	1–0
LINDY RUFF	0–1
JACQUES MARTIN	4–0
PETER LAVIOLETTE	1–0
KEN HITCHCOCK	0–2

Quinn's loss to Lindy Ruff came in the 1998/99 conference finals when Quinn was coaching the Toronto Maple Leafs against Ruff's Buffalo Sabres. Had the Leafs won it would have been their first Stanley Cup final appearance since 1966/67.

BILLY REAY versus:		
	TOE BLAKE	0–2
	PUNCH IMLACH	0–1
	EMILE FRANCIS	3–1
	HARRY SINDEN	0–1
	SCOTTY BOWMAN	0–2
	BOB PULFORD	1–0
	DON CHERRY	1–0
	FLOYD SMITH	0–1

Billy Reay's playoff win against Don Cherry came during the preliminary round of the 1974/75 playoffs. It was Cherry's first playoff appearance as an NHL head coach. The Bruins took Game 1 but the Blackhawks rebounded to steal Game 2 in overtime at home and then beat Boston 6–4 in Game 3 to win the series. It was Grapes's worst playoff performance as an NHL head coach.

ART ROSS versus:		
	PETE MULDOON	1–0
	LESTER PATRICK	2–1
	CECIL HART	0–2
	DICK IRVIN	2–2
	JACK ADAMS	0–3

Art Ross's combined 0–5 record against Cecil Hart and Jack Adams is well worth examining. Both coaches led teams with superb defences and great goaltending. Ross had better odds against Lester Patrick and Dick Irvin (both of whom were more offensive-minded).

CLAUDE RUEL versus:		
	EMILE FRANCIS	1–0
	HARRY SINDEN	1–0
	SCOTTY BOWMAN	1–0
	GLEN SATHER	0–1

Claude Ruel's series victories all came in the 1969 Stanley Cup playoffs where he beat the Rangers, Bruins, and St. Louis Blues (in that order) to win the Stanley Cup. His loss to Glen Sather came in 1980/81.

LINDY RUFF versus:

ROGER NEILSON	1–1
ALAIN VIGNEAULT	1–0
RON WILSON	0–1
JACQUES MARTIN	1–0
PAT BURNS	1–0
PAT QUINN	1–0
KEN HITCHCOCK	1–1
BRYAN MURRAY	1–1
PETER LAVIOLETTE	0–2
CLAUDE JULIEN	0–1
BRUCE BOUDREAU	0-1

Lindy Ruff's first loss against Peter Laviolette came in 2005/06 when Laviolette was coaching the Carolina Hurricanes. The 'Canes beat Ruff's Sabres in the conference finals in seven games to advance to the finals against the Edmonton Oilers. The second loss came in 2010/11 when they lost to the Flyers in a hard-fought first-round defeat.

GLEN SATHER versus:

BILL DINEEN	0–1
PAT QUINN	1–1
CLAUDE RUEL	1–0
AL ARBOUR	1–2
BOB JOHNSON	2–1
BOB PULFORD	1–0
MIKE KEENAN	2–0
ROBBIE FTOREK	0–1

Glen Sather's two wins over Mike Keenan came during the 1984/85 and 1986/87 Stanley Cup finals.

FRED SHERO versus:

SCOTTY BOWMAN	0–3
EMILE FRANCIS	1–0
AL ARBOUR	2–0
FLOYD SMITH	1–0
DON CHERRY	1–2
PAT QUINN	1–1

Both of Fred Shero's playoff wins against Al Arbour took place in the 1970s when Arbour was slowly developing his Islander teams.

His loss to Pat Quinn came in 1979/80 when Shero's New York Rangers lost in the first round to Pat Quinn's Philadelphia Flyers. I remember watching the final game on TV. It was in Philadelphia, and I recall the derisive cheering from the Flyers and the disgusted expression on Shero's face when the final buzzer sounded. It was the last playoff game Shero ever coached.

HARRY SINDEN versus:

TOE BLAKE	0–1
PUNCH IMLACH	1–0
CLAUDE RUEL	0–1
EMILE FRANCIS	1–0
BILLY REAY	1–0
SCOTTY BOWMAN	1–0
AL ARBOUR	0–1
JACQUES LEMAIRE	0–1

Harry Sinden's sole triumph over Punch Imlach was during the 1968/69 playoffs. His victories over Emile Francis, Billy Reay, and Scotty Bowman all came during the 1969/70 playoffs. The loss to Al Arbour took place in 1979/80, and the loss to Jacques Lemaire happened during the 1984/85 playoffs.

JIMMY SKINNER versus:

DICK IRVIN	1–0
TOE BLAKE	0–1

Skinner's win against Dick Irvin came during the 1954/55 Stanley Cup finals. His loss to Toe Blake took place during the 1955/56 Stanley Cup finals.

FLOYD SMITH versus:	BILLY REAY	1–0
	SCOTTY BOWMAN	1–0
	FRED SHERO	0–1
	AL ARBOUR	0–2

Floyd Smith's victories over Billy Reay and Scotty Bowman took place during the 1974/75 playoffs.

DARRYL SUTTER versus:	PAT BURNS	1–1
	SCOTTY BOWMAN	0–1
	KEN HITCHCOCK	2–2
	BOB HARTLEY	0–2
	JOEL QUENNEVILLE	2–2
	MARC CRAWFORD	1–0
	RON WILSON	1–0
	RANDY CARLYLE	0–1
	ALAIN VIGNEAULT	2–0
	DAVE TIPPETT	1–0
	TODD MCLELLAN	2–0
	BRUCE BOUDREAU	1-0

Darryl Sutter's victories against Marc Crawford and Ron Wilson both came when he led the Calgary Flames to the Stanley Cup finals in 2003/04.

His victory over Dave Tippett came during the 2011/12 Stanley Cup playoffs when he led the Los Angeles Kings to the Stanley Cup title.

His two victories against Alain Vigneault took place in 2011/12 and 2013/14 when Sutter led the Kings to the Stanley Cup. The 2011/12 victory came in the first round and the second came during the 2013/14 Stanley Cup finals.

The Sutter–Hitchcock playoff rivalry ranks with the Babcock–Tippett rivalry in terms of the number of engagements. Sutter's first two matchups against Hitchcock ended badly. Sutter's losses to Hitchcock came in 1997/98 and 1999/00 (when Sutter was coaching the San Jose Sharks and Hitchcock the Dallas Stars). The former was in the first round and the latter came in the second round. Sutter waited 12 years to get his revenge. His first defeat of Hitchcock came during the second round of the 2011/12 playoffs and the second came during the first round of the 2012/13 playoffs.

MICHEL THERRIEN versus:

ROBBIE FTOREK	1-0
BRYAN MURRAY	1–1
MIKE BABCOCK	0–1
CLAUDE JULIEN	1-0
ALAIN VIGNEAULT	0-1

Michel Therrien's loss to Mike Babcock came during the 2007/08 Stanley Cup finals. The victory over Claude Julien and the loss to Alain Vigneault both came during the 2013/14 playoffs.

DAVE TIPPETT versus:

MIKE BABCOCK	0–4
JOEL QUENNEVILLE	0–1
ALAIN VIGNEAULT	0–1
RANDY CARLYLE	1–0
RON WILSON	1–0
DARRYL SUTTER	0–1

Mike Babcock is to Dave Tippett what Pat Quinn was to Jacques Martin: the one coach he cannot lick in playoff competition. Half of Tippett's eight playoff defeats have come at the hands of Babcock. One reason why Tippett was able to reach the 2011/12 conference finals was because Babcock's Red Wings were eliminated in the first round – thus sparing Tippett a potential fifth encounter with Babcock.

ALAIN VIGNEAULT versus:

LINDY RUFF	0–1
DAVE TIPPETT	1–0
RANDY CARLYLE	0–1
JOEL QUENNEVILLE	1–2
TERRY MURRAY	1–0
TODD MCLELLAN	1–1
CLAUDE JULIEN	0–1
DARRYL SUTTER	0–2

DAN BYLSMA	1-0
MICHEL THERRIEN	1-0

Alain Vigneault's playoff wins against Joel Quenneville and Todd McLellan both came during the 2010/11 playoffs. His loss to Claude Julien came during the 2010/11 Stanley Cup finals. His victories over Dan Bylsma and Michel Therrien and the second loss to Darryl Sutter all took place in 2013/14.

COONEY WEILAND versus:

HAP DAY	1–0
JACK ADAMS	1–0

Cooney Weiland's playoff victories against Hap Day and Jack Adams came during the 1940/41 playoffs.

RON WILSON versus:

SCOTTY BOWMAN	0–2
PAT BURNS	1–0
JACQUES MARTIN	1–0
LINDY RUFF	1–0
DARRYL SUTTER	0–1
MIKE BABCOCK	0–1
MIKE KEENAN	1–0
DAVE TIPPETT	0–1

Like Terry Murray's experience, Ron Wilson's loss to Scotty Bowman in the 1997/98 Stanley Cup finals was not the first time they had met in playoff competition. Wilson had lost to Bowman the year before during the second round of the 1996/97 playoffs when Wilson's Mighty Ducks were swept by Bowman's Detroit Red Wings.

Wilson's loss to Darryl Sutter came in 2003/04 when the Sharks lost the conference finals to the Calgary Flames.

His losses to Mike Babcock and Dave Tippett both came in the second round in 2006/07 and 2007/08, the latter being the last time Ron Wilson has appeared in the playoffs thus far.

THE PROGRESSIVE CHART

By the time you reach this section, you will know who the top 50 greatest hockey coaches of all time are, but who was the best in 1917/18 or 1943/44 or 1967/68, or even 1992/93 for that matter?

Is there a way to determine which coaches were the best in seasons past? Who did Scotty Bowman surpass to become the greatest hockey coach of all time? And who did his predecessors surpass and so forth?

Applying my rating method retroactively, I was able to answer those questions on a season-by-season basis. This section identifies those key seasons when the torch of excellence was passed from coaching legend to coaching legend; it reveals long-forgotten hockey coaches who once stood among the elite ranks before fading into obscurity; it shows the high coaching quality some coaches were able to reach before misfortune set in and their stock began to fade.

When you read this section, certain things need to be explained. From 1917 to 1926 (with the exception of the 1917/18 season), I've listed only those hockey coaches with a +10 rating or higher. After the 1925/26 season, I've listed only those coaches who were at or above the +20 level, so when you see the phrase *enter the charts*, it means the coach in question had just cracked the +20 mark in coaching value. All coaches in *italic* type were actively coaching.

1917–1918

1. *Dick Carroll* +14
2. *Frank Patrick* +11
3. *Lester Patrick* +10
4. *Newsy Lalonde* +7

Dick Carroll was the head coach of the Toronto Arenas in the NHL's inaugural season. He defeated Newsy Lalonde in the NHL playoffs to face Frank Patrick, who won the PCHA title for the 1917/18 Stanley Cup by defeating his brother, Lester, in the PCHA playoffs.

Lester had the best regular-season record while Frank finished second, but Frank's Vancouver Millionaires prevailed in the PCHA playoff and were later beaten by Carroll in the 1917/18 Stanley Cup finals.

1918–1919

1. *Frank Patrick* +21
2. *Newsy Lalonde* +15
3. *Alf Smith* +10

Frank Patrick took over the #1 slot and didn't relinquish it until 1922/23, even though he failed to win the Stanley Cup despite two more attempts in 1920/21 and 1921/22.

Newsy Lalonde led the Montreal Canadiens to the 1918/19 Stanley Cup finals, thus vaulting into second place on my charts. Lester Patrick and Dick Carroll both fell off the charts because they finished last in their respective leagues.

Alf Smith was the head coach of the original Ottawa Senators during the 1918/19 NHL season and had the best regular-season record in the league, but he lost the NHL finals to Montreal. He never coached in the NHL again.

1922–1923

1. *Pete Green* +67
2. *Frank Patrick* +64

3. *Ken Mackenzie* +31
4. *Pete Muldoon* +28
5. *George O'Donoghue* +14
6. *Wesley Champ* +12
7. Alf Smith +10
8. Frank Carroll +10

Pete Green's three Stanley Cup victories in four seasons from 1919/20 to 1922/23 allowed him to overtake Frank Patrick as the greatest coach in hockey. Green would remain number one for the next 15 years.

As mentioned, Ken Mackenzie was the best coach in WCHL/WHL league history; his 1922/23 Stanley Cup finals appearance earned him the #3 slot on my charts.

Pete Muldoon's two consecutive Stanley Cup finals appearances in 1918/19 and 1919/20 also helped him enter the charts. He was nearly at his coaching peak during the 1922/23 season.

George O'Donoghue led the Toronto St. Patricks to the 1921/22 Stanley Cup over Frank Patrick's Vancouver team, which is why he is listed here.

Wesley Champ was the head coach of the Regina Capitals in the WCHL. He won the first league title in 1921/22 but failed to reach the Stanley Cup finals when he lost to Frank Patrick's Vancouver team. Champ would reach his peak rating the following season when he was +18, but he would fall off the charts in 1924/25 when he finished last in the WCHL and the Capitals folded and were sold to Pete Muldoon, who moved the team to Portland, Oregon.

Frank Carroll was O'Donoghue's predecessor at Toronto. He coached the St. Patricks for one season (1920/21) and had the best regular-season record but lost the 1920/21 NHL finals to Pete Green's Ottawa Senators. O'Donoghue avenged Carroll's loss by beating the Senators in the 1921/22 NHL finals.

1937–1938

1. *Lester Patrick* +83
2. Pete Green +82
3. *Cecil Hart* +78

4.	*Dick Irvin*	+72
5.	Frank Patrick	+70
6.	*Jack Adams*	+35
7.	Ken Mackenzie	+34
8.	Pete Muldoon	+29
9.	David Gill	+21
10.	*Art Ross*	+21

In the penultimate year of his illustrious coaching career, Lester Patrick surpassed Pete Green as the greatest hockey coach of all time. The late 1920s and 1930s were a glorious time for Patrick and the New York Rangers.

Cecil Hart entered the charts in 1928/29 (after only three seasons of coaching) and rose swiftly through the ranks. By the time he resigned as head coach in 1932, he was the second-greatest hockey coach after Pete Green (Lester Patrick was 16 points behind Hart in 1931/32). Hart returned to NHL coaching in 1936, but by then Patrick had already passed him. When Hart quit coaching for good, he was tied for third with Dick Irvin in coaching value. Seeing where he ranks among his coaching peers, it again begs the obvious question: why isn't Cecil Hart in the Hockey Hall of Fame?

When he stopped coaching in 1926, Frank Patrick was the second-greatest hockey coach, behind Pete Green. He maintained his second-place status until 1930/31, when Cecil Hart passed him. His brother, Lester, surpassed him in 1932/33. Frank's two-year coaching stint with the Boston Bruins added 13 points to his coaching value and helped him regain third place until Cecil Hart returned to coaching in 1936.

Note the presence of Dick Irvin and Jack Adams. Irvin entered the charts by 1932/33 and was gaining rapidly on the top three leaders. Jack Adams had finally entered the charts in 1935/36 after slowly building the Detroit Red Wings to prominence.

David Gill was the head coach and manager of the original Ottawa Senators from 1926/27 to 1928/29. In his rookie season as an NHL coach, he led the Sens to the 1926/27 Stanley Cup title in one of the greatest debut performances in NHL coaching history. The 1926/27 Senators had a winning percentage of .727. No other NHL rookie coach has surpassed that figure.

Art Ross, despite great coaching success with the Boston Bruins since 1926, didn't enter the charts until 1937/38. Ross's coaching record before 1926 was rather dismal, and it took him a long time to overcome the deficit and emerge on the plus side. Ross endured two losing seasons in the 1930s, which further delayed his entry on the charts.

1943–1944

1.	*Dick Irvin*	+104
2.	Lester Patrick	+89
3.	Pete Green	+77
4.	Cecil Hart	+77
5.	Frank Patrick	+70
6.	*Jack Adams*	+69
7.	*Art Ross*	+50
8.	Ken Mackenzie	+34
9.	Cooney Weiland	+31
10.	Pete Muldoon	+29
11.	*Hap Day*	+24
12.	David Gill	+21

When Lester Patrick retired as head coach of the New York Rangers in 1939, he was 12 points ahead of Dick Irvin in coaching value, and yet it took Irvin five seasons to surpass Patrick in coaching value.

When he left the Toronto Maple Leafs to become head coach of the Montreal Canadiens in 1940, Irvin took some time getting the Habs back on track. Irvin's coaching value declined slightly in the process. But when he led the Canadiens to the Stanley Cup during the 1943/44 season, it was sufficient to leapfrog him over Patrick.

Note the improvement in Jack Adams's rating. The early 1940s were a boom time for Adams and the Red Wings: the team made three consecutive Stanley Cup finals appearances and won the 1942/43 Cup in the process.

Cooney Weiland entered the charts in 1940/41 with his Stanley Cup win over the Detroit Red Wings. By 1944 Weiland was coaching in the AHL (and doing quite nicely there).

Hap Day entered the charts in 1941/42 with his first Stanley Cup win, earning him a +20 rating, but note the slight progress he made in the two years following that victory – only four extra points. What Hap Day didn't know yet was that he was on the cusp of an enormous surge that would send him to even greater heights.

1967–1968

1.	*Toe Blake*	+195
2.	Dick Irvin	+189
3.	Tommy Ivan	+95
4.	Lester Patrick	+89
5.	*Punch Imlach*	+88
6.	Hap Day	+87
7.	Jack Adams	+81
8.	Pete Green	+77
9.	Cecil Hart	+77
10.	Frank Patrick	+70
11.	Art Ross	+50
12.	Jimmy Skinner	+39
13.	Ken Mackenzie	+34
14.	Cooney Weiland	+31
15.	Pete Muldoon	+29
16.	David Gill	+21

After 1943/44, Dick Irvin continued to add to his coaching value while with the Montreal Canadiens. Irvin reached his peak in 1954/55 with a coaching value of +199. He left the Habs to coach the Chicago Blackhawks the following season and endured a last-place finish, which cost him 10 points off his coaching value.

Toe Blake entered the charts in his rookie season. At the end of his third season, he was already ranked among the top ten hockey coaches of all time. By 1959/60 (after his fifth straight Stanley Cup win), Blake was already the second-greatest hockey coach of all time, 91 points behind Irvin. During the lean years of 1960/61 to 1963/64, Blake added 33 points to his coaching value (a hefty sum for other coaches but a failure in Blake's eyes). Blake's resurgence from 1964/65 to 1967/68 made it possible for him to surpass Irvin (according to my rating system) but not without some irony in the process.

When Blake and the Montreal Canadiens lost the 1966/67 Stanley Cup finals to Punch Imlach's Toronto Maple Leafs, it was a good thing for Blake (according to my rating system). If the Habs had won the Cup, Blake planned to retire as head coach. Had he done so, his rating would have been only +180, not enough to have him surpass Irvin.

Luckily for Blake, he decided to coach one more season, and in 1967/68 he passed Irvin to become the greatest hockey coach of all time.

Tommy Ivan entered the charts in 1948/49 and by 1949/50 had already entered the top ten ranks in my rating system. By 1952/53, he was the third-greatest hockey coach who ever lived, and by the end of the 1953/54 season, he was second only to Dick Irvin.

In 1959/60 Punch Imlach had already coached two seasons in the NHL, but he wouldn't enter the charts until 1961/62 (when he won his first Stanley Cup). Punch reached his peak rank of #5 with his 1966/67 Stanley Cup win, but by 1967/68 the decline was already setting in. His failure to make the playoffs in 1967/68 presaged a greater decline and fall. By 1969, he was out as Toronto head coach and general manager.

Please take note of Hap Day's coaching value. As mentioned before: after 1943/44 Day entered into the renaissance of his coaching career. By 1944/45, he had cracked the top ten ranks. By 1948/49, he was the third-greatest hockey coach of all time (in my ranking system) and remained so when he retired from coaching in 1950.

Jimmy Skinner succeeded Tommy Ivan as Wings head coach in 1954 and had already entered the charts at the end of his rookie season. By 1956/57, he was ranked among the top ten but immediately afterwards began to decline in rank.

1992–1993

1.	*Scotty Bowman*	+202	5.	*Al Arbour*	+104
2.	Toe Blake	+195	6.	Tommy Ivan	+95
3.	Dick Irvin	+189	7.	Lester Patrick****	+89
4.	Glen Sather*	+131	8.	Hap Day	+87

9.	Punch Imlach	+86
10.	Fred Shero	+83
11.	Jack Adams	+81
12.	Billy Reay	+78
13.	Pete Green	+77
14.	Cecil Hart	+77
15.	Frank Patrick****	+70
16.	Mike Keenan	+68
17.	*Bill Dineen**	+66
18.	Art Ross	+50
19.	Claude Ruel	+46
20.	Don Cherry	+43
21.	Emile Francis	+43
22.	*Bryan Murray*	+42
23.	Jimmy Skinner	+39
24.	*Pat Quinn*	+38
25.	Tom Johnson	+36
26.	Bob Johnson	+35
27.	Ken Mackenzie	+34
28.	*Roger Neilson*	+32
29.	Cooney Weiland	+31
30.	Gerry Cheevers	+31
31.	*Pat Burns*	+31
32.	*Terry Crisp*	+31
33.	Pete Muldoon	+29
34.	*Jacques Demers**	+28
35.	Jack Kelley*	+27
36.	Harry Sinden	+25
37.	Larry Hillman*	+23
38.	Al MacNeil	+23
39.	Floyd Smith*	+22
40.	*Brian Sutter*	+22
41.	David Gill	+21

Scotty Bowman's coaching value after his first season of NHL coaching was +6. Two seasons later, Bowman entered the charts with +30. When he left the St. Louis Blues in 1971, it rose only to +33.

What followed was the mother lode: Bowman earned 127 plus points from 1971 to 1979. He cracked the top ten ranks in 1974/75, and the following year he was ranked as the third-greatest hockey coach of all time, according to my rating system. Two more Stanley Cup wins propelled Bowman even closer to Toe Blake (only 35 points behind). But when Bowman left Montreal to coach and manage the Buffalo Sabres, things began to slip.

Bowman was only creeping up the charts, whereas before he was advancing by leaps and bounds. By 1984/85, he was only five points behind Dick Irvin for the #2 spot on my charts and ten points behind Toe Blake for the top slot.

Bowman lost ground during the 1985/86 and the 1986/87 NHL seasons. When he was fired by the Buffalo Sabres, his coaching value had declined to +178 (only good for #3 on my rating charts). Bowman's rating remained static until 1991 when he took over as head coach of the Penguins when Bob Johnson died of cancer.

His Stanley Cup win in 1991/92 leapfrogged Bowman into second place, and a strong finish in 1992/93 (where the Penguins won the President's Trophy but failed to win the Stanley Cup) earned Bowman ten more plus points, which allowed him to pass Toe Blake for good as the greatest hockey coach of all time, according to my rating system. During the nine seasons that followed, Bowman added to his record in one of the finest coaching comebacks in NHL history.

Glen Sather's and Al Arbour's dynastic runs during the 1980s helped propel both men into the top five ranks. When Arbour retired for the first time in 1986, he was ranked fourth, but Sather quickly passed him in 1987/88 and secured the fourth spot (where he remains today).

Fred Shero entered the charts with his 1973/74 Stanley Cup win, and when he repeated as Cup champion the following season, he was ranked #15 on the charts. The next three seasons represented slow but steady progress, but it wasn't until he took the New York Rangers to the 1978/79 Stanley Cup finals that he cracked the top ten ranks on my charts. The following season, he peaked at eighth place.

It took Billy Reay a while before he entered the charts. His poor coaching performance with the Toronto Maple Leafs in the 1950s undermined his coaching value. But Reay's glory years with the Blackhawks in the 1960s helped to get him out of the hole. He didn't enter the charts until the end of the 1969/70 season, but during the next six seasons Reay rose swiftly up the charts and reached his peak rank of ninth place in 1975/76. His failure to win the Stanley Cup cost Reay in the long run.

There was no slow start for Mike Keenan. By his third season, Iron Mike had entered the charts and was among the top 30 hockey coaches of all time. By 1989/90, he had entered the top 20. Keenan did not realize this, but he was one season away from reaching his apex as a hockey coach and then watching his value decline during the lean years ahead for him.

Bill Dineen entered the charts with his 1973/74 Avco Cup victory. In fact, Dineen and Fred Shero ran pretty much side by side while going up the charts, according to my rating system. Interestingly, Dineen ranked slightly better than Shero during the 1970s (Shero had suffered a losing season, whereas Dineen had not). It wasn't until 1977/78 that Dineen and Shero were equal in value, and then Shero surpassed Dineen with his 1978/79 Stanley Cup finals appearance. By 1992/93, Dineen had suffered two losing seasons while coaching the Philadelphia Flyers, which reduced his coaching value even lower.

In 1992/93 Don Cherry had been out of NHL coaching since 1979/80 and yet he still ranked #20 on my charts. When he was fired by Boston in 1979, he was ranked #15.

Emile Francis didn't enter the charts until 1971/72 (the year he led the Rangers to the Stanley Cup finals). He peaked in 1973/74 but slowly began to decline in rank while his coaching value stalled out a bit.

Even though Bryan Murray started coaching in 1982, he didn't enter the charts until 1987/88 because of the poor rookie season he had (which put him in the hole, according to my rating system) and his lack of playoff success.

Pat Quinn entered the charts in 1980/81, fell off them in 1982/83, and regained a spot in 1984/85. He fell off the charts again in 1985/86 and didn't return until 1991/92 (where he has remained).

Tom Johnson's Stanley Cup triumph in 1971/72 helped him enter the charts, where he has also remained. He was the 15th-greatest hockey coach of all time when he was fired by Harry Sinden in 1973.

Bob Johnson's 1990/91 Stanley Cup win helped propel him onto the charts. He was ranked among the top 25 hockey coaches ever at the time of his death.

Roger Neilson's chart story is similar to Pat Quinn's. Neilson entered the charts in 1981/82 when he led the Canucks to their Stanley Cup appearance. By 1983/84, he fell off the charts and didn't return until 1990/91 (when he was coaching the New York Rangers).

Gerry Cheevers entered the charts in 1983/84 (the year before he was fired) and has remained there, although he will certainly be knocked off in the years to come.

Pat Burns entered the charts in 1990/91 and was slowly moving upward by 1992/93.

Note Terry Crisp's presence on the charts. Crisp's first three NHL coaching seasons were superlative in quality. By 1989/90 his coaching value was a magnificent +41, but Crisp was fired in 1990 as head coach of the Calgary Flames and didn't return to NHL coaching until 1992/93, when he became the first head coach of the expansion Tampa Bay Lightning. His years with Tampa proved to be his undoing in terms of his coaching value. As you can see above, Crisp's first season with the Lightning cost him ten points off his coaching value. By 1994/95, he would fall off the charts, though the following year (1995/96) he would briefly return (when he led the Lightning to their first playoff appearance). By 1995/97, he was off the charts for good.

Jacques Demers's Stanley Cup victory in 1992/93 helped him enter the charts, but fame would be fleeting. The following season he fell off the charts, never to return. Ironically he, too, would coach the Tampa Bay Lightning (and see his coaching value diminish further).

Jack Kelley was a famed hockey coach for Boston University (and later earned entry in the United States Hockey Hall of Fame and the Boston University Hall of Fame). He was the first head coach and general manager of the New England (later Hartford) Whalers and coached the first Avco Cup winner in 1972/73. Kelley stopped coaching the following season but did two interim stints with the Whalers and performed quite decently, which is why he is listed here.

Interestingly, it took Harry Sinden's two interim coaching stints with the Bruins in 1979/80 and 1984/85 to help him enter the charts. When he won the 1969/70 Stanley Cup, his coaching value was only +16.

Larry Hillman was a journeyman defenceman who played on the 1966/67 Toronto Maple Leafs team that won the Stanley Cup. He later played with the Winnipeg Jets in the WHA and became their head coach during the 1977/78 WHA season, winning the Avco Cup. Hillman was fired the following season and never coached major league hockey again. His 1977/78 Avco Cup triumph is the sole reason why he was on the charts.

Even though Al MacNeil led the Montreal Canadiens to the 1970/71 Stanley Cup title, he wouldn't enter the charts until 1979/80 when he was coaching the Calgary Flames. He ranked among the top 50 until 2009/10.

Note the presence of Brian Sutter. The 1992/93 NHL season was when Sutter entered the charts (thanks to his great coaching work with the St. Louis Blues and the Boston Bruins). Sutter would rank among the top 50 until 1999/00. He would briefly return in 2001/02 but fall off again the following season – never to return.

2014–2015

1.	Scotty Bowman	+309
2.	Toe Blake	+195
3.	Dick Irvin Sr.	+189
4.	Glen Sather*	+124
5.	*Joel Quenneville*	+122
6.	Al Arbour	+105

7.	*Ken Hitchcock*	+102	29.	Bryan Murray	+51
8.	Tommy Ivan	+95	30.	Art Ross	+50
9.	*Mike Babcock*	+95	31.	Jacques Lemaire	+49
10.	Lester Patrick****	+89	32.	Terry Murray	+47
11.	Hap Day	+87	33.	Claude Ruel	+46
12.	Punch Imlach	+86	34.	*Bob Hartley*	+45
13.	Mike Keenan	+85	35.	Jacques Martin	+45
14.	Fred Shero	+83	36.	Don Cherry	+43
15.	Pete Green	+82	37.	Emile Francis	+43
16.	Jack Adams	+81	38.	*Todd McLellan*	+42
17.	*Darryl Sutter*	+80	39.	Marc Crawford	+42
18.	Billy Reay	+78	40.	Roger Neilson	+42
19.	Cecil Hart	+77	41.	*Dave Tippett*	+41
20.	*Claude Julien*	+75	42.	*Lindy Ruff*	+40
21.	Frank Patrick****	+70	43.	Jimmy Skinner	+39
22.	*Alain Vigneault*	+70	44.	Tom Johnson	+36
23.	Pat Quinn	+68	45.	Bob Johnson	+35
24.	Bill Dineen*	+66	46.	Randy Carlyle	+35
25.	*Bruce Boudreau*	+63	47.	Ken Mackenzie***	+34
26.	Pat Burns	+62	48.	*Michel Therrien*	+34
27.	Dan Bylsma	+59	49.	Cooney Weiland	+31
28.	*Peter Laviolette*	+56	50.	Gerry Cheevers	+31

Note how much the charts have changed since 1992/93. Even though Scotty Bowman remains the greatest, according to my rating system, new names and positions have occupied the charts. The expansion of the NHL, which continued from 1993 to 2000, contributed significantly to an expansion of this progressive chart.

Among the newcomers was Ken Hitchcock, who entered the charts in 1998/99. Joel Quenneville, Darryl Sutter, and Bob Hartley followed in 2000/01.

In the case of Hitchcock and Hartley, it was their Stanley Cup victories in 1998/99 and 2000/01, respectively, that helped push them upward.

It was during the 2003/04 season that the 50th coach to crack the +20 value mark (Dave Lewis, who coached the Detroit Red Wings from 2002/03 to 2003/04 and later the Boston Bruins in 2006/07) entered the charts. It was Lewis's stint with the Bruins that caused him to drop off the charts, however, never to return.

Peter Laviolette entered the charts in 2005/06 after leading the Carolina Hurricanes to the Stanley Cup.

Mike Babcock and Lindy Ruff both entered the charts in 2006/07, but Babcock left Ruff (and all other active NHL coaches) behind in a cloud of dust.

Randy Carlyle entered the charts in 2007/08 after only three seasons of NHL coaching.

The 2010/11 season saw five coaches enter the charts. Claude Julien, Alain Vigneault, Dan Bylsma, Todd McLellan, and Bruce Boudreau all achieved breakthroughs. This caused Pete Muldoon, Bob Pulford, Eddie Johnston, Harry Sinden, Leo Dandurand, and Ron Wilson to lose their places among the top 50.

The 2014/15 season saw the entrance of Michel Therrien enter the charts thus displacing Robbie Ftorek from the top 50 list.

Are there any potential future occupants of the top 50 charts?

Other than John Tortorella the ranks of potential members of the top 50 list are maddeningly thin.

Although John Tortorella, technically, is only three plus points away from entering the charts, in reality he needs at least a +6 performance to enter the top 50. A +3 season will not allow him to surpass Gerry Cheevers because Cheever's ASR will still be superior to Tortorella's.

The fact that he has failed to secure an NHL coaching gig suggests that Tortorella (like Mike Keenan) has exhausted his possibilities and may never get a significant coaching opportunity which will allow him to enhance his coaching value.

After Tortorella the next potential candidate for future greatness is Jon Cooper. Cooper, in his third season as head coach of the Tampa Bay Lightning, has earned a coaching value of +14 (thanks to his reaching the 2014/15 Stanley Cup finals). If Cooper can repeat his performance in 2014/15, win the Atlantic Division title, and win the Stanley Cup then he will enter the top 50 ranks next season. If not then he will be a shoo-in for 2016/17.

After Jon Cooper there are Mike Yeo and Barry Trotz. Both coaches share a common coaching value of +9.

Yeo has done rather well leading the Minnesota Wild but he has repeatedly fallen short in Stanley Cup playoff competition.

Barry Trotz was once on the cusp of greatness in 2011/12 but two sub-par seasons with Nashville reduced his coaching value. In his first season leading the Washington Capitals in 2014/15 he regained the lost ground but he will need several strong seasons before he can crack the top 50 ranks.

After Yeo and Trotz, there are only two other possible candidates for greatness: Dave Cameron, head coach of the Ottawa Senators and Patrick Roy, head coach of the Colorado Avalanche.

Dave Cameron, after taking over from the fired Paul MacLean in 2014/15, led the Sens to a strong finish and earned a debut coaching value of +6. At his present pace, Cameron is five years away from cracking the top 50 ranks.

Patrick Roy was scintillating in his NHL coaching debut in 2013/14 with a value of +10 but his sophomore year was disastrous when Colorado finished last in the Central Division thus reducing his value to +6.

The realignment of the NHL, which, as mentioned, reduces the number of divisions from six to four (with fewer coaches earning the four points for a first-place finish), will drastically slow down the rate of progress for many of the coaches featured in the last chart above.

Claude Julien, Alain Vigneault and Bruce Boudreau made rapid progress because of their ability to dominate their divisions. Truncating the number of divisions will enhance competitive balance but will also make dominating a division a harder task to accomplish.

Is Scotty Bowman's place atop the charts vulnerable?

The answer is no.

Joel Quenneville has already surpassed Al Arbour and will easily pass Glen Sather during the 2015/16 season. But he is also entering the third period of his glorious NHL coaching career. His odds of reaching Dick Irvin and Toe Blake are remote unless he presides over a few more Stanley Cup winners besides the two he has already won; not an impossibility.

Ken Hitchcock has a solid chance to crack the top fifty ranks as long as he continues to put in solid regular season performances like he has done during the 2010s.

Mike Babcock has a more difficult task. Now that he is coaching the Toronto Maple Leafs (a team that badly needs overhauling) it may take him a while to crack the top five ranks. Indeed Babcock may lose points of his career value if the Leafs fail to respond to his coaching genius.

PART FIVE

FACTS AND FIGURES

THE RATINGS

This part lists all 394 hockey coaches who coached in the NHL, WHA, PCHA, and WCHL/WHL from 1917/18 to the end of the 2014/15 NHL season, in alphabetical order.

Hardcore hockey fans may notice the omission of two names: Boris Mayorov and Stanislav Nevesely. During the 1977/78 season, the WHA engaged in a unique promotion: from mid-December to early January, two European hockey teams – the Soviet All-Stars (led by Mayorov) and Team Czechoslovakia (led by Nevesely) – toured North America and competed against all eight WHA teams. The eight games both teams played were counted in the final standings of the WHA, as were the individual player and coaching stats. The Soviet All-Stars were 3–4–1 and the Czech team was 1–6–1.

Although both men are listed in the coaching stats of the Hockey Reference website, I've decided not to rate and list Mayorov and Nevesely for the simple reason that they did not play a complete season in the WHA.

When you read the ratings chart, please take note of the abbreviations at the top, defined here:

SC: stands for number of seasons coached

P: stands for the total number of plus points a coach has earned in his career

M: stands for the total number of minus points a coach has earned in his career

V: stands for the coach's final value

ASR: stands for the average season rating a coach has achieved in his career. As mentioned, to calculate the ASR, take the coach's value and divide it by the number of seasons the coach has coached.

Coaches listed in boldface are actively coaching at the end of the 2014/15 NHL season. The various asterisk footnotes are defined as follows:

* coached in the World Hockey Association

** coached in the Pacific Coast Hockey Association

*** coached in the Western Canada Hockey League/Western Hockey League

**** coached in both the Pacific Coast Hockey Association and the Western Canada Hockey League/Western Hockey League

COACH	SC	P	M	R	ASR
Sid Abel	16	49	42	+7	+0.438
Jack Adams	20	117	36	+81	+4.050
Gary Agnew	1	0	1	-1	-1.000
Keith Allen	2	6	2	+4	+2.000
Dave Allison	1	0	8	-8	-8.000
Jim Anderson	1	0	8	-8	-8.000
John Anderson	2	2	5	-3	-1.500
Lou Angotti	3	0	13	-13	-4.333
Al Arbour	23	137	32	+105	+4.565
George Armstrong	1	0	7	-7	-7.000
Scott Arniel	2	0	15	-15	-7.500
Mike Babcock	**12**	**98**	**3**	**+95**	**+7.917**
Bill Barber	2	13	0	+13	+6.500
Doug Barkley	3	0	15	-15	-5.000
John Bassett*	1	0	1	-1	-1.000
Andy Bathgate*	1	0	6	-6	-6.000
Bob Baun*	1	0	8	-8	-8.000
Andre Beaulieu	1	0	8	-8	-8.000
Danny Belisle	2	0	11	-11	-5.500
Red Berenson	3	11	1	+10	+3.333
Michel Bergeron	10	23	13	+10	+1.000
Bob Berry	11	30	18	+12	+1.091
Craig Berube	**2**	**5**	**2**	**+3**	**+1.500**
Nick Beverley	1	1	0	+1	+1.000
Don Blackburn*	4	2	6	-4	-1.000
Wren Blair	3	1	3	-2	-0.667
Toe Blake	13	195	0	+195	+15.00
Marc Boileau*	5	21	2	+19	+3.800
Leo Boivin	2	1	4	-3	-1.500
Frank Boucher	11	31	53	-22	-2.000
Georges Boucher	4	3	23	-20	-5.000
Guy Boucher	3	8	3	+5	+1.667
Bruce Boudreau	**8**	**69**	**6**	**+63**	**+7.875**
Scotty Bowman	30	316	7	+309	+10.30
Rick Bowness	9	3	60	-57	-6.333
Herb Brooks	7	13	11	+2	+0.286
John Brophy*	4	2	12	-10	-2.500
George Burnett	1	0	4	-4	-4.000
Charlie Burns	2	1	10	-9	-4.500
Pat Burns	14	70	8	+62	+4.429
Eddie Bush	1	0	10	-10	-10.00
Dan Bylsma	6	59	0	+59	+9.833

COACH	SC	P	M	R	ASR
Dave Cameron	**1**	**6**	**0**	**+6**	**+6.000**
Colin Campbell	4	7	2	+5	+1.250
Jack Capuano	**5**	**9**	**21**	**-12**	**-2.400**
Guy Carbonneau	3	14	2	+12	+4.000
Randy Carlyle	10	46	11	+35	+3.500
Doug Carpenter	6	1	31	-30	-5.000
Dick Carroll	2	14	10	+4	+2.000
Frank Carroll	1	10	0	+10	+10.00
Wayne Cashman	1	2	0	+2	+2.000
Bruce Cassidy	2	3	8	-5	-2.500
Dave Chambers	2	0	18	-18	-9.000
Wesley Champ***	4	18	10	+8	+2.000
Art Chapman	2	0	20	-20	-10.00
Guy Charron	2	0	10	-10	-5.000
Gerry Cheevers	5	31	0	+31	+6.200
Don Cherry	6	53	10	+43	+7.167
King Clancy	4	5	9	-4	-1.000
Dit Clapper	4	15	1	+14	+3.500
Odie Cleghorn	4	6	12	-6	-1.500
Sprague Cleghorn	1	1	1	0	0.000
Cory Clouston	3	5	9	-4	-1.333
Neil Colville	2	0	4	-4	-2.000
Charley Conacher	3	0	20	-20	-6.667
Lionel Conacher	1	0	10	-10	-10.00
Kevin Constantine	7	15	10	+5	+0.714
Bill Cook	2	0	13	-13	-6.500
Jon Cooper	**3**	**17**	**3**	**+14**	**+4.667**
Marc Crawford	15	78	36	+42	+2.800
Pierre Creamer	1	2	6	-4	-4.000
Fred Creighton	6	17	10	+7	+1.167
Terry Crisp	9	44	34	+10	+1.111
Joe Crozier*	7	6	16	-10	-1.429
Roger Crozier	1	0	5	-5	-5.000
Randy Cunneyworth	1	0	7	-7	-7.000
John Cunniff	3	3	10	-7	-2.333
Alex Curry	1	10	0	+10	+10.00
Leo Dandurand	6	37	13	+24	+4.000
Hap Day	10	91	4	+87	+8.700
Billy Dea	1	0	10	-10	-10.00
Peter DeBoer	7	15	25	-10	-1.429
Alex Delvecchio	4	0	16	-16	-4.000
Jacques Demers*	18	53	47	+6	+0.333

COACH	SC	P	M	R	ASR
Cy Denneny	2	21	10	+11	+5.500
Willie Desjardins	**1**	**6**	**0**	**+6**	**+6.000**
Bill Dineen*	9	75	9	+66	+7.333
Kevin Dineen	3	7	15	-8	-2.667
Clare Drake*	1	0	4	-4	-4.000
Rick Dudley	4	9	2	+7	+1.750
Dick Duff	1	0	1	-1	-1.000
Jules Dugal	1	1	0	+1	+1.000
Art Duncan	3	3	8	-5	-1.667
Red Dutton	5	6	16	-10	-2.000
Dallas Eakins	2	0	11	-11	-5.500
Frank Eddolls	1	0	10	-10	-10.00
Phil Esposito	2	2	0	+2	+1.000
Jack Evans	8	10	42	-32	-4.000
Gordie Fashoway	1	0	7	-7	-7.000
John Ferguson	3	1	14	-13	-4.333
Maurice Filion*	3	3	4	-1	-0.333
Bobby Francis	5	8	10	-2	-0.400
Emile Francis	13	56	13	+43	+3.308
Curt Fraser	4	0	27	-27	-6.750
Frank Frederickson	1	0	10	-10	-10.00
Robbie Ftorek	6	31	1	+30	+5.000
Bill Gadsby	2	7	2	+5	+2.500
Bob Gainey	8	15	11	+4	+0.500
Gerard Gallant	**4**	**2**	**9**	**-7**	**-1.750**
Herb Gardiner***	5	31	17	+14	+2.800
Jimmy Gardner	1	9	0	+9	+9.000
Ted Garvin	1	0	4	-4	-4.000
Jean-Guy Gendron*	2	18	0	+18	+9.000
Bernie Geoffrion	5	10	4	+6	+1.200
Eddie Gerard	11	37	33	+4	+0.364
Greg Gilbert	3	0	11	-11	-3.667
Dave Gill	3	24	3	+21	+7.000
Fred Glover	6	2	43	-41	-6.833
Bill Goldsworthy*	1	0	10	-10	-10.00
Ebbie Goodfellow	2	0	20	-20	-10.00
Jack Gordon	5	7	6	+1	+0.200
Scott Gordon	3	0	22	-22	-7.333
Butch Goring	4	3	18	-15	-3.750
Tommy Gorman	8	41	23	+18	+2.250
Johnny Gottselig	4	3	24	-21	-5.250
Phil Goyette	1	0	8	-8	-8.000

COACH	SC	P	M	R	ASR
Dirk Graham	1	0	1	-1	-1.000
Tony Granato	3	16	7	+9	+3.000
Gary Green	3	0	19	-19	-6.333
Pete Green	6	84	2	+82	+13.67
Shorty Green	1	0	10	-10	-10.00
Ted Green	3	3	14	-11	-3.667
Wayne Gretzky	4	2	19	-17	-4.250
Aldo Guidolin	1	0	10	-10	-10.00
Bep Guidolin*	5	21	19	+2	+0.400
Glenn Gulutzan	2	2	8	-6	-3.000
Glen Hanlon	4	0	24	-24	-6.000
John Hanna*	1	0	1	-1	-1.000
Ned Harkness	1	0	4	-4	-4.000
Billy Harris*	3	6	1	+5	+1.667
Ted Harris	3	1	11	-10	-3.333
Cecil Hart	9	78	1	+77	+8.556
Bob Hartley	**12**	**59**	**14**	**+45**	**+3.750**
Craig Hartsburg	7	9	15	-6	-0.857
Doug Harvey	1	1	1	=0	=0.000
Don Hay	2	3	1	+2	+1.000
Frank Heffernan	1	0	0	=0	=0.000
Lorne Henning	4	3	21	-18	-4.500
Camille Henry*	2	0	12	-12	-6.000
Larry Hillman*	2	23	0	+23	+11.50
Ken Hitchcock	**18**	**125**	**23**	**+102**	**+5.667**
Ivan Hlinka	2	3	5	-2	-1.000
Paul Holmgren	8	1	29	-28	-3.500
Peter Horachek	**2**	**0**	**10**	**-10**	**-5.000**
Harry Howell*	3	3	12	-9	-3.000
Sandy Hucul*	2	6	0	+6	+3.000
Bobby Hull*	3	13	1	+12	+4.000
Bill Hunter*	2	1	11	-10	-5.000
Dale Hunter	1	3	0	+3	+3.000
Punch Imlach	14	95	9	+86	+6.143
Earl Ingarfield	1	0	10	-10	-10.00
Billy Inglis	1	3	0	+3	+3.000
Ron Ingram*	3	4	9	-5	-1.667
Dick Irvin	27	219	30	+189	+7.000
Tommy Ivan	9	109	14	+95	+10.56
Emil Iverson	1	0	4	-4	-4.000
Bob Johnson	6	36	1	+35	+5.833
Tom Johnson	3	36	0	+36	+12.00

COACH	SC	P	M	R	ASR
Eddie Johnston	8	37	12	+25	+3.125
Marshall Johnston	3	0	28	-28	-9.333
Mike Johnston	**1**	**3**	**0**	**+3**	**+3.000**
Claude Julien	**12**	**80**	**5**	**+75**	**+6.250**
Steve Kasper	2	3	10	-7	-3.500
Duke Keats	1	0	10	-10	-10.00
Mike Keenan	20	105	20	+85	+4.250
Rick Kehoe	2	0	17	-17	-8.500
Jack Kelley*	3	28	1	+27	+9.000
Pat Kelly*	3	1	15	-14	-4.667
Red Kelly	10	14	15	-1	-0.100
Ray Kinasewich*	1	2	2	=0	=0.000
Dave King	8	17	18	-1	-0.167
George Kingston	2	0	20	-20	-10.00
Larry Kish	1	0	8	-8	-8.000
Mike Kitchen	3	3	11	-8	-2.667
Bobby Kromm*	5	30	16	+14	+2.800
Ralph Krueger	1	0	3	-3	-3.000
Orland Kurtenbach	2	0	9	-9	-4.500
Bill LaForge	1	0	8	-8	-8.000
Newsy Lalonde***	15	37	30	+7	+0.467
Lou Lamoriello	2	20	0	+20	+10.00
Jacques Laperrière	1	0	0	=0	=0.000
Ron Lapointe	2	0	15	-15	-7.500
Peter Laviolette	**13**	**65**	**9**	**+56**	**+4.308**
Hal Laycoe	3	0	24	-24	-8.000
Bob Leduc*	1	3	0	+3	+3.000
Gilles Leger*	2	0	11	-11	-5.500
Hugh Lehman	1	0	10	-10	-10.00
Jacques Lemaire	17	82	33	+49	+2.882
Pit Lepine	1	0	10	-10	-10.00
Percy LeSueur	1	0	8	-8	-8.000
Dave Lewis	4	25	7	+18	+4.500
Rick Ley	4	5	2	+3	+0.750
Ted Lindsay	2	0	18	-18	-9.000
Barry Long	3	7	4	+3	+1.000
Clem Loughlin	3	6	10	-4	-1.333
Ron Low	7	3	15	-12	-1.714
Kevin Lowe	1	3	0	+3	+3.000
Steve Ludzik	2	0	10	-10	-5.000
Parker MacDonald	2	0	7	-7	-3.500
Doug Maclean	5	11	15	-4	-0.800

COACH	SC	P	M	R	ASR
John Maclean	1	0	1	-1	-1.000
Paul Maclean	4	8	2	+6	+1.500
Billy MacMillan	3	0	16	-16	-5.333
Al MacNeil	5	24	6	+18	+3.600
Craig MacTavish	8	21	17	+4	+0.500
Keith Magnuson	2	1	2	-1	-0.500
Bill Mahoney	2	7	4	+3	+1.500
Dan Maloney	5	5	20	-15	-3.000
Phil Maloney	4	10	7	+3	+0.750
Sylvio Mantha	1	0	10	-10	-10.00
Bert Marshall	1	0	8	-8	-8.000
Jacques Martin	17	64	19	+45	+2.647
Godfrey Matheson	1	0	5	-5	-5.000
Paul Maurice	**17**	**41**	**50**	**-9**	**-0.529**
Wayne Maxner	2	0	18	-18	-9.000
Bob McCammon	8	22	19	+3	+0.375
Jack McCartan*	2	2	0	+2	+1.000
Ted McCaskill*	1	0	10	-10	-10.00
Bill McCreary	3	0	15	-15	-5.000
Pierre McGuire	1	0	6	-6	-6.000
John McKenzie*	2	0	2	-2	-1.000
Ken Mackenzie***	5	43	9	+34	+6.800
John McLellan	4	6	10	-4	-1.000
Todd McLellan	**7**	**44**	**2**	**+42**	**+6.000**
Tom McVie*	9	18	47	-29	-3.222
Howie Meeker	1	0	3	-3	-3.000
Barry Melrose	4	8	8	=0	=0.000
Mike Milbury	9	25	29	-4	-0.667
Lorne Molleken	2	0	3	-3	-1.500
Gerry Moore*	2	0	11	-11	-5.500
John Muckler	10	25	17	+8	+0.800
Pete Muldoon****	9	46	17	+29	+3.222
Kirk Muller	3	2	11	-9	-3.000
Dunc Munro	2	9	0	+9	+4.500
Bob Murdoch	3	4	11	-7	-2.333
Mike Murphy	4	1	16	-15	-3.750
Andy Murray	10	14	17	-3	-0.300
Bryan Murray	17	73	22	+51	+3.000
Terry Murray	15	58	11	+47	+3.133
Lou Nanne	1	0	10	-10	-10.00
Harry Neale*	14	25	23	+2	+0.154
Bill Needham*	2	6	0	+6	+3.000

COACH	SC	P	M	R	ASR
Roger Neilson	16	59	17	+42	+2.625
Todd Nelson	**1**	**0**	**3**	**-3**	**-3.000**
Claude Noel	4	4	15	-11	-2.750
Ted Nolan	**6**	**10**	**30**	**-20**	**-3.333**
Mike Nykoluk	4	2	21	-19	-4.750
Adam Oates	**3**	**9**	**4**	**+5**	**+1.667**
Mike O'Connell	1	1	0	+1	+1.000
George O'Donoghue	2	14	0	+14	+7.000
Ed Olczyk	2	0	18	-18	-9.000
Murray Oliver	1	3	0	+3	+3.000
Bert Olmstead	1	0	10	-10	-10.00
Terry O'Reilly	3	14	0	+14	+4.667
John Paddock	5	8	15	-7	-1.400
Pierre Page	8	9	25	-16	-2.000
Brad Park	1	0	10	-10	-10.00
Rick Paterson	1	0	8	-8	-8.000
Craig Patrick	4	3	7	-4	-1.000
Frank Patrick****	9	84	14	+70	+6.364
Lester Patrick****	21	133	44	+89	+4.045
Lynn Patrick	10	19	17	+2	+0.200
Muzz Patrick	4	0	13	-13	-3.250
Davis Payne	3	4	4	=0	=0.000
Jean Perron	4	27	10	+17	+4.250
Don Perry	3	1	16	-15	-5.000
Bill Peters	**1**	**0**	**7**	**-7**	**-7.000**
Alf Pike	2	0	16	-16	-8.000
Rudy Pilous*	7	29	10	+19	+2.714
Robert Pinder***	1	0	10	-10	-10.00
Barclay Plager	4	1	10	-9	-2.250
Bob Plager	1	0	0	=0	=0.000
Jacques Plante*	1	2	2	=0	=0.000
Jim Playfair	1	3	0	+3	+3.000
Larry Pleau	5	2	25	-23	-4.600
Nick Polano	3	2	12	-10	-3.333
Larry Popein	1	2	0	+2	+2.000
Eddie Powers	2	6	10	-4	-2.000
Joe Primeau	3	20	3	+17	+5.667
Marcel Pronovost*	3	6	10	-4	-1.333
Bob Pulford	12	37	8	+29	+2.417
Joel Quenneville	**18**	**124**	**2**	**+122**	**+6.778**
Charles Querrie	3	2	13	-11	-3.667
Mike Quinn	1	0	10	-10	-10.00

COACH	SC	P	M	R	ASR
Pat Quinn	20	92	24	+68	+3.400
Cap Raeder	1	0	4	-4	-4.000
Jerry Rafter*	1	0	1	-1	-1.000
Craig Ramsay	3	0	11	-11	-3.667
Ken Randall	1	0	7	-7	-7.000
Billy Reay	16	95	17	+78	+4.875
Larry Regan	2	0	11	-11	-5.500
Tom Renney	9	14	31	-17	-1.889
Maurice Richard*	1	0	0	=0	=0.000
Todd Richards	**6**	**11**	**15**	**-4**	**-0.667**
Doug Risebrough	2	6	1	+5	+2.500
Jimmy Roberts	3	3	1	+2	+0.667
Larry Robinson	8	34	13	+21	+2.625
Mike Rodden	1	0	8	-8	-8.000
Al Rollins*	1	0	10	-10	-10.00
Ron Rolston	2	0	14	-14	-7.000
Alex Romeril	1	0	6	-6	-6.000
Art Ross	18	98	48	+50	+2.778
Patrick Roy	**2**	**12**	**6**	**+6**	**+3.000**
Claude Ruel	5	48	2	+46	+9.200
Lindy Ruff	**17**	**59**	**19**	**+40**	**+2.353**
Ron Ryan*	2	9	0	+9	+4.500
Joe Sacco	4	5	12	-7	-1.750
Glen Sather*	16	137	13	+124	+7.750
Ted Sator	4	7	8	-1	-0.250
Andre Savard	1	0	1	-1	-1.000
Denis Savard	3	2	9	-7	-2.333
Ken Schinkel	4	6	4	+2	+0.500
Milt Schmidt	13	18	71	-53	-4.077
Jim Schoenfeld	10	16	6	+10	+1.000
Tom Shaughnessy	1	2	0	+2	+2.000
Brad Shaw	1	0	2	-2	-2.000
Brian Shaw*	2	3	0	+3	+1.500
Fred Shero	10	87	4	+83	+8.300
Joe Simpson	3	0	12	-12	-4.000
Terry Simpson	6	11	14	-3	-0.500
Al Sims	1	0	10	-10	-10.00
Harry Sinden	6	35	10	+25	+4.167
Jimmy Skinner	4	39	0	+39	+9.750
Terry Slater*	4	6	15	-9	-2.250
Cooper Smeaton	1	0	10	-10	-10.00
Alf Smith	1	10	0	+10	+10.00

COACH	SC	P	M	R	ASR
Barry Smith	1	2	0	+2	+2.000
Floyd Smith*	6	28	6	+22	+3.667
Mike Smith	1	0	10	-10	-10.00
Ron Smith	1	0	7	-7	-7.000
Conn Smythe	4	8	5	+3	+0.750
Glen Sonmor*	10	27	16	+11	+1.100
Harvey Sproule	1	0	2	-2	-2.000
Barney Stanley	1	0	8	-8	-8.000
Pat Stapleton*	3	8	14	-6	-2.000
Vic Stasiuk	4	1	19	-18	-4.500
John Stevens	5	11	10	+1	+0.200
Scott Stevens	**1**	**0**	**2**	**-2**	**-2.000**
Bill D. Stewart	1	0	10	-10	-10.00
Bill J. Stewart	2	12	5	+7	+3.500
Ron Stewart	2	1	6	-5	-2.500
Steve Stirling	2	2	3	-1	-0.500
Alpo Suhonen	1	0	3	-3	-3.000
Mike Sullivan	2	10	7	+3	+1.500
Red Sullivan	7	0	30	-30	-4.286
Bill Sutherland	2	0	12	-12	-6.000
Brent Sutter	5	22	6	+16	+3.200
Brian Sutter	13	32	23	+9	+0.692
Darryl Sutter	**15**	**91**	**11**	**+80**	**+5.333**
Duane Sutter	2	0	7	-7	-3.500
Jean-Guy Talbot*	4	2	10	-8	-2.000
Orval Tessier	3	11	1	+10	+3.333
Michel Therrien	**10**	**52**	**18**	**+34**	**+3.400**
Paul Thompson	7	11	20	-9	-1.286
Percy Thompson	2	0	20	-20	-10.00
Dave Tippett	**12**	**57**	**16**	**+41**	**+3.417**
Bill Tobin	2	4	1	+3	+1.500
Rick Tocchet	2	0	10	-10	-5.000
John Torchetti	2	0	5	-5	-2.500
John Tortorella	14	57	30	+27	+1.929
Mario Tremblay	2	4	1	+3	+1.500
Bryan Trottier	1	0	1	-1	-1.000
Barry Trotz	**16**	**46**	**37**	**+9**	**+0.563**
J. Lloyd Turner***	1	3	0	+3	+3.000
Gene Ubriaco	2	3	1	+2	+1.000
Rogie Vachon	3	0	7	-7	-2.333
Alain Vigneault	**13**	**90**	**20**	**+70**	**+5.385**
Jack Vivian*	1	1	1	=0	=0.000

COACH	SC	P	M	R	ASR
Don Waddell	2	0	3	-3	-1.500
Bryan Watson	1	0	1	-1	-1.000
Phil Watson*	9	8	30	-22	-2.444
Tom Watt	7	3	30	-27	-3.857
Tom Webster	4	14	2	+12	+3.000
Cooney Weiland	2	31	0	+31	+15.50
Bill White	1	1	1	=0	=0.000
Jim Wiley	1	0	10	-10	-10.00
Ian Wilkie*	1	0	0	=0	=0.000
Johnny Wilson*	9	7	39	-32	-3.556
Larry Wilson	1	0	10	-10	-10.00
Rick Wilson	1	2	2	=0	=0.000
Ron Wilson	18	64	44	+20	+1.222
Trent Yawney	2	0	7	-7	-3.500
Mike Yeo	**4**	**12**	**3**	**+9**	**+2.250**
Garry Young	3	3	9	-6	-2.000

ALL-STARS

This section lists all the NHL, WHA, PCHA, and WCHL/WHL All-Stars who played for the coaches featured in this book. The coaches are listed alphabetically, whereas the players are listed in chronological order along with the years they were honoured.

JACK ADAMS:

John Ross Roach	1932/33
Cooney Weiland	1934/35
Ebbie Goodfellow	1935/36–1936/37, 1939/40
Larry Aurie	1936/37
Marty Barry	1936/37
Normie Smith	1936/37
Sid Abel	1941/42
Jack Stewart	1942.43, 1946/47
Johnny Mowers	1942/43
Flash Hollett	1944/45
Syd Howe	1944/45
Bill Quackenbush	1946/47

AL ARBOUR:

Denis Potvin	1974/75–1978/79, 1980/81, 1983/84
Glenn Resch	1975/76, 1978/79

Clark Gillies	1977/78
Mike Bossy	1977/78–1978/79, 1980/81–1985/86
Bryan Trottier	1977/78–1978/79, 1981/82, 1983/84
John Tonelli	1981/82, 1984/85
Billy Smith	1981/82
Roland Melanson	1982/83

MIKE BABCOCK:

Paul Kariya	2002/03
Nicklas Lidstrom	2005/06–2009/10
Henrik Zetterberg	2007/08
Pavel Datsyuk	2008/09
Marian Hossa	2008/09

TOE BLAKE:

Bert Olmstead	1955/56
Maurice Richard	1955/56–1956/57
Jean Beliveau	1955/56–1959/60, 1963/64, 1965/66
Tom Johnson	1955/56, 1958/59
Doug Harvey	1955/56–1960/61
Jacques Plante	1955/56–1959/60, 1961/62
Dickie Moore	1957/58–1958/59, 1960/61
Henri Richard	1957/58–1958/59, 1960/61, 1962/63
Bernie Geoffrion	1959/60–1960/61
Jean-Guy Talbot	1961/62
Jacques Laperrière	1963/64–1965/66
Charlie Hodge	1963/64–1964/65
Claude Provost	1964/65
Bobby Rousseau	1965/66
Gump Worsley	1965/66, 1967/68
J. C. Tremblay	1967/68

BRUCE BOUDREAU:

Alex Ovechkin	2007/08–2010/11
Mike Green	2008/09–2009/10
Francois Beauchemin	2012/13
Ryan Getzlaf	2013/14
Corey Perry	2013/14

SCOTTY BOWMAN:

Glenn Hall	1968/69
Yvan Cournoyer	1970/71–1972/73
J. C. Tremblay	1970/71
Ken Dryden	1971/72–1972/73, 1975/76–1978/79
Frank Mahovlich	1972/73
Guy Lapointe	1972/73, 1974/75–1977/78
Guy Lafleur	1974/75–1978/79
Steve Shutt	1976/77–1977/78
Larry Robinson	1976/77–1978/79
Serge Savard	1978/79
Danny Gare	1979/80
Jim Schoenfeld	1979/80
Don Edwards	1979/80
Tom Barrasso	1983/84–1984/85, 1992/93
Kevin Stevens	1991/92–1992/93
Mario Lemieux	1991/92–1992/93
Larry Murphy	1992/93
Sergei Fedorov	1993/94
Paul Coffey	1994/95
Vladimir Konstantinov	1995/96
Chris Osgood	1995/96
Nicklas Lidstrom	1997/98–2001/02
Brendan Shanahan	1999/00, 2001/02
Steve Yzerman	1999/00
Chris Chelios	2001/02

PAT BURNS:

Chris Chelios	1988/89
Patrick Roy	1988/89–1991/92
Raymond Bourque	1998/99
Byron Dafoe	1998/99
Martin Brodeur	2002/03–2003/04
Scott Niedermayer	2003/04

DAN BYLSMA:

Evgeni Malkin	2008/09, 2011/12
Sidney Crosby	2009/10, 2012/13-2013/14
James Neal	2011/12
Chris Kunitz	2012/13
Kris Letang	2012/13

RANDY CARLYLE:

Scott Niedermayer	2005/06–2006/07
Chris Pronger	2006/07
Corey Perry	2010/11
Lubomir Visnovsky	2010/11

GERRY CHEEVERS:

Raymond Bourque	1980/81–1984/85
Rick Middleton	1981/82
Pete Peeters	1982/83

DON CHERRY:

Phil Esposito	1974/75
Bobby Orr	1974/75
Brad Park	1975/76, 1977/78

MIKE CRAWFORD:

Sandis Ozolinish	1996/97
Markus Naslund	2001/02–2003/04
Todd Bertuzzi	2002/03

LEO DANDURAND:

Aurel Joliat	1934/35

HAP DAY:

Sweeney Schriner	1940/41
Syl Apps	1940/41–1942/43
Wally Stanowski	1940/41
Turk Broda	1940/41–1941/42, 1947/48
Gord Drillon	1941/42
Bucko McDonald	1941/42
Lorne Carr	1942/43–1943/44
Babe Pratt	1943/44–1944/45
Paul Bibeault	1943/44
Gaye Stewart	1945/46
Ted Kennedy	1949/50
Gus Mortson	1949/50

BILL DINEEN:

Mark Recchi	1991/92

EMILE FRANCIS:

Eddie Giacomin	1966/67–1970/71
Harry Howell	1966/67
Don Marshall	1966/67
Rod Gilbert	1967/68, 1971/72

Jim Neilson	1967/68
Brad Park	1969/70–1973/74
Vic Hadfield	1971/72
Jean Ratelle	1971/72
Steve Vickers	1974/75

ROBBIE FTOREK:

Luc Robitaille	1987/88–1988/89
Wayne Gretzky	1988/89
Bill Guerin	2001/02
Joe Thornton	2002/03

CECIL HART:

Aurel Joliat	1930/31–1931/32
Howie Morenz	1930/31–1931/32
Sylvio Mantha	1930/31–1931/32
Wilf Cude	1935/36–1936/37
Babe Siebert	1936/37–1937/38
Toe Blake	1937/38–1938/39

BOB HARTLEY:

Peter Forsberg	1997/98–1998/99
Joe Sakic	2000/01–2001/02
Raymond Bourque	2000/01
Rob Blake	2000/01–2001/02
Patrick Roy	2001/02
Ilya Kovalchuk	2003/04

KEN HITCHCOCK:

Mike Modano	1999/00
Steve Mason	2008/09
Alex Pietrangelo	2011/12, 2013/14
Vladimir Tarasenko	2014/15

PUNCH IMLACH:

Allan Stanley	1959/60–1960/61, 1965/66
Johnny Bower	1960/61
Dave Keon	1961/62
Carl Brewer	1961/62–1962/63, 1964/65
Frank Mahovlich	1962/63–1965/66
Tim Horton	1962/63–1963/64, 1966/67–1968/69
Borje Salming	1978/79–1979/80

DICK IRVIN:

Charlie Gardiner	1930/31
Busher Jackson	1931/32–1934/35, 1936/37
Charlie Conacher	1931/32–1935/36
King Clancy	1931/32–1933/34
Joe Primeau	1933/34
Bill Thoms	1935/36
Gordie Drillon	1937/38–1938/39
Syl Apps	1937/38–1938/39
Maurice Richard	1943/44–1954/55
Elmer Lach	1943/44–1945/46, 1947/48, 1951/52
Butch Bouchard	1943/44–1946/47
Bill Durnan	1943/44–1946/47, 1948/49–1949/50
Toe Blake	1944/45–1945/46
Glen Harmon	1944/45, 1948/49
Ken Reardon	1945/46–1949/50
Doug Harvey	1951/52–1954/55

Bert Olmstead	1952/53
Gerry McNeil	1952/53
Ken Mosdell	1953/54–1954/55
Bernie Geoffrion	1954/55
Jean Beliveau	1954/55

TOMMY IVAN:

Ted Lindsay	1947/48–1953/54
Bill Quackenbush	1947/48–1948/49
Jack Stewart	1947/48–1948/49
Sid Abel	1948/49–1950/51
Gordie Howe	1948/49–1953/54
Red Kelly	1949/50–1953/54
Leo Reise, Jr.	1949/50–1950/51
Terry Sawchuk	1950/51–1953/54
Alex Delvecchio	1952/53
Ed Litzenberger	1956/57

BOB JOHNSON:

Lanny McDonald	1982/83
Al MacInnis	1986/87
Kevin Stevens	1990/91

TOM JOHNSON:

John Bucyk	1970/71
Ken Hodge	1970/71
Phil Esposito	1970/71–1972/73
Bobby Orr	1970/71–1972/73

EDDIE JOHNSTON:

Tony Esposito	1979/80
Randy Carlyle	1980/81
Jaromir Jagr	1994/95–1996/97
Larry Murphy	1994/95
Mario Lemieux	1995/96–1996/97

CLAUDE JULIEN:

Martin Brodeur	2006/07
Zdeno Chara	2007/08–2008/09, 2010/11–2011/12, 2013/14
Tim Thomas	2008/09, 2010/11
Tuukka Rask	2013/14

MIKE KEENAN:

Pelle Lindbergh	1984/85
Mark Howe	1985/86–1986/87
Bob Froese	1985/86
Tim Kerr	1986/87
Ron Hextall	1986/87
Doug Wilson	1989/90
Chris Chelios	1990/91
Ed Belfour	1990/91
Adam Graves	1993/94
Brian Leetch	1993/94
Jarome Iginla	2007/08–2008/09
Dion Phaneuf	2007/08

PETER LAVIOLETTE:

Eric Staal	2005/06
Shea Weber	2014/15

JACQUES LEMAIRE:

Scott Stevens	1993/94, 1996/97
Martin Brodeur	1996/97–1997/98
Scott Niedermayer	1997/98

JACQUES MARTIN:

Alexei Yashin	1998/99
Zdeno Chara	2003/04

TODD MCLELLAN:

Dan Boyle	2008/09
Joe Pavelski	2013/14

BRYAN MURRAY:

Rod Langway	1982/83–1984/85
Pat Riggin	1983/84
Larry Murphy	1986/87
Scott Stevens	1987/88
Daniel Alfredsson	2005/06
Zdeno Chara	2005/06
Dany Heatley	2005/06–2006/07

TERRY MURRAY:

Al Iafrate	1992/93
John LeClair	1994/95–1996/97
Eric Lindros	1994/95–1995/96
Pavel Bure	1999/00–2000/01
Drew Doughty	2009/10

ROGER NEILSON:

Borje Salming	1977/78–1978/79
Darryl Sittler	1977/78
Brian Leetch	1990/91–1991/92
Mark Messier	1991/92
John Vanbriesbrouck	1993/94
Eric Desjardins	1998/99–1999/00

FRANK PATRICK:

Dit Clapper	1934/35
Eddie Shore	1934/35–1935/36
Tiny Thompson	1934/35–1935/36
Babe Siebert	1935/36

LESTER PATRICK:

Bun Cook	1930/31
Bill Cook	1930/31–1932/33
Frank Boucher	1930/31, 1932/33–1934/35
Ching Johnson	1931/32–1933/34
Earl Siebert	1934/35
Cecil Dillon	1935/36–1937/38
Art Coulter	1937/38–1938/39
Dave Kerr	1937/38
Neil Colville	1938/39

BOB PULFORD:

Rogie Vachon	1973/74–1974/75, 1976/77
Marcel Dionne	1976/77
Doug Wilson	1981/82

JOEL QUENNEVILLE:

Chris Pronger	1997/98, 1999/00, 2003/04
Al MacInnis	1998/99, 2002/03
Roman Turek	1999/00
Patrick Kane	2009/10
Duncan Keith	2009/10, 2013/14
Jonathan Toews	2012/13

PAT QUINN:

Bill Barber	1978/79, 1980/81
Luc Robataille	1986/87
Kirk Maclean	1991/92
Pavel Bure	1993/94
Alexander Mogilny	1995/96
Mats Sundin	2001/02
Bryan McCabe	2003/04

BILLY REAY:

Glenn Hall	1963/64, 1965/66–1966/67
Bobby Hull	1963/64–1971/72
Stan Mikita	1963/64–1967/68, 1969/70
Moose Vasko	1963/64
Pierre Pilote	1963/64–1964/65, 1966/67
Kenny Wharram	1963/64, 1966/67
Pat Stapleton	1965/66, 1970/71–1971/72
Tony Esposito	1969/70, 1971/72–1973/74
Bill White	1971/72–1973/74
Dennis Hull	1972/73

ART ROSS:

Dit Clapper	1930/31, 1943/44
Eddie Shore	1930/31–1933/34, 1937/38–1938/39
Tiny Thompson	1930/31, 1937/38
Bill Cowley	1937/38, 1942/43–1944/45
Bobby Bauer	1938/39
Frank Brimsek	1938/39, 1941/42–1942/43
Jack Crawford	1942/43
Flash Hollett	1942/43
Herb Cain	1943/44

CLAUDE RUEL:

Jean Beliveau	1968/69
Yvan Cournoyer	1968/69
Ted Harris	1968/69
Jacques Laperrière	1969/70
Guy Lafleur	1979/80
Larry Robinson	1979/80–1980/81
Steve Shutt	1979/80

LINDY RUFF:

Dominik Hasek	1997/98–1998/99, 2000/01
Ryan Miller	2009/10
Jamie Benn	2013/14–2014/15

GLEN SATHER:

Wayne Gretzky	1979/80–1987/88
Paul Coffey	1981/82–1985/86
Grant Fuhr	1981/82, 1987/88
Mark Messier	1981/82–1983/84
Jari Kurri	1983/84, 1985/86–1986/87, 1988/89

FRED SHERO:

Bobby Clarke	1972/73–1975/76
Barry Ashbee	1973/74
Bernie Parent	1973/74–1974/75
Bill Barber	1975/76
Reggie Leach	1975/76

HARRY SINDEN:

Bobby Orr	1966/67–1969/70
John Bucyk	1967/68
Phil Esposito	1967/68–1969/70
Ted Green	1968/69
John McKenzie	1969/70
Raymond Bourque	1979/80, 1984/85

JIMMY SKINNER:

Bob Goldham	1954/55
Red Kelly	1954/55–1956/57
Terry Sawchuk	1954/55
Glenn Hall	1955/56–1956/57
Gordie Howe	1955/56–1956/57
Ted Lindsay	1955/56–1956/57

FLOYD SMITH:

Rick Martin	1974/75–1976/77
Rene Robert	1974/75
Gilbert Perreault	1975/76–1976/77
Borje Salming	1979/80

DARRYL SUTTER:

Ed Belfour	1992/93, 1994/95
Chris Chelios	1992/93, 1994/95
Jerome Iginla	2003/04
Miikka Kiprusoff	2005/06
Jonathan Quick	2011/12
Drew Doughty	2014/15

MICHEL THERRIEN:

Jose Theodore	2001/02
Sidney Crosby	2006/07
Evgeni Malkin	2007/08
P. K. Subban	2012/13, 2014/15
Carey Price	2014/15

DAVE TIPPETT:

Derian Hatcher	2002/03
Marty Turco	2002/03
Sergei Zubov	2005/06
Ilya Bryzgalov	2009/10
Ray Whitney	2011/12

ALAIN VIGNEAULT:

Jose Theodore	2001/02
Roberto Luongo	2006/07
Daniel Sedin	2009/10–2010/11
Henrik Sedin	2009/10–2010/11

COONEY WEILAND:

Bobby Bauer	1939/40–1940/41
Frank Brimsek	1939/40–1940/41
Dit Clapper	1939/40–1940/41
Woody Dumart	1939/40–1940/41
Milt Schmidt	1939/40
Bill Cowley	1940/41

RON WILSON:

Paul Kariya	1995/96–1996/97
Teemu Selanne	1996/97
Olaf Kolzig	1999/00
Sergei Gonchar	2001/02
Joe Thornton	2005/06, 2007/08
Brian Campbell	2007/08
Evgeni Nabokov	2007/08

PCHA ALL-STARS

1912–1924

PETE MULDOON:

Moose Johnson	1914/15, 1917/18
Eddie Oatman	1914/15
Bernie Morris	1915/16–1916/17, 1918/19, 1920/21–1922/23
Hap Holmes	1915/16–1916/17, 1918/19–1922/23
Frank Foyston	1916/17, 1918/19–1923/24
Bobby Rowe	1916/17, 1918/19–1919/20, 1922/23
Jack Walker	1916/17, 1918/19–1921/22, 1923/24
Cully Wilson	1918/19
Jim Riley	1919/20–1922/23
Archie Briden	1922/23
Gord Fraser	1922/23–1923/24

FRANK PATRICK:

Newsy Lalonde	1911/12
Smokey Harris	1912/13, 1918/19–1919/20, 1921/22
Frank Patrick	1913/14, 1916/17
Fred Taylor	1913/14–1914/15
Mickey Mackay	1914/15–1918/19, 1920/21–1922/23
Frank Nighbor	1914/15
Hugh Lehman	1914/15–1915/16, 1917/18–1923/24
Lloyd Cook	1915/16, 1917/18–1920/21, 1922/23
Gord Roberts	1916/17
Barney Stanley	1917/18
Art Duncan	1918/19–1919/20, 1921/22–1923/24

Alf Skinner	1919/20–1920/21, 1922/23
Jack Adams	1920/21–1921/22
Frank Boucher	1922/23–1923/24
Corb Denneny	1922/23
Ernie Parkes	1922/23

LESTER PATRICK:

Tommy Dunderdale	1911/12–1914/15, 1919/20, 1921/22
Lester Patrick	1912/13, 1914/15–1917/18, 1919/20
Bert Lindsay	1912/13
Dubbie Kerr	1913/14
Walter Smaill	1913/14
Ran McDonald	1915/16
Hec Fowler	1916/17–1917/18
Frank Foyston	1917/18
Bernie Morris	1917/18
Bobby Rowe	1917/18
Moose Johnson	1918/19
Frank Fredrickson	1920/21–1923/24
Clem Loughlin	1920/21–1923/24
Wilf Loughlin	1920/21
Harold Halderson	1921/22–1922/23
Harry Meeking	1921/22–1922/23
Gizzy Hart	1923/24

WCHL/WHL ALL-STARS

1921–1926

KEN MACKENZIE:

Ty Arbour	1921/22
Art Gagne	1921/22–1922/23, 1925/26
Duke Keats	1921/22–1925/26
Joe Simpson	1921/22–1922/23, 1924/25
Bob Trapp	1921/22–1922/23
Earl Campbell	1922/23
Hal Winkler	1922/23
Eddie Shore	1925/26

PETE MULDOON:

George Hay	1925/26
Bob Trapp	1925/26

FRANK PATRICK:

Frank Boucher	1924/25
Mickey Mackay	1924/25–1925/26

LESTER PATRICK:

Gord Fraser	1924/25
Hap Holmes	1924/25
Frank Fredrickson	1925/26

WHA ALL-STARS

1972–1979

BILL DINEEN:

Gordie Howe	1973/74–1974/75
Mark Howe	1973/74, 1976/77, 1978/79
Don McLeod	1973/74
Ron Grahame	1974/75–1975/76
Poul Popiel	1974/75
Ernie Wakely	1977/78
Rick Ley	1978/79

GLEN SATHER:

Al Hamilton	1977/78
Dave Dryden	1978/79
Wayne Gretzky	1978/79
Dave Langevin	1978/79
Paul Shmyr	1978/79

FLOYD SMITH:

Robbie Ftorek	1978/79

TROPHY WINNERS

This section lists all the players who won major individual trophies in the NHL for the coaches featured in this book. It does not cover all the NHL trophies but focuses only on the following: the Calder, Conn Smythe, Hart, Jennings, Lady Byng, Norris, Maurice Richard, Ross, Frank Selke, and Vezina trophies.

For those who coached in the WHA, PCHA, and WCHL/WHL, I've listed the category for which the player won the award: whether they were the MVP or Gentleman player or best goalie and so on.

All the trophies listed below were created years or decades after the founding of the NHL in 1917. For those who led the league in a specific category before their trophy was established, I have listed the category they led and cited the player's name and the season in which he led.

The coaches are listed alphabetically, whereas the trophy winners are listed chronologically in the order they won the trophies along with the years they won them.

JACK ADAMS:

Calder:	*Carl Voss, 1932/33*
Goals Scored (NHL):	*Larry Aurie, 1936/37*
Hart:	*Ebbie Goodfellow, 1939/40*
Lady Byng:	*Marty Barry, 1936/37*
Vezina:	*Normie Smith, 1936/37*
	Johnny Mowers, 1942/43

AL ARBOUR:

Calder:	*Denis Potvin, 1973/74*
	Bryan Trottier, 1975/76
	Mike Bossy, 1977/78
Conn Smythe:	*Bryan Trottier, 1979/80*
	Butch Goring, 1980/81
	Mike Bossy, 1981/82
	Billy Smith, 1982/83
Goals Scored (NHL):	*Mike Bossy, 1978/79, 1980/81*
Hart:	*Bryan Trottier, 1978/79*
Jennings:	*Roland Melanson/Billy Smith, 1982/83*
Lady Byng:	*Mike Bossy, 1982/83–1983/84, 1985/86*
	Pierre Turgeon, 1992/93
Norris:	*Denis Potvin, 1975/76, 1977/78–1978/79*
Ross:	*Bryan Trottier, 1978/79*
Vezina:	*Billy Smith, 1981/82*

MIKE BABCOCK:

Conn Smythe:	*Jean-Sébastien Giguère, 2002/03*
	Henrik Zetterberg, 2007/08
Jennings:	*Chris Osgood/Dominik Hasek, 2007/08*
Lady Byng:	*Pavel Datsyuk, 2005/06–2008/09*
Norris:	*Nicklas Lidstrom, 2005/06–2007/08, 2010/11*
Selke:	*Pavel Datsyuk, 2007/08–2009/10*

TOE BLAKE:

Calder:	*Ralph Backstrom, 1958/59*
	Bobby Rousseau, 1961/62
	Jacques Laperrière, 1963/64
Conn Smythe:	*Jean Beliveau, 1964/65*
	Serge Savard, 1967/68
Goals Scored (NHL):	*Jean Beliveau, 1955/56, 1958/59*

	Dickie Moore, 1957/58
	Bernie Geoffrion, 1960/61
Hart:	*Jean Beliveau, 1955/56, 1963/64*
	Bernie Geoffrion, 1960/61
	Jacques Plante, 1961/62
Norris:	*Doug Harvey, 1955/56–1957/58, 1959/60–1960/61*
	Tom Johnson, 1958/59
	Jacques Laperrière, 1965/66
Ross:	*Jean Beliveau, 1955/56*
	Dickie Moore, 1957/58–1958/59
	Bernie Geoffrion, 1960/61
Vezina:	*Jacques Plante, 1955/56–1959/60, 1961/62*
	Charlie Hodge, 1963/64
	Gump Worsley/Charlie Hodge, 1965/66
	Gump Worsley/Rogie Vachon, 1967/68

BRUCE BOUDREAU:

Hart:	*Alex Ovechkin, 2007/08–2008/09*
Richard:	*Alex Ovechkin, 2007/08–2008/09*
Ross:	*Alex Ovechkin, 2007/08*

SCOTTY BOWMAN:

Calder:	*Ken Dryden, 1971/72*
	Tom Barrasso, 1983/84
Conn Smythe:	*Glenn Hall, 1967/68*
	Yvan Cournoyer, 1972/73
	Guy Lafleur, 1976/77
	Larry Robinson, 1977/78
	Bob Gainey, 1978/79
	Mario Lemieux, 1991/92
	Mike Vernon, 1996/97

	Steve Yzerman, 1997/98
	Nicklas Lidstrom, 2001/02
Goals Scored (NHL):	*Steve Shutt, 1976/77*
	Guy Lafleur, 1977/78
	Danny Gare, 1979/80
Hart:	*Guy Lafleur, 1976/77–1977/78*
	Mario Lemieux, 1992/93
	Sergei Fedorov, 1993/94
Jennings:	*Tom Barrasso/Bob Sauve, 1984/85*
	Chris Osgood/Mike Vernon, 1995/96
Norris:	*Larry Robinson, 1976/77*
	Paul Coffey, 1994/95
	Nicklas Lidstrom, 2000/01–2001/02
Ross:	*Guy Lafleur, 1975/76–1977/78*
	Mario Lemieux, 1991/92–1992/93
Selke:	*Bob Gainey, 1977/78–1978/79*
	Craig Ramsey, 1984/85
	Sergei Fedorov, 1993/94, 1995/96
	Steve Yzerman, 1999/00
Vezina:	*Glenn Hall/Jacques Plante, 1968/69*
	Ken Dryden, 1972/73, 1975/76
	Ken Dryden/Michel Larocque, 1976/77–1978/79
	Bob Sauve/Don Edwards, 1979/80
	Tom Barrasso, 1983/84

PAT BURNS:

Calder:	*Sergei Samsonov, 1997/98*
Jennings:	*Patrick Roy/Brian Hayward, 1988/89*
	Patrick Roy, 1991/92
	Martin Brodeur, 2002/03–2003/04
Norris:	*Chris Chelios, 1988/89*
	Scott Niedermayer, 2003/04

Selke:	*Guy Carbonneau, 1988/89, 1991/92*
	Doug Gilmour, 1992/93
Vezina:	*Patrick Roy, 1988/89–1989/90, 1991/92*
	Martin Brodeur, 2002/03–2003/04

DAN BYLSMA:

Conn Smythe:	*Evgeni Malkin, 2008/09*
Hart:	*Evgeni Malkin, 2011/12*
	Sidney Crosby, 2013/14
Richard:	*Sidney Crosby, 2009/10*
Ross:	*Evgeni Malkin, 2008/09, 2011/12*
	Sidney Crosby, 2013/14

RANDY CARLYLE:

Conn Smythe:	*Scott Niedermayer, 2006/07*
Hart:	*Corey Perry, 2010/11*
Richard:	*Corey Perry, 2010/11*

GERRY CHEEVERS:

Lady Byng:	*Rick Middleton, 1981/82*
Selke:	*Steve Kasper, 1981/82*
Vezina:	*Pete Peeters, 1982/83*

DON CHERRY:

Goals Scored (NHL):	*Phil Esposito, 1974/75*
Lady Byng:	*Jean Ratelle, 1975/76*
Norris:	*Bobby Orr, 1974/75*
Ross:	*Bobby Orr, 1974/75*

MARC CRAWFORD:

Calder:	*Peter Forsberg, 1994/95*
Conn Smythe:	*Joe Sakic, 1995/96*

LEO DANDURAND:

Best Goalie (NHL):	*Georges Vezina, 1923/24–1924/25*

HAP DAY:

Calder:	*Gaye Stewart, 1942/43*
	Gus Bodnar, 1943/44
	Frank McCool, 1944/45
	Howie Meeker, 1946/47
Goals Scored (NHL):	*Gaye Stewart, 1945/46*
Hart:	*Babe Pratt, 1943/44*
Lady Byng:	*Syl Apps, 1941/42*
Vezina:	*Turk Broda, 1940/41, 1947/48*

BILL DINEEN:

Best Defenceman (WHA):	*Rick Ley, 1978/79*
Best Goalie (WHA):	*Don McLeod, 1973/74*
	Ron Grahame, 1974/75, 1976/77
MVP (WHA):	*Gordie Howe, 1973/74*
Playoff MVP (WHA):	*Ron Grahame, 1974/75*
Rookie of the Year (WHA):	*Mark Howe, 1973/74*

EMILE FRANCIS:

Calder:	*Steve Vickers, 1972/73*
Lady Byng:	*Jean Ratelle, 1971/72*
Norris:	*Harry Howell, 1966/67*
Vezina:	*Eddie Giacomin/Gilles Villemure, 1970/71*

PETE GREEN:

Best Goalie (NHL):	*Clint Benedict, 1919/20–1922/23*
Goals Scored (NHL):	*Punch Broadbent, 1921/22*
	Cy Denneny, 1923/24
Hart:	*Frank Nighbor, 1923/24*
Lady Byng:	*Frank Nighbor, 1923/24–1924/25*
Top Scorer (NHL):	*Punch Broadbent, 1921/22*
	Cy Denneny, 1923/24

CECIL HART:

Goals Scored (NHL):	*Howie Morenz, 1927/28*
Hart:	*Herb Gardiner, 1926/27*
	Howie Morenz, 1927/28, 1930/31–1931/32
	Babe Siebert, 1936/37
	Toe Blake, 1938/39
Top Scorer (NHL):	*Howie Morenz, 1927/28, 1930/31*
Vezina:	*George Hainsworth, 1926/27–1928/29*

BOB HARTLEY:

Calder:	*Chris Drury, 1998/99*
Conn Smythe:	*Patrick Roy, 2000/01*
Hart:	*Joe Sakic, 2000/01*
Lady Byng:	*Jiri Hudler, 2014/15*
Jennings:	*Patrick Roy, 2001/02*
Richard:	*Milan Hejduk, 2002/03*
	Ilya Kovalchuk, 2003/04

KEN HITCHCOCK:

Calder:	*Steve Mason, 2008/09*
Conn Smythe:	*Joe Nieuwendyk, 1998/99*
Jennings:	*Ed Belfour/Roman Turek, 1998/99*

	Roman Cechmanek/Robert Esche, 2002/03
	Brian Elliott/Jaroslav Halak, 2011/12
Selke:	*Jere Lehtinen, 1997/98–1998/99*

PUNCH IMLACH:

Calder:	*Dave Keon, 1960/61*
	Kent Douglas, 1962/63
	Brit Selby, 1965/66
	Gilbert Perreault, 1970/71
Lady Byng:	*Red Kelly, 1960/61*
	Dave Keon, 1961/62–1962/63
Vezina:	*Johnny Bower, 1960/61*
	Johnny Bower/Terry Sawchuk, 1964/65

DICK IRVIN:

Calder:	*Syl Apps, 1936/37*
	John Quilty, 1940/41
	Bernie Geoffrion, 1951/52
Goals Scored (NHL):	*Charlie Conacher, 1931/32, 1933/34–1934/35*
	Bill Thoms, 1935/36
	Gordie Drillon, 1937/38
	Maurice Richard, 1944/45, 1946/47, 1949/50, 1953/54–1954/55
	Bernie Geoffrion, 1954/55
Hart:	*Elmer Lach, 1944/45*
	Maurice Richard, 1946/47
Lady Byng:	*Joe Primeau, 1931/32*
	Gordie Drillon, 1937/38
	Toe Blake, 1945/46
Norris:	*Doug Harvey, 1954/55*
Ross:	*Elmer Lach, 1947/48*
	Bernie Geoffrion, 1954/55

Top Scorer (NHL):	*Busher Jackson, 1931/32*
	Charlie Conacher, 1933/34–1934/35
	Gordie Drillon, 1937/38
	Elmer Lach, 1944/45
Vezina:	*Bill Durnan, 1943/44–1946/47, 1948/49–1949/50*

TOMMY IVAN:

Calder:	*Jim McFadden, 1947/48*
	Terry Sawchuk, 1950/51
Goals Scored (NHL):	*Ted Lindsay, 1947/48*
	Sid Abel, 1948/49
	Gordie Howe, 1950/51–1952/53
Hart:	*Sid Abel, 1948/49*
	Gordie Howe, 1951/52–1952/53
Lady Byng:	*Bill Quackenbush, 1948/49*
	Red Kelly, 1950/51, 1952/53–1953/54
Norris:	*Red Kelly, 1953/54*
Ross:	*Ted Lindsay, 1949/50*
	Gordie Howe, 1950/51–1953/54
Vezina:	*Terry Sawchuk, 1951/52–1952/53*

BOB JOHNSON:

Calder:	*Gary Suter, 1985/86*
Conn Smythe:	*Mario Lemieux, 1990/91*
Lady Byng:	*Joe Mullen, 1986/87*

TOM JOHNSON:

Conn Smythe:	*Bobby Orr, 1971/72*
Goals Scored (NHL):	*Phil Esposito, 1970/71–1972/73*
Hart:	*Bobby Orr, 1970/71–1971/72*

Lady Byng:	*John Bucyk, 1970/71*
Norris:	*Bobby Orr, 1970/71–1972/73*
Ross:	*Phil Esposito, 1970/71–1972/73*

EDDIE JOHNSTON:

Goals Scored (NHL):	*Mario Lemieux, 1995/96*
Hart:	*Mario Lemieux, 1995/96*
Lady Byng:	*Rick Kehoe, 1980/81*
Norris:	*Randy Carlyle, 1980/81*
Ross:	*Jaromir Jagr, 1994/95*
	Mario Lemieux, 1995/96
Selke:	*Ron Francis, 1994/95*

CLAUDE JULIEN:

Conn Smythe:	*Tim Thomas, 2010/11*
Jennings:	*Tim Thomas/Manny Fernandez, 2008/09*
	Tim Thomas/Tuukka Rask, 2009/10
Norris:	*Zdeno Chara, 2008/09*
Selke:	*Patrice Bergeron, 2011/12, 2013/14–2014/15*
Vezina:	*Martin Brodeur, 2006/07*
	Tim Thomas, 2008/09, 2010/11
	Tuukka Rask, 2013/14

MIKE KEENAN:

Calder:	*Ed Belfour, 1990/91*
Conn Smythe:	*Ron Hextall, 1986/87*
	Brian Leetch, 1993/94
Jennings:	*Bob Froese/Darren Jensen, 1985/86*
	Ed Belfour, 1990/91
Selke:	*Dave Poulin, 1986/87*
	Dirk Graham, 1990/91

Vezina:	*Pelle Lindbergh, 1984/85*
	Ron Hextall, 1986/87
	Ed Belfour, 1990/91

PETER LAVIOLETTE:

Conn Smythe:	*Cam Ward, 2005/06*
Selke:	*Michael Peca, 2001/02*
	Rod Brind'Amour, 2005/06–2006/07

JACQUES LEMAIRE:

Calder:	*Martin Brodeur, 1993/94*
Conn Smythe:	*Claude Lemieux, 1994/95*
Jennings:	*Martin Brodeur/Mike Dunham, 1996/97*
	Martin Brodeur, 1997/98, 2009/10
	Manny Fernandez/Nicklas Backstrom, 2006/07

JACQUES MARTIN:

Calder:	*Daniel Alfredsson, 1995/96*

KEN MACKENZIE:

Best Goalie (WCHL):	*Hal Winkler, 1922/23*
Goals Scored (WCHL):	*Duke Keats, 1921/22*
Top Scorer (WCHL):	*Duke Keats, 1921/22*
	Art Gagne, 1922/23

PETE MULDOON:

Best Goalie (PCHA):	*Hap Holmes, 1916/17, 1918/19–1921/22*
Goals Scored (PCHA):	*Bernie Morris, 1915/16*
	Frank Foyston, 1919/20–1920/21

Goals Scored (WHL):	*Dick Irvin, 1925/26*
Top Scorer (PCHA):	*Bernie Morris, 1916/17*

BRYAN MURRAY:

Jennings:	*Pat Riggin/Al Jensen, 1983/84*
Norris:	*Rod Langway, 1982/83–1983/84*
Selke:	*Doug Jarvis, 1983/84*

TERRY MURRAY:

Hart:	*Eric Lindros, 1994/95*
Richard:	*Pavel Bure, 1999/00–2000/01*

ROGER NEILSON:

Hart:	*Mark Messier, 1991/92*

FRANK PATRICK:

Best Goalie (PCHA):	*Hugh Lehman, 1914/15, 1917/18, 1922/23–1923/24*
Goals Scored (PCHA):	*Newsy Lalonde, 1911/12*
	Cyclone Taylor, 1913/14, 1917/18–1918/19
	Mickey Mackay, 1914/15, 1923/24
	Gordon Roberts, 1916/17
	Jack Adams, 1921/22
	Art Duncan, 1923/24
Goals Scored (WCHL):	*Mickey Mackay, 1924/25*
Hart:	*Eddie Shore, 1934/35–1935/36*
Top Scorer (PCHA):	*Newsy Lalonde, 1911/12*
	Gordon Roberts, 1916/17
	Cyclone Taylor, 1913/14–1915/16, 1917/18–1918/19

	Jack Adams, 1921/22
	Art Duncan, 1923/24
Vezina:	*Tiny Thompson, 1935/36*

LESTER PATRICK:

Best Goalie (PCHA):	*Bert Lindsay, 1912/13–1913/14*
Best Goalie (WCHL):	*Harry Holmes, 1924/25–1925/26*
Goals Scored (PCHA):	*Tommy Dunderdale, 1912/13–1913/14, 1919/20*
	Frank Frederickson, 1922/23
Lady Byng:	*Frank Boucher, 1927/28–1930/31, 1932/33–1934/35*
	Clint Smith, 1938/39
Top Scorer (PCHA):	*Tommy Dunderdale, 1912/13*
	Frank Fredrickson, 1920/21, 1922/23
	Jack Walker, 1924/25
Top Scorer (NHL):	*Bill Cook, 1926/27, 1932/33*

BOB PULFORD:

Lady Byng:	*Marcel Dionne, 1976/77*
Norris:	*Doug Wilson, 1981/82*
Selke:	*Troy Murray, 1985/86*

JOEL QUENNEVILLE:

Calder:	*Barret Jackman, 2002/03*
Conn Smythe:	*Jonathan Toews, 2009/10*
	Patrick Kane, 2012/13
	Duncan Keith, 2014/15
Hart:	*Chris Pronger, 1999/00*
Jennings:	*Corey Crawford/Ray Emery, 2012/13*
	Corey Crawford, 2014/15
Lady Byng:	*Pavol Demitra, 1999/00*

Norris:	*Al MacInnis, 1998/99*
	Chris Pronger, 1999/00
	Duncan Keith, 2009/10, 2013/14
Selke:	*Jonathan Toews, 2012/13*

PAT QUINN:

Calder Memorial:	*Luc Robataille, 1986/87*
	Pavel Bure, 1991/92
Goals Scored (NHL):	*Pavel Bure, 1993/94*
Lady Byng:	*Alexander Mogilny, 2002/03*

BILLY REAY:

Calder:	*Frank Mahovlich, 1957/58*
	Tony Esposito, 1969/70
Goals Scored (NHL):	*Bobby Hull, 1963/64, 1965/66–1968/69*
Hart:	*Bobby Hull, 1964/65–1965/66*
	Stan Mikita, 1966/67–1967/68
Lady Byng:	*Ken Wharram, 1963/64*
	Bobby Hull, 1964/65
	Stan Mikita, 1966/67–1967/68
Norris:	*Pierre Pilote, 1963/64–1964/65*
Ross:	*Stan Mikita, 1963/64–1964/65, 1966/67–1967/68*
	Bobby Hull, 1965/66
Vezina:	*Glenn Hall/Denis De Jordy, 1966/67*
	Tony Esposito, 1969/70, 1973/74
	Tony Esposito/Gary Smith, 1971/72

ART ROSS:

Goals Scored (NHL):	*Cooney Weiland, 1929/30*
	Nels Stewart, 1936/37

	Roy Conacher, 1938/39
Hart:	*Eddie Shore, 1932/33, 1937/38*
	Bill Cowley, 1942/43
Top Scorer (NHL):	*Cooney Weiland, 1929/30*
	Herb Cain, 1943/44
Vezina:	*Tiny Thompson, 1929/30, 1932/33, 1937/38*
	Frank Brimsek, 1941/42

CLAUDE RUEL:

Norris:	*Larry Robinson, 1979/80*
Vezina:	*Richard Sevigny/Denis Herron/Michel Larocque, 1980/81*

LINDY RUFF:

Calder:	*Tyler Myers, 2009/10*
Hart:	*Dominik Hasek, 1997/98*
Jennings:	*Dominik Hasek, 2000/01*
Ross:	*Jamie Benn, 2014/15*
Vezina:	*Dominik Hasek, 1997/98–1998/99, 2000/01*
	Ryan Miller, 2009/10

GLEN SATHER:

Best Goalie (WHA):	*Dave Dryden, 1978/79*
Conn Smythe:	*Mark Messier, 1983/84*
	Wayne Gretzky, 1984/85, 1987/88
Goals Scored (NHL):	*Wayne Gretzky, 19881/2–1984/85, 1986/87*
	Jari Kurri, 1985/86
Hart:	*Wayne Gretzky, 1979/80–1986/87*
Lady Byng:	*Wayne Gretzky, 1979/80*
	Jari Kurri, 1984/85
MVP (WHA):	*Dave Dryden, 1978/79*

Norris:	*Paul Coffey, 1984/85–1985/86*
Rookie of the Year (WHA):	*Wayne Gretzky, 1978/79*
Ross:	*Wayne Gretzky, 1980/81–1986/87*
Vezina:	*Grant Fuhr, 1987/88*

FRED SHERO:

Conn Smythe:	*Bernie Parent, 1973/74–1974/75*
	Reggie Leach, 1975/76
Goals Scored (NHL):	*Reggie Leach, 1975/76*
Hart:	*Bobby Clarke, 1972/73, 1974/75–1975/76*
Vezina:	*Bernie Parent, 1973/74–1974/75*

HARRY SINDEN:

Calder:	*Bobby Orr, 1966/67*
	Derek Sanderson, 1967/68
	Raymond Bourque, 1979/80
Conn Smythe:	*Bobby Orr, 1969/70*
Goals Scored (NHL):	*Phil Esposito, 1969/70*
Hart:	*Phil Esposito, 1968/69*
	Bobby Orr, 1969/70
Norris:	*Bobby Orr, 1967/68–1969/70*
Ross:	*Phil Esposito, 1968/69*
	Bobby Orr, 1969/70

JIMMY SKINNER:

Calder:	*Glenn Hall, 1955/56*
Goals Scored (NHL):	*Gordie Howe, 1956/57*
Hart:	*Gordie Howe, 1956/57*
Lady Byng:	*Dutch Reibel, 1955/56*
Ross:	*Gordie Howe, 1956/57*
Vezina:	*Terry Sawchuk, 1954/55*

DARRYL SUTTER:

Calder:	*Evgeni Nabokov, 2000/01*
Conn Smythe:	*Jonathan Quick, 2011/12*
	Justin Williams, 2013/14
Jennings:	*Ed Belfour, 1992/93, 1994/95*
	Miikka Kiprusoff, 2005/06
	Jonathan Quick, 2013/14
Norris:	*Chris Chelios, 1992/93*
Richard:	*Jarome Iginla, 2003/04*
Vezina:	*Ed Belfour, 1992/93*
	Miikka Kiprusoff, 2005/06

MICHEL THERRIEN:

Calder:	*Evgeni Malkin, 2006/07*
Hart:	*Jose Theodore, 2001/02*
	Sidney Crosby, 2006/07
	Carey Price, 2014/15
Jennings:	*Carey Price, 2014/15*
Norris:	*P. K. Subban, 2012/13*
Ross:	*Sidney Crosby, 2006/07*
Vezina:	*Jose Theodore, 2001/02*
	Carey Price, 2014/15

DAVE TIPPETT:

Selke:	*Jere Lehtinen, 2002/03*

ALAIN VIGNEAULT:

Hart:	*Henrik Sedin, 2009/10*
Jennings:	*Roberto Luongo/Cory Schneider, 2010/11*
Ross:	*Henrik Sedin, 2009/10*
	Daniel Sedin, 2010/11

Selke:	*Ryan Kesler, 2010/11*

COONEY WEILAND:

Byng:	*Bobby Bauer, 1939/40–1940/41*
Hart:	*Bill Cowley, 1940/41*
Ross:	*Milt Schmidt, 1939/40*
	Bill Cowley, 1940/41

RON WILSON:

Goals Scored (NHL):	*Peter Bondra, 1997/98*
Hart:	*Joe Thornton, 2005/06*
Lady Byng:	*Paul Kariya, 1995/96–1996/97*
Richard:	*Jonathan Cheechoo, 2005/06*
Ross:	*Joe Thornton, 2005/06*
Vezina:	*Olaf Kolzig, 1999/00*

GREATEST COACHES

This section lists the head coach with the most wins for all franchises competing in the NHL as of the end of the 2013/14 season. The franchises are listed in alphabetical order.

ANAHEIM DUCKS	RANDY CARLYLE
ARIZONA COYOTES	DAVE TIPPETT
BOSTON BRUINS	ART ROSS
BUFFALO SABRES	LINDY RUFF
CALGARY FLAMES	BOB JOHNSON
CAROLINA HURRICANES	PAUL MAURICE
CHICAGO BLACKHAWKS	BILLY REAY
COLORADO AVALANCHE	MICHEL BERGERON[242]
COLUMBUS BLUE JACKETS	TODD RICHARDS
DALLAS STARS	KEN HITCHCOCK
DETROIT RED WINGS	MIKE BABCOCK

242 The team was still called the Quebec Nordiques when Michel Bergeron was coaching.

EDMONTON OILERS	GLEN SATHER
FLORIDA PANTHERS	JACQUES MARTIN
LOS ANGELES KINGS	ANDY MURRAY
MINNESOTA WILD	JACQUES LEMAIRE
MONTREAL CANADIENS	TOE BLAKE
NASHVILLE PREDATORS	BARRY TROTZ
NEW JERSEY DEVILS	JACQUES LEMAIRE
NEW YORK ISLANDERS	AL ARBOUR
NEW YORK RANGERS	EMILE FRANCIS
OTTAWA SENATORS	JACQUES MARTIN
PHILADELPHIA FLYERS	FRED SHERO
PITTSBURGH PENGUINS	DAN BYLSMA
SAN JOSE SHARKS	TODD MCLELLAN
ST. LOUIS BLUES	JOEL QUENNEVILLE
TAMPA BAY LIGHTNING	JOHN TORTORELLA
TORONTO MAPLE LEAFS	PUNCH IMLACH
VANCOUVER CANUCKS	ALAIN VIGNEAULT
WASHINGTON CAPITALS	BRYAN MURRAY
WINNIPEG JETS	BOB HARTLEY[243]

243 The team was still called the Atlanta Thrashers when Bob Hartley was coaching.

NHL COACHING RECORDS

SEASONS COACHED

1.	Scotty Bowman	30		Jack Adams	20
2.	Dick Irvin	27	7.	*Ken Hitchcock*	18
3.	Al Arbour	23		*Joel Quenneville*	18
4.	Pat Quinn	20		Art Ross	18
	Mike Keenan	20		Ron Wilson	18

GAMES COACHED

1.	Scotty Bowman	2,141	6.	Mike Keenan	1,386
2.	Al Arbour	1,607	7.	*Joel Quenneville*	1,375
3.	Dick Irvin	1,449	8.	*Lindy Ruff*	1,329
4.	Ron Wilson	1,401	9.	*Ken Hitchcock*	1,322
5.	Pat Quinn	1,400	10.	Jacques Martin	1,294

POINTS

1.	Scotty Bowman	2,812	6.	Pat Quinn	1,556
2.	Al Arbour	1,812	7.	Mike Keenan	1,527
3.	*Joel Quenneville*	1,691	8.	Ron Wilson	1,488
4.	Dick Irvin	1,614	9.	*Lindy Ruff*	1,487
5.	*Ken Hitchcock*	1,601	10.	Jacques Martin	1,426

WINS

1.	Scotty Bowman	1,244	6.	Pat Quinn	684
2.	Al Arbour	782	7.	Mike Keenan	672
3.	*Joel Quenneville*	754	8.	*Lindy Ruff*	652
4.	*Ken Hitchcock*	708	9.	Ron Wilson	648
5.	Dick Irvin	692	10.	Bryan Murray	620

LOSSES

1.	Al Arbour	577	6.	Dick Irvin	527
2.	Scotty Bowman	573	7.	*Barry Trotz*	505
3.	Ron Wilson	561	8.	*Paul Maurice*	495
4.	Mike Keenan	531	9.	*Lindy Ruff*	494
5.	Pat Quinn	528	10.	Jacques Martin	481

WINNING PERCENTAGE[244]

1.	Dan Bylsma	.670	6.	*Todd McLellan*	.637
2.	*Bruce Boudreau*	.664	7.	Toe Blake	.634
3.	Scotty Bowman	.657	8.	*Mike Babcock*	.627
4.	Claude Ruel	.648	9.	Floyd Smith	.626
5.	Pete Green	.640	10.	*Joel Quenneville*	.615

PLAYOFF APPEARANCES

1.	Scotty Bowman	28	6.	Toe Blake	13
2.	Dick Irvin	24		*Ken Hitchcock*	13
3.	Al Arbour	16		Mike Keenan	13
	Joel Quenneville	16		Bryan Murray	13
5.	Pat Quinn	15		*Darryl Sutter*	13

---

244 I've only listed those coaches who have coached a minimum of five seasons in the NHL.

PLAYOFF GAMES COACHED

1.	Scotty Bowman	353	6.	Mike Keenan	173
2.	Al Arbour	209	7.	*Darryl Sutter*	165
3.	*Joel Quenneville*	204	8.	Pat Burns	149
4.	Dick Irvin	190	9.	*Ken Hitchcock*	148
5.	Pat Quinn	183	10.	*Mike Babcock*	144

PLAYOFF WINS

1.	Scotty Bowman	223	6.	Pat Quinn	94
2.	Al Arbour	123	7.	Glen Sather	89
3.	*Joel Quenneville*	115	8.	*Darryl Sutter*	88
4.	Dick Irvin	100	9.	*Mike Babcock*	82
5.	Mike Keenan	96		Toe Blake	82

PLAYOFF LOSSES

1.	Scotty Bowman	130	6.	Mike Keenan	77
2.	*Joel Quenneville*	89		*Darryl Sutter*	77
	Pat Quinn	89	8.	*Ken Hitchcock*	72
4.	Dick Irvin	88	9.	Pat Burns	71
5.	Al Arbour	86	10.	*Mike Babcock*	62

PLAYOFF WINNING PERCENTAGE[245]

1.	Glen Sather	.705	6.	Hap Day	.613
2.	Toe Blake	.689	7.	Tommy Gorman	.600
3.	Claude Ruel	.667	8.	Larry Robinson	.596
4.	Scotty Bowman	.632	9.	Al Arbour	.589
5.	Leo Dandurand	.625[246]	10.	Peter DeBoer	.583

245 Again, I've listed only persons who have coached a minimum of five years in the NHL.

246 This includes the interleague playoff games Dandurand coached in 1924 and 1925.

STANLEY CUP FINALS[247]

1.	Dick Irvin	16	6.	Punch Imlach	6
2.	Scotty Bowman	13	7.	Hap Day	5
3.	Toe Blake	9		Tommy Ivan	5
4.	Lester Patrick	7[248]		Al Arbour	5
	Jack Adams	7		Glen Sather	5

STANLEY CUP WINS

1.	Scotty Bowman	9		Glen Sather	4
2.	Toe Blake	8	7.	Pete Green	3
3.	Hap Day	5		Lester Patrick	3[249]
4.	Punch Imlach	4		Jack Adams	3
	Al Arbour	4		Tommy Ivan	3
				Joel Quenneville	3

STANLEY CUP LOSSES

1.	Dick Irvin	12		Mike Keenan	3
2.	Lester Patrick	4[250]	10.	Lynn Patrick	2
	Sid Abel	4		Milt Schmidt	2
	Scotty Bowman	4		Don Cherry	2
5.	Frank Patrick	3		Fred Shero	2
	Art Ross	3		Pat Quinn	2
	Jack Adams	3		*Mike Babcock*	2
	Billy Reay	3		*Alain Vigneault*	2

247 I've listed only those appearances made from 1918 to 2015.

248 This does not count Lester Patrick's Cup final appearance in 1914 when he was coaching in the PCHA, but it does include his finals appearances in 1925 and 1926 when he was coaching in the WCHL/WHL.

249 This figure includes Lester Patrick's 1925 Cup win when he was coaching in the WCHL.

250 This figure includes Lester Patrick's 1926 Cup loss when he was coaching in the WHL.

PCHA COACHING RECORDS

GAMES COACHED

1.	Frank Patrick	272
2.	Lester Patrick	272
3.	Pete Muldoon	228
4.	Edward Savage	42
5.	Jimmy Gardner	30

WINS

1.	Frank Patrick	143
2.	Lester Patrick	120
3.	Pete Muldoon	117
4.	Edward Savage	22
5.	Jimmy Gardner	15

LOSSES

1.	Lester Patrick	149
2.	Frank Patrick	127
3.	Pete Muldoon	109
4.	Edward Savage	20
5.	Jimmy Gardner	15

POINTS

1.	Frank Patrick	288
2.	Lester Patrick	243
3.	Pete Muldoon	236
4.	Edward Savage	44
5.	Jimmy Gardner	30

WINNING PERCENTAGE

1.	Frank Patrick	.529
2.	Edward Savage	.524
3.	Pete Muldoon	.518
4.	Jimmy Gardner	.500
5.	Lester Patrick	.447

LEAGUE CHAMPIONSHIPS

1.	Frank Patrick	6
2.	Pete Muldoon	3
3.	Lester Patrick	2
4.	Jimmy Gardner	1
	Edward Savage	1

WCHL/WHL COACHING RECORDS

GAMES COACHED

1.	Ken Mackenzie	142
2.	Herb Gardiner	118
3.	Newsy Lalonde	118
4.	Wesley Champ	112
5.	Lester Patrick	58
	Frank Patrick	58

WINS

1.	Ken Mackenzie	78
2.	Newsy Lalonde	57
3.	Herb Gardiner	57
4.	Wesley Champ	55
5.	Lester Patrick	31

LOSSES

1.	Ken Mackenzie	58
2.	Herb Gardiner	57
3.	Wesley Champ	55
4.	Newsy Lalonde	54
5.	Frank Patrick	34

POINTS

1.	Ken Mackenzie	162
2.	Newsy Lalonde	121
3.	Herb Gardiner	118
4.	Wesley Champ	112
5.	Lester Patrick	66

WINNING PERCENTAGE

1.	Ken Mackenzie	.570
2.	Lester Patrick	.569
3.	Newsy Lalonde	.513
4.	Herb Gardiner	.500
	Wesley Champ	.500

LEAGUE CHAMPIONSHIPS

1.	Lester Patrick	2
2.	Wesley Champ	1
	Ken Mackenzie	1
	Herb Gardiner	1

WHA COACHING STATS

GAMES COACHED

1.	Bill Dineen	545
2.	Harry Neale	404
3.	Jacques Demers	311
4.	Terry Slater	258
5.	Joe Crozier	239

POINTS

1.	Bill Dineen	664
2.	Harry Neale	437
3.	Jacques Demers	310
4.	Terry Slater	244
5.	Joe Crozier	231

WINS

1.	Bill Dineen	318
2.	Harry Neale	208
3.	Jacques Demers	144
4.	Terry Slater	116
5.	Joe Crozier	109

LOSSES

1.	Bill Dineen	199
2.	Harry Neale	175
3.	Jacques Demers	145
4.	Terry Slater	130
5.	Joe Crozier	117

WINNING PERCENTAGE[251]

1.	Bobby Kromm	.621
2.	Jean-Guy Gendron	.616
3.	Bill Dineen	.609
4.	Glen Sather	.553
5.	Harry Neale	.541

PLAYOFF GAMES COACHED

1.	Bill Dineen	71
2.	Harry Neale	65
3.	Bobby Kromm	33
4.	Glen Sather	23
5.	Jack Kelley	21

251 I've listed only those WHA coaches who coached a minimum of two complete seasons.

PLAYOFF WINS

1.	Bill Dineen	44
2.	Harry Neale	32
3.	Bobby Kromm	23
4.	Jack Kelley	14
5.	Marc Boileau	12

PLAYOFF LOSSES

1.	Harry Neale	32
2.	Bill Dineen	27
3.	Glen Sather	15
4.	Jacques Demers	12
5.	Jean-Guy Gendron	11

PLAYOFF WINNING PERCENTAGE[252]

1.	Bobby Kromm	.697
2.	Jack Kelley	.667
3.	Bill Dineen	.620
4.	Bobby Hull	.500
5.	Harry Neale	.492

AVCO CUP FINALS APPEARANCES

1.	Bill Dineen	3
2.	Bobby Kromm	2
3.	Jack Kelley	1
	Bobby Hull	1
	Pat Stapleton	1
	Jean-Guy Gendron	1
	Marc Boileau	1
	Larry Hillman	1
	Harry Neale	1
	Tom McVie	1
	Glen Sather	1

AVCO CUP WINS

1.	Bill Dineen	2
2.	Jack Kelley	1
	Bobby Kromm	1
	Marc Boileau	1
	Larry Hillman	1
	Tom McVie	1

252 I've listed only those WHA coaches who coached a minimum of two playoff appearances.

PART SIX

THE WORST OF THEIR TIMES

LOSING COACHES

So far, this book has been devoted to rating and ranking hockey's most successful head coaches, but who were the worst hockey coaches of all time? Since my rating system balances a coach's success against his failures, which coaches came out on the bottom of my ratings? Who were the unluckiest members of the coaching fraternity?

This part lists the ten worst coaches in hockey history in descending order of futility from the tenth worst to the absolute worst head coach of all time.

10. PAUL HOLMGREN

PLUS: 1
MINUS: 29
VALUE: -28
AVERAGE SEASON: -3.500
SEASONS COACHED: 8
LOSING SEASONS: 7
LAST-PLACE FINISHES: 2

In the 1970s and 1980s Paul Holmgren was a crushing, bruising player who played briefly in the WHA for the Minnesota Fighting Saints (Bruce Boudreau was a teammate of his) before returning to the NHL to play for the Philadelphia Flyers (where he was a member of the 1979/80 Flyers team that lost the Stanley

Cup finals to the Islanders) and the Minnesota North Stars (Holmgren was born in Minnesota).

When his playing career ended in 1985, he became an assistant coach under Mike Keenan when Keenan manned the Flyers. When Keenan was fired, Holmgren took over and lead the Flyers to the 1988/89 conference finals before losing to Pat Burns's Montreal Canadians.

It was the high point of Holmgren's coaching career.

Afterwards, Holmgren led the Flyers and later the Hartford Whalers to seven consecutive losing seasons and two last-place finishes. He was the second-worst head coach in the NHL during the 1990s with a -29 value, according to my rating system.

After 1996, Holmgren returned to Philadelphia to work in the front office: working as director of pro scouting, director of player personnel, and assistant general manager under Bobby Clarke before becoming the Flyers general manager in 2006. Holmgren managed the Flyers until the end of the 2013/14 Season when he stepped down to work as an adviser to Flyers owner Ed Snider – where he remains today. (If you applied my rating system to analyze Holmgren's career as a general manager, his managerial value was a solid and respectable +20).

9. MARSHALL JOHNSTON

PLUS: **0**
MINUS: **28**
VALUE: **-28**
AVERAGE SEASON: **-9.333**
SEASONS COACHED: **3**
LOSING SEASONS: **3**
LAST-PLACE FINISHES: **3**

Although tied with Paul Holmgren with a coaching value of -28, Marshall Johnston did a far worse job as a coach than Holmgren did. He had the worst average season of all hockey coaches with at least three seasons of head coaching experience in their careers.

Johnston was a defenceman who played for the Minnesota North Stars and the hapless California Golden Seals from 1967 to 1974. Seals teammate Gary Jarrett later told Seals chronicler Brad Kurtzberg, "[Johnston] was steady. You wouldn't necessarily notice him much but when you graded him out, you would never find many mistakes he made. He always did his job but in a non-spectacular fashion."[253]

Johnston took over as the Seals' head coach when Fred Glover was fired in 1974 (Johnston immediately retired as a player). The Golden Seals were one of the worst franchises in NHL history, and Johnston was doomed to spend two seasons as its head coach, unable to get the team out of the cellar.

He later told Brad Kurtzberg, "In retrospect, now, I realize I had no business coaching the team. I had no prior coaching experience. It was an opportunity to coach and to see if I had an aptitude for it."[254]

Johnston took up NCAA coaching before returning to the NHL to work for the Colorado Rockies (another hapless expansion franchise struggling to earn respectability). He returned to coaching when Rockies head coach Bert Marshall was fired during the 1981/82 season. Johnston led the team to a miserable last-place finish. (It would prove to be the team's last season in Colorado. The following year they relocated to North Jersey, where they would become the New Jersey Devils.)

Johnston never coached in the NHL again but worked in the Devils' front office before becoming general manager of the Ottawa Senators in 1999 and then retiring from hockey in 2002.

8. TOM MCVIE

PLUS: 18
MINUS: 47
VALUE: -29
AVERAGE SEASON: -3.222

---

253 *Shorthanded: The Untold Story of the Seals*, Brad Kurtzberg, p. 215.

254 Ibid, p. 216.

SEASONS COACHED: **9**
LOSING SEASONS: **7**
LAST-PLACE FINISHES: **3**

Tom McVie was the third-worst coach of the 1980s, according to my rating system.

With one exception, McVie had the misfortune of coaching the wrong teams at the wrong times, but at least he maintained his sense of humour about his predicament. He would later tell Dick Irvin Jr.: "I'm the one guy walking around who has coached three expansion teams and can actually carry on a half-decent conversation. Anyone who has coached as many as two is usually with Jack Nicholson in the cuckoo's nest."[255]

McVie was a career minor league player before he took up coaching. His first coaching gig came with the Washington Capitals, a team that was first in war, first in peace, but last in the NHL. After three seasons with the Caps, McVie's coaching value was already -26.

His one lucky break came during the 1978/79 season when the Winnipeg Jets hired McVie to take over as head coach from the newly fired Larry Hillman. The Jets were in a stall, and McVie energized the team in the nick of time to lead them to the final Avco Cup playoffs in WHA history (14 of his 18 plus points come from that season).

McVie coached the last Avco Cup champion, but when the Jets entered the NHL their glory days were over. The Jets were drawn, quartered, and bowelled, never to be a factor in the league. McVie endured two horrific seasons with the Jets before being fired.

His next stop in his descent into the centre of hell was with the New Jersey Devils (another laughing-stock in the NHL). After another miserable season, McVie coached in the AHL, where he performed creditably.

He returned to the Devils in 1991 and coaxed two playoff appearances out of the team before being fired for good.

---

255 *Behind the Bench,* Dick Irvin, p. 205.

7. GEORGE "RED" SULLIVAN

PLUS: 0
MINUS: 30
VALUE: -30
AVERAGE SEASON: -4.286
SEASONS COACHED: 7
LOSING SEASONS: 7
LAST-PLACE FINISHES: 1

George "Red" Sullivan played 12 seasons as a centre in the NHL with the Boston Bruins and the Chicago Blackhawks before ending up with the New York Rangers (and serving as the team's captain until 1961, when he was sent down to the minors).

Sullivan ended his playing career and was hired by the Rangers to be their head coach. The Rangers at that time were in terrible disarray. During Sullivan's coaching reign, the team would vie with the Boston Bruins over who would occupy the NHL cellar. According to my rating system, Sullivan was the third-worst coach of the 1960s with a -22 coaching value for the decade.

When Emile Francis took over as Ranger's general manager, he replaced Sullivan 20 games into the 1965/66 season.

When the NHL expanded in 1967, Sullivan became the first head coach of the Pittsburgh Penguins, but he still couldn't shake his losing ways. In two seasons of coaching in Pittsburgh, Sullivan failed to reach the playoffs twice.

He wouldn't return to NHL coaching until the 1974/75 season, when he became the second head coach in Washington Capitals history. During their inaugural season in the NHL, the Caps were a disaster in the making, and Sullivan was at ground zero of that disaster.

6. DOUG CARPENTER

PLUS: 1
MINUS: 31

VALUE: **-30**
AVERAGE SEASON: **-5.000**
SEASONS COACHED: **6**
LOSING SEASONS: **4**
LAST-PLACE FINISHES: **3**

As mentioned, Doug Carpenter has the third-worst average season rating of all hockey coaches with at least five years' coaching experience, and he was the worst coach of the 1980s, with a coaching value of -23.

Carpenter (like Tom McVie) was a career minor league player in the Eastern Hockey League and International Hockey League. He took up coaching in junior in the 1970s before coaching in the AHL in 1980/81. In 1984/85 he succeeded McVie as head coach of the New Jersey Devils but (like McVie) could not get the team to escape its ineptitude.

The Devils finished last in the Patrick Division twice during his reign. Carpenter was fired in 1988 but two years later was made the head coach of the Toronto Maple Leafs (where he earned his sole plus point – a playoff appearance in 1989/90). When Carpenter was fired the following season, the Leafs were in last place.

5. JOHNNY WILSON

PLUS: **7**
MINUS: **39**
VALUE: **-32**
AVERAGE SEASON: **-3.556**
SEASONS COACHED: **9**
LOSING SEASONS: **6**
LAST-PLACE FINISHES: **3**

As noted earlier, Johnny Wilson was the uncle of former Maple Leafs head coach Ron Wilson. He was also a key player in the Detroit Red Wings dynasty teams of

1950 to 1955, playing left wing and showing great endurance, splendid two-way skills, and solid fundamentals.

Wilson took up coaching in the AHL in 1967 and by the 1969/70 season was coaching the Los Angeles Kings in the NHL to a last-place finish. He returned to coaching in the AHL (leading the Springfield Kings to the 1970/71 Calder Cup) before becoming head coach of the Red Wings that same year. The Wings were in the worst decade of their existence. Wilson coaxed a winning season out of the team during the 1972/73 season but was fired as head coach.

Wilson fared no better in the WHA, spending two seasons coaching there with no results. He returned to the NHL in 1977 with the Pittsburgh Penguins, but his teams were inconsistent. He was the second-worst coach in hockey during the 1970s, according to my rating system.

4. JACK EVANS

PLUS: 10
MINUS: 42
VALUE: -32
AVERAGE SEASON: -4.000
SEASONS COACHED: 8
LOSING SEASONS: 6
LAST-PLACE FINISHES: 5

Before he took up coaching, Jack Evans was a defenceman who played with the New York Rangers and the Chicago Blackhawks during the 1950s and 1960s. His greatest moment as a player came during the 1960/61 Stanley Cup finals when the Hawks beat the Red Wings. Although teammate Glenn Hall drew considerable attention with his superb goaltending, Hall also received able assistance from Evans.

In interviews with former Wings players who played in that series, Evans's name was repeatedly mentioned as playing an unsung hero role in blunting the Wings' offence during that series.

When Evans's playing career ended in 1972, he took up coaching in the minors before accepting the head coaching job with the California Seals (who later became the Cleveland Barons).

Like all the other coaches who preceded him, Evans, too, saw his coaching record tarnished by being forced to lead this travesty of an NHL franchise. As it turned out, his stint with the Seals/Barons made him the third-worst hockey coach of the 1970s, according to my rating system, with a coaching value of -27.

Despite this, Evans made a positive impression. Brad Kurtzberg writes that Evans "set to cut down the Seals goals against [average] and helped bring a system to the Seals on and off the ice. . . . While Evans was not very vocal, he did earn his players' respect."[256]

After 1978, Evans returned to minor league coaching before returning to the NHL in 1983 to lead the Hartford Whalers. The Whalers during their NHL years were a weak franchise, with the 1980s being particularly horrific for them.

The team remained beached in last place during Evans's first two seasons; however, by 1985 he led Hartford to two winning seasons and a divisional title in 1986/87 (thus earning all ten plus points in his career). When the Whalers floundered again in 1987/88, Evans was fired as head coach, never to return to the NHL again.

He died in 1996.

3. FRED GLOVER

PLUS: 2
MINUS: 43
VALUE: -41
AVERAGE SEASON: -6.833
SEASONS COACHED: 6
LOSING SEASONS: 6
LAST-PLACE FINISHES: 4

256 *Shorthanded: The Untold Story of the Seals*, Brad Kurtzberg, p. 31.

In 2006, when the AHL Hall of Fame was established and its inaugural class was inducted, Fred Glover was one of the seven initial inductees (along with Johnny Bower and Eddie Shore, to name a few).

Glover had made a reputation for himself in the AHL as a player and a coach. He was a centre for the Cleveland Barons teams that dominated the AHL during the 1950s and 1960s. He led the league in scoring twice and was named league MVP three times, in 1959/60, 1961/62, and 1963/64.

Glover became the Barons' head coach in 1962 and spent the next six seasons with an uneven record. He led the Barons to two Calder Cup appearances (winning the 1963/64 Calder Cup) while also enduring two last-place finishes, in 1964/65 and 1967/68. Still, Glover was named head coach of the Oakland Seals and brought a sense of professionalism to a horrible situation. Veteran broadcaster Tim Ryan tells Brad Kurtzberg: "Freddie brought a new atmosphere to the club. He had an understanding of what we were up against and the team's financial problems were acknowledged. He knew he had to be fan-friendly. He got the players into the community. He was good with the media. It wasn't his personality, but he did it."[257]

Despite the team's limitations, Glover coaxed two playoff appearances from the Seals (the only ones in their franchise history) and was named NHL coach of the year by *The Hockey News* for his performance during the 1968/69 season.

Glover brought intensity and pugnacity to the team. He also stood between the players and their eccentric and egocentric owner, the late Charles O. Finley, whenever Charlie O's aesthetic excesses got in the way of the team doing its job – yet he never lost Finley's respect. That is why it's sad to note that Glover was the worst hockey coach of the 1970s. His -41 value for the decade is the third-worst decade performance, according to my rating system.

His -6.833 ASR is the worst of all hockey coaches with at least five years' coaching experience. And the reason his record was so lousy is because he coached (and managed at times) the hapless Oakland/California Golden Seals team and the Los Angeles Kings without ever having a winning season in six seasons of coaching. In five of those six seasons, his teams finished below .400 in winning percentage. He endured four last-place finishes.

Seals historian Brad Kurtzberg eulogizes Glover's unfortunate NHL coaching

---

257 Ibid, p. 69.

career this way: "Despite all the difficulties he faced – coaching an expansion team, low attendance, a team constantly on the verge of being moved and/or sold and a talent poor roster – Fred Glover persevered. He led the Seals to their greatest successes and kept them together through their toughest times. He genuinely loved coaching in Oakland despite facing so many problems."[258]

That is how Fred Glover should be remembered. Even though his years with the Seals dimmed his coaching record in terms of numbers, his goodness and character transcends the statistics. He was a decent man and a hardworking head coach trapped in an impossible situation. Let no one cast a stone against him.

Glover quit coaching in 1974 and lived quietly in the San Francisco Bay area until his death in 2001.

2. MILT SCHMIDT

PLUS: 18
MINUS: 71
VALUE: -53
AVERAGE SEASON: -4.077
SEASONS COACHED: 13
LOSING SEASONS: 10
LAST-PLACE FINISHES: 6

As of 2015, Milt Schmidt is a living legend as a hockey player and one of the game's best goodwill ambassadors. Schmidt succeeded Eddie Shore as Boston's greatest player and was the backbone of the team during the late 1930s, the 1940s, and the early 1950s, leading the Bruins to the 1938/39 and 1940/41 Stanley Cup title. Long before the arrival of Bobby Orr, Schmidt commanded the love and devotion of Bruins (and hockey) fans across North America.

When his playing career ended in 1954, he took over as head coach of the Bruins. At first he started off quite well, leading the team to two winning seasons

258 Ibid, p. 71.

and two Stanley Cup finals appearances, in 1956/57 and 1957/58 (losing twice to the Montreal Canadiens). By 1958/59, his coaching value was a respectable +14.

It was after 1959 that Schmidt and the Bruins entered the abyss, cursed by the fact that during the 1960s the Bruins usually had to live off the scraps left over from other teams.

Indeed, as mentioned, Schmidt was the worst coach of the decade and his -49 coaching value during the 1960s is the worst of all time, according to my rating system. Furthermore, he was the second-worst head coach during the Original Six era, with a coaching value of -35. (Frank Boucher was the worst, with a value of -52.)

Schmidt's troubles were not confined solely to the Bruins. He (along with Red Sullivan) did interim coaching work with the expansion Washington Capitals in their inaugural season.

The Caps suffered an 8–67–5 record, which is the worst performance ever for an NHL expansion franchise. Many hockey historians today consider the 1974/75 Caps the worst team in NHL history.

1. RICK BOWNESS

PLUS: 3
MINUS: 60
VALUE: -57
AVERAGE SEASON: -6.333
SEASONS COACHED: 9
LOSING SEASONS: 8
LAST-PLACE FINISHES: 7

Stan Fischler in his book *Coaches* titled his chapter on Rick Bowness "The Losingest Coach," and that's exactly what Rick Bowness was – the worst coach in hockey history.[259] And not only that: he was the worst coach of the 1990s. Indeed,

259 *Coaches*, Stan Fischler, p. 85.

his is the worst coaching performance of all time since the NHL expanded in 1967, all according to my rating system.

Before he took up coaching, Bowness was a journeyman centre alternating between the NHL and the minors with the Atlanta Flames, Detroit Red Wings, St. Louis Blues, and Winnipeg Jets.

When his playing career ended in 1984, he took up coaching in the AHL with mixed results. He succeeded Mike Milbury as head coach of the Boston Bruins, and during the 1991/92 season he led the team to a winning season and a conference final loss to Scotty Bowman's Pittsburgh Penguins. That was the sole winning season and playoff appearance in his lacklustre coaching career (his three plus points all derive from that season). What followed were seven seasons of coaching futility with the Ottawa Senators (he was their first head coach), the New York Islanders, and the Phoenix Coyotes.

Bowness's teams didn't just lose. They lost badly, and in seven of his nine seasons of NHL coaching, his teams finished last.

Since 2006 Rick Bowness has worked as an assistant coach under Alain Vigneault for the Vancouver Canucks until he and Vigneault were fired in 2013.

Bowness went to the Tampa Bay Lightning as an assistant coach to Jon Cooper, overseeing the team's defence and penalty-killing, where he remains today.

ACKNOWLEDGEMENTS

First and foremost, I offer my thanks to God in the name of the Father, the Son, and the Holy Spirit. Amen.

To my departed mother and father, for making me possible and for making everything else possible; my thanks also to my brothers, Frank Jr. and Chris; and their wives, Joann and Kristin; to my nephews, Frank III and Christopher Karl; and to my nieces, Amanda and Kelsey.

My deepest and most heartfelt thanks to my agent, Curtis Russell, from P.S. Literary Agency, who believed in my project, nurtured and improved my book proposal, and got the deal done with Random House while helping a literary greenhorn like me go through the publishing process. None of this would have been possible without him; thanks also to B. D. Gyulai and Irene Merritt, who worked alongside Curtis at P.S. Literary Agency in getting the deal done.

I also want to thank Paul Taunton, who did a lovely and brilliant job in editing the earlier drafts of the manuscript. Paul's delicate touch and insightful comments during those early stages really helped out. He was so helpful and I am most grateful to him for his kindness and professionalism.

To Elizabeth Kribs and Zoe Maslow who picked up where Paul Taunton left off with regards to the editing, my deepest thanks to you both for your fine and brilliant efforts.

To Brad Martin, president and CEO of Penguin Random House Canada; Kristin Cochrane, president of the Penguin Random House Publishing Group; and Jordan Fenn, publisher of Fenn/M&S: a major league "thank you" for having faith in me; to Valerie Gow and Scott Loomer, in sales, and to the production and design departments for their glorious work; and, especially, to Ruta Liormonas – my publicist – for getting my name up in lights. I just love it! A major debt of gratitude to Mike Wyman and Kevin Greenstein at *Inside Hockey* for allowing me to join their team and test the insights and materials contained in this book with hockey fans everywhere. The words *thank you* are insufficient reward for their kindness, encouragement, and generosity.

I want to especially thank Mrs. Claire Arbour (the wife of Al Arbour), Mr. Jim Devellano, and Mr. Scotty Bowman for their considerable help in making the foreword to this book possible. It was Mrs. Arbour who suggested I reach out to Jim Devellano to see if he would pass on my request to Scotty Bowman to write the foreword. It was Mr. Jim Devellano, a brother member of the Society of International Hockey Research/SIHR, who very nobly and generously sent my request to Mr. Bowman. And last but never least, my eternal thanks to Mr. Scotty Bowman for writing the foreword.

I said it before and I will say it again, Mr. Bowman, you are the greatest, sir!

To Brian Kennedy, who helped me develop and polish my book proposal until it shone like a diamond.

An even greater debt of gratitude goes out to the former NHL players and head coaches I interviewed in person or over the telephone during the past seven years. Their names are listed in the bibliography section of this book. I cannot begin to thank them enough for their kindness, hospitality, generosity, and willingness to share their memories, insights, and stories.

To Joe Kadlec, Joe Watson, and Joe Siville with the Philadelphia Flyers; and Ian Ott with the Buffalo Sabres.

To David Nairn and Chris Wojcik with the Arizona Coyotes for arranging my interview with Dave Tippett.

To Dylan Wade, the manager of marketing and media with the NHL Alumni Association, for arranging my interviews with Gerry Cheevers, Floyd Smith, Bill Dineen, and Eddie Johnston; and to Gerry Cheevers, Floyd Smith, Bill Dineen, and Eddie Johnston for being so kind and generous with their time and their insights.

To Cindy Brueck for helping me get in contact with Bob Pulford, and to Bob Pulford for sharing his coaching wisdom.

To Michael Caruso and Dan O'Neill from the St. Louis Blues for helping me arrange a lovely telephone interview with Ken Hitchcock; and to Ken Hitchcock for his very perceptive and informative insights about coaching.

To Bob Rotruck with the Adirondack Phantoms, who arranged my telephone interview with Terry Murray; and to Terry Murray for his memories and insights about his coaching career and for helping to arrange my interview with his brother, Bryan Murray.

To Jaime Holtz at the Knuckles Group for her help in arranging my interview with Chris Nilan, and to Chris Nilan for being so generous with his time and insights.

To Jason Beck and Cecilia Olmos at the B.C. Sports Hall of Fame; and to Sherry Bell and Paula Aurini Onderwater at the City Archives of Edmonton.

My thanks to Andrew Marenus and to Robert "Rocky" Larocque.

A big thank-you to Paul Kitchen, who very kindly loaned me his background notes regarding Pete Green. Thanks to Paul, my section on Pete Green was much better.

Thanks also to Tom "Chico" Adrahtas, Todd Denault, D'Arcy Jenish, Jay Moran, Kevin Shea, and Brad Kurtzberg, hockey authors all, for their advice, input, and assistance in making this book a much better book. *Mucho appreciado.*

A big thank-you to George Grimm (a hockey writer in his own right) for graciously allowing me to quote excerpts from an interview he had with former New York Ranger Ted Irvine. The material enhanced my section on Emile Francis.

To Dave Soutter in Utah; and to Jeff Marcus for helping resolve some questions regarding PCHA hockey coaches.

To everyone at the Society of International Hockey Research.

My love and thanks to my cousins Mrs. Ruth Anne Labate and Miss Julia K. DiBiase. To paraphrase Bob Dylan, they stood behind me when the game got rough.

To Darlene and James Young (and their children) and to Amber and Michael Owens (and their children): for keeping the faith; and to the Drago family: Elliott, Vanessa, John, and Freida. Love always.

My thanks and appreciation to my colleagues at the National Archives at Philadelphia: Leslie Simon, Gail Farr, Heather Glasby, Stephen Charla and Andrea Reidell.

My eternal thanks to Jefferson Moak, who stood with me on St. Crispin's Day.

To Patrick Connelly, who makes the workplace a fun place to be. *Erin Go Bragh!*

To Kathleen Groch, for being such a dear friend through thick and thin.

My thanks to Diane Doerner, you're a real trooper, and to Mike Laskowski, stay thirsty, my friend! And to Grace D'Agostino, future archivist in the making, your day will come!

To Beth Haines Levitt: good luck in all your endeavours.

To Dr. Robert Plowman: thanks for everything you did for me and thanks for believing in me always. I said it before when you retired and I'll say it again: I love you.

To Glenn Brahin for helping a computer illiterate like me overcome the technical glitches of life.

To Monsignor Arturo Banuelas at St. Pius X in El Paso, Texas, and Sister Marie Magdalena at Camilla Hall in Immaculata, Pennsylvania: thanks for teaching me many a vital lesson about faith.

And for reasons known only to me: HHS and NT . . . if only . . . if only . . . if only.

BIBLIOGRAPHY

Adrahtas, Tom. *The Man They Call Mr. Goalie: Glenn Hall* (Kingston, RI: Albion Press, 2003).

Baun, Bobby, with Anne Logan. *Lowering the Boom: The Bobby Baun Story* (Toronto: Stoddart Publishing, 2000).

Boucher, Frank, with Trent Frayne. *When the Rangers Were Young* (New York: Dodd, Mead & Company, 1973).

Boudreau, Bruce, and Tim Leone. *Gabby: Confessions of a Hockey Lifer* (Washington, D.C.: Potomac Books, Inc., 2009).

Bower, Johnny, with Bob Duff. *The China Wall: The Timeless Legend of Johnny Bower* (Bolton, ON: Fenn Publishing Co. Ltd., 2008).

Brunt, Stephen. *Searching for Bobby Orr* (Chicago, IL: Triumph Books, 2006).

Chelios, Chris, with Kevin Allen. *Made in America* (Chicago, IL: Triumph Books, 2014).

Cherry, Don, and Stan Fischler. *Grapes: A Vintage View of Hockey* (Scarborough, ON: Prentice-Hall, 1982).

Clancy, King, with Brian McFarlane. *Clancy: The King's Story* (Toronto: ECW Press, 1997).

Cole, Stephen. *The Last Hurrah: A Celebration of Hockey's Greatest Season '66-'67* (New York: Viking, 1995).

Coleman, Charles L. *The Trail of the Stanley Cup Vol. 1 1893–1926 inc.* (Dubuque, IA: Kendall/Hunt Publishing Company, 1964).

———. *The Trail of the Stanley Cup Vol. 2 1927–1946 inc.* (Sherbrooke, QC: Progressive Publications Incorporated, 1969).

———————. *The Trail of the Stanley Cup Vol. 3 1947–1967 inc.* (Sherbrooke, QC: Progressive Publications Incorporated, 1976).

Cox, Damien, and Gord Stellick. *'67: The Maple Leafs, Their Sensational Victory, and the End of an Empire* (Toronto: John Wiley & Sons, Canada Ltd., 2004).

Denault, Todd. *A Season in Time: Super Mario, Killer, St. Patrick, the Great One, and the Unforgettable 1992–1993 Season* (Toronto: John Wiley & Sons, Canada Ltd., 2012).

———————. *Jacques Plante: The Man Who Changed the Face of Hockey* (Toronto: McClelland & Stewart, Ltd., 2009).

Diamond, Dan, Ralph Dinger, James Duplacey, and Eric Zweig. *The Official Encyclopedia of the National Hockey League: Total Hockey second edition* (Kingston, NY: Total Sports Publishing, 2000).

Diamond, Dan, James Duplacey, and Eric Zweig. *The Ultimate Prize: The Stanley Cup* (Kansas City: Andrews McMeel Publishing, 2003).

DiManno, Rosie. *Coach: The Pat Burns Story* (Toronto: Doubleday Canada, 2012).

Dupuis, David. *Sawchuk: The Troubles and Triumphs of the World's Greatest Goalie* (Toronto: Stoddart Publishing Co. Ltd., 1998).

Ellis, Ron, with Kevin Shea. *Over the Boards: The Ron Ellis Story* (Bolton, ON: Fenn Publishing, 2002).

Esposito, Phil, and Peter Golenbock. *Thunder and Lightning: A No B.S. Memoir* (Chicago: Triumph, 2003).

Fischler, Stan. *Coaches: The Best NHL Coaching Legends from Lester Patrick to Pat Burns* (Toronto and Los Angeles: Warwick Publishing Co., 1995).

———————, and Chris Botta. *Pride and Passion: 25 Years of the New York Islanders* (New York Islanders Hockey Club in cooperation with H & M Productions, Inc. Marceline, MO: Walsworth Publishing Co., Inc., 1996).

Greenburg, Jay. *Full Spectrum: The Complete History of the Philadelphia Flyers* (Toronto: Dan Diamond and Associates, 1997).

Gretzky, Wayne, with Rick Reilly. *Gretzky: An Autobiography* (New York: HarperCollins Publishers, 1990).

Hadfield, Vic, with Tim Moriarty. *Vic Hadfield's Diary: From Moscow to the Playoffs* (Garden City, NY: Doubleday & Company, Inc., 1974).

Hiam, C. Michael. *Eddie Shore and That Old Time Hockey* (Toronto: McClelland & Stewart, 2010).

Holzman, Morey, and Joseph Nieforth. *Deceptions and Doublecross: How the NHL Conquered Hockey* (Toronto: Dundurn Press, 2002).

Howe, Mark and Jay Greenberg. *Gordie Howe's* Son (Chicago, IL: Triumph Books LLC, 2013.

Hunter, Douglas. *Champions: The Illustrated History of Hockey's Greatest Dynasties* (Chicago: Triumph Books, 1997).

————. *Scotty Bowman: A Life in Hockey* (Chicago: Triumph Books, 1998).

Imlach, Punch, with Scott Young. *Hockey Is a Battle: Punch Imlach's Own Story* (New York: Crown Publishers, Inc., 1969).

Irvin, Dick. *Behind the Bench: Coaches Talk About Life in the NHL* (Toronto: McClelland & Stewart Inc., 1993).

————. *The Habs: An Oral History of the Montreal Canadiens* (Toronto: McClelland & Stewart Inc., 1991).

James, Bill. *The Bill James Guide to Baseball Managers: From 1870 to Today* (New York: Scribner, 1997).

Jenish, D'Arcy. *The Montreal Canadiens: 100 Years of Glory* (Toronto: Doubleday Canada, 2008).

Johnston, Mike, and Ryan Walter. *Simply the Best: Insights and Strategies from Great HOCKEY Coaches* (Surrey, B.C.: Heritage House Publishing, 2004).

Kitchen, Paul. *Win, Tie, or Wrangle*: *The Inside Story of the Old Ottawa Senators 1883–1935* (Manotick, ON: Penumbra Press, 2008).

Lahman, Sean. *The Pro Football Historical Abstract: A Hardcore Fan's Guide to All-time Player Rankings* (Guilford, CT: Lyons Press, 2008).

MacSkimming, Roy. *Gordie: A Hockey Legend* (Vancouver: Greystone Books, 2003).

Mancuso, Jim, and Scott Peterson. *Hockey in Portland: Images of Sports* (Charleston, SC; Chicago, IL; Portsmouth, NH; and San Francisco, CA: Arcadia Publishing, 2007).

McFarlane, Brian. *Best of the Original Six* (Bolton, ON: Fenn Publishing Company Ltd., 2004).

————. *50 Years of Hockey* (Toronto: Pagurian Press Ltd., 1967).

Obermayer, Jeff. *Hockey in Seattle* (Charleston, SC; Chicago, IL; Portsmouth, NH; and San Francisco, CA: Arcadia Publishing, 2004).

Official Guide & Record Book, 2004 (Toronto: Dan Diamond and Associates, Inc. and Chicago: Triumph Books, 2004).

Official Guide & Record Book, 2009 (Toronto: Dan Diamond and Associates, Inc. and Chicago: Triumph Books, 2009).

Official Guide & Record Book, 2013 (Toronto: Dan Diamond and Associates, Inc. and Chicago: Triumph Books, 2013).

Orr, Bobby. *Orr: My Story* (New York: G.P. Putnam's Sons, 2013).

Prato, Greg. *Dynasty: The Oral History of the New York Islanders 1972–1984* (Greg Prato; printed and distributed by Lulu.com, 2012).

Robinson, Larry, with Kevin Shea. *The Great Defender: My Hockey Odyssey* (Toronto: Fenn/McClelland & Stewart, 2014).

Roenick, Jeremy, with Kevin Allen. *J.R.: My Life as the Most Outspoken, Fearless and Hard Hitting Man in Hockey* (Chicago: Triumph Books, 2012).

Sanderson, Derek, with Kevin Shea. *Crossing the Line: The Outrageous Story of a Hockey Original* (Toronto: HarperCollins Publishers Ltd., 2012).

Scanlan, Wayne. *Roger's World: The Life and Unusual Times of Roger Neilson* (Toronto: McClelland & Stewart Ltd., 2004).

Smythe, Conn, with Scott Young. *If You Can't Beat 'Em in the Alley: The Memoirs of the Late Conn Smythe* (Toronto: McClelland & Stewart Ltd., 1981).

Whitehead, Eric. *The Patricks: Hockey's Royal Family* (Toronto: Doubleday Canada Ltd., and Garden City, NY: Doubleday & Company, Inc., 1980).

Willes, Ed. *The Rebel League: The Short and Unruly Life of the World Hockey Association* (Toronto: McClelland & Stewart Inc., 2004).

Williams, Tiger with James Lawton. *Tiger: A Hockey Story* (Vancouver: Douglas and McIntyre Ltd. 1984).

PERSONAL INTERVIEWS

Lou Angotti	January 16, 2009
Al Arbour	January 16, 2008
Jean Beliveau	March 31, 2007
Gerry Cheevers	October 1, 2013
Bill Dineen	December 29, 2010
	October 8, 2013
Ron Ellis	June 6, 2008
Emile Francis	January 13, 2009
Ray Getliffe	April 1, 2006
Glenn Hall	September 11, 2009
Ken Hitchcock	October 14, 2013
Earl Ingarfield Sr.	September 7, 2009
Dick Irvin Jr.	April 27, 2007
Doug Jarrett	July 15, 2007
Eddie Johnston	November 10, 2008
	October 8, 2013
Red Kelly	June 4, 2008
Ted Lindsay	February 13, 2006
Fleming Mackell	April 26, 2007
Howie Meeker	January 30, 2010
Doug Mohns	May 18, 2010
Bryan Murray	October 26, 2013
Terry Murray	October 21, 2013
Phil Myre	October 11, 2013
Eric Nesterenko	September 13, 2006
Chris Nilan	October 29, 2013
Bob Pulford	October 14, 2013
Henri Richard	April 28, 2007
Bobby Rousseau	April 23, 2007
Ed Sandford	May 17, 2010
Harry Sinden	May 26, 2010
Floyd Smith	October 2, 2013

Vic Stasiuk	September 8-9, 2009
Gaye Stewart	June 10, 2008
Dave Tippett	August 21, 2013
Gilles Tremblay	April 25, 2007
Bryan "Bugsy" Watson	December 19, 2006

WEBSITES

http://aol.sportingnews.com/nhl/story/2010-05–20/sn-nhl-coach-year-dave-tippett-phoenix-coyotes?developing-stories-sport-NHL=MLB – background article on Dave Tippett.

http://bleacherreport.com/articles/1621175-why-detroit-red-wings-playoff-berth-proves-mike-babcock-is-best-coach-in-nhl – background article on Mike Babcock.

http://espn.go.com/boston/nhl/story/_/id/7292119/claude-julien-boston-bruins-mutual-respect-breeds-success – background article on Claude Julien.

www.hhof.com – the Hockey Hall of Fame's official website.

www.hockeydb.com – the Internet Hockey Database: an excellent source of information for major league and minor league hockey.

www.hockey-reference.com – another splendid hockey source.

http://hsp.flyershistory.com – website for the Hockey Summary Project: a website dedicated to digitizing the results of all NHL regular season and playoff games.

www.nhl.com – the National Hockey League's official website.

http://stars.nhl.com/club/news.htm?id=674757 – article on Lindy Ruff's hiring by Dallas.

http://www.nytimes.com/2000/03/25/sports/on-hockey-ftorek-did-not-bend-causing-devil-breakup.html – profile article on Robbie Ftorek.

http://www.nytimes.com/2010/05/30/sports/hockey/30muldoon.html?_r=1&ref=sports – nice article by author Morey Holzman on Pete Muldoon.

http://www.post-gazette.com/pg/09207/986478-87.stm – profile article on Eddie Johnston.

www.prosportstransactions.com/hockey/index.htm – a website dedicated to listing all player drafts, trades, free-agent transactions, and retirements; and all coaching and front office personnel hiring and firings that take place in the NHL.

http://rangers.lohudblogs.com/2013/08/12/guest-blogger-george-grimm-an-interview-with-teddy irvine/?utm_source=feedburner&utm_medium=email&utm_campaign=Feed%3A+RangersReport+%28Rangers+Report%29 – contains insights on Emile Francis.

www.sihr.org – the official website for the Society of International Hockey Research.

http://www.si.com/vault - the official website for back issues of *Sports Illustrated*.

http://slam.canoe.ca/Slam/Hockey/NHL/Ottawa/2005/03/06/952149-sun.html – background article on Bryan Murray.

http://sports.espn.go.com/espn/eticket/story?page=doncherry – article on Don Cherry.

http://sports.espn.go.com/nhl/news/story?id=3909857 – article on Dan Byslma.

http://sports.groups.yahoo.com/group/hockhist – website dedicated to the discussion of hockey history.

http://www.tsn.ca/nhl/story/?id=390788 – March 19, 2012, Jonas Siegel story on Ron Wilson.